The Polish Shades and Ghosts of
JOSEPH CONRAD

by Gustav Morf

ASTRA BOOKS

NEW YORK

ASTRA BOOKS, NEW YORK
Box 392, Times Square Station
New York, N.Y. 10036

Distributed by
Twayne Publishers:
A Division of G. K. Hall Co.
70 Lincoln St., Boston, Massachusetts 02111

This book has been published with help of a grant
from the Humanities Research Council of Canada,
using funds provided by the Canada Council.

The Polish Shades
and Ghosts of
JOSEPH CONRAD

One's literary life must turn frequently for sustenance to memories and seek discourse with the shades.

(A Familiar Preface, *A Personal Record*)

And now . . . these shades may be allowed to return to their place of rest where their forms in life linger yet, dim but poignant, and awaiting the moment when their haunting reality, their last trace on earth, shall pass forever with me out of the world.

(Author's Note *A Personal Record*, 1919)

That which in their grown-up years may appear to the world about them as the most enigmatic side of their natures and perhaps must remain for ever obscure even to themselves, will be their unconscious response to the still voice of the inexorable past from which his work of fiction and their personalities are remotely derived.

A Personal Record

CONTENTS

Acknowledgments

This book could not have been written without the kind help of a number of people. I wish to thank especially the director and the staff of the Jagiellonian Library and the staff of the PAN Library, both in Cracow, Prof. P. Mroczkowski (Jagiellonian University), and Mrs. Bronisława Zamarska in Cracow. I am indebted for valuable suggestions to Mr. Leszek Prorok, Sec'y. Gen., of the Polish Writer's Union, Mr. A. Braun, writer, and Prof. St. Zabierowski. Finally, I wish to thank my wife who typed successive versions of the manuscript, as well as Miss Marguerite Pałczyńska who typed most of the final version.

I am obliged to Oxford University Press and the Conrad estate for two quotations from Najder's *Conrad's Polish Background*, and to the publishers of *Conrad Żywy* (The Living Conrad), B. Świderski, who allowed me to quote freely from this work.

List of Illustrations

I.

THE FAMILY HERITAGE

In 1850, a young man of twenty-one, called Tadeusz Bobrowski graduated from Petersburg University with the degree of *magister legum*. He was a Pole, a Catholic, and a gentleman, as the saying went. His father, Józef (Joseph), was an outstanding representative of the land-owning gentry which played such a great part in the Western Ukraine of the time. Józef's wife, Michała (Michaela) Biberstein-Pilchowska, came from similar stock. Both families were proud of their tradition; both had their coat of arms; both were Polish to the core, well off, and respected. They had not taken part in the ill-fated Polish rising of 1831 and therefore had been able to keep and increase their property. They were known to be progressive and democratic in their dealings with their numerous serfs.

Living in a country where the liberty of expression was very restricted, the name given to a child often amounted to a confession of political faith on the part of the parents. When, on the 19 March 1829, a third son was born to Józef Bobrowski, he was christened Wilhelm (William) in honor of William Tell, the Swiss freedom fighter, Jerzy (George) in honor of George Washington, and Tadeusz after the Polish general Kościuszko. Later, the son would only use the Polish Christian name, Tadeusz.

The young student had hardly obtained his degree of M.LL. when he received an urgent message. His father had died suddenly, and he was called home to act as "head of the family." He had intended to continue his studies and to go into public service, but without hesitation he gave up his career.

According to Róża Jabłkowska, the estate he was to

administer was enormous. It consisted of 4250 acres of fertile land, dotted with 120 small farms and inhabited by 360 peasants, not counting the women and children. It included a distillery, two water-driven flour mills, an orthodox church. Part of the market town Oratov belonged to the estate too. Tadeusz sold a good deal of the property in order to satisfy his siblings. He kept only one part, the Kazimierówka, a village still numbering about 200 peasants and a mansion for himself. Although this property was rightfully his (and his mother's as long as she lived), he always considered it as family holdings, and freely sent money to any of his relatives whenever they were in need. His accounts were kept neatly, and he never failed to enter those contributions in the books. When he started this practice, he could not know that in later years by far the greatest strain on the estate's finances would be caused by a difficult nephew, Józef Konrad.

Tadeusz Bobrowski was of small stature and he sometimes complained of this handicap (as Conrad would do later), but his character was anything but average. He had none of the vices common to many sons of Polish landowners of that time. He neither drank nor gambled; was no spendthrift, no braggart. He never made debts and never fought a duel. He was rather sedentary, perspicacious, realistic, somewhat pedantic. He believed in the supremacy of reason and therefore got the nickname "Frenchman" from his fellow students. His friend Spasowicz called him "a child of the French Enlightenment." He was just and democratic. One of his first actions as head of the estate was to liberate his serfs, long before the liberation of the serfs was imposed by law. His servants were treated like members of the family and could look forward to old age with confidence. Bobrowski, who had the reputation of a "Voltairean" in Petersburg, was very tolerant and got along well with people of very different background, language and religion, such as Ukrainians, Russians, Jews, and Poles.

He rose early and did his work systematically and conscientiously according to a schedule made out weeks or months in advance. He became justice of the peace of the district of Lipoviets, to which Oratov belonged. Later, he was given the title of honorary judge of the district court. His advice was sought by many who had dealings with the civil law. According to Jabłkowska, between

Conrad's uncle and guardian, Tadeusz Bobrowski

1861 and 1875 Bobrowski handled a total sum of 18.5 million roubles (worth almost as many dollars) in the form of marriage contracts, last will settlements, liquidations of property, curatorships for minors, etc. In all these dealings, he was scrupulously honest. He got very little for his work. He lived mainly off the proceeds of his estate, the Kazimierówka.

Tadeusz Bobrowski was a sociable man. During the long winter evenings, he would invite friends to his mansion, and they would come gladly, for he was a good storyteller. He had an excellent memory, and his stories were factual, for he had neither the imagination nor the inclination to invent anything. A number of these stories and anecdotes appear in his *Memoirs* (*Pamiętniki*, 1900), among them the pathetic story of Prince Roman Sanguszko which Conrad later retold under the title "Prince Roman." Telling stories and anecdotes of times gone by was a favorite pastime among Polish gentlemen (the women were excluded, for this was strictly men's talk). Such stories were called "gawęda" which could be translated as "tales of hearsay." Bobrowski had the reputation of an entertaining *gawędziarz* or teller of such stories.

Tadeusz was preceded by two brothers, Michał and Stanisław. The first died early. Stanisław became a soldier in the Grodno hussars corps and lived a rather unruly life. After Tadeusz came Kazimierz who became an officer in the Russian army. Tadeusz also had two younger sisters, Ewa and Teofila. The Benjamin of the family was Stefan. Tadeusz would outlive all of his siblings who died of "consumption" in their twenties or thirties, except Stefan who perished at the age of 23. He was actively preparing the uprising of 1863 when he was tricked into fighting a duel against a political opponent who killed him.

When Tadeusz Bobrowski reached the age of 28, he took a wife. His bride was a beautiful and rich lady considerably younger than himself, Józefa (Josephine) Lubowidzka. She came also from a well-known and respected family, connected with the Bobrowskis by bonds of friendship. The marriage was of short duration. Less than a year after the wedding, in April 1858, his wife died after giving birth to a daughter. The child was christened after her mother, and affectionately called Józia. She would die at the age of twelve, probably of tuberculosis. Tadeusz never remarried, and after the death of his only beloved child his nephew Conrad who was only a few months older than Józia, would take the first place in his heart.

Tadeusz had come of age on the 19 March 1849. A near friend of his who was courting his sister Ewa, Apollo Korzeniowski (The pronunciation is best rendered in French transcription: Kojéniofski), sent him a belated letter of congratulation dated 11 May. The wishes were expressed in verses and said this (my translation):

> Fit is your boat—in outstretched sails
> There blows a wind, caressing.
> In midst of treacherous whirls of life
> Some never go astray.
>
> May cowards tremble at lofty waves—
> To you they bring good fortune.
> The hidden reefs are known to you,
> You fought before with tempests.
>
> Your eager boat, with eagle's wings,
> Will make a rapid passage,
> And steered by reason, led by will,
> Will surely reach the shores of fame.
>
> When, resting from your journey
> In the golden realm of fortune,
> Recall, regret, and mourn the many
> Who perished in those tempests!

The author of these verses was nine years older than Tadeusz. He lacked the latter's fortunate disposition. He was known to be unpredictable, impulsive, easily fanatic in his opinions, often elated but sometimes also gloomy. Whatever his mood, he was always unrealistic. The ominously prophetic turn of his poem is obvious. The author must have felt that he too might "perish in those tempests," while Bobrowski, sailing on a more even keel, would survive and achieve success.

Eight years later, the poet would become the father of Joseph Conrad. Again, after thirty more years, the manuscript of this poem would be the only piece of handwriting of his father which Conrad possessed. It had been given to him by Bobrowski during one of his visits to the Kazimierówka. It appeared in print in Bobrowski's *Memoirs*. The poem is very much a work of that time. Its imagery, where nature (and this includes the wind-propelled boat) is used as a mirror reflecting human feelings and actions, is very romantic. The partly inflated style ("the shores of fame") is also typical of the epoch. This was the thing to say, even if all that was meant was that Bobrowski would be successful.

The father as a writer

Joseph Conrad's personality cannot be understood fully without a good knowledge of his father, Apollo Korzeniowski (1820-1869). Fortunately, so much has been written about this curious man that the problem is the wealth rather than the lack of information.

Already in 1870, at the first anniversary of Apollo's death, his former schoolmate and life-long friend, Stefan Buszczyński, published a tribute entitled *A little known poet*. In 1900, Tadeusz Bobrowski's *Memoirs* shed new light on his brother-in-law's controversial figure. In 1914, Michał Rolle devoted a chapter to Conrad's father in his book *In illo tempore*. The chapter's very title, "*A forgotten poet*," was significant.

Buszczyński, among other things, wrote: "The outstanding part of his poetry is still slumbering in his manuscripts. Numerous copies have been circulated in the whole country, passing from hand to hand, eagerly copied, often deformed, and always under a different name. . . . The manuscripts are all in [my] possession, looking for a publisher." Of Apollo, he said this: "All things noble and beautiful lifted him up and carried him into a sort of ecstasy. When he spoke, his eyes sparkled with tears and his face, normally sombre and careworn, in those moments of elation and rapture took an expression of strange beauty and pure spirituality."

Rolle, while recognizing Apollo's gifts, also noted his defects: "He was weak in German . . . English he learned only later, just enough to read the language. Generally speaking, he had no thorough knowledge in any branch. His assets were good taste and intuition, plus an inborn ability for poetry."

For eight decades, the forgotten poet was only known as the father of Conrad. Apollo himself had foreseen this. From his Russian exile, he once wrote in a letter: "I had the fantasy that one day, though unknown and forgotten, through my son I shall be somebody."

Indeed, it was only in 1949 that a Polish critic, Maria Kasterska, drew attention to Apollo as a writer in his own right. Her essay was entitled " A Play by Apollo Korzeniowski" and it was published in the London Polish weekly *The News*. Then, at long last a thorough study of Conrad's father as an author appeared in Poland: *Apollo Korzeniowski: the Last Romantic Playwright* (1957), by Roman Taborski.

Despite the title, Taborski does not only describe Apollo as a dramatic writer, but also as a poet. His talents as a playwright were not remarkable, while his poetry had distinction. Apollo saw the poet as a man who gets his inspiration from above, "and then, god-inspired, returns to the people where we find the tears, the misery, and the toil." The poet, according to Apollo, was an agent of social change, a harbinger of new ideas which would transform the nation. In 1855, when the peasants of the district of Skwira rioted for reasons which Apollo found justified, he exclaimed:

> Follow the sun, brothers, the rising sun,
> Follow the people, for there's your strength,
> Follow the people, in it find the saving word!
> Poland must be a people's nation,
> So that she may live for ever and ever!

Like Victor Hugo's poetry, which Apollo admired very much, Apollo's verses often appear too exalted, too pathetic. There is a discrepancy between the fairly simple ideas and the inflated form—a discrepancy which at times can also be noticed in Conrad's first novels. There is also a strong element of narcissism: he displays his verbal skill as a ringmaster in the circus displays his trained horses. What Heyst says of his father, "He was a great master . . . of beautiful words . . . and noble ideals." (*Victory*, 195), literally applies to the father of Joseph Conrad.

Apart from its pathos, Apollo's poetry is also characterized by the then fashionable tendency to personify the abstract e.g., Poland is a mother lying in her grave (the symbol is from Adam Mickiewicz); youthful idealism is likened to the flight of eagles. He loved to invoke the absolute: eternity, immortality, humanity. He believed in all or nothing, in life or death; he never compromised. Beauty too has to be absolute—so he translates prose into verse—and the same holds true of liberty as opposed to mere liberties; of love, patriotism, faith, fidelity, courage. Apollo wrote, lived, suffered and died for ideas. He educated his only son for an idea. Unlike Heyst's father, he believed in progress, in Western civilization, in mankind, in God.

Contrary to Bobrowski, Apollo had absolutely no gift as a storyteller. But like his son, he was endowed with a most powerful sarcastic sense of humor which not only was his main weapon in his frequent polemics, but also made him "the terror" of social parties. In a reply to an article in which somebody had said that the main thing in art was "grace and skill," Apollo, seized by a holy wrath, exploded:

> So there is to be nothing else behind art but grace and skill? So literature becomes a toy for those who live only for their bread and a pastime for idle moments between digging beetroots, cheating the Jew, and counting one's money? So when people with a sincere and upright heart look at our literature as at a rainbow in which shine all the colors of our national life and which is a promise of harmony and full of divine thoughts—how can a voice be raised wanting to turn that arch of life into a senseless puppet-show?

Because of its exaggerated, not to say hysterical pitch, Apollo's attack caused quite an uproar and did more harm than good. Basically well-mannered as he was, he felt the need to justify himself:

> As to what they say about my sarcastic talent, one honest acquaintance once told me that the more angry I am the better I write . . . such a talent is very necessary at certain moments and produces good effects. Society very often resembles a cutlet: the more you beat it the better it becomes. (*The Living Conrad, Conrad Żywy*, London: B. Świderski, 1957, p. 147)

Apollo's sarcasm is best expressed in his plays. These are fairly realistic, although always strongly biased in favor of the poor, the helpless, who are at the same time the innocent, pure and honest. To be rich and influential is almost a sure sign of corruption. In his *Comedy* he describes a wealthy town magnate called the "President" as follows: "he administers the fortune of young Lydia to his profit and educates her to her damage." And of course, when the poor but honest "proletarian" and poet, Henryk, asks him for Lydia's hand, the President refuses, despite the fact that Henryk is a nobleman by birth. In another play whose title could be best translated as *For the Beloved Dollar*[1], Apollo expresses his contempt for the new breed of industrialists who, for the sake of profit, were sacrificing the old values:

> This world, where everyone runs, crawls or walks
> Toward a new Colchis and its golden fleece,
> On the way, the heart is crushed, the feelings go.
> Dedication? Ridiculous! Faith? As many falsehoods!
> Virtue? Fading! Happy in their animal smartness
> They holler senselessly—for they have more roubles.

Apollo, however, also wrote two plays strictly for entertainment: *What Shall I Do with This Pawn?*[2] (for the amateur theatre), and *The Little Whip* (to be played by children). The latter was based on an anecdote according to which the Polish national hero Tadeusz Kościuszko once bought a little whip from a poor saddler and thereby made him well-known and prosperous. The charming work must have been played fairly often; it was reprinted as late as 1902 in Chociszewski's *Comedies for Children and Young People*.

Apollo's comedies, written in verse, had some success. *For the Beloved Dollar* was played in Kiev, Zhitomir, Wilno, and Lublin, from 1859 to 1861. According to the Warsaw *Daily Gazette*, the play, being so topical, had great success with the general public, but met with icy reserve on the part of the well-to-do. His *Comedy* never made it to the stage, but it was printed and reviewed in three dailies and a periodical, in 1855 and 1856. Three of the reviews were very critical, one was favorable.[3] Most critics found the social satire exaggerated and biased. Moreover, they noted that the plot of Apollo's play rather closely followed a (still well-known) Russian comedy by Alexander Griboyedov, entitled *Gorie ot uma* ("Knowledge is a curse"). This is true, but while Griboyedov wanted to entertain, Apollo sought to chastise.

There is perhaps a similarity between Apollo and Conrad, for in Conrad's works, too, we find names, descriptions, and sometimes whole passages borrowed from other authors, and in *A Personal Record* whole pages are based on Bobrowski's *Memoirs*.

Much like Conrad himself, Apollo poured sarcasm on those who made a fortune in industry (just then, the beet sugar industry was flourishing in the Ukraine), and he thought little of high finance and industrial capitalism. But both father and son must be suspected of having been jealous of men who possessed those financial talents which the Korzeniowskis conspicuously lacked. Apollo was also critical of the higher nobility because these influential people, in wanting to keep their prerogatives and estates, were generally on good terms with the Russian authorities. With rare exceptions, like Prince Roman Sanguszko, they were not inclined to risk everything in what they considered as a dangerous political speculation. Nor had they any confidence in young artists, littérateurs and intellectuals, who had never proven their worth in practical life.

Presumably for its historical interest, Apollo's *Comedy* was taken out of the dusty archives and actually had its premiere almost one hundred years after it was written, namely in 1952, in Wrocław. In 1954, it was presented in Lódź, and in 1956 in Opole.

Although, as Bobrowski testified in his *Memoirs*, Apollo was called a socialist and a "red" by many of his contemporaries, he was no Marxist in the modern sense of the word. But he very strongly sided with the Russian and Ukrainian peasants who, between 1855 and 1860, expressed their dissatisfaction in over 300 riots.

Despite his high opinion of the common people, Apollo's political ideas were far from clear. Bobrowski writes in his *Memoirs* that they were in many ways more conservative than his own. For instance, Apollo did not see the necessity for the peasants to have political rights. This is not as paradoxical as it seems. Apollo's conviction was that the great masses of people should be given a better social status. They should contribute to the life of the nation by developing their own culture; they should play *their* role, but not on the government level. His conception of society was paternalistic, but with fathers who understood the needs of those who depended on them. It is significant, that when Apollo moved to Warsaw in

1861 in order to prepare the resistance, he did not address himself to the working people, but to the students, artists and young intellectuals who accepted him readily as their leader.

Apollo excelled in the field of translation. His Polish version of de Vigny's *Chatterton* (where he used verse instead of the original's prose) is still read. The same is true of his translation of *Hard Times* by Charles Dickens. In both cases, Apollo was attracted by works containing a lot of social criticism. In *Chatterton*, a poet complains of his plight in an increasingly industrialized and materialistic society, while *Hard Times* is one of the saddest and most anti-capitalistic stories by Dickens. As a translator, Apollo showed a great intuition. This and his real gift for linguistic expression made his translations outstanding. His texts read like Polish originals.

Hard Times was reprinted as late as 1955, in Warsaw. The editor justified the revival of Apollo's 89-year-old translation thus: "We found that it was right to make this version available to our readers because of the beauty of its original 19th century prose, and because it renders so well the genuine Dickens spirit."

As Conrad did in his preface to the *Nigger of the "Narcissus"*, Apollo expressed his artistic creed in his preface to his Polish translation of *Chatterton*. At a time, he says, when the spiritual values are sacrificed to "the circus of material interests," the poet remains the sole defender and representative of the spirit. Art, beauty, honesty, and goodness are inseparable:

> While the original drama . . . exclusively defends the situation of the poet in a money-obsessed world, in the Polish translation the drama comes to the defense of all the poor but honorable men still surviving in our affluent and money-ridden society who refuse to trade their principles and ideals for material advantages, and who are cast aside by a prosperous and rich society. This is why I translated this drama.

The burden of the Nałęcz

Apollo Nałęcz (pronounced Nallainch) Korzeniowski was born 21 February 1821 in Honoratka near Lipoviets, Ukraine. This was part of what the Poles called the Polish borderland. The great majority of the inhabitants were Ukrainians, but the Polish minority (about 10%), due to its superior education, its strong ethnic convictions and Western cultural traditions, played an ascendant role and was generally well accepted by their Ukrainian peasants.

Apollo's parents were Teodor and Julia, née Dyakiewicz. Teodor had fought under Napoleon when young, then had taken to estate managing. When Apollo was ten, his father, on the news of the outbreak of the 1831 Uprising, immediately enlisted, was made captain and, having himself distinguished in battle, was decorated. After the defeat, Teodor went back to estate managing.[4]

There are many Polish families bearing the name of Korzeniowski. Conrad's ancestors distinguished themselves by a coat of arms showing a kerchief with two corners tied together. Nałęcz means "tied together." Conrad believed that he and his sons were the only descendants of the "Korzeniowski of the Nałęcz arms," but this is not correct.

Tradition has it that the Nałęcz arms were bestowed by a king either to chiefs of pagan tribes who had adopted Christianity as a symbol of their attachment to the new faith, or to a soldier who had dressed a royal wound. At any rate, the coat of arms expressed the idea of absolute fidelity. The founder of the Nowodworski College, later St. Anne's, in Cracow bore the Nałęcz arms already in 1616.

According to the Polish historian, St. Mleczko (*New Polish Courier*, 29 and 31 August 1923), one remarkable member of the Nałecz Korzeniowski was Kajetan, chancellor of the principality of Lithuania (1775). A daughter of his married Count Pociej who distinguished himself in the unfortunate battle of Praga against the Russians (1794). Pociej is immortalized by Mickiewicz (*Pan Tadeusz*, Book VI, verses 697-708) who wrote that the count received no less than 23 wounds in that battle and was "riddled like a sieve."[5]

Contrary to his ancestors who had actually dropped the "Nałęcz," Apollo was very proud of it, and had letters patent issued confirming his and his descendants' right to bear the Nałęcz arms. In his Polish letters, Conrad for some time used to sign his name as Józef N. Korzeniowski.

We have four testimonies concerning Conrad's paternal grandfather Teodor: two by Conrad, one by Stefan Buszczyński, and one by Tadeusz Bobrowski. In a letter to an American friend, published in *New Republic* (USA), Conrad wrote:

> My paternal grandfather served in the Polish army from 1817 to 1820, when he sold his land in Podolia and came to live on his wife's estate in Volhynia. Their fortune, which descended to my father, his brother, and his sister, was confiscated by the Russian government in consequence of the rebellion of 1863.

This letter is not quite accurate. Teodor was already lieutenant in the Polish army in 1807. He had five brothers and three sisters. He was a poor man long before 1863, and there was not much to confiscate.

This is what Conrad wrote to Edgar Garnett:

> My parental grandfather, Teodor N. Korzeniowski, served in the cavalry. Decorated with the cross "Virtuti[6] Militari" (a plain white enamel with a green wreath of laurel and these words in the center), something in the nature of V.C. Attained the rank of captain in 1830, when the Russo-Polish war occured, after which the so-called Polish army ceased to exist. Two wounds. Retired to a little hereditary estate adjoining the extensive possessions of the family of Sobański (they are in the Almanach de Gotha), great friends and, I fancy, distant relatives. Administered the territorial fortune of Madame Melanie Sobańska.[7]

This letter also contains inaccuracies. Teodor became captain during the Uprising of 1831, not in 1830. After the defeat, he administered a government estate, not Mrs. Sobańska's. (It was Apollo who administered Melanie Sobańska's estate, at the time of Conrad's birth). Conrad got the cross from his uncle. In the center there are no words, but the Polish white eagle, flanked by two branches of laurel. The words VIR-TUTE MILI-TARI are written in the four arms of the Maltese cross.[8]

Stefan Buszczyński, in his *Little Known Poet*, praises Teodor for his outstanding patriotism and devotion to the Polish cause. Bobrowski's judgment, on the other hand, is very unfavorable.[9] As an example of Teodor's boastfulness, Bobrowski mentions that when Apollo was studying in Petersburg the proud father told acquaintances that his son wrote letters in Arabic which he, Teodor, was able to read.

Teodor had three sons: Robert, Hilary, and Apolinary who later used the more poetic name Apollo. The irrepressible story-teller, Bobrowski, describes Conrad's Uncle Robert as a drunkard and gambler who, when once sent to the Kiev cattle market with about fifty oxen and some farmhands, gambled the animals away during the journey and finally returned home empty-handed. He died during the Uprising of 1863, "no longer young, having contributed not a little to the decline of the family."

Conrad's other uncle, Hilary, is described by Bobrowski as "an utopian just like his father and not less sarcastic than his brother Apollo, but without the latter's pleasant manners." He also dabbled in estate-managing and was a victim of delusions all his life. Bobrowski says he was "whipping the sand," meaning that he worked more for effect than for substance. He was arrested shortly before the Uprising of 1863 and exiled to Tomsk, Siberia. Even there he continued to live according to his dreams and (one thinks of Almayer) "sought gold" and speculated. "He died in 1873, very much in debt."

Bobrowski makes a point of stating that Apollo was the only one who was free from that passion for speculating which had obsessed his father and his two brothers. He pointed out other traits of the Nałęcz Korzeniowski family: an unpractical romanticism, taking dreams for reality, and too vivid an imagination leading to boastfulness and untruthfulness. "The Nałęcz, from time immemorial, were an excitable lot, and the Korzeniowski were known as gifted, eloquent and sarcastic." In financial matters, the Nałęcz Korzeniowski invariably showed bad judgment and were over-optimistic. This, of course, had disastrous consequences. They were fiercely devoted to the Polish cause, but were also fierce individualists. They thought with nostalgia of Poland's former might and military splendor. The Russian writer, V. Korolenko, who lived at Zhitomir during the rising of 1863, writes in his *History of my Contemporary* (1910) that "the romance which attracted the young [Polish] noblemen so much was a bad training for war . . . the crude and unromantic attack of a handful of peasants against the Cossacks had no resemblance to the beautiful pictures of battles as they imagined them." Korolenko knew what he was talking about. He had a Polish mother, had been brought up in Polish, had married a Polish wife, and had witnessed the terrible repression ("Russification") which had taken place after the unfortunate insurrection of 1863.

The romantically warlike spirit of the Polish gentry lives in many pages of Conrad's shorter works: "The Duel," "The Warrior's Soul," "Gaspar Ruiz," "Prince Roman."

Bobrowski's opinion of Conrad's paternal ancestors explains why he so often warned his nephew about giving in to the Nałęcz Korzeniowski strain. In 1876 he wrote to the 19-year-old Conrad who, by sheer carelessness, had just lost all his belongings: "You disturb me with your disorder and negligence . . . you remind me much more of the Korzeniowskis than of my dear sister, your mother." In another letter of the same year he made this reproach: "You have by your extravagance in two years already spent your allowance for the whole third year too." In 1877 he recognized Conrad's gift for sarcasm (*la répartie facile et suffisamment acérée*) as a typical Nałęcz Korzeniowski trait, but he failed to find any of the caution and common sense characterizing Conrad's maternal ancestors and advised him to "work on his character."

In 1880, the 22-year-old Conrad received the following admonition, "You would not be a Nałęcz, my dear boy, if you were steadfast in your actions and did not constantly change your plans." At the same time Uncle Bobrowski conceded that the "Nałęcz have a spirit of initiative and enterprise greater than that which is in my blood."

One year later, Conrad had again run out of money and, in order to avoid any further reproaches, invented the story that he had been involved in the shipwreck of the *Anna Frost* when in fact he had never served on that ship.[10] The uncle immediately sent £10, expressing his sympathy, but at the same time wondering whether Conrad was not insured against such an accident. In the same letter, he sternly warned his "dear boy" against speculating with borrowed money: "As you are a Nałęcz, beware of risky speculations which rest on nothing but [vain] hope, for your grandfather [Teodor] wasted his property on speculations, and your uncle [Hilary] got into debt speculating with other people's money, causing them losses and finally dying heavily in debt." In the same year, possibly as a warning, the uncle mentions that Conrad's former tutor, Marek Adam Pulman, had once borrowed 600 roubles from him and that, despite the fact that Pulman was now married to a prosperous woman and was practicing medicine in Sambor, he did not even acknowledge the letters addressed to him, and that it was known that he was being sued for other debts too. Bobrowski suggested that Conrad write to Pulman himself, but Conrad never complied.

In 1891, when Conrad was 34, his uncle, in reply to a request from his nephew, again made an inventory of his nephew's faults. He did not seem to have improved much, for Bobrowski mentioned instability of character, lack of steadfastness and perseverance, an inclination to be carried away by dreams and illusions, and prone to depression when the dream does not come true. This, of course, is the Nałęcz strain, so visible in Conrad's paternal forebears.[11]

In another letter during the same year, Bobrowski points out that "geniuses and visionaries" are not as necessary to the world as are conscientious workers securing their daily bread. He tells Conrad that an active and useful life is the best antidote for depression and pessimism and recommends his own philosophy: steadfastness and a serene outlook on life, as expressed in his motto *Usque ad finem*. He considers Conrad to be a dreamer, by individual disposition as well as by heritage. In another passage, he qualifies Conrad as "a penniless dreamer," certainly not a compliment for a 34-year-old British captain.

When reading Bobrowski's family chronicle, one understands his concern for Conrad. Indeed, it might be Bobrowski describing one of the Korzeniowskis when Richard Curle writes about Conrad: "When success came to him late in life, the natural princeliness of his nature made him lavish, and he put by next to nothing. Theoretically a wonderful man of business and full of elaborate projects, in actual practice he was entirely lacking in the money sense."[12] Or again, when John Galsworthy says, "A sailor and an artist, he had little sense of money."[13] F. M. Ford called him "a magnificent business man of the imaginative type" and "the most unrivalled hatcher of schemes for sudden and unlimited wealth."[14] It is well known that when Conrad, after his uncle's death, received a substantial inheritance of 16.200 roubles[15]—then almost $6000—he quickly lost most of it in a speculation connected with a gold mine in South Africa.

Apollo had justified his Nałęcz defects by pointing out that he was a poet: "When a poor man puts his conscience and the moral obligations deriving from it, and his dignity, above material interests, we exclaim: That's a poet!" What excuse could an English captain offer?

c. Apollo: from School to Calvary

Apollo went to four different classical colleges (*Gimnazja*): in Kamieniets Podolski, Niemirov, Vinnitsa, and finally in Zhitomir.[16] Buszczyński who went to school with him at Vinnitsa, describes him thus: "His exuberant adolescent mind, his fiery soul, and his independent character won the hearts of his co-students but, on the other hand, forced him to change school several times. The Russian authorities always persecuted him for his free thinking."

An echo of this can be found in *Under Western Eyes* (138): "In the educational establishment for girls where Miss Haldin finished her studies she . . . was suspected of holding independent views on matters settled by official teaching. Afterwards . . . both mother and daughter . . . had earned for themselves a reputation of liberalism."

Having finished his studies at Zhitomir, around 1840, Apollo applied for a passport to go to Berlin for studies. In view of his reputation as a liberal, the passport was refused and he had to go to Petersburg, where he registered himself as a student of law and oriental studies. Although he stayed at the University from 1842 to 1846, he never pursued any regular studies. In his writings there is no trace of academic knowledge in any of the fields mentioned. He obviously used his status as a student in order to take part in literary circles. He must have read a lot, and improved his knowledge of French, the classical language of European liberalism. He may also have begun to study English at that time, probably for the same reason. Western literature was the only legitimate vehicle by which Western liberal ideas could penetrate into Russia.

It was in Petersburg that Apollo began to write. He

first translated Victor Hugo's *Les Burgraves* into Polish verse, then started on his first original work: *Verses from Purgatory*. The *Burgraves* was published in a small Warsaw literary paper, the *Verses* only circulated in handwritten copies, for they would not have passed the Censor.

In 1846 Apollo returned to the Ukraine. He was 26, had not completed any studies, and just lived with his father Teodor who administered an estate near Berdyczów (Berdichev). During that time he was often in touch with the Bobrowski family and became attracted to Tadeusz's sister Ewa—or Ewelina as they affectionately called her. Her parents strongly opposed the match. It was only in 1856, when he was newly married, that he tried to make a living, but he fell heavily in debt.

While "studying" in Petersburg, Apollo must have lived very merrily. In 1849, three years after his return to Podolia, he wrote this poem:

> How long, how vilely did I close
> My life to passion, inspiration!
> Within me was an awesome night
> The night of hell—where in gloom and twilight
> Life's villainy reigned supreme.
> In the midst of death and mourning
> In the midst of moans and agony
> I only knew and loved myself.
> When the dawn of my young years
> Fell on naught but tombs,
> No tears sprang from my eyes,
> No sobbing stirred my breast,
> No pain my youthful heart!
> God, o God, o pardon me!

From this moment on, Apollo must have decided to live and to write no longer for himself, but for his country. But the full consequences of this resolution would only show ten years later.

The first English translation of Bobrowski's portrait of Conrad's father was published in my book, *The Polish Heritage of Joseph Conrad* (1930):

> In the neighborhood he had an established reputation of being not nice but exceedingly spiteful. Indeed, he was not handsome, not even attractive, but he had a very lovely expression of the eyes, and his malice was only verbal and confined to living room

conversation, for neither in his feelings nor in his actions did I ever notice it. His feelings were impetuous and expansive; he sincerely loved people, but was unpractical in his actions and often helpless. In word and writing often unyielding, in daily life he was frequently more than lenient, perhaps in compensation as I told him more than once, as I also told him that he had two weights and measures—one for the little and simple ones and another for the great ones of this world. (*Memoirs*, I, 361).

The Bobrowski family then lived at the wife's estate at Novofastov (Nowofastów), Podolia, near the Volhynian border. Their opinion about Apollo is reported by Bobrowski as follows:

My parents both liked [Apollo] Korzeniowski as a nice and well-bred guest, but both, although for different reasons, with displeasure saw him courting their daughter. My mother suspected him of being lighthearted and unstable in his feelings (for he was often sarcastic) while father thought he was unpractical, helpless and lazy, for although he was supposed to assist his father in estate-managing, he preferred reading, writing and traveling around to working. (*Memoirs*, II, 66).

It seems that the resistance of the parents rather strengthened Ewelina's weakness for Apollo; but the marriage took place only after ten years of courtship and several years after the death of father Bobrowski. The wedding was celebrated on 8 May 1856 in Oratov; but even then Tadeusz as the head of the family had to give his permission. A number of Ewelina's relatives protested against the marriage and refused to attend. By then Apollo was 35. The newly-weds lived in Łuczyniec for a year, but when Ewelina's dowry was paid they rented another estate named Derebczynka and Ewelina's mother, also having invested some money there, moved in with them. Łuczyniec (pronounced Loochiniets) is situated 30 km N. of Mogilev Podolski and 80 km SSW of Vinnitsa, on the river Niemiya. According to the *Geographical Dictionary of the Polish Kingdom* (Warsaw 1880), the estate over 2200 acres belonged to Mrs. Melanie Sobańska. She also owned a much smaller estate (240 acres) named Derebczynka, situated east of Mogilev Podolski, and this was probably the estate Apollo rented after his marriage. He was not only an incompetent administrator; he must not even have lived there, for Conrad was born far away, in a mansion situated in the Eastern outskirts of Berdichev. The building is now called Ivankovtsy. The Russian writer D. Urnov visited it in 1971, identifying it from an old photograph he got from Borys Conrad. Whether this mansion was also called Derebczynka (as Urnov believes) is a matter of conjecture. Apollo then dated his letters from Berdichev. During that time, on 21 November 1857, (3 December Western Calendar) their son was born there. Naturally, Apollo was overjoyed. He gave him the names of both his grandfathers Józef and Teodor, and the symbolic name Konrad. He wrote a letter to the well-known Polish novelist Kraszewski asking him to bless his son, "I take the liberty of asking you for a blessing for my son. I feel, I have the confidence that my son will become a man of honor and honesty, if at the threshold of his life he is greeted by the sign of the cross from your hand and by your wishes." Kraszewski complied, although only by writing. Apollo thanked him in these words, "Your letter will be a talisman for my son." Later, however, Kraszewski came over from Zhitomir to visit the young family and acted as godfather.

For the baptism of his son, Apollo wrote a "little song" (piosenka) which was published for the first time by Rafał Blüth in *Literary Scene*, 1932. It is a most pathetic document, linking the plight of Poland with the fate of the child. Conrad never knew this most oppressing song in which his father places his own burden of national mourning on his small son's shoulders. He foresees that his son will grow up "under the shadow of alien spirits" and dates the song "in the 85th year of Moscow bondage."

This song renders so well the spirit and atmosphere in which Apollo intended to bring up his son that it seems worthwhile to reproduce it in full. The only known manuscript of this intriguing lullaby is in the Jagiellonian Library in Cracow. It is not in Apollo's hand and three lines are incomplete. Since Blüth left out the two incomplete verses, the following represents the first complete version, albeit in an English translation:

The mansion in which Conrad was born still stands in Berdichev.
It is now used as a sports club.
(Drawing by E. Tabachnikova, 1971.)

My child and son—no fear, just
Sleep and Sleep—The world is dark
No home is yours, no country.
Yet sleep with God—poor you are,
Yet springs baptismal flow for you,
God's spirit dwells in you already
Has taken soul and bears a name.
   Sleep, my Son, my Little One.

My Child and Son, O sleep in peace.
Amid the shades of foreign spirits
Two loving hearts are all you own,
Your only shield remains the Cross.
These precious three will never fail,
The world cannot corrupt them.
Now close your eyes and doze.
   Sleep, my Son, my Little One.

My Child and Son, with a thousand songs
I shall lull you, Son, to sleep.
May they transform, enchant your life
And be your stars, your flowers, and your sun.
May beauty, goodness, ever be your lot.
And as they carry you upon their wings
They will enlighten this dark world for you.
   Sleep my Son, my Little One.

My Child and Son, may holy baptism
Give you the strength to live, endure·
The courage, too, to face the shades.

                              when God permits

That one and only Mother Poland
Be raised from her dark tomb of bondage.
   Sleep, my Son, my Little One.

My Child, my Son—do sleep . . . Baptismal strength
Flows through your soul, your body.
Heaven, Divinity all around thus
Bless my little child; Be a Pole!
If foes with riches try to lure you,
Reject them all—preferring misery.
   Sleep, my Child, my Little One.

My Child, my Son, and if your foe
Should call you nobleman and Christian:
Then tell yourself—I must be pagan
And my nobility—corruption.
If foe tempts me with slimy gold
And I do not reject his world
Renounce your father-renegade.[17]
   Sleep, my Son, my Little One.

My Child and Son, so tell yourself:
While Mother Poland lies entombed
No country yours will be, no love,
No homeland, no humanity.
Your grief will be your only kin,
Your only faith, demanding sacrifice.
   Sleep, my Son, my Little One.

My Child and Son, without [your Mother Poland]
Without her
Without her
There's no salvation without her!
As days go by, and comes the time to be:
Grow up in this strong thought:to
Give your country—and yourself—Immortality!
   Sleep, my Son, my Little One.
                              Berdyczów, 23 November 1857

As we see, Apollo conjured up several spirits to his son's
cradle: the spirit of literature (Kraszewski), but also the
spirit of invincible but hopeless patriotism, of gloom and
national mourning. Here was a father who was obviously
too narcissistic to understand the monstrosity of denying
all happiness to the child, a father who just wanted his
son to feel like himself, be a reflection of himself. And,
as we shall see, the boy *did* grow up in the gloomy atmosphere evoked in the song: his mother usually wearing black as a sign of national mourning, his father
fighting with the wrong means for the Polish cause.
   Ewa's father had been right. Apollo was no more able
to make a success of estate-managing than he had been
to make a success of his studies. According to Taborski,
Ewa's dowry and her mother's investment were lost
within two years, in 1859 they had to give up Derebczynka. The little family moved first to Terekhova, a
small estate belonging to the Pilchowskis. This later gave

rise to the assertion, repeated in the last edition of the *Ukrainian Encyclopedia*, that Conrad was born there. From Terekhova, they went to live in Zhitomir, the capital of Volhynia with a population of about 30,000.

The intellectual climate there was very stimulating; there were three Polish publishers, a Polish classical college, and a Polish playhouse. Kraszewski and other Polish authors lived there; they and a number of doctors, lawyers, journalists gave the town its cachet as a Polish intellectual center. And there was a multitude of ladies interested in reading the latest novels and watching the newest plays. When Apollo came to this town from lonely Terekhova he must have felt like a fish in a fresh mountain stream. He began to produce at great speed and quickly became known as a writer of poetry and plays, for one of the latter was presented at the local "Theatre of Volhynian Nobility." He also worked as a free lance writer and provincial correspondent for some national newspapers and periodicals. As a journalist he gave free rein to his sarcastic and polemic tendencies.

Things appeared to go better when Apollo got a job as secretary and co-editor in a newly formed publishing firm. If ever there was an ideal work for Apollo, this was it; yet after about six months he resigned his post because of differences of opinion with the president of the company. The latter had to think in terms of profit and loss while Apollo remained the idealist who thought a publishing firm should not pay attention to financial considerations. He left his job in November 1959, having lost 500 roubles in the venture.

Apollo was already 39 years old and had no steady source of income. He tried to found a weekly paper but nobody would advance the money. It seems that he wrote a satirical comedy, *A Practical Man*, but it was never printed and got lost. He regularly contributed to Warsaw newspapers, reporting on the intellectual and economic life of the province. In economic questions he was singularly conservative. For instance, he was absolutely against the expansion of industry, believing that this would destroy agriculture. One contemporary critic said Apollo's ideals were medieval and belonged to the age of knights.

We believe that Apollo's pessimism was not only due to the Muscovite bondage. After all, many patriotic Poles—such as T. Bobrowski—found happiness and self-fulfilment despite the Czarist regime. Apollo was a man who failed in everything he did. He may have earned a living for a year or two in his life; for the rest he was living at the expense of someone else, all the time pointing his finger at the materialists who thought of nothing else but making a living. He had a remarkable gift for brilliant verbal expression but he lacked original ideas. His poetry was a flight into another world; his plays were, at best, an attempt to grapple with life as seen by a doctrinarian. The characters in his plays are stereotypes.

When we consider these facts we find it probable that Apollo's patriotic pessimism to a great extent was a projection of his own sense of failure. Instead of blaming himself in the first place, he put all the blame on the political situation. These are hard words to say, but Conrad himself, when describing his numerous idealists, reformers, and extremists, tended to see it in this light and mistrusted their motives.

In April 1861, the representatives of the Polish gentry in the border provinces were meeting at Zhitomir. Among other things, they decided to send a petition to the Czar, humbly asking for a stronger union of the border provinces with Lithuania and Western Ukraine. Apollo was strongly in favor of the move, while Tadeusz Bobrowski opposed it as dangerous. Before the petition could be drafted, news came of tumultuous manifestations in Warsaw, and of Russian troops firing at the crowd. The news shocked the assembly, and it was decided to dispatch two delegates to the capital to establish contact. One of the delegates was Apollo. He arrived on 25 May, ostensibly to prepare the launching of a new periodical to be called *Fortnightly*, but in reality in order to participate in a resistance movement.

For a man like Apollo, in whom patriotism and religion were inseparable, the decision to go to Warsaw probably had a deep, even archetypal meaning. He certainly knew that to disseminate his patriotic faith in the capital meant courting disaster, yet he felt a compelling need to defy the ruling powers. It does not seem farfetched to assume that his behavior was determined by an archetype of Jesus Christ going to Jerusalem. There was a strong messianic urge in Apollo. The conviction that even apparent defeat would in some mysterious way lead to the resurrection of Poland was part of the then widespread Polish politico-religious faith known as "messianism". As for Ewelina, did she not resemble Mary following the master?

On his arrival in Warsaw Apollo first lived at the Saski Hotel. After his wife and son (Konradek or little Konrad) had joined him in July, they stayed at 45 Nowy Świat, a fashionable central street. His activities were twofold: he worked for the launching of the new periodical (he himself wrote a prospectus and tried to find a number of contributors), and he got more and more involved in political activities. The plans for the periodical were overly ambitious: the subjects included almost everything from economics to travel, from literature to jurisprudence; it is very doubtful whether it would have been a sound venture financially. As for the more or less clandestine political activities, Apollo soon became the leader of the extremists or "Reds" who wanted liberty at all costs, contrary to the "Whites" who would have been satisfied with cultural autonomy, and believed this could be obtained by pacific means. The Reds consisted mostly of students and artists of whom quite a number had studied for many years without ever passing any examinations—much like Apollo himself. It was to this inflammable material that he appealed, and it was their enthusiastic response that inspired him.

There was a patriotic committee in Warsaw, and in this body Apollo had an important voice as the representative of the Reds. It was he who suggested that the picture of St. Nicholas should figure on the emblem of this committee besides the Polish white eagle. The members of this body wore a ring which bore the emblem; Apollo's ring was preserved and later given to Conrad.[18]

Apollo was exceedingly active. Far from hiding himself, he became a conspicuous figure in the streets of Warsaw, wearing the provincial peasant garb with high black boots in the sophisticated metropolis where men dressed like the French. He must have written several political pamphlets, for they unmistakably betray his exalted style. At one time there were elections to the Municipal Council, approved by the Russian authorities as well as by the patriotic committee, but at the last moment Apollo decided to tell the citizens not to vote as a sign of protest. This is how an eye-witness recalled the scene:

Two days later people came in great numbers to the
Church of the Holy Cross and to the Building of
the Academy where the elections were to be held.
We saw many students of the Art school and other
people, young and old, belonging to the extremists,
among them Apollo Korzeniowski, a sincere but overly ar-
dent patriot. They passed through the crowd that
had assembled to vote, distributing leaflets and
whispering to those to whom they handed them.
One of our party succeeded in snatching one of
these leaflets which had been printed in great haste,
and we saw with astonishment that, in spite of the
agreement, this was an urgent appeal not to vote.
We tried in vain to remind them of their promise
[that they were not to oppose themselves to the elec-
tion], but it was impossible to calm the effervescence
and to stop the noisy propaganda in the streets and
in front of the Academy of Art. People of the moderate party were obliged to intervene and there en-
sued, unfortunately, a struggle between the two
wings which was not without scandalous scenes. The
moderates were victorious, and the opposition trying to enter the building were thrown out and limited themselves to distributing their pamphlets.

The Reds insulted the students of the Academy,
and one of the extremists, Apollo Korzeniowski, a well-
known personality, full of genuine patriotism and leader
of the Red faction, was obliged to take back his words
publicly before the students.

(Daniłowski, *Notes*, 60-64. My italics.)

Apollo was not a politician but a political dreamer who
believed that the future Poland should encompass
Lithuania and the Eastern provinces including Kiev! It is
true that these territories, where only a few per cent of
the population were Polish, had once been part of Poland, but this was at a time when neither Russia nor
Germany was a European power. It was completely
unrealistic—as people like Tadeusz Bobrowski always
maintained—to demand that the "one and indivisible"
Poland should be restored in its former grandeur.

In August or September 1861 the home of the Nałęcz
Korzeniowski on Novy Świat Street became the gathering place of patriots. Conrad later wrote that he vaguely
remembered stealthy visits and mysterious gatherings.
Apollo was known to the police as a subversive. Ewelina
herself had been under police surveillance in Zhitomir

and she had been warned that her husband would be arrested if he returned there.

The unrest in Warsaw grew and big patriotic demonstrations were planned for 10 October 1861 to celebrate the centenary of the historic union of Lithuania with Poland. Apollo was one of the most active organizers. This great manifestation, and the funeral of a Polish archbishop scheduled for the same day, were the last celebrations permitted. On 14 October, the Russians declared a state of war in Warsaw and made it illegal to assemble. This forced the Polish patriots underground. The municipal committee became a clandestine national government in which Apollo was again to be a leading member.

One Polish historian, Bronisław Szwarce, states that "the poet Apollo Korzeniowski, from the Ukraine, and brother-in-law of Stefan Bobrowski, was the first founder of the insurrectionist committee."

Apollo was one of the first to be arrested. It happened during the night of 20-21 October, a week after the declaration of the state of war and only four days after the foundation of the secret national government. He was imprisoned in the infamous Pavilion 10 of the Citadel, the Pavilion of the political prisoners. The police seized all his papers including the letters he had (clandestinely) sent to his wife and which she had been imprudent enough to bring with her to Warsaw. Apollo was tried by a war tribunal before which he appeared four times during the following four months. The minutes of the trial were duly filed away and, when Poland became free in 1919, were kept in the Warsaw *Archives of Historical Documents*. Jean-Aubry saw them there in 1927, but in 1944, in consequence of the last of the Polish risings,[19] the inner town was systematically destroyed by the Germans as a measure of retaliation, and only a few shreds of the minutes remained.

The Russian court did not use any means of coercion and it must be said that it tried to be just according to the law in force. After weighing the evidence, the court came to the conclusion that although it could not be proven that Apollo took practical steps to overthrow the government, his pamphlets and letters showed that he was not just a participant but the main agitator in the subversive riots and manifestations connected with the *Scientific College* and the *Academy of Art*, the chairman of

The side gate access to the Tenth Pavilion of the Warsaw Citadel, as it looked when Apollo was imprisoned there.

the secret committee, and the author of subversive leaflets in which he tried to convince the population of Warsaw that Lithuania, White Russia, and the Western Russian provinces, including Kiev, should be part of Poland. Therefore, and mindful of the defendant's "arrogant manners" and of his written declaration that he was a Pole and wanted Poland's happiness, the court resolved that "literator" Apollo Korzeniowski and his wife be "sent out" to Perm under strong police escort to live there in forced residence and under police supervision[20]. The sentence was carried out immediately and the convoy left 8 May 1862. (Apollo's "arrogant manners"—or what we would call contempt of court—consisted in his refusal to answer or to answer in Russian).

It is well-known that the place of forced residence was changed on the insistence of the Perm governor who had been a friend of Apollo's at Petersburg, and that the exiles were sent to a more Northern place—Vologda. (Conrad, basing himself on his uncle's version, repeated in the latter's *Memoirs*, always believed that his mother voluntarily followed her husband into exile, but in fact she was sentenced together with her husband). Both Konradek and Ewa fell ill on the journey and a Moscow physician and former friend of Apollo's is credited with having saved the boy's life. Bobrowski writes that Apollo remembered that a former tutor he had had at Vinnitsa Classical College, Dr. Młodzianowski, was now a well-known physician and professor at Moscow University. A traveler bound for Moscow promised to transmit a message for him. "This very competent doctor arrived quickly and saved the child from a severe inflammation of the brain. Thanks to his numerous Moscow connections the doctor obtained that the journey be interrupted for a few days until the child was able to travel."

At Nizhni Novgorod, again according to Bobrowski, Ewelina became very weak and had to be carried from the carriage to the inn. A note was transmitted to the governor of the province who ordered the journey to be interrupted for a few days. They finally arrived at their place of exile, Vologda, end of June 1862, after a journey of over one month. Bobrowski writes, "In Vologda were 21 Polish men, mostly priests . . . My sister was no. 22 and her son no. 23 of the Polish colony there. From the point of view of treatment by the authorities the life there was quite tolerable; but the climate took its own.

Almost all the men fell ill with scurvy, but my sister and her son were free of it. However, they lost their strength because of the change of climate and the living conditions."

Shortly after his arrival in Vologda, Apollo wrote a long letter to his relatives Gabrielle and Jan Zagórski. The address given is Kozlinaya Street, House Dzieviatkov. In this letter, Apollo uses his sarcastic humor as a defence against the authorities, but probably still more against his own depressive moods.

Dear Gabrielle and Jan,
This is our 16th day in Vologda. We are in good health, unless we count as illness my nostalgia for my country. The authorities thoughtfully and paternally dealt with me, for when they saw that I worked on my *Fortnightly*, they gave me a prescription of powerlessness, speechlessness and immobility for seven months. Then, noticing that the dose was too great, they arranged to have me moved over a distance of two thousand and several hundred verst [kilometers]. Now they should have the same motherly regard and send me back to my country, say to tend unhorned cattle—which would always be nicer, more distinguished, more virtuous, more religious, and more splendid than to occupy the first rank here. I would ask that they do me the favor of not organizing my return journey, for you cannot imagine the unbearable conditions of the journey behind me. As long as we were in the country, blue-eyed people gathered by the dozens around the post station; they were incredibly nice to us.[21] But as soon as we had passed Mohilev we were isolated, and the people became terribly nasty. They were obviously afraid, while there [in Poland] people behaved like heroes. I shall not describe the journey, but only pick out one of the thousand disagreeable facts, an event typical for the civilization of this country. In Białokamienna the child gets pneumonia; the doctor is maintaining him with fluids and calomel—that's fine. But then they harness the horses. Naturally I oppose the continuation of the journey, especially as the doctor clearly states that in this case the child may die. My firm opposition stops the journey for the time being, and my protector goes to the local oracle. This civilized oracle, having heard the report, expresses the opinion that we should leave at once since children are born

in order to die (*sic*). So the order is to travel, but owing to my obstinate refusal we get some twenty hours' respite. By the way, God obviously blessed and comforted me, for he permitted that I should not be obligated to anyone, not even for sheer humanity,[22] and ordered that I should be only grateful to myself that I could keep my little son during this hard journey. In Nizhnyi Gorod, Ewelina fell sick. While the telegraph was ticking about the question whether one might treat her or not, some days passed and although the answer was No, we at least heard that the itinerary had been changed. Otherwise, we would have traveled to Perm and then would have traveled West for another 1500 verst. Enough, we arrived in Vologda on 16 June [Eastern calendar].

What is Vologda? A Christian being need not know this, Vologda is one great swamp of several square miles, over which, in parallel and crossing lines, boards are placed, all rotten and sagging under the feet. They are the only means of communication for the inhabitants. By these boardwalks pickets have been driven and on these are built Italian-style cottages for the provincial gentry who all live here. The climate has two seasons: white winter and green winter, the first lasting nine and a half months, the second two and a half. We are at the beginning of the green winter; rain has been falling steadily for the last 21 days. In the white winter the frost reaches [minus] 25-30 degrees [Réaumur] and the wind from the White Sea, unimpeded by anything, carries with it rumors of polar bears. According to statistics there are about 17,000 people here—why and for what purpose I do not know. But during our pilgrimage in search of a residence in the course of 15 days we met the following living beings: 62 cows, 17 goats, 33 dogs, and 29 living dead who pass here for human beings. Vologda is developed according to its civilization. I got acquainted with two of its expressions: the presence of police and of thieves. To the police I was addressed like merchandise. The thieves daily make their presence known. The question is who came first. The genesis is unknown. For us Vologda as such does not exist, only as a group of deported persons.

[A list of ten Polish names follows.] We arranged and are maintaining a chapel which is the center around which we live. We pray a lot, fervently and

The Pavilion of the political prisoners in the Warsaw Citadel, with the "kibitka", wagon used for the transportation of arrested persons. (Photo "Ruch")

sincerely. Around us are people deported in the years 1830, 1846, and 1848. They could have returned from 1856 on, but they got acclimatized, they married and—even more important—they multiplied.

For them, our arrival was like drops of water upon quick lime. It made them remember the language, the customs, the church. Priests are teaching their children, we hold common prayers and meetings, for it would be a pity if the sheep would disperse. Vologda serves as a place for people who love their country and want to work for her, for prostitutes, and for thieves. Our group is as numerous as incongruous. Now you know all about Vologda. When we arrived, we asked the savages here about Vologda: everywhere I saw their faces become red . . . we received one and the same answer: the Governor is good and the fish are cheap. This is obviously the A and Z of human happiness. The Governor is good all right, for he did us no harm, neither here nor at home. About the fish I don't know. By the way, there are emanations of swamps in the air: the odor of burning tar, and the smell of whale oil; this is what we breathe. One has no desire to speak, for one has the impression that the voice does not carry and will not get through to the ear of the listener. One does not want to write, for it looks as if the ink would not leave a trace on the paper. One only prays out of confidence, with blind faith, for our judgment says that, from here, prayers can in no way reach heaven, that God constantly looks in another direction, because otherwise the state of the world would fill him with disgust. We have not yet received a letter from anyone. We have written a lot and to many people.

We do not consider our deportation as a punishment, but as a new phase and form of service to the country. For us there can be no punishment, for we are innocent. This form of serving the country is necessary too, for it helps others to live, May therefore God and Christ crucified be praised, that he grants us such a reward beyond our merits. Curious how many serene faces you find here, with noble foreheads and with eyes looking proudly and penetratingly. Because of what we saw and what God looked at, there remained a reflection in our eyes which nothing can obscure and with which, as

if with a written testimonial, we shall once stand before God's judgment. So do not pity us, and above
all do not consider us as martyrs. We are servants
richly rewarded for our service.

(Translated from *People of the Year 1863*,
London 1963, 241-244).

Apollo's description of the Vologda climate is highly
poetical, but has been taken for granted by all Western
critics. Jean-Aubry and Baines called the climate "murderous" and the epithet is repeated in the latest edition
of *The Encyclopedia Britannica* (1975). In fact, the climate
is the same as in most Northern countries. What was
murderous was the way people like Apollo lived. They
would never do any physical work, have no physical
exercise. The women were wearing corsets which deprived them of one third of their breathing capacity. The
windows very likely remained closed during the cold season which lasted 7-8 months. The quarters were
cramped. To set the matter straight we have to compare
Apollo's sarcastic description with the meteorological
facts. This is what the *Great Soviet Encyclopedia* (2nd edition, 1952) says about them:

> The county (oblast') of Vologda is characterized by
> a very continental climate, mostly determined either
> by marine masses of air coming from the North-
> west, or by dry arctic air from the Northeast. The
> arctic winds bring dry and clear weather, the
> Northwestern winds are more humid . . . The mean
> January temperatures descend to −11 C. in the
> West to −14° C in the East; the corresponding
> temperatures in July fluctuate between 17° and 18°
> C. The annual precipitation is 550-600 mm, of
> which 400 fall during the warm season. The winter
> is long and icy. The snow remains on the ground
> for 160 days. The climate is favorable for the pro-
> duction of field vegetables and the breeding of
> animals. The wet and cool summer is particularly
> beneficial for the culture of flax.

As we can see the climate of Vologda is anything but
murderous. The population of the town which was only
8000 in 1800, increased steadily, and in 1914 reached
45,000, in 1939 95,000, it is now 200,000. True, the
winter is as long as in Canada, but the air is mainly dry

and the temperatures are much more moderate. The summer is short and wet, but the annual precipitation is about that of the English East coast and far below that of the West coast of England or the region of Vancouver in Canada.

Apollo soon·became the leader of the twenty-one Polish exiles. Once a week, they assembled in Apollo's tiny home for "tea with sweets" and discussion. After some time, Apollo's health deteriorated. It was the beginning of a tuberculosis of the lungs. He applied for permission to move to a warmer climate. The permission was granted and in summer 1863 the family settled in Chernikov,[23] 130 km (80 miles) North of Kiev.

Apollo felt much better in this town. Here began his last creative phase, lasting less than two years, until the death of his wife which occurred on 18 April 1865. In 1863, he wrote a long pamphlet entitled *Poland and Moscow*. It was published anonymously in the Polish emigrants' paper *Fatherland* (Ojczyzna) in Leipzig, 1864, nos. 17-50. For Apollo, Moscow is barbarism undiluted, while Poland represents civilization at its best. The Russians are but the heirs of the Tartars, while the more refined Poles defend the Eastern outpost of Western culture.[24]

Since this pamphlet reflects faithfully the fanatical views in which young Konrad was brought up, it deserves our attention. Apollo begins by describing his Warsaw prison, the Citadel, as "a well-built destructive machine . . . an immense dungeon in which Czarism buries Polish patriotism." He then quotes the text of the sentence (see Note 20).

After this, Apollo expresses his disappointment with the attitude of the Western powers, "This is the way Poland is grabbed by Moscow with the consent of the peoples and governments of Europe. If one day all the prisons of Europe were thrown open, letting out hordes of criminals ready for anything, one certainly would take the necessary measures . . . Yet the nations and governments [of Western Europe] look at Moscow and remain quiet . . . although at times they may shake with disgust, they do not recognize the gravity of the danger. As if the hypothetical liberation of all the criminals in the world were not a minor issue compared with the constant threat of a Moscow organized and prepared to swamp Europe with its millions of felons." For Moscow "has its own peculiar civilization, camouflaged with a semblance of Western ideas which Moscow adores like an idol . . . Moscow's goal is to ruin all human progress. It is therefore not astonishing that she is hiding her intentions. Were it not for her actions, I might be accused of prejudice. But history proves that whenever Moscow interfered in European affairs she threw herself with rage upon every holy principle evolved in the civilized world and, when she could not destroy it, she at least hurt it dangerously." Whatever the Russians print or write "is a lie, a shameless and downright lie, from the first to the last letter . . . Falsehood is piled upon falsehood. The partition of Poland was a moral crime. But everything was done to make the nations and governments of Europe blind with regard to Moscow." The Western powers did not understand that the partition of Poland was only the first act of the destruction of Europe, for "Europe will either be free or belong to the Cossacks." In the course of the years the Western powers forgot. For the sake of peace, Poland was written off. When, during the Crimean war (in 1854) the Polish diplomat, Richard Bielicki, was sent to Paris with a plan for a Polish insurrection—which, creating a second front, would have helped the Western powers—he found that the West was not interested and that the French government considered Poland as dead and buried. Yet, "only an independent Poland can guarantee the peace of Europe."

Ninety years ago European governments and nations looked on as the locusts invaded the most fertile fields, as the miasmas of the most prolific plague spred in a murderous way, as the infectious muds from the sea swallowed a whole civilization, its light, its faith in God and in the future of mankind—in one word: as Moscow overpowered Poland. There was England, this England rightly proud of her liberties established by the efforts of her people. During the ninety years since Moscow plays a role in Europe, she has been a constant threat to the West. At the Vienna Congress they trembled before her. In 1831, England had to bow to the tyranny of Nicholas. In the Crimean war she could not obtain those concessions to which she was entitled, and finally, in 1863, she had to look on when her first statesmen were humiliated by Moscow's minister.

"There was France, this France where not so long ago the Polish noblewoman had been a queen [and for which the Poles fought so often and so valiantly]... this same France today can no longer remember clearly what she stands for, what is in her blood and in her soul—namely, liberty and independence; confronted with the Polish problem she is intimidated by Moscow and mute."

As an example of Muscovite tyranny, Apollo reminds the West that the Russian censor had forbidden the Poles to print such words as Poland, fatherland, tyranny, liberty, dedication, victim, patriot, and numerous others of the kind. Apollo's article culminates in the following two statements: "Moscow is no nation, only an autocracy (gosudarstwo)..." "The centuries old history of Poland has shown her vocation—to be a guard and a defense of Europe against the designs of barbarism."

Apart from *Poland and Moscow*, Apollo worked mostly on translations. Shakespeare, Victor Hugo, and Dickens were his favorite authors. He translated the *Comedy of Errors* and *Much Ado about Nothing*. Of Hugo's work, he translated *Les travailleurs de la mer, Marion Delorme, Hernani*; and from Dickens: *Hard Times*. (Conrad mentions in *A Personal Record* that he read *The Two Gentlemen of Verona* in his father's translation, but there is absolutely no evidence that Apollo translated this play).

Bobrowski and others after him also reported that Apollo translated Heine, but no such translation has been found.

Apollo's philosophy of art is expressed in an article on Shakespeare, written in exile and published in *Warsaw Library*, Vol. II, 1868. All the pathos and the absoluteness of a Nałęcz are present in this essay:

> Shakespeare! It is enough to pronounce this name and at once a whole world of alluring visions fascinates the mind... the dramatic work he created shines all the more brilliantly on the new road he opened up. After three hundred years it still stands eminent, unique, and apart.

Then Apollo explains that the dramatist creates out of the fullness of the people's heart. Dramatic conflicts necessarily are basic human conflicts. This is why dramatic art has always existed, why it never had to be invented:

Apollo Korzeniowski (right) in Vologda, together with two other exiles: Count M. Szembek and J.G. Sabinski

There can be no history of the birth of dramatic
art . . . like every natural phenomenon, like inspiration, it was perfect and distinct from the very beginning. In primitive ages, it manifested itself
through the souls of magicians and prophets, and
later in geniuses. Even today whenever it manifests
itself, it does so in its perfection.

Apollo then discusses the philosophy of Shakespeare
as reflected in his tragedies:

The well-known [Polish] proverb, "Man fires, but
God carries the bullet" seems to be the principle
upon which Shakespeare's dramatic art is
built . . . God permits man to use his free will, but
to fulfill plans which man did not invent himself.
He permits him to carry out, of his own free will,
tasks which he did not set himself.

Reading this one wonders whether this is not actually
Apollo's life philosophy. Towards the end of his life he
felt he had done his share—the final outcome was in
God's hands. The Polish proverb was, of course, well-
known to Conrad. He quotes it in "Gaspar Ruiz," followed by a bitter comment which stands in strange contrast to the religious resignation of his father:

[The proverb] evolved out of the naive heart of the
great Russian people, "Man discharges the piece,
but God carries the bullet," is piously atrocious and
at bitter variance with the accepted conception of a
compassionate God. It would indeed be an inconsistent occupation for the Guardian of the poor, the
innocent, and the helpless to carry the bullet, for
instance, into the heart of a father.
(*A Set of Six*, 18).

Once more, Conrad chose to camouflage a Polish
memory by attributing a well-known Polish proverb to
the Russians. As for the expression "Guardian of the
poor, the innocent, and the helpless," it is an allusion to
Conrad's childhood prayers. The sarcasm of father and
son are of the same kind, but, contrary to Apollo, Conrad directed his at targets which his father would have
respected. Apollo's irony was strictly aimed at human institutions; Conrad's was cosmic and included the whole
scheme of the universe.

A contemporary critic, Leonard Sowinski, said this about Apollo: "His wit bites to the bone, his irony kills. His laughter is a kind of snarl, followed by a deep bite. He is as unwilling as unable to reprove gently; simple faults and crimes alike he nails on the pillory of shame and contempt."[25]

A modern critic, Mieczysław Lisiewicz, characterized Apollo as follows: "For a politician he was too violent, too uncompromising. He considered it as his strict duty to tell everyone the truth to his face."[26]

During the last illness of his wife and after her death, which coincided with the fateful and unsuccessful insurrection of 1863, Apollo seems to have drifted ever stronger towards "messianism". He likened his country to the Messiah who had been tortured and crucified, but had risen in the end:

> As he did on the cross, so you died from torture
> He—for salvation—you for liberation
> And as he rose from his dark tomb
> Thus you too—O Polish people—from the
>   dead will rise again.

This mystic tendency even expressed itself in the way Apollo dressed and behaved. In a picture taken at that period, he looks like a sad Old Testament prophet. Speaking of the years 1863 to 1866, Bobrowski once said to his former ward, twenty-year-old Perłowski: "After the insurrection, Korzeniowski, by his pose as a despondent seer and poet, disheartened everyone." (Barbara Kocówna *Reminiscences*, 119)

Lisiewicz adds, however: "There *was* tragedy, but some role playing as well. Apollo finds himself in a truly hopeless situation, so he strikes up a certain pose. Role playing and taking up a pose was in the style of that epoch. Whatever a man did had to be deadly serious, and every woman had to be not only an angel, but an angel of self-sacrifice."

Much happened during Apollo's stay at Chernikov, from 1863 to January 1868. The insurrection broke out in January 1863. Apollo was not happy when he heard this. He thought the insurrection was not prepared well enough. His comment was: "That's how we do things in Poland—either too early or too late." Yet the rising was first successful, but in the absence of any substantial aid from outside, it was brutally repressed and came to an end in 1865. Apollo's brother Robert lost his life at the beginning while his younger brother Hilary was deported to Siberia.

In 1864, Ewelina was allowed to spend three months with her brother Tadeusz in Novofastov, accompanied by Konradek. Although dangerously ill, she had to return to Chernikov under circumstances which Conrad later described in detail following his uncle's *Memoirs* (*A Personal Record*, 65-67) Only a few weeks later, she was no more. Apollo's father also died in the same year.

During his exile, Apollo wrote about twenty letters to his friend Kazimierz Kaszewski (not to be confused with the novelist Józef I. Kraszewski), a well-known critic and translator living in Warsaw, who transmitted Apollo's manuscripts to the publishers or journals. After the death of his wife, Apollo's letters (they are preserved at the Jagiellonian Library in Cracow) became very gloomy. First he planned to entrust Konradek to Kaszewski, but this did not materialize. He asked Kaszewski to send him school books, so he would be able to teach his son. He also told Kaszewski that he was sitting for hours, if not days, at Ewelina's grave. And he added, "My only link with life is through Konradek. I can do less and less for him. Soon I will not be able to do anything."

For almost another year, he kept his son with him, before he allowed him to go and live with his uncle, where at long last the boy was able to learn and to play with other children and live a normal life. But less than two years later Apollo, finally freed from exile, would claim his son again.

To a suggestion by Kaszewski that he write and publish his memoirs to increase his income, Apollo replied: "I don't want to throw the pearls of my holy suffering and lifelong grief on the garbage heap of daily life—but I must live, unfortunately." It is not likely that he ever began to write his autobiography. If he did, he must have destroyed the manuscript shortly before his death.

One of the last things he wrote in Chernikov was a long poem entitled "The Sea—the People." He compared the masses of water to the masses of people. Just like the sea, the people might be quiet and content at one time, but when they revolt they can destroy thrones as the sea may destroy ships. The poem is interesting because it is the only one with so much sea imagery.

However, Apollo got his description of the sea from Victor Hugo's *Les travailleurs de la mer* rather than from personal experience. Throughout, the sea is only used as a simile.

A letter dated 16 January 1866 to Gabrielle and Jan Zagórski reflects the state of Apollo's mind during his last years at Chernikov:

> The orphan keeps me at my duty, it's not likely I should relax in my care for him. That's how I live, dear friends. I love what was is left for me to love as strongly as when I could give something to those I loved, while today I have nothing to offer. No dedication, no sacrifices are left, for I have nothing to dedicate or to sacrifice. Sad is the fate of the man to whom those two only ways of realizing the image and semblance of God are closed, but such is the will of the Providence. I read your cherished letter whenever fever and sweat come over me, filling me with proud despair and a sort of divine sadness—tears flow, the spring [of tears] gives relief and more composed I take up life again which, today, is centered in Konradek alone. I protect him against the influence of the [Russian] atmosphere around us, and the little boy grows up as in a monk's cell. The grave of our Unforgotten One serves us as a holy Memento mori . . . We shiver with cold, we die of hunger, we share the misery and the prayers of our nearest friends here . . . My situation is that of a man standing at locked doors behind which the most cherished being is in agony, but he cannot even protect her forehead from the mortal sweat. We look at something which Dante did not describe, for his soul, although terrified by all sort of horrors, was too Christian to have such inhuman visions. That's our life!
>
> (Translated from *Illustrated Weekly*, 15 May 1920).

Apollo in Galicia

In January 1868, Apollo, with his ten-year-old son, crossed the Russian border and went to Lwów (Lemberg). It was the first time Apollo set foot outside of Russia. He knew he would never return. Lwów was in Galicia, as the Austrian slice resulting from the partition was called.

After his arrival on Austrian soil, Apollo wrote frequently to his former schoolmate and lifelong friend,

Stefan Buszczyński who lived in Cracow at the time. He was a journalist and the author of a pamphlet *Patience and Revolution* (1862), in which he warned his compatriots against starting an uprising. He had also written a voluminous book *La décadence de l'Europe* (Paris 1867), in which he criticized "the -isms in the name of which well-meaning men want to save humanity" without realizing that in doing so they only "opened chasms of calamities with their own hands."

The letters to Buszczyński are preserved in the Library of the Polish Academy of Sciences (PAN) in Cracow. In the first letter, dated 17 March 1868, Apollo expresses his satisfaction at being able "to write openly," i.e. without interference of the censor. Knowing the nature of his illness, he says, "I don't know whether I can live on my work in Lwów—whether with the last breath of my lungs I can do something useful here." Then he criticizes Lwów, "Up to now Lwów did not at all endear itself to me. At once I was struck by its hatred against Cracow, from which Lwów would take away everything it could . . . If at least one could notice here any sign of a new and powerful idea . . . I came to the conclusion that there is no question of my staying here, nor of finding here a way of supporting myself . . . In this town, there is no Polish spirit . . . My second, if not my first, goal here is to bring up Konradek not as any democrat, aristocrat, demagogue, republican, or monarchist—nor as a lackey or servant of these factions—but just as a Pole; but I doubt whether under the conditions prevailing in Lwów, this can be done if he goes to a government school . . . It is quite possible that one day I move to Cracow, if I may ask your help . . . The next months will decide this." But in the same letter, Apollo also mentions that Konradek is having German lessons "so that he may attend school here."

The next three letters are dated from April 1868. In the first, Apollo reports that he had made a journey to Przemyśl (two and a half hours by train) and that he returned sicker than before: "My Dearest, . . . one who has fever every day and in the night sweats profusely, does not need any imagination to recognize his state of health. By the way, I follow the doctor's advice strictly. The doctor, who was recommended to me by honest friends, prescribed for me Obersalzbrünn [mineral water] and later sheep's milk. He ordered me to go to the countryside. So, around the 5 May I will travel to Kruchel Wielki . . . later I definitely will travel to Topolnica (the earliest on the 20 May if the funds allow)." In the same letter, Apollo mentions that he received an invitation to contribute to the *Literary Journal* of Galicia. The journal had financial difficulties, but Apollo said, "One must be practical," and suggested that small capitalists be approached for financial support.

About the 20 April, Apollo writes to Buszczyński: "Tomorrow, they drive me to Topolnica for the sheep's milk cure . . . The doctor in Lwów actually forces me to go . . . Of course, Konradek will accompany me." From Topolnica, on 26 April, Apollo writes that he is taking sheep's milk, but that he is not well: "I cannot take upon me to teach Konradek. Reading in itself for me has become real work. But if my health returns, I shall be in Cracow at the end of July."

On 10 May, we find Apollo at Kruchel Wielki, a village not far from Przemyśl. In a very disorderly, unnaturally large handwriting he tells Buszczyński, "In the old fashion I kiss Ofelia's little hands . . . Konradek kisses the hands of his uncle [Buszczyński] . . . he will write you. By himself, without being told, he does not write, well—he likes what he likes . . ." On 16 May, this revealing admission: "The weight of my guilt which they throw upon me and for which I paid with my best blood. One can do nothing about it. But I was astonished at Pawlimiecz. The people here [in Lwów] all hurt my heart and my conscience with their reproaches . . . I best stay at Kruchel—for the schools in Lwów are stupid . . . My son deteriorates, for I am not even able to look after his education."

On 29 May, Apollo writes a long commentary on Buszczyński's *La décadence de l'Europe* which he had received in April. In October 1868, in an unusually tiny handwriting, Apollo reports from Przemyśl that he would like to live in the mountains, and quotes Heine's verse "Auf die Berge möcht ich steigen" (I would like to climb mountains). He adds, "In four days I shall travel to Lwów. I sit in a corner and my one and only preoccupation is the teaching and upbringing of Konradek."

The next letter is dated from 19 November 1868. Apollo then lived at 11, Szeroka Street, in Lwów. "I am sick and hardly ever go outside. I look after Konradek better, giving him lessons." On 29 December he reports that his illness keeps him confined not only to his apartment, but to his room.

In January, Apollo, who still hopes that his health may improve, speaks of a projected daily newspaper, *Kraj*. On 1 February, he sends a telegram for Ofelia's birthday and again discusses the newspaper project. On 7 February, he tells Buszczyński of his forthcoming arrival in Cracow: "On the 20th I shall travel to Cracow. I will be a member of the editorial board. British affairs are assigned to me." He will have to contribute an article per week. Yet, he has misgivings: he feels very sick, "every movement is difficult". He will have to make the [ten hours'] journey in two days, being unable to travel in the morning nor late in the evening. Then he asks Buszczyński to find an apartment near the newspaper office, on the ground floor or no higher than the first floor, dry, warm, furnished, and provided with a kitchen. "Unfortunately my health is not good—I need some comfort and household help . . . I am father and mother to a sick little child." Then he strikes a cheerful note: "Vivat! We shall see each other. Incredible how great my joy is—if only God will permit this to become reality."

Apollo, accompanied by his eleven-year-old boy, arrived in Cracow toward the end of February. Less than three months later, on 23 May 1869, Apollo Nałęcz Korzeniowski died at the age of 49. He had not been able to write a line for the newspaper. Part of his manuscripts he must have entrusted to Buszczyński, another part he burned shortly before his death—a scene described in Conrad's *A Personal Record* (10).

Apollo's death was reported by only three Polish newspapers and by *Warsaw Library*. The funeral itself was described anonymously (actually by Buszczyński) in the Cracow daily *Time* (Czas):

> Yesterday at 6 p.m. an immense crowd filled the Grodzka and Poselska streets in order to pay their last homage to the poet and distinguished son of Poland. The clergy, the trade-guilds with their flags, the professors of the University and higher schools, the youth of the schools, the members of the Learned Society and the Friends of Cultural Progress surrounded the coffin . . . behind them were several thousand people . . . It is a long time since Cracow saw such an impressive funeral, impressive not by its external pomp, but by the deep-

Conrad's father, Apollo Korzeniowski, towards the end of his life. The eyes of a dreamer and visionary, a leonine mane. . .

The house in Cracow where Apollo died in May 1869. The sickroom must have been upstairs and to the right; it was connected by a door with the boy's room behind. On the other side of the passage, the Canon of the Cathedral had his study and bedroom. The housekeeper lived below on one side, dining room and kitchen being on the other side. (See "Poland Revisited", *Life and Letters*, p. 167-168)

WDOMU KTÓRY STAŁ NATEM MIEJSCU
MIESZKAŁ ZALAT MŁODZIEŃCZYCH
OKOŁO ROKU 1869
JÓZEF KONRAD KORZENIOWSKI
JOSEPH CONRAD
SYN|POETY=TUŁACZA
WNIÓSŁ DUCHA POLSKIEGO
WPIŚMIENNICTWO ANGIELSKIE
KTÓREGO STAŁ SIĘOZDOBĄ
x
IT WAS IN THAT OLD ROYAL AND ACADEMICAL
CITY THAT I CEASED TO BE A CHILD=BECAME
A BOY HAD KNOWN THE FRIENDSHIPS THE
ADMIRATIONS THE THOUGHTS AND THE
INDIGNATIONS OF THAT AGE ·

The Polish text of this tablet reads "In the house which stood at this place, there lived in his youthful years—around 1869—Józef Konrad Korzeniowski—Joseph Conrad—son of the exiled poet. He brought the Polish spirit into English literature, in which he became outstanding." The rest, in English, is from *Poland Revisited*.

"...the Florian Gate, thick and squat under its pointed roof, barred the street with the square shoulders of the old city wall...its black archway stood out small and very distinct." (*Poland Revisited*)

felt sympathy shown and the tears shed by the citizens.

Conrad himself described the funeral twice in his later works, in his Author's Note (1921) to *A Personal Record*, and in "Poland Revisited" (*Notes on Life and Letters*, 169), Conrad mentions the "Youth of the Schools, the grave Senate of the University, the delegations of the Tradeguilds," and the nature of the homage paid to his father.[27] In fact, the funeral took place in the evening, not in the afternoon as Conrad has it, so that the whole population might attend. And the boy did not walk alone in an empty space behind the hearse. Stefan Buszczyński, who acted as his tutor, was walking beside him.

After the funeral, Buszczyński opened a subscription in *Time* to collect the funds for a proper monument. It was designed by a well-known Cracovian sculptor, Walery Gadomski. It still stands in the same place. Built from rough hewn fieldstones, topped by a small cross, it well symbolizes Apollo's simple but unyielding personality. A slab in front bears the inscription:

> To Apollo Nałęcz Korzeniowski
> Victim of Muscovite Tyranny
> Born 21 February 1830
> Died 23 May 1869
> To the man who loved his country
> Worked for it and died for it
> His Compatriots

Ivy has been growing around the tomb for more than a hundred years. And each year, on the day of Apollo's death and on Allsaints Day, flowers appear mysteriously on the tomb. The poet may be forgotten, the patriot is not.

Looking back on Apollo's life, one is inclined to agree with Taborski that Conrad's father could be called a typically Conradian hero. He would have fitted perfectly into *Nostromo*. This man, verbally so gifted, certainly was a figure as pathetic and as romantic as any of Conrad's characters.

At Apollo's death, the following of his works had been published:

Apollo's tomb in Cracow

Conrad's mother, Ewelina

Drama: *Comedy*, three acts, Warsaw 1854 and 1855.

> *For the Beloved Dollar*, a comedy in three acts, St. Petersburg 1859.
>
> *What to do with this Pawn?*, one act, Warsaw 1861.
>
> *The Little Whip*, Comedy for children in two acts, Lwòw 1861.
>
> *No Hope*, unfinished drama, Warsaw 1866.

Poetry: *Ave Maria*, St. Petersburg 1844.

> *Verses at Random*. Wilno 1856 (together with *Comedy*).

Articles: Numerous articles in newspapers on political, social and literary subjects.

> Article on Shakespeare, Warsaw 1868.

Translations: Some scenes from *Les Burgraves* (Victor Hugo) Warsaw 1846.

> *Chatterton*, by A. de Vigny, told in Polish. Kiev 1857.
>
> *Légende des Siècles* (Victor Hugo) [Excerpts] translated by Adam Pług and Apollo N. Korzeniowski, Żytomierz (Zhitomir) 1860.
>
> *Hernani* (Victor Hugo), Warsaw 1862.
>
> *Marion Delorme* (Victor Hugo), Warsaw 1863.
>
> *Comedy of Errors* (Shakespeare), Warsaw 1866.
>
> *Hard Times* (Dickens), Warsaw 1866.

After Apollo's death, the following of his works appeared in print:

Drama: First Act, comedy in one act, Lwów 1869.

Verses: *To Józef Ignacy Kraszewski*, Warsaw 1898 and 1954.

> *Fit is your Boat*, in Bobrowski's *Memoirs*, Lwów 1900.
>
> *Words from the Cross to Mother Poland*, Warsaw 1928.
>
> *Unpublished Verses*, on the Peasant Revolt in the Ukraine, (*Literary Album* 1955, no. 4).

d. The Mother

As for Conrad's mother, she too would fit into Conrad's work. Her image remained somewhat hazy to him, for he knew her mostly as a very weak and ailing woman, but one who always had a smile for him. She must have been a highly intelligent, most sensitive, and extremely active person. In the pictures which have been preserved of her, she looks physically delicate. She was well educated and, among other things, mastered French. From the few letters that have been preserved of her correspondence with Apollo, one understands that she subordinated her life completely to that of her husband. Although highly gifted herself, she personified the ideal of a woman and wife of that time: she was self-effacing and never questioned her husband's ideas or plans but identified herself with them. She helped him with his translations from the French, whenever he demanded it. Her short life was sacrificed for her husband, her child, and her country. She too believed that nobody had a right to personal happiness as long as Poland was under foreign tyranny. After 1860, she always dressed in black. While in exile, she often made her little son wear black, too, as a sign of mourning for "Mother Poland in her grave."

Conrad may have thought of his mother when, in his Author's Note to *Under Western Eyes*, he wrote of Miss Haldin's "idealistic faith . . . great heart . . . and simple motives."

In his *Memoirs* Bobrowski wrote an evaluation of his sister Ewelina, Conrad's mother, which Conrad has almost copied in *A Personal Record*:

Bobrowski

My oldest sister had a beautiful appearance and was better used to the manners of the great world than most of the educated women of our rank at that time. She also had high qualities of mind and heart. At that time she found it difficult to adjust and expected more attention than she would or could give to others. Of rather delicate health, and torn between her love for her husband-to-be, and the declared opposition of her father whose memory and convictions she respected, she was in a moral turmoil. Not at peace with herself, she could not give others what she lacked herself. Only after she had become united with the man she loved, did she develop uncommon qualities of heart and mind. In the midst of the most adverse events in her life, where all national and social aspirations ended in failure, she was able to stand fast, fulfilling her obligations as a wife, mother and patriot, and winning the respect and admiration of her relatives as well as of strangers, sharing the exile of her husband and representing worthily the ideals of Polish womanhood.

Conrad:

Your mother—of far greater beauty, exceptionally distinguished in person, manner and intellect, had a less easy disposition. Being more brilliantly gifted, she also expected more from life . . . she was torn by the inward struggle between her love for the man she was going to marry and her knowledge of her dead father's objection to that match. Unable to bring herself to disregard that cherished memory and that judgment she had always respected and trusted, and, on the other hand, feeling the impossibility to resist a sentiment so deep and true, she could not have been expected to preserve her mental and moral balance. At war with herself, she could not give to others that feeling of peace which was not her own. It was only later, when united at last with the man of her choice, that she developed those uncommon gifts of mind and heart which compelled the respect and admiration even of our foes. Meeting with calm fortitude the cruel trials of life reflecting all the national and social misfortunes of the community, she realized the highest conceptions of duty as a wife, a mother and a patriot, sharing the exile of her husband and representing nobly the ideal of Polish womanhood.

(A Personal Record, 28-29)

II.

Conrad's Education

Józef Teodor Konrad was born in the Polish borderland, that large fertile plain between Poland and Russia proper where practically all intellectuals, estate owners and estate managers were Poles, while the farmhands and servants were mostly illiterate Ukrainians. When the boy was three, his parents moved to the provincial capital, Zhitomir. A photograph taken shortly before Ewa's and Konradek's departure for Warsaw and published in Taborski's biography (128), shows the four-year-old boy sitting on a balustrade, holding a gun in his left hand. His face is surrounded by long dark hair, and at the same time expresses determination and sensibility. There is an unmistakable likeness to his mother. The boy is wearing a military coat. His light-colored pants are closed below the knees: in short, he presents the figure of a freedom fighter in miniature.

Another photograph, taken in Chernikov and published in Jean-Aubry's *LL* (22) and in Barbara Kocówna's *Conrad's Polonitas* (Polskość Conrada, 48), shows the seven-year-old boy in long grey pants and a dark jacket, sitting fearlessly upon a horse.

After his arrival in Warsaw (1861) and up to 1866, when he was almost nine, the boy lived with his parents under circumstances which can hardly be called normal. He intimately shared their anxieties, their sorrows, their extreme poverty, their narrow quarters in exile, their illnesses. He never went to school. He had only one teacher—his father. Writing, reading, and memorizing the most exalted passages of Polish romantic literature were the main subjects, followed by French. Apollo had learned English by a self-teaching method (Robertson)[28] and he adapted the method to French for his boy. As we

55

know from Apollo's letters to Kaszewski, Konradek was also taught arithmetic.

The boy read Polish fluently at the age of six. He was often left to himself, with no other companion than a book. From the age of four to the age of nine there was not much room for play, no cheerfulness, no carefree humor in his life. Apollo was aware of this. Four months after the death of his wife, he wrote to Kaszewski: "The poor child does not know what it is to have a friend of the same age. He looks at the sadness of my decrepitude and who knows whether this sight does not put wrinkles in his young heart and will not cover with hoar frost his awakening soul."[29] Despite this insight, it took Apollo a year to decide to let his son join the Bobrowski family in the Ukraine. This happened in the spring of 1866. Here, at last, Konradek could work and play with other children in a happy rural atmosphere. Here, also, he had the opportunity of speaking French, for Bobrowski, like everybody of his status, had a French governess, Mlle Durand,[30] for his daughter, Józia. This happy period, however, was to last hardly two years, for in January, 1868, Apollo was released from exile and allowed to leave Russia. Although already suffering from pulmonary tuberculosis, he went to the Ukraine and took the eleven-year-old boy with him to Lwów in Austria, and later to Cracow. In his narcissism, he wanted to bring up the boy all by himself and to make a second self out of him.

Indeed, the very name Konrad was a profession of Polish patriotism. In a talk with Marian Dąbrowski in 1914, Conrad stated that his father read to him aloud (and made him read aloud) the Polish national poems *Pan Tadeusz* and *Konrad Wallenrod*, and "not just once or twice." Both poems are by Mickiewicz whom the Poles call a seer-poet or a bard (*wieszcz*). The first extols, in a rather nostalgic mood, the pathos of old time Polish country life and preparations for liberating the country from the Muscovites with the help of the approaching Napoleonian army, while *Konrad Wallenrod* is a camouflaged description of Poland's fight for freedom. Konrad is a patriot fighting the Teutonic Knights who here stand for imperialistic Russia. Of course, Konrad is really a German name (the middle-German *Kuonrat* means "bold in counsel") used by Mickiewicz to camouflage a Polish identity. Another Konrad is the hero of Mickiewicz's dramatic poem *The Forefathers* in which a certain Gustaw changes his name to Konrad. Because of Mickiewicz (who was only 20 years older than Apollo) Konrad became the name for a patriotic Pole. This fact was well-known to the Russians of the borderland, and the Russian writer, Korolenko, relates the story of a Russian priest who hated the Polish name so much that he obliged a Polish pupil bearing it to change it to *Kodrat*.

It is improbable that Konrad went to school while living with his father in Lwów. In his free time he was often left to himself and read whatever he chose. By some extraordinary stroke of luck, two persons who knew him well during his sojourn in Lwów reported their reminiscences in Polish periodicals shortly after Conrad's death. One is the daughter of Apollo's physician, Dr. Tokarski. She was one year older than Konrad and became one of his playmates. These are the reminiscences of Jadwiga Kałuska née Tokarska:

> My mother, wanting to relieve the father [Apollo] of the trouble of looking after the lively boy, asked that he should visit us children in his free time. Whether Konrad then went to school or whether his father taught him, I do not know—I cannot remember. Thus Konrad stayed with us every free day, and when the weather was bad, also overnight. He astonished us all with his memory: he recited whole paragraphs of *Pan Tadeusz* and entire ballads by Mickiewicz. Already his inclination to write showed itself. He wrote small plays, distributed the parts among us three and became very angry when my brother and I did not memorize the text. Big cardboards painted with a red and a blue colored pencil served as decorations. The subject of these productions was the fight against the Muscovites. If necessary I too had to don masculine clothing, borrowed from one of my brothers. [Stage directions]: 'The rebels (wearing confederate caps) sit around the camp fire, together with their chief, singing patriotic songs.' Konrad knew the latter by heart and ordered us to repeat the refrains. 'Afterwards Muscovites arrive silently and there is a battle.'—which was enacted with tables and chairs. I remember this all very well, for these times were cheerful and carefree. The little despot governed us and we listened to him as our chief. The most beautiful production was a drama called *The Eyes of King Sobies-*

ki . . . In everything he did, Konrad expressed his
great love for his unfortunate country. And his
father instilled into the son what he felt himself.[31]

Mrs. Kałuska also remembered that Konrad proudly
wore the red confederate cap with a square top trimmed
with white lamb's wool and adorned with a feather—a
headgear as Polish as Tartan kilts are Scottish. Unfortunately for Jadwiga and her brother, Apollo decided,
after nine months, to move to Cracow, and these happy
days came to an end. It was only five years later, in September 1873, when Konrad was 16 years old and an orphan, that Jadwiga saw him again. He came to Lwów to
live in a boarding house run by a relative, Antoni Syroczyński, and he naturally visited the Tokarskis. This is
how Jadwiga remembered Konrad the adolescent:

> I did not recognize him at first; he had grown up,
> had long hair combed backwards, was quite a young
> man with a hint of moustache. He used to twinkle
> his eyes in such a way that he seemed to look at you
> through narrow slits. This gave him a somewhat
> fierce look . . . He read a lot, mainly about traveling.
> His desire was to know more about the world. A
> weekly called *Traveler* was being published at the
> time; it was Konrad's favorite paper. Konrad was
> also most interested in natural science and in litera-
> ture, and I know he was a very ardent student . . . I
> do not know where he studied.[32]

It was well-known that Uncle Bobrowski had strongly
opposed Konrad's plan to go to sea. Jadwiga and her
parents were all the more astonished when, about a year
later, in October 1874, this worthy guardian told them
that a Cracow doctor had said that, Konrad's father having died of pulmonary tuberculosis, the young man
could only be saved from the same fate by living near
the sea for a long time, and that he had therefore decided to send his nephew to Marseilles. We do not think
that this was just a face-saving pretext to explain his
change of mind. Too many people in Bobrowski's family
had died of tuberculosis: his sisters Ewa and Teofila, his
brother Kazimierz, Apollo, his only daughter Józia: and
Konrad's health had been a constant worry to both
Apollo and to Tadeusz. About the nature of his ailments
we know nothing, except that he had nervous attacks

and stomach cramps.[33] But we do know that he was overprotected and supposed to be delicate.

A second witness, Mrs. Wojakowska, wrote the following account:

> I saw Konradek for the first time 57 years ago (in 1868) and during his eight months' stay at Lwów I saw him often. Every Thursday and Sunday I went to bring the eleven year old Konradek to our apartment where we had also rented a great garden full of beautiful trees and flowers. We did our best to entertain and cheer up the pale and delicate boy. His father Apollo, a very sensitive poet and a melancholic person, discouraged by the failure of the insurrection and the recent death of his wife, had arrived from Vologda [actually Chernikov] and, in the Żółkiewski suburb, had rented two rooms where the sun never penetrated. He taught the boy himself, but apart from that could not occupy himself with him, perhaps from lack of energy, for he was in a state of apathy. In their dwelling I noticed an enormous amount of books from which Konradek read what he liked. Already at that time he made up little plays which we children were supposed to play; but it never came to that. Once, having entered their dwelling, I found Apollo sitting immobile before his wife's portrait. He did not look up, and Konradek, who came with me, put his finger on his mouth and said: 'Let's go silently through the room, for father, on the anniversary of Mammy, always looks at her portrait and neither speaks nor eats.' Konradek remembered with joy his two months stay by the sea (as a ten year old he had been taken to Liman beach[34] near Odessa by his uncle Bobrowski). He told me he wanted to become a sailor and travel a lot, and for the purpose very diligently learned geography and foreign languages. From Lwów they soon moved to Cracow where his father later died of pneumonia. Then his maternal grandmother, the mother of Tadeusz and Stefan, traveled to Cracow and for his sake took up residence there. She had a nice apartment on a first floor. From there, Konrad went to the classical college (Gimnazjum) for several years, and, as supervisor of studies, had a Mr. Pochman [really: Adam Pulman] whom he liked very much. We visited him there, and after the death of his grandmother in 1873, my father took him in our family. He spent ten months with us, attending class seven of the

classical college. Very developed intellectually, he
did not like the school routine which tired and
bored him. He said he had a good talent and would
become a great writer. This statement, the sarcastic
expression of his face, and his numerous critical
remarks, provoked astonishment in his teachers and
laughter in his fellow students. He did not like to be
bothered. At home, at school, and in the living
room especially, he lounged on a chair. He used to
have very severe migraine headaches and nervous
attacks at that time, and the doctors said that he
might get cured by a sojourn on the sea. This broke
the opposition of his uncle and guardian, Bobrowski, who up to then in no way wanted him to
become a sailor. (On the sea, he had those attacks
but very rarely; however, he once had an attack
while at the top of a mast, fell on deck and broke a
leg.[35] From that time on he limped). He had brown
hair, black eyes, and a mat complexion. He was
rather ugly, but there was something distinguished
and original about it.[36]

Despite some obvious inacuracies, the memories of
Mrs. Jadwiga Kułaska and Mrs. Wojakowska, recorded
more than fifty years after the events, are very revealing.
They prove that those who always had surmised that
Conrad did not tell everything in his *Personal Record*
were right. Certainly Joseph Conrad must have remembered the youthful plays and the battles with tables and
chairs against the Muscovites. Why did he not mention
them, but gave the impression that he was living with his
father in strict seclusion? Why did he forget to mention
his patriotic fervor that made him write his plays? And
why did he maintain that it was only at the age of sixteen that he decided to become a sailor when he had actually expressed this desire at the age of twelve? And,
last, but certainly not least, why did he write that he had
never thought of becoming a writer before the acceptance of his first manuscript, *Almayer's Folly*, when we
have the testimony of at least one witness that he declared already in Cracow that he would one day become
a great writer?

Looking back at Konrad's Polish years, one can only
marvel that he could make a success of his life at all. He
was an only child who lost his mother at the age of seven
and his father at eleven. Of the first eleven years of his

"To our right the unequal massive towers of St. Mary's Church soared aloft into the ethereal radiance of the air, very black on their shaded sides. . ." (*Poland Revisited*)

The Line A-B, to which Conrad devoted a full page in *Poland Revisited* (Notes on Life and Letters, 165-166). The cast iron tablet described by him became a victim of the German-Austrian war effort 1914-1918 and has been replaced by an enamel plate.

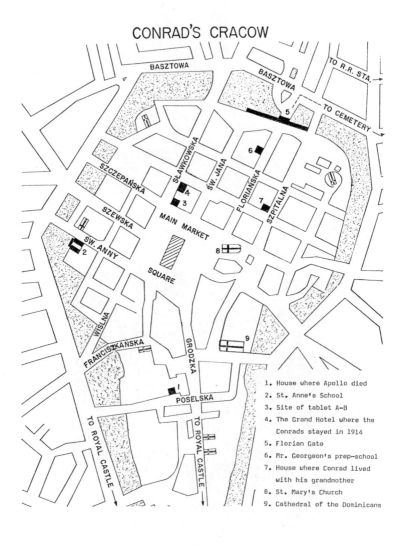

CONRAD'S CRACOW

1. House where Apollo died
2. St. Anne's School
3. Site of tablet A-B
4. The Grand Hotel where the Conrads stayed in 1914
5. Florian Gate
6. Mr. Georgeon's prep-school
7. House where Conrad lived with his grandmother
8. St. Mary's Church
9. Cathedral of the Dominicans

life, from 1857 to 1868, only the first three can be called somewhat normal. The following five were completely overshadowed by the exile, the illness and death of his mother, and the sadness of his father. Konrad only led a normal schoolboy's life from the spring of 1866 to January 1868 when he lived with his uncle's family in the Ukraine and was taught by a French governess. From January 1868, and until Apollo's death in May 1869, his father once more monopolized his thinking and feeling.

Several Polish scholars, among them Ludwik Krzyżanowski[37] and Czesław Witowski[38], have done some research into Conrad's life in Cracow, where the eleven-year-old boy arrived in Spring 1869 and where his father was to die in May of the same year. The boy was extremely backward in all subjects but Polish[39]. Concerning the three months between the arrival in Cracow and the death of his father, Conrad himself gave a short account from which we extract the following:

> . . . a small boy of eleven, wending his way, not very fast, to a preparatory school for day pupils on the second floor of the third house down from the Florian Gate. It was in the winter months of 1869.[40] At eight o'clock of every morning that God made, sleet or shine, I walked up Florian Street . . . Every evening at seven, turning my back on the Florian Gate, I walked all the way to a big old house in a quiet narrow street a good distance beyond the Great Square.
> ("Poland Revisited", *Notes on Life and Letters*, 167).

Konrad's way to school and back can be followed on the map of old Cracow, reproduced here (page 62, illustration No. 12). The Great Square is, of course, Cracow's famous Main Market Place (Rynek Główny). As we know from Witowski, the "big old house" was on Poselska Street, No. 12.[41] A picture of it appeared with this author's article in *Trends* (Kierunki) in 1958. The building was a typical, middle class, two-storied town house. It was later destroyed to make space for an administrative building. Where the house stood, a tablet has been placed (See illustrations No. 7,8, p. 48).

Conrad must always have remembered his father, a sad figure with an "ambrosial head"[42], wheezing, coughing feebly from time to time, not able to speak aloud,

St. Anne's classical High School as it looked a century ago.
There are in fact three buildings, arranged in form of a U and
enclosing a stylish courtyard. The buildings are now used as
the medical school of the Jagiellonian University. (Drawing by
Walery Eljasz, 1888)

The courtyard of St. Anne classical school, built by Jan
Laitner in 1689-1705 in the barock style. The entrance is visible on the right. (Drawing by Leon Getz)

half-lying, half-sitting in his bed, in the gloomy atmosphere created by the drawn curtains. The boy would only enter, kiss his father's emaciated hand, then withdraw. He felt his father's eye upon him, but he also felt that his father's life was all turned inside, that while still breathing he had died to the world already. Emaciated and dying people are frequent in Conrad's works: Almayer and Willems before their end, Wait the "Nigger," Kurtz, Yanko Goorall, and others.

And then, after the coughing and wheezing had ceased, a still figure with "a leonine mane"[43] in a white funeral shirt. And the last glimpse: his father's coffin wobbling through the town on a hearse, turning northwards to the big cemetery at the town limit, the boy following right behind. Then a man who made a speech praising Apollo as a political martyr, but not saying a word about his literary work[44], and finally, the prayer of a priest while the coffin was lowered into the grave, and somebody handing the boy a shovel to throw some earth on the casket. He must have felt very lonely in the huge crowd and at the same time very exposed. His uncle had not been able to come, but Stefan Buszczyński took care of the boy.

After Apollo's death on 23 May 1869, Konradek's grandmother, Teofila, made the necessary arrangements for the boy's education. Less than three weeks after Apollo's burial, she wrote to Kaszewski:

> My beloved orphan, following a wish of his father, was placed in the boarding house *The Cracovian*, of Mr. Georgeon (20 Florian St.). For lack of German and Latin, he could only be admitted to class 2 [grade 5], but we hope that he will be able to attend class 4 in a year's time, for the director of studies as well as every one of his teachers commend him for his assiduity and his interest—may God give him health—he gives every free minute to this purpose. His guardian, on the other hand, says that he doesn't know a child more easy to guide and having a more noble heart.

According to Witowski, Konradek went with his grandmother to the spa Wartenberg (now Straz), Bohemia, during the summer holidays of 1869, and returned to Mr. Georgeon for the autumn term. Apollo's friend, Buszczyński, also lived on Florian Street, and his son Konstantyn became Konrad's friend. (He was to meet him again in 1914).

Since the classical college at that time began with the fourth school year (at the age of nine), Konrad was two years behind his age group. The new school year began in spring, and if the boy wanted to catch up with those of his age, he had to do grade 4, 5 and 6 till April 1870.

It seems that, contrary to the grandmother's expectations, Konrad was not promoted to class 4 (grade 7) of the classical school in April 1870, but only in September of that year. In June 1870 Uncle Bobrowski arrived in Cracow, from where he took his mother to Italy. Konrad spent the summer in the well-known mountain resort, Krynica, in the Carpathians. In August 1870, the City Council of Cracow officially nominated the grandmother, Teofila Bobrowska, as Konrad's guardian. Being a woman, she had to be "assisted" by a man, Professor Mniszek—a mere formality. Uncle Tadeusz could not legally be Konrad's guardian since (technically) he lived in a foreign country.

When Grandmother Teofila returned from a prolonged cure in Italy she took up residence at 9 Hospital Street (Szpitalna) and Konrad lived with her there from November 1870 to May 1873. During the summer holidays of 1871 and 1872, he went again with Pulman to Krynica. He left school in May 1873, after having graduated from class 6 (grade 9) in the spring of that year. In order to go to university, he would have had to do two more years.

In May 1873, Konrad was sent with Pulman on a long journey to Germany, Austria, Switzerland and Italy, of which Conrad has given several glimpses in his *Personal Record*. The boy and his companion traveled to Vienna ty train, then by boat up the Danube to Linz and Passau, thence to Munich and Schaffhausen, Switzerland, by train. At Schaffhausen, they visited the Falls of the Rhine and then took the steamboat up the Rhine to Lake Constance. From there they took the train to Zurich. From there, they very probably took the steamboat to Rapperswil, at the other end of the Lake of Zurich, to visit the Polish Museum which, ever since its opening in 1870, had become a place of pilgrimage for the Poles abroad. The museum contained many relics of the Polish insurrections, such as arms, banners, historical documents, uniforms, the heart of Kościuszko; things that could not be exhibited in Poland. One of the biggest rooms was called Falck Room, because it contained nine famous steel engravings by the Polish artist Jeremias Falck (1610-1677), portraits of Polish kings, nobles, and high dignitaries. (One remembers that Falk is the title of a short story by Conrad). Back to Zurich, the two travelers would go to Lucerne by train and from there take the boat to Vitznau. Conrad tells us they visited the Rigi, but he forgot to say that this mountain had become one of the greatest tourist attractions of the century not only because of its celebrated panorama of the Alps. In 1871, the first rack railway of the world had begun to climb up and down the steep flank of the mountain, and nobody walked up any more. At Rigi Kulm Konrad had to get up at four in the morning to admire the "obligatory sunrise" (*Personal Record*, 43). Back to the lake, they went by steamer to Fluelen; from there on foot up the valley of the Reuss to Goeschenen, where they spent a night in a barrack built for the men working at the St. Gothard tunnel. On the following day they walked to Andermatt, Hospental, and over the Furka Pass. It seems that it was on top of that pass, in view of the majestic Finsteraarhorn, that the final argument about Konrad's desire to go to sea took place. At any rate, that mountain remained associated in Conrad's mind with his tutor's remark that he was a mania-afflicted, incorrigible Don Quixote.

It seems that after this dispute the arguing ceased. They went down to Gletsch, admired the Rhone Glacier together with droves of other tourists, crossed the Grimsel pass, and went down the Hasli valley to Brienz, where they very likely took the steamboat to Interlaken. From there, they probably made the day-long excursion to Lauterbrunnen and the Staubbach Falls immortalized by Goethe. Then they would leave Interlaken by boat for Thun and by train for Berne. It is probably in this town that they received a letter from Uncle Bobrowski saying that owing to a number of cases of cholera in Cracow they should prolong their journey and visit Upper Italy. If they followed the flow of tourists, they would go over the Simplon pass to Porlezza on the Lago Maggiore and from there travel to Milan. They would not possibly miss that Jewel of the lake, the Isola Bella. In Milan, it was of course the famous dome which constituted the main attraction. From Milan, they traveled to Venice. Conrad states in his *Personal Record* that it was in Venice that he saw the sea for the first time. They crossed by boat to Trieste, then an Austrian navel base. From there, the train took them to Vienna and finally to Cracow. They had been away for three months and were back at the end of July, 1873.

In spring, 1873, Konrad had been promoted to grade 10, but probably refused to return to school, for there is no other reason why Bobrowski would let him go on a long journey hardly two weeks after the beginning of the new school year. It is probable too that the good uncle hoped to quench Conrad's thirst for travel in this way, but when Conrad returned after three months, he was as obstinate as ever. Having missed school during the first quarter, he could hardly go back. He made life miserable for everyone. His grandmother could not cope with him anymore. All this explains why, at the beginning of September, we find Conrad in Lwów, under the guardianship of a distant relative, "Uncle" Antoni Syroczyński. He was an educator who directed a home for orphans of the 1863 Rising, to which Konrad was admitted. The language in the home was French. This was about the only thing which suited Konrad, for the rest, he proved a most undesirable boarder. He obviously did not go to any school, but passed his time reading light literature and especially the works of Jules Verne who had been a great traveler in imagination[45]. He may have read Verne's *A 15-Year-old Captain*. According to Bernard Meyer, Konrad must have read also Sacher-Masoch's *Venus in Furs*. Uncle Antoni disliked Konrad's ways, his laziness, his lack of discipline, the fact that he courted his daughter Tekla in a most disagreeable way (she made fun of him, though), the fact that he talked of nothing else but going to sea. Konrad developed bad manners, did what he liked, made a nuisance of himself. Syroczyński called him a "wałkoń"—that is a lazy tramp.

When this worthy educator told Bobrowski that he could no longer keep Konrad in the house, and when a Cracow doctor advised that Konrad should for some time live in a warmer climate and near the sea in order to escape the danger of consumption, Uncle Tadeusz was ready to let him go. In September, 1874, Konrad was back in Cracow, preparing for his journey to France. When he finally left for Marseilles on 14 October 1874, duly provided with letters of recommendation to two honorable citizens living in the French city, Konrad became Conrad, much as Mickiewicz's Gustaw had changed his name to Konrad. Shortly afterwards, Conrad would only be known as Monsieur Georges. But he was to find that shedding the past was not as easy as shedding a name.

Conrad's Schooling

Despite intensive searching, it has not been possible to determine with certainty which classical school Conrad attended while in Cracow. As we have seen, he first went to a private school on Florian Street, which prepared pupils for the entrance examinations to the classical school. The death of his father occurred after the beginning of the new school year, and his grandmother attempted to get him admitted to the leading classical college, St. Anne's.

Conrad had always maintained that he had gone to St. Anne's. It therefore came as a shock when Zdzisław Najder discovered that his name could not be found on the list of students published in 1888 in Jan Leniek's *Tricentenary Book*. The list is claimed to be fairly complete for all students attending the school between 1810 and 1880: each name is followed by the year of admission. Students having graduated from the top class are designated by an asterisk. In all, there are 12,952 entries. During the years 1870-1872, the school had between 600 and 700 students. For 1870, when Conrad is supposed to have been admitted to St. Anne's, 151 names are entered on the list as new students. According to Leniek, the pupils (all boys) belonged mainly to the middle class. Half of them had scholarships. The drop-out rate was high: only 15% of the 151 eventually graduated from the top class.

The curious fact that neither Józef Konrad Korzeniowski, nor Konstantyn Buszczyński, nor the Taube brothers can be found on this list does not necessarily mean that they did not attend the school. The list was compiled by two students of St. Anne's. Since each name is followed by the year of admission, it seems very likely that they simply copied the names entered as new pupils at the beginning of each school year. In this way, the few students who were admitted during the school year would not appear on the list, since at the beginning of

the following school year they would not be classified as
new pupils. This would explain why the Taube brothers,
Konstantyn Buszczyński, and Józef Konrad Korzeniowski
were overlooked, for they arrived from outside and were
admitted during the school year.

A perusal of the list of students shows that the name
Konrad does not occur once and that there are no middle names. In fact, there are no German first names at
all which means that it was the policy of the school to
eliminate them. (The name Konrad was only patriotic in
Russian Poland). There is some evidence that Józef Konrad Korzeniowski entered the school as Józef Korzeniowski, for L. Krzyżanowski found the following note
in the minutes of the school: "Józef Korzeniowski was
admitted to class 4 [grade 7] on 17 September 1870."
Despite the fact that the name Józef Korzeniowski was
not uncommon, this was the period when Konrad must
have been admitted to the school. The fact that the
above Józef Korzeniowski is not on Leniek's list of students seems to prove that our theory is correct. There is
only one Józef Korzeniowski on the list, but he entered
the school some years after Konrad had dropped
out—he would become the librarian of the Jagiellonian
University who sent Conrad Bobrowski's *Memoirs*.

Conrad himself told Mégroz that he had been to St.
Anne's High School, a school "of five hundred boys":

> St. Anne's where I was a scholar . . . the school was
> on the classical side, you know, along old-fashioned
> lines . . . I was good at mathematics, fairly good at
> history, and my composition could always pull me
> up in the class. But I was not good at grammar.

In a letter to the Polish writer, Bruno Winawer, dated
23 November 1922, Conrad wrote:

> While I was a boy in a great public school, we were
> steeped in classicism to the lips and, though our his-
> torical studies were naturally tinted with Ger-
> manism, I know that all we boys, the six hundred of
> us, resisted that influence with all our might."
>
> (*LL*, II, 289)

As we have seen, St. Anne actually had exactly 660
pupils in 1873, when Conrad left the school. The only
other gimnazjum in Cracow, St. Jacek's, was much smal-

ler. St. Anne's, with its almost three hundred-year-old Polish tradition, was of course the school the son of a Polish patriot would attend. It is preposterous to think that Conrad should have told a senseless lie to Mégroz. And how could he have known the approximate number of boys after so many years, if he had not attended the school?

According to my research carried out in Cracow libraries, it is probable that Conrad was admitted, in September 1870, to the fourth class of the Nowodworski Gimnazjum, better known as St. Anne's Gimnazjum because of its location on St. Anne Street, opposite St. Anne's church. In Spring 1871, he was promoted to class five (grade 8). In the summer, he was sent with his tutor to the mountain resort Krynica, where he had already passed the summer of 1870. They stayed in a boarding house called "Pod husarami i Górą parkową." In Spring 1872 he was promoted to class 6 (grade 9), and once more passed the summer holidays in Krynica. He must have done rather badly at school, for his uncle promised him a journey to Central Europe if he succeeded in his next exam. This seems to have helped, for he was promoted to class 7 (grade 10) in Spring 1873. He left in May with Pulman[46] for his long journey, after which he dropped out of school, having completed grade 9.

Since Conrad was not a good student, his education was very fragmentary, and he had no thorough knowledge in any subject. The lack of formal knowledge remained a handicap all his life, and he must often have thought of his uncle's words, written after Apollo's death, "Without a thorough education you will not be anybody in this world."

In the already quoted letter to Winawer, Conrad admits that he was never "an average and able boy. As a matter of fact, I was not able at all. In whatever I achieved afterwards I have simply followed my instinct: the voice from inside." As we see it now, the trouble was not lack of ability, but that the boy had not been brought up normally, that for many years he could practically do what he liked and was never submitted to any real work discipline. The school may have been dull, as Conrad claims in *A Personal Record*, yet it produced very remarkable men. Though only 15% actually graduated from the top class (grade 11) and went to University, those who left at grade 9 went into an apprenticeship of some kind, especially commerce.

The school curriculum at that time, and the schoolbooks used at St. Anne's have been preserved at the PAN and Jagiellonian Libraries in Cracow. The teaching had been in German till 1869, when the working language became Polish. A perusal of the teaching program of 1870 shows, however, that the "imperial-royal Gymnasium of St. Anne's" was actually quite German in spirit. Apart from Polish, the curriculum was the same as for all other Austrian "Gymnasia," and these again were closely modeled on the German schools of the same kind. Latin was the leading subject (six hours weekly), German the second (four hours), Polish came behind with only three hours.

In *Latin*, the following texts were used:

Class 3 (grade 6) Cornelius Nepos, *Nine Life Stories of Famous Leaders*. (This Conrad must have studied at Mr. Georgeon's prep school).

Class 4 (grade 7) Caesar, *De Bello Gallico, Books* I, III, IV, V, VI.

Class 5 (grade 8) Livius, *Books I* (1-46), II (1-33) XXI (1-54).

Ovidius, *Tristia*, Book I, Elegy 3 (*Exile* and Good-bye to Rome), Book IV, Elegy 10 (autobiography of the exiled author).

Ovidius, *Metamorphoses*, Book I (89-162) Revolt of the Giants against Jupiter:

Book VI (146-312) Niobe's tragedy;

Book VIII (138-235 and 611-728) The Labyrinth, Ariadne;

Book X (1-77) Orpheus and Eurydice;

Book XIII (1-398) Death of Ajax.

Class 6 (grade 9) Sallustus, *De Bello Jugurth.* Ch. 1-60.

Vergil, *Eneid*, Lib. I, IV.

Caesar, *De Bello Civile*, Lib. 1-36.

The students had to do major homework in Latin every two weeks, and pass a written exam once a month.

German: In the classes 4-6, the grammar of Janota was used. Each rule was exemplified by one or several quotations, sometimes of proverbs, but mostly of two-line classical verses. Besides the German grammar, a reader was used: the *Lesebuch* by J. Mozart, with a different volume for each grade. In class 6 (grade 9), the reader contained the best ballads by Goethe (*Erlkönig, König von Thule, Zauberlehrling, Schatzgräber*), and *Die Kraniche des Ibicus* by Schiller. Uhland, Grillparzer, Körner, Rückert were represented as well, together with Lenau's nostalgic-sentimental "Last Postilion." The artificial and pretentious versifications of Klopstock and Voss, now practically unreadable, took quite some place too. The prose section contained either biographies of heroic figures, mostly from antiquity, and quite a number of extremely romantic descriptions of nature: "A snowstorm in the Alps," "The Rhine," "The Aetna" (by Goethe). Perhaps the most typical of these descriptions is one of the Falls of the Rhine (near Schaffhausen, Switzerland) by Meyer.

The reader of Conrad will no doubt find something familiar in this nature description:[47] the scandalized rocks shaking their black heads at the fury of the water. Especially in his first works, Conrad often endowed rivers, trees, and of course the sea, with human feelings and passions.

Polish: The teaching was modeled on that of Latin and German. The students had a grammar and a reader. Politically engaged writers were ignored, while historical figures were favorites: Elegies by Jan Kochanowski (a 16th-century poet), Ballads by Mickiewicz, writings by Norwid. Galician writers were also being studied, but anything that could rouse Polish patriotic feelings was carefully avoided. Polish literature had to extol a great past gone forever.

History and geography were taught with the help of German textbooks translated into Polish, i.e. from the German point of view.

Since Conrad, in his letter to Winawer, mentioned that he was good at writing essays, it is of some interest to hear what kinds of essays the students of St. Anne's were asked to compose. Here are some of the subjects in Polish for class 6 (grade 9):

> Contents and meaning of Elegy 19 of Jan Kochanowski.
> How can we improve ourselves by learning from others' faults?
> The place of Klonowicz in literature.
> Causes and effects of the Yugurthian war.
> On the epic poems of Polish literature of the 16th century.
> Are explanations necessary when reading our poets?
> Ferro nocentius aurum. [Gold is more harmful than iron]
> Kromer as a historian, statesman, and priest. [Kromer lived in the 16th century]

The German essays were in the same vein: subjects

from antiquity, essays on the uses of certain materials, ethical or philosophical dissertations. The following were some of the subjects given in classes 5 and 6 (grades 8 and 9):

> The uses of glass.
> Straw, its kinds and uses.
> Relate the ballad "Baszyna" in form of a tale.
> Water: where does it occur in nature? How does it serve man, and in other ways?
> Paper: its kinds and uses.
> What do you think when contemplating your drawing-room window?
> What I know about the different qualities and uses of metals?
> The third Persian campaign.
> How I spent the Easter holidays.
> Dialogue between winter and spring.
> The forest and the sea—compare.
> Flowers and hopes—compare.
> Relate in prose Schiller's ballad "Die Kraniche des Ibicus."
> What resolutions should a student make at the beginning of the school year?
> Reflections on the meaning of life.

The philosophy of the German and Austrian higher schools was based on the teachings of Schiller, Herder, Novalis who had said that education was necessary to form courageous men and good citizens. The ideal was the Roman citizen, and biographies of the leading men of antiquity always formed a part of the curriculum. The main problem was not to impart knowledge, but to form character and virility (this excluded co-education). To educate the heart was as important as to educate the mind. This is why nature descriptions played such a role—they appealed to the sensitivity. The approach to nature was that of Rousseau and of the Romantics: not to grab from nature, but to be enriched by it spiritually, was the idea behind the cult of nature. For Novalis, the whole world was a sort of mirror in which the human mind recognized itself. Schlegel said, "It is only through education that man becomes a human being. The highest, the only useful value is education" Hölderlin (1770-1845) wrote in *Hyperion*, the goal of knowledge was "to become one with everything that lives." The German Romantics postulated an educational ideal in which the subjective, personal, and even the "dreamlike irrational, and mysterious" (Jean Paul) would have its place.

Novalis wrote, "Nothing is more accessible to the human spirit than the infinite." The teachers had to appeal to the idealism of youth to promote love and understanding, and to use the beautiful to form the personality of their students. Behind school's like St. Anne's was Jean Paul's conviction that every boy carried some hidden genius within, which the school had to bring out. W. von Humboldt in Prussia, and Vinzenz E. Milde in Austria, were the leading educators who gave these junior colleges their final form which would not change for almost eighty years. They were convinced that classical antiquity was the best means of education. They postulated a "harmonious development of the mind" through the study of Greek, Latin, and German on one hand, and mathematics on the other. Milde added that the goal of education was twofold: on one hand the development of the humanity of the student, on the other of his usefulness as a citizen.

These then were the ideas and ideals behind St. Anne's. They are clearly reflected in the curriculum. The authorities at that time believed in the formative value of education, i.e. in the possibility and necessity of moulding, through appropriate schooling, strong characters and useful citizens able to form the elite of the nation and assure its future.

Memories of Conrad's fragmentary school knowledge pop up in many of his works, most of them quite unexpectedly and without adding much to the story. Thus, Prometheus is mentioned twice (*Arrow of Gold*, III; *Freya* in *Twixt Land and Sea Tales*, (208). Helen of Troy makes a veiled appearance in *The Rescue* (22), Caligula in *The Secret Agent* (83). The end of *The Secret Sharer* brings us up to the gates of Erebus, while *The Arrow of Gold* winds up with the King of Thule. Danae is mentioned in *The Arrow of Gold* (37), and in the same book we read: "A Latin tag came into my head about the facile descent into the abyss." (276) an allusion to Vergil's Eneid, book IV, 126 (Facilis descensus Averno). In *The Return* we find this curious paraphrase of the birth of Diana: "Divine wisdom springing full grown, armed and severe out of a tried heart" (*Tales of Unrest*, 183). The unhappy Niobe, too, appears in Conrad's works, and the legendary Phoenix, and nymphs and a centaur and other mythological figures with whom the boy had become familiar.

The students of St. Anne's were not only "steeped in classicism," but also in religion. They went to mass together once a month and to confession several times a year. The boys knew their Bible, and it is partly from this stock of knowledge that Conrad drew for the rest of his life, for he never went to church again except to be married and to have his children baptized. He must also have read the King James version of the Bible (it was on board every ship and was used for burials and other services), for biblical allusions and turns of phrases couched in that idiom are as frequent in his works as allusions to antiquity.

In *Lord Jim* (211), Conrad makes Stein quote this German verse:

Nun halt ich endlich es in meinen Händen
Und nenn es in gewissem Sinne mein.

The verse is from Goethe's play *Torquato Tasso*, Act I, scene 3. Since this play is not on the curriculum of St. Anne's, the verse was probably quoted as an example of the grammatical use of the possessive pronoun. It is astonishing that he should have kept the verse in mind for 27 years, for it is not likely that he had Goethe's works or Janota's German grammar with him when writing *Lord Jim*.

Since none of Conrad's allusions to ancient mythology, nor the above verse contributes anything to the story itself, one may well ask oneself whether Conrad did not feel a need to display his fragments of "classical" knowledge precisely because he was self-conscious about his lack of higher education. He must have suffered from feelings of inadequacy and inferiority in that respect, and it is not unreasonable to assume that his passionate ambition to become a great English writer included an element of over-compensation. By the way, his German quotations in *Lord Jim* (Stein, Yucker) are not free of elementary grammatical and spelling errors. In her Polish translation, Aniela Zagórska quietly and tactfully corrected them all—the English publisher did not.

Jean-Aubry believes that Konrad's decision to leave Poland may have been strengthened by an unhappy first love (*LL*, I, 24). Frankly, I do not share this view. That young Konrad was in love at one time, while attending school in Cracow, is known from his preface to *Nos-*

tromo[48] in which he draws a portrait of the girl who served as a model for Antonia Avellanos.

In a canceled passage from *The Arrow of Gold*, Conrad described the same girl as follows:

> A great austerity of feeling and conviction is not a very common phenomenon in youth. But that young girl seems to have been an uncommon personality, the moral centre of life. Her own education appears to have been not finished at the time. But she had the power of an exalted character.

> Of that time he reminds her at great length (in a letter). And no wonder. He was in love with her. But he never betrayed this sentiment to her, to anybody. He rather affected resistance to her influence. He even tried to cheat his own self in that respect.

Then Conrad goes on explaining that he also had been in love with a girl whom he describes as wicked, since she "had made him suffer . . . to her heart's content." Then he continues:

> In the case of the other young girl (the one he is writing to after all these years) she obviously awed him a little. And yet it was she who, at the last, put some heart into him. It was very little that she had done. A mere pressure of the hand. But he had remembered it for five and thirty years of separation and silence!

These passages, autobiographical as they no doubt are, are nevertheless not exactly clear. The "first love" in the first quotation cannot be the "first love" in the second, for the latter concerned a girl who had nothing but scorn for him. Obviously, the girl he is writing to in the second quotation is the girl with the handshake.

Konrad knew two girls well while going to school; one was Janina Taube, the sister of his friends, the Taube brothers. She later became the baroness de Brunnov. The other girl was Ofelia, two years older than Konrad, and the daughter of Apollo's friend, Stefan Buszczyński. Like her father, she was a great patriot. Her "austere, unanswerable invective" could be nothing else but *Zdrajco!* (Traitor!). Janina Taube would not fit Conrad's description, for she was only nine at the time. As to the girl who had nothing but scorn for him and made him suffer, this was Tekla Syroczyńska in Lwów.

In the following passage from *The Arrow of Gold* ("First note",), however, he clearly writes about Janina:

> They had parted as children, or very little more than children. Years passed. Then something recalled to the woman the companion of her young days, and she wrote to him: "I have been hearing of you lately. I know where life has brought you. You certainly selected your own road. But to us, left behind, it always looked as if you had struck out into a pathless desert. We always regarded you as a person that must be given up for lost. But you have turned up again, and though we may never see each other, my memory welcomes you, and I confess to you that I should like to know the incidents on the road which had led you where you are now

This is certainly a very poetical elaboration of what Janina de Brunnov actually did write, after having heard of Joseph Conrad as a novelist. She simply asked (in a letter written in French) whether he still remembered her and what his plans were. Conrad answered (in French), in October 1897:

> I have a certain—literary—reputation, but the future is anything but certain, for I am not a popular author and probably never shall be. This does not disturb me, for it was never my ambition to write for the all-powerful masses. I have no liking for democracy—and democracy has no liking for me. I have come to be appreciated by a few chosen minds and I have no doubt that I can sell well enough—on a limited scale, of course—to earn my living. I have no dreams of making a fortune—and anyhow you don't find fortunes in inkwells. But I will admit that I dream of peace, of a little fame, and of being able to devote the rest of my life to the service of art, free from material worries. *Et voilà, Madame, le secret de ma vie.*[49]

In *The Arrow of Gold*, as befits a piece of fiction, the answer is more poetic:

> I believe you are the only one now alive who remembers me as a child. I have heard from you

from time to time, but I wonder what sort of person you are now. Perhaps if I did know, I wouldn't dare to put pen on paper. But I don't know. I only remember that we were great chums. In fact, I chummed with you even more than with your brothers. But I am like the pigeon that went away in the fable of the *Two Pigeons*. If I once start to tell you, I would want you to feel that you have been there yourself. I may overtax your patience with the story of my life, so different from yours, not only in all the facts, but altogether in spirit. You may not understand. You may even be shocked. I say all this to myself; but I know that I shall succumb. I have a distinct recollection that in the old days, when you were about fifteen, you always could make me do whatever you liked.

In this passage which mixes reality with fiction, we find an allusion to a very old fable of Hindu origin, retold by Lafontaine in his second book of fables, and by Russia's greatest fable teller, Ivan Krylov (1768-1844). Krylov's fables, translated by Gliński, were very popular in Poland. There is no doubt that Konradek must have known them very early. The expression "if I once start to tell you, I would want you to feel that you have been there yourself" is almost a quotation from Krylov's text.

The fable is the story of two pigeons who loved each other dearly. But one pigeon felt a strong urge to see the wide world and "went away." In the translation of Bernard Pares' *Krylov's Fables* (London 1926), the relevant passages are rendered as follows:

There lived two pigeons; each to each was dear as brother

. . . one birdie yearned to take a distant flight
And get to know by sight
The wide world's wonders without end. . . .
(The other bird admonishes him thus)
"How can you . . . shame upon you! . . .
Think of the ravening birds, the dreadful storms, the traps!"
. . . .(But) he dearly longs to go.
The wish in all his hopes, in all his thoughts appears.
"Don't cry, my pretty one," 'tis so he calms her fears,

For just three days, no more, I'll go awandering:
I'll notice everything so quickly as I fly,
And when I've seen the sights,—the ones that catch
my eye,
I'll soon be back again. . . .
. . . . . I'll mention every place:
There's nought you shall not hear,—their doings
and their ways
And every marvel that I see,
'Twill almost as I talk, lie there beneath your gaze,
As if you too had flown all round the world with
me.
(But the pigeon that went away finally comes back
in a most pitiful state and the poet draws this con-
clusion for his young readers):
Oh, you who so much yearn to travel without end

  The whole wide world to view,
  First read my little fable through.
Haste not your happiness on that far road to send,
Whatever joys that dream has promised to your
mind;
No distant search, be sure, a fairer land will find
Than that which holds your love, your true devoted
friend.

The fact that Conrad remembered this fable so well
more than fifty years after his childhood, certainly
throws an interesting light on his conflict.

III.

Conrad's Contacts with Poland

Joseph Conrad Korzeniowski stayed three and a half years in Marseilles during which time he spent barely 18 months at sea. At first he must have made friends easily, and was quite popular as Monsieur Georges; but he seems to have finally alienated most, if not all of his friends. When, in 1914, Mr. Dąbrowski asked Conrad what he had actually done during those years he got the answer: "I amused myself, I lived merrily." Small wonder that Uncle Bobrowski was not satisfied with this playful conception of a seafaring career.

Conrad's contacts with Poland were mainly through his uncle whom he saw in March 1878 in Marseilles, after his suicide attempt. He visited his uncle in 1883, meeting him for a month in Marienbad and Teplitz (Teplice), Bohemia. Later, having become a British subject, Conrad was able to travel to Russia. He visited Uncle Bobrowski in the latter's homestead, Kazimierówka, in 1890 and again in 1893. Bobrowski died in January 1894 without knowing that his "beloved nephew" had just given up his maritime career. In the intervals between the visits there was a steady correspondence, mostly prompted by Conrad's need for money and Bobrowski's apprehensions about his nephew's behavior and future. While most of Bobrowski's letters to Conrad have been preserved and are available in English in Najder's *Conrad's Polish Background*, those written by Conrad apparently were destroyed during the Russian Revolution of 1917.[50]

A curious document concerning Conrad's visit to the Bohemian spa remains. Bobrowski, having heard that Stefan Buszczyński was holidaying at Teplice, traveled there with Conrad. To their disappointment,

Buszczyński had just left. Nine years after his departure from Poland Conrad wrote to Buszczyński:

Teplitz, 14 August, 1883

Most Honored and Respected Sir!

We hoped—Uncle Tadeusz and I—that we would be able to meet you here in Teplitz, but we heard that you had been here but had left.

Since I cannot personally greet you and obtain your pardon for my transgressions, I hasten to do this in writing, enclosing my photograph in the hope that, in memory of your friendship with the father, the son may find in you friendly memories and, for his letter—despite such a long silence—a kind reception.

Although a long time absent from our country and perhaps even apparently forgetful of those whose kindness I experienced, I have, in reality, never forgotten my country, my relatives, nor those who have been kind to me—among them you, dear Sir. My warden at the time of my becoming an orphan must always occupy the first place.

I would ask you politely, dear Sir, to remember me to beloved Kostuś—if I may call him so [familiarly]. Surely, I gave him reason to forget our friendship in Cracow; I myself never forgot, even if it seems such a long time since! Perhaps he, too, would like to remember those times and will accept my sincere greetings and friendly handshake.

In a few days I shall leave for London; from there I don't know yet where fate will lead me. In the course of the last few years, that is, since my first examination, I was not too lucky in my travels. I [almost] drowned, I was burnt out; otherwise, I am in good health. I have good courage, as well as a liking for my work and an attachment to my profession. Moreover, I always remember your recommendation at the moment of my departure from Cracow. "Remember," you said, "wherever you go sailing, you will sail towards Poland!"

This I never forgot, and never will forget. Hoping that my sins will be forgiven, I ask to be remembered kindly, and remain with attachment, gratitude and my highest regards,

your humble servant
Konrad N. Korzeniowski
6 Dynevor Rd., Stoke Newington, London N.

This curious letter, written on Conrad's personal stationery embossed with the initials C.K., is written in the Polish style of the period. But the attitude as well as the handwriting, are those of a school boy. Yet Conrad was then 26 years old! The photograph he enclosed had been taken at Marienbad and shows him with beard and moustache (Conrad never shaved in his life). The contrition shown about his "transgressions" (meaning the fact that he never wrote to Buszczyński or to Konstantyn) probably reflects Uncle Bobrowski's feelings rather than Conrad's. As for the quotation "Wherever you go sailing, you will sail towards Poland," it may seem to be a variation of the well-known proverb, "All roads lead to Rome." In fact, it is very likely an allusion to a famous verse by Juliusz Słowacki, from a nostalgic song entitled "Hymn" (1836):

> For I well know that my vessel,
> Sailing through the wide world,
> Will *not* sail to my country.

What Buszczyński probably meant was that, like Słowacki, Conrad would always feel the attraction of his country, but that, unlike the Polish poet, he would be able to return to Poland one day.

Of Conrad's first visit to his native Ukraine, in 1890, we have two accounts. One is by Conrad himself. In *A Personal Record*, he describes his journey by way of Berlin where he almost lost his bag and with it the unfinished manuscript of *Almayer's Folly*, and finally the eight hours' sleigh ride through snow drifts from the station to Bobrowski's estate, the *Kazimierówka*. *(See map of Podolia on endsheets.) Conrad tells very little of his stay with his uncle, but he mentions that he did not place his manuscript in a drawer but in full view on the table.

Fortunately, we have a second report by an eye witness called Jan Perłowski. He was a young man who, like Conrad, had lost his father rather early and had become one of Bobrowski's numerous wards. Perłowski wrote that none of Conrad's biographers, or Conrad himself, did justice to this uncommon man. Perłowski remembered Bobrowski as a short man, bald, vivacious, perspicacious, absolutely honest, endowed with the shrewd mind of a lawyer, and representing, in that Western part of the Ukraine, the best of Polish social tradition and culture. He was widely known, most respected; many sought his advice. He was very tolerant despite his sarcastic sense of humor.

After Conrad had arrived, Bobrowski invited a number of neighbors to come and meet his nephew. They had all known Conrad's parents, if not Konradek himself, and were eager to meet this son of the Polish borderland turned sailor. Though able to speak Polish fluently Conrad was reluctant to make contact. Perłowski, who was only 18 while Conrad was 32, tried to get through the reserve of Bobrowski's nephew. He told him about a lady called Regina Korzeniowska who had been known throughout the Ukraine for her patriotism. To his astonishment, "Conrad became embarrassed and his face expressed displeasure. Avoiding [my] subject, he began to talk very fast of something else." Then Perłowski showed him an antique clock standing on the mantelpiece. Conrad immediately began to praise the British sea chronometers. Perłowski left the room and went out to the porch. The snow was thawing. Conrad followed him. The rest of the story is best told in Perłowski's own words:

> Before, whenever he needed the Polish equivalent of an English expression, I had offered him the right word. Now, he approached me, keeping his hands deep in his pockets in the English fashion and called in that cheerful tone which the English adopt amongst themselves in such circumstances [in English]: *"A breezy day! Very fine, isn't it?"* I was considerably younger than Conrad, but he did not impress me at all. None of us yet knew about his extraordinary talent. Only once Mr. Tadeusz had mentioned casually to me that his nephew was writing something in English. I answered him, smilingly but not very politely: "Couldn't it be in Polish?" He lifted his head, frowned and turned his face away. At that moment, some others came out and with them a young yet full-size dog who jumped at us, threatening us with his dirty paws. Conrad stooped, turned to the dog in the snow and patted him contentedly for a long time, repeating tenderly and defiantly, half to him, half to me: *"Doggy, doggy, doggy . . . you dirty dog."*[52]

So Perłowski had his answer—in English. He left the same evening and never saw Conrad again. But, as he explains in his report, he later understood that "while Conrad had irritated [me, I] had hurt him." Indeed, the budding novelist must have taken Perłowski's gentle rebuke as referring to his writing as well. He did not yet know how often Poles would try to "repolonize" him.

Perłowski also wrote in his article that in their society it was all right to emigrate and even to write in a foreign language as long as everybody knew the author was a Pole and as long as he tried to work, albeit indirectly, for the sake of Poland. In this respect, he found Conrad badly wanting.

As for Bobrowski, he probably thought that *Almayer's Folly* was actually Conrad's folly—another speculation that would fail. Even Apollo, despite great gifts, had not succeeded in making himself a name. The uncle never dreamt that his nephew might one day become a famous writer. But he was proud of Conrad's success in the British merchant navy and happy to prove to his former critics how right he had been in allowing his nephew to go to sea.

Perłowski also mentioned Bobrowski's opinion of Apollo. It seems that his private judgement was even more severe than the characterization given in his *Memoirs*. To Perłowski, Tadeusz said that Apollo had been a man who was "helpless in practical matters;" and it was evident that he still had not forgiven his brother-in-law for having ruined his sister Ewa's life through a political activity which, as Bobrowski had always maintained, was unrealistic and doomed to end in disaster.

During the visit of the 32-year-old Conrad at Kazimierówka, Uncle Bobrowski gave him a complete report concerning the administration of Apollo's and Conrad's finances. From this so-called "Bobrowski document" (available in English in Najder's *Conrad's Polish Background*) we see that Bobrowski acted as a trustee for the whole Korzeniowski family, collecting bequests, inheritances and interests. Part of the funds thus accumulated were used to support Apollo and his son. It was Bobrowski who provided for Apollo's upkeep after 1863 and during his stay in Galicia; for Konrad's schooling in Cracow and Lwów; for his medical bills and three or four prolonged holidays prescribed by the doctors, and eventually for his journey to Marseilles. From his arrival in Marseilles in 1874 till 1881 when he was 24, Conrad received from Bobrowski a regular allowance of

2400 francs ($500) per year, a sum which was then suffi-
cient to cover the cost of modest living of one person.
After 1881, the allowance was reduced to one half and
the amount of 1200 francs ($250) was paid yearly till
1887, when Conrad reached the age of thirty! (Apollo
himself had begun to earn a living only at the age of
32). Moreover, Bobrowski had to make extra payments,
especially when Conrad reached the age of 21 and "lived
merrily." Later, Bobrowski paid almost every extra expense; provided the money for Conrad's journey to
Marienbad and Teplice; paid his examination fees for
the mate's certificate and later for the captain's diploma;
he supported the cost of Conrad's naturalization; and
sent small extra amounts whenever his nephew was hard
up. But when his "dear boy" reached the age of thirty,
Bobrowski found it was time he supported himself completely, so the regular allowance was stopped. Yet Conrad continued to receive money from Bobrowski. As that
worthy guardian remarked with a touch of irony: "Making a man out of Mr. Konrad" cost 17,454 roubles (a-
bout $9000), quite apart from a capital of 3600 roubles
and Conrad's inheritance which he received only after
his uncle's death. This is an amount which at that time
would have seen two persons comfortably through medical studies. Yet Jerry Allen, obviously surveying the situation from the height of North American affluence, calls
Bobrowski "parsimonious" and "provincial!"

Where did Bobrowski get the money from? There is
something very ironical in the fact that the money Bobrowski sent to Apollo and Conrad came partly from the
sugar industry which Apollo had loathed so much. For a
long period, this industry paid dividends of 25% or
more; and when this finally fell to 8%, Bobrowski
thought he was a poor man.

A close study of Conrad's seafaring career explains
why he had to be supported to such an extent up to the
age of 30. This career lasted 19 years, during which time
Conrad served on twenty-one different vessels. On six
vessels he stayed less than two months. Only on four he
served for more than one year. He never served on a
ship twice, except on the *Torrens*. The actual time during
which Conrad was gainfully employed during these
nineteen years was eleven years and 49 days. In other
words, almost half the time Conrad was on shore, earning nothing. Only once was he employed as a captain—

on the sailing barque *Otago*. Curiously enough, he left
this most satisfactory employment after 427 days of his
own accord and returned to London at his own expense
to face unemployment until his ill-fated journey to the
Congo. It must be said that Conrad's record as a sailor
betrays all too well the unruly "Nałęcz Korzeniowski
strain." At age of 36 he found it already quite impossible to get employment, probably in view of his overly
chequered working record.

Another bond with Poland were Karol Zagórski and
his wife Aniela who was a distant cousin of Apollo. The
couple had two daughters, Karola and Aniela. The latter
remained unmarried and later became the distinguished
translator of many of Conrad's earlier works (*Outcast,
Lord Jim*). On his way to the Ukraine, in 1890 and 1893,
Conrad visited the Zagórskis in Lublin. Moreover, he
corresponded with the family in Polish (Karol did not
understand English at all), and fifteen of these letters
have been published in English in Jean-Aubry's *Life and
Letters*. Finally, during their memorable journey to Poland in 1914, the Conrads were the guests of Mrs.
Aniela Zagórska in Zakopane.

On his way to the Ukraine, Conrad stopped at Warsaw, and in February 1883, unsuccessfully tried to meet
the editor of the paper *Słowo* (not Henryk Sienkiewicz,
as it has been claimed). During his second journey to the
Ukraine, from August till October 1893, Conrad again
stopped in Warsaw where he came in touch with the
young writers of the avant-guarde publication *Chimera*.

After Bobrowski's death in January 1894, the
executors of the will invited Conrad, as the nearest relative, to come to the Ukraine and attend the opening of
the testament. But since they did not send the money
for the journey, as Bobrowski had always done, Conrad
was unable to go. Had he made the journey, they would
most probably handed him his letters to Bobrowski.

The Spiridion-Kliszczewski Incident

During one of his voyages Conrad had met a Polish
sailor named Komorowski (later a business man in
Chicago) and had promised him to settle a debt that the
latter owed a Polish watchmaker called Spiridion
Kliszczewski, of Duke Street, Cardiff, Wales. While his
ship *Tilkhurst* was being loaded at Cardiff, from end of
May to 5 June, 1885, Conrad set out to find the watch-

maker. He was very well received. Actually, this was the first English home which opened to him, and this casual meeting developed into a friendship with the whole family to which we owe Conrad's famous letter of 13 October 1885, where he tells the son, Joseph Spiridion (Kliszczewski) that Poland was lost for ever:

> We have passed through the gates where "Lasciate ogni speranza" is written in letters of blood and fire, and nothing remains for us [Poles] but the darkness of oblivion. In the presence of such national misfortune, personal happiness is impossible in its absolute form of general contentment and peace of heart.
>
> *(LL* I, 81)

Conrad could hardly have used stronger words than those Dante put on the gates of hell, nor could he have come much nearer to what his father wrote in his "Song for the baptism of my son."

In another letter to Joseph, Conrad wrote about his plans to go whaling and asked Joseph's advice. The Polish watchmaker, who had inherited his father's business, sensed that Conrad would ask him for a loan—which a Pole could not well refuse another Pole—and dissuaded him at once.[53]

The second visit took place at Joseph's home and lasted over a week. This must have been in June or July 1889, shortly after Conrad had returned as a passenger from the East where he had given up his command of the *Otago*. This visit has found no reflection in any letters. Father Spiridion Kliszczewski had died, and the son had dropped the Polish surname, adopting Spiridion instead, because it was easier on the English ears.[54]

In 1895, Conrad's *An Outcast of the Islands* was accepted by Allen & Unwin Ltd. on condition that the author pay £60 towards the cost of printing. Since he had only £50, he asked Joseph for a small loan which he got. He paid the sum back a few months later. The whole correspondence pertaining to this business matter has been destroyed, probably at Conrad's request.

The third visit took place at Christmas 1895, after the publication of the *Outcast* and following Conrad's honeymoon. His wife accompanied him. They had a wonderful Christmas with the Spiridion (Kliszczewski) family in which the Polish language was sadly declining, but not Polish hospitality. Conrad was then working at the *Nigger of the "Narcissus."*[55] He was given a quiet room where he spent most of the day writing. On 30 December, he visited the Cardiff public library where he entered his name as "Jph Conrad (Korzeniowski)." The couple must have left Cardiff soon afterwards. Mrs. Conrad was expecting her first baby any day.

While in Cardiff, Conrad was interviewed by a young man called Arthur Mee who published his report, "A New Novelist on Dickens," in the Yearbook *Western Mail*, January 1897. Mee was even newer at interviewing than Conrad was at writing novels; but it speaks for his journalistic flair that he thought of interviewing this practically unknown author at all. Among other things, Mee mentioned that Conrad, "like many of his compatriots," had dropped his surname because the English could not pronounce it.

This third visit was to end on a discordant note. Although brought up in England, Joseph Spiridion who was roughly the same age as Conrad, had strong patriotic feelings for his father's country. One day he quite innocently asked Conrad why he did not tell the English about Poland's sufferings. Conrad's reaction was so violent and unexpected that Joseph remembered it for the rest of his life. Lifting both arms in horror, Conrad answered: *"Ah, mon ami, que voulez-vous? I would lose my public!"*

But worse was to come. In his article published just after Conrad had left Cardiff, Mee had mentioned that Conrad was the son of a Pole exiled to Sibèria (*sic*) for political activity and as a small boy had shared the exile with his parents. This information had been given in good faith by Joseph Spiridion without Conrad's knowledge. When Conrad got the article, he was furious and practically broke with the Spiridions. As Joseph and his sons later told the Polish critic, Witold Chwalewik[56], they were astonished that such a great man should be so terribly sensitive about matters of his origin. It was only more than three years later that Conrad tried to make good by sending Joseph Spiridion his latest book, *Tales of Unrest*, together with a very cordial letter in which he reminded Joseph of his last visit (*LL*, I, 273-274). But this was the last his "dear old friend" would hear from him.

Chwalewik, who corresponded with and personally

visited the Spiridion family, provides some interesting details on Conrad's visits. The first time (June 1885), the old watchmaker Spiridion Kliszczewski was ill. While Conrad was sitting at his bedside, Spiridion's grandson Hubert came in, and Conrad asked him some questions. The bright youngster later remembered that he wondered how a man who spoke English so badly could be entrusted with a British ship. Conrad was then first mate. At the second visit, Hubert found that Conrad, now a captain, spoke English much better, and was also well dressed. But being brought up *à l'anglaise*, the boy found it amusing to watch Conrad bow deep and kiss his mother's hand in the most distinguished Polish fashion. Hubert reported to Chwalewik that the conversation was all in English and concerned mainly Poland and international politics. Echoes of the conversation can be found in the letters which Conrad wrote to his Cardiff friends during the years 1885 to 1886, and which were published in Jean-Aubry's *LL*. Poland was a subject which the author was loath to touch with his English friends, but he discussed the matter freely with the Spiridions.

The Emigration of Polish Talent and of Conrad's in Particular.

In 1896, the Polish philosophy professor, Wincenty Lutosławski, visited Conrad, having heard of him through Henry James. He was the first Pole to visit Conrad in his home. Jessie Conrad describes him almost as a clown[57], blissfully unaware of the fact that this man had written a remarkable book in English, entitled *The Origin and Growth of Plato's Logic*, was professor at the Swiss university of Fribourg, and had just been invited to lecture in several American universities. Conrad did not like the intruder either. Lutosławski not only had a superior college education and spoke English very well, he also let everybody know that he was not only a Pole but intended to remain one, while Conrad wanted to develop his English *persona* at the expense of the Pole.

Two years after his fleeting visit to Conrad, Lutosławski decided to write an article, *The Emigration of Talent* (what in today's journalese is called "the brain drain"). The article appeared in the Polish nationalistic weekly, *Homeland* (Kraj), of March and April 1899, and was to cause quite an uproar. The editor of *Homeland* explained that he could not refuse a contribution by such an eminent personality, but he made sure that Lutosławski's opinions were followed by a refutation by T. Żuk-Skarszewski.

In his article, Lutosławski reported that he had asked Conrad: "Why don't you write in Polish?" Conrad's reply had been: "My dear Sir! I hold our Polish literature in too high esteem to spoil it with my unskilled work. For the English, my abilities are sufficient and they provide me with bread." Lutosławski agreed with this, explaining to the readers of *Homeland* that Polish literature was indeed noble and aristocratic by nature, while English literature was not so exclusive. He also said that it was to Poland's advantage if capable Poles emigrated. Not only did they have much better opportunities abroad to develop their talents; for some it was the only chance of developing at all. Besides, most of these emigrants kept in touch with their native country and not a few came back to spend the rest of their life there. In any case, the reputation they gained abroad enhanced Poland's prestige in the eyes of the world.

Lutosławski's article appeared in Nos. 12 and 14 of *Homeland*. In No. 14, Żuk-Skarszewski replied by attacking Conrad for having forsaken his native language. He wrote that any teacher in some obscure Polish town did more for Poland than a Pole going abroad and writing in a foreign language.[58]

But the worst attack upon Conrad came from a leading Polish novelist, Mrs. Eliza Orzeszkowa, in *Homeland*, April 1899. She also wrote Conrad a personal letter in which she vehemently accused him of betraying his Polish heritage. The letter has not been preserved, but we know that it must have hurt Conrad to the quick. In her article, Mrs. Orzeszkowa said that it was all right for engineers or opera singers to go abroad, but certainly not for writers: "When it comes to books, I must say that this gentleman who writes novels in English nearly gave me a nervous fit. I felt, when reading about him, something slippery and disgusting coming up in my throat." To make the measure full, another leading Polish novelist, *Bolesław Prus* also wrote against the emigration of talents, but without mentioning names (in the *Daily Courier*, Warsaw, No. 104, 1899).

It is not likely that Conrad ever read Żuk-Skarszewski's or Mrs. Orzeszkowa's articles (he did not read *any* Polish periodicals), but her letter, certainly written in the same vein as her article, reached him just at the crucial moment when he was beginning to write *Lord Jim* for good

Although Conrad obviously destroyed Orzeszkowa's letter, we get a good idea of what she wrote him from her words addressed to the Rev. Father Czeczott, dated 14 November 1899:

> My little article on emigration was prompted by my indignation caused by Mr. Lutosławski's article ... otherwise an eminently respected man and the best of patriots. (Then Mrs. Orzeszkowa mentions that Lutosławski could have had a professorship at an American university, but after some years abroad preferred to return to Poland to put his talent at the service of his country). I have for a long time now, with great alarm and painful astonishment, been watching the unheart-of lightheartedness with which some leave these lands and with which others look at these abandoned territories deprived of their best forces without doing anything at all to prevent the disaster. The indifference and carelessness of our society in this respect—and in others—not infrequently exceeds even the limits of the most pessimistic conjectures and stands in a truly tragical contrast with the importance and the dangers of the historical moment in which we live. Neither the written nor the spoken word is of any help ... one has to live here in order to see the full consequences of this emigration: the deserted land, the moral and physical misery, the dreamy apathy and the trembling fear which reign here and stifle those who remained behind—when everybody young and energetic and able to fight lives at the other end of the world.[59]

The latent antagonism between Conrad and Lutosławski came to a head many years later, in 1911, when the philosophy professor sent him some Polish publications. We know Conrad's reaction by a letter he wrote to Garnett on 20 October, 1911:

> I had a letter and some books from Mr. Lutosławski. I ought to have written him before—though really and truly I don't know what he wants with me. I don't understand him in the least. His illuminations seem to me a very naive and uninteresting thing. Does he imagine I am likely to become his disciple? He worries and bores me. But I won't tell him that when I write (as I must in common de-

cency) because I believe he is a good man—though confoundedly inquisitive[60].

We do not know the kind of material Conrad received from Lutosławski, but it is probable that the latter had sent him, among other things, his articles published in *Sparks from Warsaw* (1911) where Lutosławski had once more given an account of this views on the Conrad affair. Conrad destroyed this material as well as the letters from the Polish philosopher.

Conrad had good reasons to be puzzled and even to take offence. What Lutosławski had written about him in *Sparks from Warsaw* was certainly no compliment. In a belated rebuttal of the late Mrs. Orzeszkowa (who had died in 1910) he declared that had Conrad come back to Poland after his maritime career, "he would not have dared to write in the language of Sienkiewicz." Instead, "he began to write in English to make a living, and has given the English a number of novels sparkling with Polish spirit and from which Polish influence radiates to the race now dominating the world . . . If Conrad had written those exotic novels in Polish, they would not have had the success they had in England." According to Lutosławski, Conrad's works, although full of Polish qualities, lack that commitment to renew the nation which inspired Mrs. Orzeszkowa; therefore, even if written in Polish, they would not have contributed to keep up the Polish morale.

Then, with a sudden turn against Conrad, Lutosławski concluded: "We should not envy the English for a second class writer who, in any case, would not have enriched our literature since he himself admitted that gain was the motive of his creative activity. We are rich enough to give many such writers to all the nations of the earth, keeping for ourselves only the best who will express their souls in Polish."

In 1929, Lutosławski once more wrote about his visit to Conrad. This time he reported Conrad's answer as follows: "Writing in Polish is fine. But to do that one would have to be a writer like Mickiewicz or Krasiński. I am a common man, I write to make a living and to support my wife and I do this in the language of the country which gave me asylum."

Another link with Poland was Marguerite Poradowska, née Gachet, a Belgian lady married to a

Polish freedom fighter who was a cousin to Apollo. The couple lived in Galicia and Marguerite made Poland's cause her own. She had a modest gift for writing and in her stories she tried to present the Ruthenian folk to the West. She returned to her native Brussels with her husband, and in 1890 was instrumental in getting Conrad his ill-fated assignment in the Congo. Poradowski died in 1890 while Conrad was on his way to the Ukraine.

At the beginning of 1914 Conrad received a Polish journalist, Marian Dąbrowski, whose wife Maria later wrote a series of essays on Conrad. His conversation with Conrad was published in the *Illustrated Weekly* (Warsaw, May 1914) and has since been reprinted in Mrs. Dąbrowska's *Sketches on Conrad* (1959) and in *Polska* (1960). This interview is remarkable for two reasons: first, it is one of the rare interviews ever granted by Conrad to a journalist (he normally hated journalists and interviews); second, as far as we know it is the first occasion that Conrad openly discussed his Polish heritage with anyone.

Conrad was telling his interviewer how in 1878 he had met a few Russian warships when on his way to the Azov Sea and had seen the Russian ensign flying. He then added, "This gave me a creepy feeling. My father, you know—" After some minutes of silence, during which Conrad seemed absorbed by his memories, the interviewer said, "I would like to discover Poland's immortal genius in the English writer," to which Conrad replied: "The genius of Poland? You—and me. Who ever doubts it exists? The English critics—since I am in fact an English writer—when discussing me always note that there is something in me which cannot be understood, nor defined, nor expressed. Only you can grasp this undefinable factor, only you can understand the incomprehensible. It is *polskość*[61] (*polonitas*), that *polskość* which I took into my work from Mickiewicz and Słowacki. My father read *Pan Tadeusz* to me and made me read it aloud. And not just once or twice. I liked especially [Mickiewicz's] *Konrad Wallenrod* and *Grażyna*[62]. Later, I preferred Słowacki. Do you know why Słowacki? *Il est l'âme de toute la Pologne, lui*."

At the end of the interview, Dąbrowski asked Conrad to give him a short message for the Poles at home, "as a Pole to another Pole." To this Conrad answered, "I am neither a great man, nor a prophet. Yet your immortal fire burns in me too. It is small and insignificant, more in the nature of a *lueur* [glimmer], but it is there and it persists. When I think of the present political situation, *c'est affreux!* I am unable to think often of Poland, for this is bitter, painful, bad. I could not live! The English, when taking leave use the expression *Good luck!* I could not [as a Pole to a Pole] say this to you. Yet, despite of everything, faced with the threat of extermination, we still stay alive [as a nation]."

In these words, Conrad expressed his deepest feelings for Poland, feelings he normally kept in the dark. As he said, he could not have gone on living if he had brooded too much over the plight of his unfortunate country. Yet the bitterness, the pain, and the sadness engendered by "the political situation" were always with him. He could not share these feelings with anyone, for who would have understood? At long last, in 1919, he could tell the English that the partition of Poland had been a crime, but he could never have told them how much he was hurt—as his father had been hurt—by the fact that England and France throughout the years were on excellent terms with the criminals while caring little for the victim. These feelings of latent despair, of hurt, of sad resignation, and of pessimism he had to hide from others and even from himself, but they pervaded his whole work and gave them that specifically Conradian haunting quality.

Little could Conrad know that a few years later Poland's immortality would assert itself and that, after over one and a half century of virtual foreign occupation and division, the country would become one and free. It seems that Dąbrowski's interview moved Conrad to accept Mrs. Retinger's invitation to visit her in Poland. He wanted his sons to see his native country and yet he dreaded stirring up early or painful memories.

Before leaving, he wrote to Galsworthy: "As to this Polish journey, I depart on it with mixed feelings. In 1874 I got into a train in Cracow (Vienna Express) on my way to the sea, as a man might get into a dream. And here is the dream going on still. Only now it is peopled mostly by ghosts and the moment of awakening draws near." (*LL*, II, 157)

The "Konstantynówka" on 7 Jagiellońska Street in Zakopane.
The Conrads lived on the ground floor with the ladies
Zagórska.

As is well-known, this trip took place in July 1914. Conrad and his family were surprised by the outbreak of the first world war while in Poland. Before their departure could be arranged, the Conrads stayed at Mrs. Aniela Zagórska's boarding house, "Konstantynówka", situated at No. 7 Jagiellońska Street, Zakopane, a health resort south of Cracow, in the midst of the Tatra mountains (see photograph). The Zagórska family consisted of Mrs. Aniela Zagórska, who had become a widow in 1898, and her two daughters Aniela and Karola. During the two months and four days that the Conrad family stayed at the Konstantynówka, Conrad seems to have lived in a world of his own, far away from England but also from his English wife and children. Aniela assiduously provided him with modern Polish novels which he read avidly. He also met the Polish novelist, Żeromski, but no real communication was established by the two men.

Back in England Conrad wrote an account of his Polish journey for the *Daily Mail* ("Poland Revisited", reprinted in *Notes on Life and Letters*). As usual, this report is remarkable not so much for what it says, but for what it conceals. Like Sigmund Freud, Conrad, when telling about himself, made a distinction between the things that may be said; those that are private, but may be mentioned to a few intimate friends, and finally those that are "privatissimi" (Freud's expression), i.e. ever to be kept to oneself. After Conrad's death, Mrs. Jessie Conrad described the Polish journey as she saw it in her book *Joseph Conrad as I knew Him* (Ch. V). Fortunately, his niece and translator, Miss Aniela Zagórska, later also wrote her memories concerning Conrad's ten weeks' stay at the Konstantynówka. They were published in Warsaw's leading literary weekly, the *Literary News* (December 1929, No. 51) and have been reprinted lately in Barbara Kocówna's *Reminiscences and Essays* (Warsaw 1963, 89-102).

Aniela Zagórska writes that Conrad and his family arrived at Zakopane on the third or fourth of August 1914. She had never met him before. "He was a graying elderly gentleman with a severe physiognomy and a distinguished appearance." During the whole stay at Zakopane, Conrad was in an exceptionally relaxed and agreeable mood. "His wife remarked on this several times, adding that this was only natural," meaning that he felt thoroughly at home in the Polish countryside. Jessie Conrad told Miss Aniela Zagórska that at home, in England, her husband's mood was very uneven and unpredictable and that "visitors wanting to make his acquaintance never knew in what mood they would find him." But at the Konstantynówka, "he spoke freely and warmly."

Only once was there an exception. Miss Zagórska had invited a Mr. Rembowski, an admirer of *Lord Jim*, anxious to make the personal acquaintance of the author. But Conrad hardly said a word, nor did the visitor. Finally supper was served, but Conrad remained taciturn. Miss Zagórska felt very badly and when the guest was leaving, tried to apologize. To her great astonishment, Rembowski answered, "I am enchanted by Conrad, he is immensely sympathetic." As for Conrad, he was also delighted and afterwards said, "This Rembowski is really charming, I was very impressed by him." When his niece then asked why he had not said more, he answered simply, "I was not in the mood." Having reported this event, Miss Zagórska continues with the following remarks:

> Only later did I understand Conrad's silence. I noticed that when he was especially interested in someone, when he wanted to win the sympathy of someone he liked, he became unnatural and awkward. He then either spoke too much and with too much emphasis (as when he met Żeromski), or he became mute and sombre. It seems to me I know what he felt then. He was demoralized and frozen by the uncertainty: "What does this man think of me? Does he, too, take me for a deserter?"

Indeed, as Miss Zagórska remarks in this connection, Conrad could never forget "the bitter and painful experience" of getting that letter from Mrs. Orzeszkowa. Even after her death, Conrad could not forgive her now twenty-year-old rebuke.

> That letter must have been rather crude and ruth-less, especially as it touched his most sensitive feel-ings and thoughts. I have no doubt that Conrad's double allegiance, his dichotomy between England and Poland—with the stress on England—was pro-ducing in him a constant tension and discord. This conviction of mine is not only based on my observa-tions but also on his own words. Only once during our numerous talks did he touch the subject. He did no more than mention it, but I saw that even that cost him a great effort. One day I wanted to give him Orzeszkowa's novel *On the Niemen* to read. "Bring me nothing of the kind," he exclaimed. "But Conrad . . ." "Don't bring me anything by her,"[63] he interrupted me vehemently. "You don't know, but she once wrote me such a letter."

Conrad spent a great deal of his time in Zakopane reading modern Polish novels and some verse. Accord-ing to Miss Zagórska, who provided him with books from the local library, he read fast and indefatigably:

> In these two months, he devoured nearly every-thing worthy of being read in the domain of (con-temporary) novels and drama. "Devoured" is the right word. He read with incredible speed. I con-stantly brought him new books. He lost patience when, having finished one book, he had not already another one waiting for him on the table. His judgment not only of the work but of the style of each writer was absolutely infallible.

Once, having read Wyspiański's *A Warsaw Woman* (Warszawianka) he exclaimed, "How I would love to translate this!" He especially liked Żeromski's *Ashes* and *The Works of Sisyphus*. Once Conrad had started to read the works of Bolesław Prus, he wanted to read every one of his novels, even his first ones which Miss Zagórska herself found "honestly boring." Upon discussing with his niece an Egyptian novel by Prus, she asked him whether he thought the description of the Egyptian landscape to be faithful. "Not at all," Conrad answered, "but there is no harm in that. The theme of the book is

important." He said that Prus was better than
Dickens—certainly a remarkable judgment on the part
of Conrad who admired Dickens so much.

But Miss Zagórska got to know Conrad not only as
an indefatigable reader, but also as a supreme teller of
stories:

> The nicest part of the whole day was the evening.
> The house was quiet and we gathered in the living
> room—my mother, Conrad, and I—and we talked
> until late at night. Conrad was an absolutely first
> class causeur. Once he told us an episode of his
> youth. It happened on one of the islands of the
> Pacific inhabited by cannibals. Conrad went ashore
> with some other sailors to look for a man who had
> got lost and had not returned to the vessel. After
> many efforts they found their comrade. He had
> been caught by the cannibals and bound. After a
> struggle, the sailors managed to free him and bring
> him back on deck. From this whole story I re-
> member the return best, but I do not only re-
> member Conrad's story but also the expression of
> his face—so dramatic and so well adapted to the
> various details he was describing.

During one of those memorable evenings Miss
Zagórska decided to read aloud from Słowacki (as
Apollo had read aloud to his boy). The effect on Conrad
was rather unexpected:

> Once I resolved to read from Słowacki in the even-
> ing, and the whole day the thought gladdened my
> heart. After supper, we sat down as usual in the liv-
> ing room. I began to read from *Agamemnon's Tomb*.
> I read aloud and without interruption, never lifting
> my eyes from the book. Finally, having finished, I
> looked at Conrad—and was frightened. There he
> sat with an irritated and painful face. Suddenly he
> got up and left without a word, not looking at me
> or my mother, like a deeply grieved man. There
> was in this flight from the recited verses something
> so very profound that I never dared to allude to it.
> The common reading of Słowacki remained buried
> forever. It is probable that the verses, not heard for
> a long time, had unexpectedly touched such a sensi-
> tive chord in Conrad that he could not dominate
> and hide his feelings of painful shock.

Why should Conrad have wanted to translate Wyspiański's *A Warsaw Woman* (Warszawianka)? As Wit Tarnawski recently pointed out (*News*, London, 24 January 1971), the plot of this novel must have appealed to Conrad because it deals with a man's Hamlet-like hesitation and indecision in face of a situation which calls for immediate action—a subject very dear to Conrad.

And why did *Agamemnon's Tomb* make such a deep, even ghastly impression upon Conrad? Agamemnon's funeral vault visited by Słowacki is of course reminiscent of Mother Poland in her grave. In this poem of 126 lines, the poet conjures up all the buried hopes, aspirations, and the glorious past of Poland. He blames his contemporaries for their lack of faith. The refrain "I feel sad" expresses the poet's feeling of sorrow looking at the grave of Polish greatness.

Confronted with those beautiful verses which come as near to music as human language can, Conrad must have felt stripped of his English overlay, stripped naked of his acquired personality as a prolific, well-known English author. Faced with the Polish genius, Conrad would but feel very small, if not annihilated. He knew he would never be able to write like Słowacki; not in Polish where he never got beyond the school boy level, nor even in English. And he too must have felt condemned for his lack of patriotic faith, for Słowacki had become more intensely Polish while living and writing abroad.

Conrad's works were hardly ever discussed during those two memorable months (Miss Zagórska knew little more than *Lord Jim* at the time), but once Conrad explained to her how the title *Heart of Darkness* should be rendered in Polish. His suggestion—literally: *The Core of Darkness* (Jądro Ciemności) was later adopted.

Once, while standing beside her seated uncle, Miss Zagórska noticed a scar on the top of his head and asked what this was due to. Conrad answered that he might have acquired it during a brawl in some port. Then his niece asked him point blank, "Didn't you have a duel once?" Apparently Conrad was caught off guard, for he said nothing for a while, just looked in front of himself and reflected. Finally he answered with a smile, "Yes. Then I got quite something, he shot me here," pointing to his breast. Then suddenly lifting his head, he said with a malicious twinkle in his eye: *Mais moi, je lui ai fracassé la patte* ("But I smashed his paw"). Aniela appeared to be convinced by her uncle's story.

The Conrads left Zakopane on 8 October, 1914. In the evening of that day everybody was assembled in the living room, waiting for the "góral" (mountain peasant) who, with horse and buggy, was to bring them to the nearest open railway station. The man was two hours late. According to Miss Zagórska, the mood at the Konstantynówka was good, even elated. Everybody was convinced the war would be over in a few months and then, so the Conrads promised, they would be back in Poland for another and longer holiday. They left after midnight and arrived at Chabówka station at six or seven in the morning. On the way they had been kept awake by a population of fleas nesting in the sheepskins that kept them warm, a fact duly noted by Mrs. Conrad. Two days later the family left Poland for Austria and Italy. Conrad never set foot in Poland again.

One must ask oneself why he never visited his native land after her resurrection. Did his "double allegiance" bother him? Żeromski suspected this when, writing about Conrad in his *Elegies*, he said, "He must have been torn in our direction, for Poland is so rich in sentiment that no noble soul can detach itself from her bonds." One may also ask oneself what would have happened if Conrad and his family had been obliged to stay in Poland for the duration of the war. Would the scope and contents of his inspiration have changed? Would not the conflict. of allegiance have become unbearable, for Galicia was part of Austria and thus at war with Great Britain? Fortunately, the order to detain him and his family on Austrian soil came too late.

After 1914, Conrad's relations with Poland were only casual. Occasionally, as Jessie Conrad and John Conrad[64] have mentioned, he uttered the wish to retire to his native country, but it seemed rather a dream, not a serious project.

In England, Conrad never seems to have owned up to the deep impression Polish books had made upon him in Zakopane. Retinger went as far as stating, "He knew Polish literature but slightly, with the exception of a few novels he read in Zakopane in 1914, or after the war. They did not find favor with him, with the exception of a young writer, Bruno Winawer, whose *Book of Job* he spontaneously translated into English."[65] It is likely that

Retinger's statement concerning Conrad's opinion of Polish modern literature was a misinterpretation of Conrad's reticence concerning his Polish readings in Zakopane. Mrs. Conrad also was quite unaware of the impact these Polish readings had on her husband.

Conrad was very much at home in Zakopane, discussing with Poles for hours, borrowing money freely, sitting in cafés (where he took good meals behind his wife's back while she thought he was starving[66]), and becoming friendly with complete strangers. During those two months, he must have identified himself with the Poles to an extent he never did either before or afterwards. Somehow the spirit of the country got hold of him, even claimed him more than he would ever admit, and it seems reasonable to believe that it was the fear of this claim which prevented him from ever visiting Poland again.

During the first world war, Conrad naturally became interested in the future of Poland. Contrary to his former convictions, there was now a possibility of a free Poland arising out of the turmoil of the war. Conrad had always been interested in political questions, a fact amply illustrated by his political novels. In 1905, he had written a remarkable political essay entitled "Autocracy and War" in which he tried to present the dark side of Czarist Russia to a rather naive West. He argued that the existence of an autocratic European power was by necessity a threat to Western democracy. Of course, Conrad was then preaching in the wilderness: Western democracy was not conscious of any danger. There is in Conrad's article much which reminds us of his father's political essay "Poland and Moscow," in which Moscow stands for a sinister form of autocracy, barbarism, and aggression while Poland represents liberty, tolerance, and civilization. "Autocracy and War" in fact is a pamphlet. Conrad rendered the sinister and Byzantine aspect of Czarist autocracy much better in his novel, *Under Western Eyes*, and it is here that he actually settled his and his father's account with Russia.

At the beginning of World War I, while staying in Galicia, Conrad had many political talks with Polish friends living in Zakopane, and especially with the Cracow lawyer, Dr. Teodor Kosch, and Mr. Zajaczkowski, a businessman. The gist of these conversations was put down in a "Memorandum" which Conrad wrote in

Polish. The curious document was left with Dr. Kosch who finally published it in March 1934 in the Cracow paper, *Time* (*Czas*). It has been reproduced, both in English and in Polish, in Ludwik Krzyżanowski's *Joseph Conrad: Centennial Essays* (123-125, and 138-139 respectively). It is a discussion of Poland's future after the war. Conrad did not believe that Germany would be defeated, but he hoped for a political compromise. Since Russia was fighting on the side of Britain, he feared that Britain would not really stand up for a free Poland; all he hoped for that she would exert "moral pressure" on Russia to release the Poles from bondage. At the time he thought that Britain should become a friend of Austria which, in the past, had allowed the Poles the greatest cultural autonomy. Political propaganda must therefore be directed at the British public to get it interested in the future of Poland. The tone of the document is only moderately optimistic; all that Conrad (and his Polish friends) wanted was that Poland should become a protectorate of the Western powers.

During his short stay in Vienna, Conrad also discussed the Polish question with Mr. Marian Biliński: "I had the pleasure and profit to talk with him for several hours, extensively, exhaustively on the Polish question in general, on the way of how it might be put before a European Congress, of the hopes, fears, and possibilities connected with it." At a second meeting, they discussed "chiefly of how to present the Polish question in England . . . it will be necessary to look around, to sound out the hearts and minds of influential people, and only then start some action, if action is possible, on the question which lies in our hearts."[67]

In a letter addressed to Mr. Biliński and written aboard the ship which brought the Conrad family back to England, Conrad promised: "Already tomorrow I'll try to see a few influential persons in the journalistic world."[68] But Conrad appears to have run into difficulties and we hear nothing more about the Polish question till 1916. On 20 August of that year, he wrote to Richard Curle about "the hopeless state of the Polish question" (*LL*, II, 174). He admired the relentless efforts of Joseph Retinger who gave all his energy to pave a way for Poland's independence in British and French political circles. He added, "I too have dipped my fingers in diplomacy by writing a memorandum on the peace settlement on the Eastern front which got into the Foreign Office." Here, Conrad alludes to his *Note on the Polish Problem*, reprinted in *Notes on Life and Letters*.

This *Note*, written primarily for the British government, but also addressing itself to the public, is a well-written, extremely moderate and objective essay. It is completely bare of that pathos and emotionality which characterized Apollo's (and Retinger's) political writings. Conrad began by stating that "Polonism", i.e. the Polish cultural and national spirit was different from "Germanism" (which the Poles hate) and from "Slavonism" with which it was "incompatible". Therefore, the new Poland could not be dependent on either Germanism or Slavonism. This was why Poland always looked to the West, i.e. to France and Great Britain, if not for help, so at least for moral support. In temperament, feeling, and mind, the Poles are more Western than the Russians, Germans or Austrians. This gives the Poles the right to exist as a nation. They have resisted foreign domination so long only because of their unbroken faith in the West and it would be unsafe for the Western powers to overlook this fact. Poland should receive her freedom, her constitution, the right to have an army, etc. from the hands of Great Britain and France, with the concurrence of Russia. Poland's status should be that of a "triple protectorate."

Conrad actually had an interview with a Mr. Clark of the Foreign Office, to whom he submitted his plan. In a letter dated 21 August, 1916, written in French and addressed to Joseph Retinger, Conrad reports Clark's reaction as follows: that the Poles themselves should make "a well-founded demand supported by well-known personalities representing as completely as possible the political opinions and social strata of Poland." Therefore, wrote Conrad, it was now Retinger's task to unite all Polish parties to approve the plan, "for it is better to receive the gift of national independence from the hands of friends than from that of enemies." The first thing was "to begin to live, to breathe, to take shape. Afterwards the fight of ideas will develop within the framework of the basic political institutions as in every free country."

On 31 August, 1916, Conrad wrote to Christopher Sandeman, "The cause to which you are so friendly . . . I look at from the English point of view, which is only tinged with the ineradicable sentiments of origin—as indeed is but natural. That is why I wrote a short memoir, motived as much by my sentiments of allegiance as by my sentiment of origin. It (the triple protectorate) is the only arrangement under which I could be sure . . . that the Poles would never be drawn into antagonism to England." (*LL*, II, 174).

On 19 March, 1917, Conrad wrote to Hugh R. Dent, "Can't say that I am delighted at the Russian revolution." A revolution was bound to weaken Russia and its alliance with the West. Nor was Conrad delighted when the Russians, in a proclamation, paid lipservice to the idea of an independent Poland.[69] He also feared that the Poles, having had no political experience for generations, might make big mistakes: "We can't expect certain virtues from people conscious of having been regarded for ages as a political nuisance."[70]

On 25 January 1919, Conrad wrote to Hugh Clifford, "Of course my concern is for England, which engages all my affections and all my thoughts . . . As for Poland, I have never had any illusions and I must render the Poles the justice to say that they too had very few."[71] From the English point of view, Conrad did everything to plead the cause of an independent Poland. True, he did this with his usual pessimism and not without some bitter remarks on the "idealism, stupidity, or hypocrisy" of the British politicians. From the Polish point of view, however, Conrad was far from being committed.

Perłowski, in his article "On Conrad and Kipling," tells the following story:

When the war broke out, I found myself in Switzerland, where a group of Poles took to work. In Vevey a committee was formed to bring relief to the war victims in Poland, under the direction of Sienkiewicz and Paderewski. In fact, the goals of the committee were much wider. We were not only concerned with material help, but also with public relations. We wanted to prove to the world that the Poles do exist, that Poland wants to live and has established rights to this. Conrad refused to collaborate with our committee with the pretext that some "ambassador of Czarist Russia" took part in it. He gave lessons of Patriotism to a Sienkiewicz, a Paderewski! I remember the moment when the

vice-president of the committee, Osuchowski, a
skinny old man with eyes still glowing with the most
noble fire, told us (with bony hands trembling in
the air and stammering with emotion) that 'Mr.
Konrad Korzeniowski, famous English writer, disappointed our expectations'. There was a deep silence. We were astonished, since we knew about
Conrad's (Polish) past. Well, even foreigners who
wished Poland well, worked with us. Why this lack
of good will? Sienkiewicz gave us the answer, as always, quietly and directly: "This is a simple matter.
Often a man revenges himself for his own bad
deed."[72]

As a matter of fact, the Polish committee had invited the Russian ambassador in London, Count D. A.
de Benckendorff, to participate. Benckendorff was married to a Roman Catholic, was liberal-minded, and was
believed to understand the Polish aspirations. Moreover,
he naturally had some influence in Russia which was
Great Britain's ally. Conrad's stubborn refusal was
bound to shock the Polish patriots. And it was another
example of the historical fact that Polish individualism
had so often led to inner division.

Conrad refused his cooperation in a telegram addressed to Paderewski, Claridge Hotel, London. It read:
"With every deference to your illustrious personality I
cannot join a committee where I understand Russian
names will appear. Conrad." The original telegram form
was found and first published by W. Berbelicki in the
Polish *Library Yearbook,* 1961, from which we copied it.
Paderewski showed the telegram to Retinger in March,
1915, shortly before the great pianist left for the United
States where he wanted to use his influence for the liberation of Poland.

Conrad's attitude was rather unique in so far as no
other high ranking Pole is known to have refused his
cooperation on these or similar grounds. In 1919, four
years after the event, he gave a rather long-winded explanation to a Polish editor of the Chicago *Daily News,* Antoni Czarnecki, who had visited Conrad in England. It is
probable that it was agreed that the conversation should
not be made public at that time. At any rate, it was only
published on 31 July 1924, three days before Conrad's
death, and only in a Polish paper, the *Ameryka Echo,*
printed in Toledo, Ohio. The title of Czarnecki's article

Conrad's telegram to Paderewski (1915)

> Paderewski Garidges Hotel
> London
>
> With very deference to your
> illustrious personality I can not
> join a committee where I
> understand Russian names
> will appear. Conrad.

is "An Evening with Conrad." This is how Conrad explained his refusal:

They came to me asking my permission to add my name to the list of members of the Committee. My principle is not to accept a membership in any committee, if I have no time to devote to it, nor to attend its meetings. Moreover, I would not belong to a committee without knowing the names of the other members with whom I have to work. I explained this to my visitors and they showed me a list of the people invited to participate. There were names of outstanding Poles and Englishmen, but there was among them also the Czarist ambassador to Great Britain who had already given his assent.

My father had fought to get rid of the foreign yoke in Poland and was exiled from his fatherland by order of the Czar when I was still a small boy. The partition of Poland for me had always been a crime, and the brutal persecution of the Polish people by foreign despots I always condemned violently. The Russian Czar, the German Kaiser and the Austrian Emperor were to me always symbols of tyranny, and so were their representatives and agents. I am proud of my Polish blood and of being born in Poland. To help the Polish cause was the principle of my whole life. I have been and still am always ready to do my part to help the needy and the suffering. I am always ready to serve the cause for which my father fought, but as a free man living in this country (England). Looking at the Polish problem, I could not with good conscience assist the Committee to bring help to Poland with, at my side, one of the arms of the despot who during the whole past had done everything to crush the Polish nation and destroy its ideals, principles, and aspirations. It was not my business to pass judgement on those who organized this Committee. When I noted that the ambassador of Czarist Russia had accepted the membership, I asked the Polish leaders to excuse me for not being able to cooperate. I understood then quite well that the Czarist government in its hour of need was an ally of my adopted country, Great Britain, which is not only my residence and the country of my choice, but also the place where I found recognition and with which, of my own free will, I am connected by the bonds of citizenship.

As an Englishman, I could not give the Polish leader the reasons why I did not want to serve on the Committee. My friends understood and did not need any explanations. Others stubbornly refused to understand, interpreting my attitude wrongly. They did not even try to get to the truth of the matter. This event motivated some Polish leaders to consider me as one who had forgotten the country of his fathers. What I did in fact for the Polish cause within a strictly English or strictly Polish context only those can tell who worked together with me.

Throughout my whole life I have tried to be a really loyal Englishman. Such is the principle of all Englishmen of Polish descent. The same question arose with you, American citizens of Polish origin. Traditions, literature, ideals, the history of our native country, like the love of our mother, accompany us throughout our lives. We are always ready to help our compatriots. We are equally ready to spread the truth about Poland, to make people see her real worth and character, the nobility of heart of her people. We who are far away from Poland and citizens of another country can give the best demonstration of this character by being the most loyal and most useful citizens of the country we chose voluntarily.

How did Paderewski, the famous pianist and later prime minister of the Polish Republic (1918-1921), take Conrad's refusal? He may have been offended at first, but when he met Conrad for the first time, eight years later, they seemed to understand each other well. The meeting took place during Conrad's American tour, in

May 1923, at a lunch arranged by Colonel House in New York.[73] A few weeks later, on 17 June 1923, Jean-Aubry happened to meet the famous musician on board a channel steamer. This is Jean-Aubry's report: "Paderewski spoke of the great novelist with sincere sympathy. I got the impression that the half-hour discussion between the two great Poles had not been about music but about actual political problems." When, shortly afterwards, Jean-Aubry asked Conrad about Paderewski, he replied: "What an extraordinary man! In half an hour I learned considerably more from him about my fatherland than during the last fifteen years of my life".[74]

In 1919, Conrad wrote another political essay concerning Poland: *The Crime of Partition*, again an objective and unemotional piece of work, trying not just to present to a rather obtuse British public the Polish point of view, but to show that such a crime (unfortunately not uncommon in the days of absolutism), even after a hundred and thirty years remains unacceptable and must be corrected. What Conrad demands in his essay is justice for Poland and he expects the Western powers (Great Britain and France) to take an active part in the restoration of Poland. Soon afterwards the independent Polish Republic was established by the Treaty of Versailles with Paderewski as prime minister. It is strange that from now on Conrad did not seem to be interested in Poland any more. He appeared annoyed when, arriving at New York in May 1923, he was greeted by a group of Polish girls in Polish costumes. He never took part in any festivities connected with the restoration of Poland, nor did he visit the reborn country. The dreams of his father had finally become reality—but the son did not seem elated. Did Conrad, who always has been afraid of becoming a victim of illusions, distrust the leaders of the new Poland? Or did he distrust the Western powers who had created the Polish Republic?

A few months before his death, Joseph Conrad came in contact with Poland for the last time. He was invited to a reception at the Polish embassy in London. We can imagine his feelings when, for the first time in his life, he was confronted with a representative of a free and united Poland. After all, Poland had not been lost!

We have no less than three accounts of this event. One is by Jean-Aubry, who accompanied Conrad and

wrote about it in the Warsaw *Illustrated Weekly*. The sec-
,ond report, by Edward Raczyński, was published in the
London Polish paper *News*, Nos. 176-177, 1949. The
third and most interesting report is by Roman Dyboski,
who then met Conrad for the first time; it was printed
in the venerable Cracow paper, *Time*, No. 71, 1932, the
very paper which had published Buszczyński's biography
of Apollo. In answer to a question by Dyboski, Conrad
bluntly stated he "had enough of the sea." Asked whether
he wanted to take part in a Literary Association of
Friends of Poland, Conrad said his name could be used
as one of the sponsors, but he would not take any active
part in the society, nor be its honorary president.

Dyboski explained to Conrad that the society had
first been founded in 1831 and now was to be resur-
rected in order to do a public relations job for Poland in
the West. Conrad then became quite emphatic, maintaining that Poland did not require any propaganda abroad:
"That's all right for those other nations who recently
emerged from the ruin of their former masters and
from the dust of oblivion: for the Serbs who for hundreds of years were Turkish slaves, or the Czechs so
long buried under a crust of Germanization. But we
Poles, who through more than a hundred years of
foreign domination remained what we had been for almost a thousand years, we do not need such efforts.
Whoever so desires will find us in the same bastion of
Europe where we always defended her civilization!"

"The same bastion of Europe where we always defended her civilization"—here Conrad was literally
speaking the language of his father. And thus, near the
end of his life, his Polish heritage claimed him once
more, and the Pole and "Korzeniowski of the Nałęcz
arms" broke through the *persona* of the English novelist.

The Lingard Trilogy

There are three books by Joseph Conrad dealing either directly or indirectly with a seaman called Tom Lingard. This man, who might have stepped out of one of Marryat's books, is described as an excellent sailor, an astute pilot, a gallant fighter, a bold adventurer, and a first class trader. His brig can outsail any other vessel. Lingard is known all over the Eastern archipelago as Rajah Laut, or "the King of the Sea." He is popular with the Malays because of his gallantry, his sense of justice, and his urbanity, while the pirates fear his swift revenge and the Arab traders hate him as a superior rival.

Beneath his outward appearance of roughness, Tom Lingard has a kind heart. Like a good father, he wants to make other people happy, to the extent of adopting the daughter of a pirate that he killed, or by picking up human flotsam in Eastern ports. He wants to plan their lives, arrange their marriages, find jobs for them. "I carry everything right through" is one of his favorite sayings, and "I always get my way"[75] another.

The Lingard trilogy consists of three episodes in the life of this fabulous man: an overture, so to speak (*The Rescue*), where Tom Lingard is beginning his career as an independent ship owner and trader. He commits a moral mistake by betraying a native prince in exchange for saving a rich English couple with whom he has nothing in common except his origin. In *An Outcast of the Islands*, in his turn the same Lingard is betrayed by the very man he had tried to rehabilitate. He also loses his unique "Lightning" in a shipwreck, and his power over the Malay river settlement whose fortune he had made. In *Almayer's Folly*, Lingard is but a name, a vague hope, a memory of great times irretrievably gone. In *The Rescue*,

Lingard is the main character; in the *Outcast* this is
Peter Willems, a man whom Lingard "made" and who,
in return, is going to destroy him: whereas *Almayer's Folly*
is the story of the fall of another Lingard protégé, Kaspar Almayer, and of the final loss of Lingard's economic
kingdom.

Contrary to what one would expect, Joseph Conrad
wrote the three novels of the trilogy in reverse order,
beginning with *Almayer's Folly,* continuing with the *Outcast*
(which is set about fifteen years earlier), and concluding
with *The Rescue*, in which he describes events that happened approximately 25-35 years before. When writing
Almayer's Folly, Joseph Conrad did not expect to write
anything else, least of all a trilogy. As for *The Rescue*, this
novel is only connected with the other two by the hero,
Lingard, and it was finished only very late in Conrad's
writing career.

Apart from the three novels which form the Lingard trilogy, there are two short stories entitled "The Lagoon" and "Karain" which, in style, inspiration, and time of
writing, belong to the same period. Since these two
stories (they form part of his *Tales of Unrest*) are typical
of Conrad's first period of writing—a period which he
himself called his "Malayan phase"[76]—we shall include
them in this chapter.

What then were Conrad's three characters—
Lingard, Willems, and Almayer—like, and in which way
did their character also become their fate? What attracted him in people like Karain and Arsat? Why did
he create these characters at all?

1. *Almayer's Folly*

This novel naturally occupies a key position in Conrad's writings. It is his first book, and the only one he
did not write primarily for publication, but rather as a
hobby, in odd moments of leisure over the course of
four years which were partly filled with sea voyages. The
slowly and fitfully growing manuscript accompanied its
author all over the East, to the Ukraine, and finally up
the Congo river where it almost got lost. He must have
written quite a lot of it on the *Torrens*, for there he got
the nickname "the scribbling mate."[77] *Almayer's Folly*
marks the transition between Captain Korzeniowski and
Joseph Conrad the writer. It is the end of a period and

the beginning of an entirely new adventure in life which had already known quite a number of perilous vicissitudes.

Kaspar Almayer[78] is described as the son of a subordinate Dutch official at Buitenzorg, Java. At about eighteen, Almayer "had left his home with a light heart and a lighter pocket, speaking English well, and strong in arithmetic; ready to conquer the world, never doubting that he would". Almayer had gone to Macassar, Celebes, "to woo fortune in the godowns of old Hudig". Tom Lingard was one of Hudig's customers. He took a fancy to young Almayer and placed him as his agent in Sambir, a trading post.

Lingard was supposed to be very rich. "He had discovered a river." This meant that he alone knew the entrance to the Pantai river; and he was therefore the only one who could trade with that place where he would exchange Manchester cotton goods, brass gongs, rifles and gunpowder for rattan, gutta-percha, and other tropical products. Almayer's future seemed brilliant. The old seaman told him "of his past life, of escaped dangers, of big profits in his trade, of new combinations that were in the future to bring bigger profits still."

Lingard was also a benefactor. He had adopted a girl, the only survivor of a band of Malayan pirates. She was being brought up in a convent. If Almayer married his Malayan girl, he would make them his heirs. Almayer sees, "as in a flash of dazzling light, great piles of shining guilders."[79] He promptly marries the girl whom he despises as belonging to an inferior race, and thus commits his first folly. Lingard installs the young couple in Sambir,[80] on the mysterious Pantai river along which he has the monopoly of trade. A child—Nina—is born to the incongruous couple. This girl soon becomes everything to Almayer. He pampers her, spoils her, plays with her, and finally sends her to Macassar to get the sort of education that would make her acceptable to Amsterdam society—for this is where Almayer, once become rich, intends to retire.

At the beginning of the novel Almayer is shown "contemplating the wreckage of his past in the dawn of new hopes." For wreckage there is. Nina has returned unexpectedly from Macassar where she had been increasingly rejected by the white people, and as the brittle veneer of her education peels off, her real nature starts showing. She hates the whites, distrusts her father, takes the part of her primitive mother, and soon falls in love with a young native. On top of all this, Almayer's trade is completely wrecked by the arrival and establishment of Arab traders (brought in by the treachery of his partner Willems), by the disappearance of Lingard, and by political intrigues. Yet, in the midst of all this wreckage, new hopes are dawning. Almayer has "enchanting visions" of a glorious future.

Lingard, too, had become a victim of illusions some time before. He had spent all his money exploring the interior in the hope of finding gold. Then old Hudig went bankrupt, and Lingard lost the rest of his money there. We meet him, finally, an old man "with the fire of fever burning in his sunken eyes", but still undaunted and convinced that "untold riches were in his grasp" if he only had more money "to realize a dream of fabulous fortune." He finally disappears, going to Europe "to raise money for the great enterprise." People would rush in with their money. But nobody did, apparently, and his last letter only mentions that he was ill and lonely. The rest is silence.

Almayer soon commits his second folly. Believing that the British would take over that part of the archipelago, he starts building a house "for the reception of the Englishmen." The Arab traders, on the other hand, put their trust in the Dutch, who actually take over. Almayer has to play host to Dutch officers, reveals the meaning of the new house to them, and they promptly christen it "Almayer's Folly."

After a while, Almayer's plans seem to take shape. A young Malay trader has arrived—Dain Maroola. Almayer tells him his secrets, not aware that Dain is only interested in his daughter and in the illegal acquisition of gunpowder. Almayer also prepares boats for that expedition to the goldfields up the river which is to make his fortune. In his daydreams, his imagination carries him away to the West, "where the paradise of Europe" is "awaiting the future Eastern millionaire."

Almayer needs money for his expedition. Since all legitimate trade is now in the hands of the Arabs, the only "combination" left to Almayer is the illegal sale of gunpowder to the Malays.

Almayer sees his hopes crumble. Nina disappears with Dain. Mrs. Almayer forsakes her husband, as do most of the servants. Almayer becomes an opium smoker, the only goal of his last months being "to forget," "never to forgive," and finally, to die.

What made Conrad choose Almayer (Olmeijer) as the hero of his first book? What attracted him to the remote little world of Malays, Arabs, white traders and colonizers as the scene for his first novel? Did he call it Sambir after Sambor, the market town in Eastern Galicia where his former tutor, Pulman, worked as a physician? Did the Arab traders, with their orthodox religion, remind him of the ubiquitous Jewish merchants so typical of the Poland he had known? And could it be that his strong bias against the colonizers, "the more sophisticated pioneers of [our] glorious virtues," reflected the feelings that every Pole naturally had for his German, Austrian, or Russian overlords?

Conrad's first book may be interpreted as an attempt to grapple with his Polish shadows and with the Nałęcz Korzeniowski strain within himself. Most of his forebears had lived on financial as well as political illusions, and had died ruined. In Conrad himself, the temptation to speculate was far from absent. As we have seen earlier, he lost all he had in a South African gold mine (1895-1896) and he was always "full of elaborate projects," wanted to invest money in whaling, etc. The very decision to go out into the world (one year younger than Almayer) resembles that of young Almayer.

Just how much of *Almayer's Folly* was related to Conrad's Polish background was given away by the author himself. In the last sentence of his "Author's Note" he says of his characters: "Their hearts—like ours—must endure the load of the gifts from Heaven: the curse of facts and the blessing·of illusions, the bitterness of our wisdom and the deceptive consolation of our folly." When we think of Polish history since the partitions ("the curse of facts"), the history of Conrad's father and relatives ("the blessing of illusions"), of Apollo's belief in his mission ("the deceptive consolation of our folly"), the formula of *Almayer's Folly* obviously stems from Conrad's Polish background and heritage.

2. An Outcast of the Islands

This second book of Joseph Conrad's, published one year after *Almayer's Folly*, begins on a sarcastic note. "When he stepped off the straight and narrow path of his peculiar honesty, it was with an inward assertion of unflinching resolve to fall back again into the monotonous but safe stride of virtue as soon as his little excursion into the wayside quagmires had produced the desired effect." Peter Willems, another protégé of the fabulous Captain Lingard, has committed an embezzlement at the expense of his employer, old Hudig. Like Almayer and old Lingard, Willems is a victim of illusions. He imagines "that he could go on afterwards looking at the sunshine, enjoying the shade, breathing in the perfume of flowers in the small garden before his house. He fancied that nothing would be changed" once he had put back the embezzled sum.

Willems was thirty and the confidential clerk of old Hudig, whose moral principles were not too strict either. Illegal deals in opium and gunpowder, smuggling firearms and so forth were, as Hudig called it, merely "pushing the principles of trade to their furthest consequences." "The wise, the strong, the respected, have no scruples. Where there are scruples there can be no power." Only "the fools, the weak, the contemptible" believe in strict honesty. That's what Hudig the trader had taught his clerk Willems. The teaching had not fallen on deaf ears. Willems "had appropriated some of Hudig's money." It had been "a deplorable necessity" to be judged with "the indulgence that should be extended to the weaknesses of genius."

Willems' youth resembles that of Conrad. He came from Rotterdam where his father was an "outdoor clerk of some shipbroker." The mother was dead. "The boy was quick in learning, but idle in school." Attracted by "the spirit of the sea," Peter ran away from home at the age of 17, but soon found the sea "that had looked so charming from afar" rather "hard and exacting on closer acquaintance." As luck (or fate) would have it, the boy had run into Captain Lingard who picked him up "like a starved cat", made him his protégé, and after a few years turned him over to old Hudig.

The years passed. Hudig made him marry a half-caste girl—an illegitimate child of his—without disclosing her origin. He had a house built for the young couple, and they had a son, Leonard. Willems had never liked his wife, and she was afraid of his outbursts. The in-laws too were constantly hanging around, perpetually asking for money. He was often seen drinking and gambling, and with "a run of bad luck at cards" had seen himself obliged to secretly "borrow" that money from Old Hudig.

It happened instinctively. "Almost before he was well aware of it he was off the path of his peculiar honesty." For what kind of honesty had he anyhow? He had no other guide to moral conduct than "his own convenience and that doctrine of success which he had found for himself in the book of life—in those interesting chapters that the Devil has been permitted to write in it, to test the sharpness of men's eyesight and the steadfastness of their hearts."

Hudig found out about the embezzlement and Willems was fired. After a scene with his wife and his brother-in-law, Willems runs away. In a flash-back, he sees the house fronts of his native Rotterdam and the "faded face of a weary man earning bread for the children that waited for him in a dingy home"—his father. No, he would never go back. "He had cut himself adrift from that home many years ago."

Willems is picked up a second time by the ubiquitous Lingard, fourteen years after their first meeting. The King of the Sea places him as an assistant with Almayer, Lingard's trade agent in Sambir, on that fabulous river accessible to Lingard's *Flash* alone.

Willems' arrival is first greeted with alarm by the three exiled Malayan chiefs, the blind Omar, Lakamba, and Balabatchi. These people are powerless now; but, like many old Poles, have never given up their dreams, "cherishing that persistent and causeless hope of better times, the possession of which seems to be the universal privilege of exiled greatness." But soon the three change their minds. Instead of being an asset to Almayer, Willems soon becomes a liability. He promptly falls in love with Omar's daughter, Aissa, without noticing that he has been caught in a trap. Moreover, Almayer and Willems do not get along with each other. "Those two specimens of a superior race" often quarrel now,

Finally, Willems becomes ready for his ultimate treachery. He gives in to the dark girl's seductive charms, and, as he perfectly well knows, is thus not only betraying his race and his upbringing, but also his benefactor, Lingard. For a long moment he struggles; but "it was a vain effort . . . He seemed to be surrendering to a wild creature the unstained purity of his life, of his race, of his civilization . . . He struggled with the sense of certain defeat . . . With a faint cry and an upward throw of his arms he gave up as a tired swimmer gives up: because the swamped craft is gone from under his feet; because the night is dark and the shore is far—because death is better than strife".[81]

Yet, as in a good tragedy, one more desperate chance to avert disaster presents itself. Willems makes a last attempt to leave the girl and be reconciled with Almayer, and also to tell him of the Arabs' evil intentions. But Almayer refuses to have a reasonable dialogue.

Willems' only refuge is now with Aissa, the brown girl, and her friends. Having surrendered to her, he is at the mercy of her people. Yet, when looking at her calmly, he realizes "their hopeless diversity," that they "had nothing in common," that "he could not make clear to her the simplest motive of any act of his," but he cannot detach himself. He remembers Hudig's saying: "Scruples are for imbeciles." His own happiness has to prevail. "Did he ever take an oath of fidelity to Lingard? No."

Were *Outcast* a play, everything would now move swiftly towards the inevitable end. Willems would bring in the Arab traders and then, not being useful any longer, would be disposed of in the guise of an accident. Almayer would die of poison while drunk. Coming back to "his" Sambir, Lingard would fall into an ambush. But Conrad is a master of suspense. Willems' treason happens around the middle of the novel. While we know perfectly well that the hero is trapped and doomed, Conrad tells fate to linger. For dozens of pages, time appears to stand still.

In due time, Willems compounds his treason and pilots Abdulla, a well-known Arab trader, up the river. The latter is cheered like a hero who has just won a decisive battle. Nobody goes to bed that night. There is "a big bonfire in the palm grove" and everybody is rejoicing. Only Almayer is left out; he feels "utterly alone and helpless." His only "protection" is the Union Jack flying from his flagpole, while on the other side of the river a Dutch flag has been hoisted.

Misfortune seldom comes singly. Lingard, in the meantime, has no luck either. He has lost his famous brig on a reef. So when he finally arrives in Sambir, it is with a hired vessel and a strange crew. He has brought with him Willems' wife, Joanna, and her small son, with the well-meant but now quite incongruous intention of reuniting the family. Almayer is furious, he knows that Lingard's sentimental plan cannot possibly work.

Lingard realizes that his chances as a trader are gone as far as Sambir is concerned. But the vacuum is filled with dreams. There is gold in the interior. "He had been in the interior before, There [were] immense deposits of alluvial gold there. Fabulous." Of course, it would be "dangerous work," but it would pay. "What a reward! . . . He would explore and find. Not a shadow of a doubt." First, they would keep the thing quiet and get "as much as they could for themselves . . . Then after a time, form a company. In Batavia or in England. Yes, in England. Much better. Splendid!" Nina would be "the richest woman in the world." The only trouble would be "to pick up the stuff." They would be rich—"rich is no name for it."

While indulging in these fantasies, Lingard is actually building a house of cards for the prospective "richest woman in the world." Having reached three stories, the light structure stands for a moment, then suddenly collapses—a symbol expressive of the fragility of Lingard's dreams.

Then Lingard's thoughts go back to the past. He sees himself; first as a poor boy in Falmouth Bay, England; then as a young sailor in a south-bound ship, "ignorant and happy"; later as "a commander of ships, then shipowner, then a man of much capital, respected wherever he went," his name a household word throughout the Malayan archipelago—the Rajah Laut. And now he realizes that for the first time in his life "doubt and unhappiness" are taking hold of him. He who used to describe himself as a man who "had been a fool in his time" but whom "hard knocks had taught . . . wisdom" feels his assurance and self-confidence fail him. The man who had given advice to many and had always known what to do is at a loss. Sambir owed him everything, and now, like an ungrateful child, rejects him.

Almayer plots to get rid of Willems' wife and child. Joanna is extremely noisy, accusing Almayer of keeping her husband from her. The situation rapidly become unbearable.

Lingard soon makes up his mind about Willems. He

is not going to rehabilitate him a third time. Almayer's ideas go in the opposite direction: he plans to save Willems behind Lingard's back and get rid of the cumbersome Mrs. Willems and her brat at the same time.

Both plans are executed with excellent timing. Lingard sees Willems and tells him coolly that he is going to leave him to his fate in the Malay jungle where Aissa jealously watches every move he makes. Some days later, Almayer puts *his* plan into execution. Mrs. Willems is told to visit her husband with her son and to take Willems out of the region. A canoe with hired men is provided. Everything seems to be working well. Willems, who feels that his life is not much worth now, tries to avail himself of the unique opportunity, even if this means being reunited with his wife. But before he can sneak away Aissa appears on the scene and intuitively recognizes the half-caste woman as her rival and the child as Willems' offspring. Exasperated, she snatches Willems' revolver and shoots him. When Almayer comes to fetch the body, the inconsolable Aissa has to be torn away. Later, the incorrigibly sentimental Lingard spends one hundred and fifty dollars on a tombstone with the inscription: "Peter Willems, Delivered by the Mercy of God from his Enemy." The book closes with an outburst of Almayer's: "The world's a swindle! A swindle! What have I done to be treated so?"

The theme of treason, already present in *Almayer's Folly* becomes dominant in *Outcast*. We believe this to be connected with Conrad's moral conflict arising from his "double allegiance." The two Malay stories summarized below also take up the theme of betrayal.

3. *"The Lagoon"*

This is the first short story Conrad wrote. It was published in the *Cornhill Magazine* in January 1897, and included in *Tales of Unrest*. It is the account, told in the first person, of the one fatal moral failure in a man's life.

A white man (it might be Lingard), has made the acquaintance of a good and trustworthy Malay called Arsat. Although coming from an old and venerable family, Arsat and his wife live alone by a lagoon—a very unusual thing for any Malay and especially one of a distinguished family. Passing up the river on business, the white man decides to stop for the night at Arsat's clearing.

He finds Arsat in despair, for his wife is dying from high fever. Under the stress of his emotions and guilt feelings, Arsat tells his white friend his whole story. He has good reasons to expect the worst. His beloved one had been one of the Rajah's slaves. Overpowered by his passion for the girl, he had kidnapped her with the help of his brother. Together, the three had reached the lagoon when a group of the Rajah's men almost caught up with them. In this predicament the brother told him to run ahead with the girl in order to take possession of a canoe, while he would keep the enemy at bay with an old rifle. He would join them as soon as possible, and they were supposed to wait for him with the canoe.

Mad with love and fear alike, Arsat left his brother behind to save himself and the girl. His brother "shouted: 'I am coming!' The men were close to him. I looked. Many men. Then I looked at her. Tuan, I pushed the canoe! I pushed it into deep water . . . Tuan, I heard him cry my name twice, and I heard voices shouting 'Kill! Strike!' I never turned back. I heard him calling my name again with a great shriek, as when life is going out together with the voice—and I never turned my head . . . My brother! Three times he called—but I was not afraid of life. Was she not there in that canoe? And could I not with her find a country where death is forgotten—where death is unknown?"

Then, after a long moment of silence, Arsat says quietly: "Tuan, I loved my brother," only to burst out after another pause: "What did I care who dies? I wanted peace in my own heart." Then the sun rises above the horizon. A white eagle[82] takes flight from one of the trees, and flying higher, disappears at last "as if it had left the earth forever." Arsat rushes into the hut where his beloved wife is groaning. After a while, however, the noise subsides and Arsat reappears with the simple words, "She burns no more."

The white man offers to take him away after the burial, but Arsat refuses. "There is no light and no peace in the world; but there is death for many. We are sons of the same mother—and I left him in the midst of enemies . . ." He will not eat or sleep in that hut any more; he will go back and face his punishment. As the white man leaves, Arsat is standing immobile in the sunshine, looking "beyond the great light of a cloudless day into the darkness of a world of illusions." Descended from a ruling family, this dark man who had been the swordbearer of the native ruler and according to his own words had been "more fit than any to carry on (his) right shoulder the emblem of power" had forfeited his life—not because of the kidnapping, not because he had to kill a man in order to get the canoe, but because he had let his brother die in order to save his own skin.

4. "Karain: A Memory"

This second of Conrad's Malayan short stories was written about a year after the "Lagoon" and immediately following the completion of the *Nigger of the "Narcissus."* It was first published in *Blackwood's Magazine* (1897), then included in *Tales of Unrest*. It is the story of a Malay of noble descent who, after a moral failure in his life, had become an adventurer of the sea, an outcast, and a ruler. This man, Karain, buys rifles and gunpowder from the fictitious narrator of the story (who could well be another Lingard).

Karain suffers from a phobia. "He had the dislike of open space behind him" and was constantly followed by a faithful swordbearer whose presence alone would give him a comparative sense of security.

On the narrator's last visit—he had decided to discontinue the illicit traffic of firearms—an extraordinary event took place. Karain did not invite the ship's officers to come ashore as he was wont to do. Incidentally, the also learn that the old swordbearer and servant had died. Then, one night, during a terrific thunderstorm, Karain suddenly appears in the doorway of the cabin, dripping wet, scared, looking over his shoulder like one pursued. He comes alone as a fugitive who has swam to safety away from some mortal danger. "His cheeks were hollow, his eyes sunk." He is not only exhausted physically, but his face shows still "another kind of fatigue," "a tormented weariness," "the fear of a struggle against a thought, an idea . . ." What was he afraid of? Obviously of something irrational that "cannot be grappled: a shadow, a nothing, unconquerable and immortal, that preys upon life."

Step by step, the whole story unfolds itself as Karain starts confessing. He has run away from a voice that pursued him right to the water's edge. As the old bodyguard was no longer, the ghost had come back to pursue him. Karain was unable to face it any longer, and had to run away in the middle of the night to find refuge in the midst of the white men who, being unbelievers, are not tormented by shadows.

As Karain's story goes on, the origin of his anxiety neurosis becomes manifest. Karain had been chief of a stockade and collector of tolls on one of the rivers. One day a Dutch trader had come and built a house upstream. Shortly afterwards he had fallen in love with a native girl of noble birth, the sister of Pat Matara, the Malay ruler, and had enticed her to leave her people and come to live with him. Matara was naturally very indignant and demanded her return, for she was promised to one of his men. The Dutchman refused. Not feeling safe any longer, the couple left the region shortly afterwards. According to the native laws of honor, the girl "had broken faith, and therefore must die." Matara said: "Now they have left our land their lives are mine. I shall follow and strike—and, alone, pay the price of blood." Karain decides to go with him. The two friends strike out for a strange odyssey all over the archipelago, earning a modest living by doing all kinds of menial jobs or begging their way long, but always on the lookout for the Dutchman and his renegade wife.

During these endless travels Karain has a strange experience. He often sees the face of the young woman they are pursuing, and hears her whisper. The sounds of her footsteps follow him wherever they go. The never-to-be-forgotten face and the voice become his constant companions.

Then the day arrives when the two weary wanderers unexpectedly come across their intended victims. One morning, the opportunity presents itself to strike the deadly blow. The unwary couple are sitting in front of their house, shamelessly happy. Matara decides to creep close and kill the girl with his criss, while Karain would shoot the Dutchman. But as so often happens in Conrad's books, the carefully thought-out plan goes amiss. Karain is afraid of losing his faithful companion, the girl he loves, so when he sees Matara leaping towards her, he kills him with a sure shot. He is soon surrounded by people. The Dutchman thanks him with effusion, offers him money, hospitality; but Karain denies having had anything to do with Matara, so they let him go.

Karain is an outcast now. He becomes a fighter for other people. The vision of the girl disappears forever, but only to be replaced by the frightening vision of the friend he had killed. Karain tries in vain to escape from this oppressive presence.

Some time later Karain meets an old man just back from a pilgrimage during which his son, his son's wife, and their child had died. People consider this old man as a sorcerer, perhaps because of his survival. He becomes Karain's companion, confidant, swordbearer, and servant. He has the power of keeping Matara's shadow at bay. Now he is dead and the strange presence is back, more obsessive than ever. It haunts Karain day and night, and one night it is so bad that he has to seek refuge with his white friends who do not believe in strange presences.

Unlike most of Conrad's stories, "Karain" has a happy ending. Yet—and this is perhaps typical of Conrad—this is no real cure, only its caricature. One of the ship's officers, Hollis, has an idea for exorcising Karain's evil spirit. He makes an amulet ("a thing like those Italian peasants wear") out of a gilt Jubilee sixpence and a piece of soft leather. Hanging it around Karain's neck, he explains to him that this charm with "the image of the Great Queen, and the most powerful thing the white men know" (meaning money!) will protect him forever against any ghost. The sacrilegious exorcism works: the following morning Karain returns to his land free of his phobia, unafraid of the ghosts of the past, and commanding more prestige than ever.

In inspiration and pathos, both short stories remind one very much of Mickiewicz's ballads which, as we have seen in Chapter I, young Conrad knew by heart. In these beautiful ballads, war, exile, honor, love, treason, and revenge are the eternal themes. It does not come completely as a surprise, therefore, to discover that "Karain" was actually inspired by a ballad of the famous Polish romantic. As Juliusz Kleiner showed in an article "An Echo of a Mickiewicz Ballad in a Tale of Conrad" (published in *The Literary Journal* of 5 June 1949), Conrad's story seems to be related with Mickiewicz's Ukrainian ballad "The Watch" (Czaty) dated 1829. It is a story of a *voivode* (governor of a province) who suspects his wife of clandestine meetings with her former lover. One evening he orders his cossack to take a gun and come with him: "They took their arms, left the house, crept into the garden where bushes overgrow a shelter. After some fruitless waiting, something shines in the shade: a woman in a white dress. A man is kneeling before her. Clasping her knees, he says: "Everything is lost to me, even your sighs, even the pressure of your hands now belong to the voivode. I loved you dearly all these years and will love you and moan evermore. *He* never loved, never sighed, only rattled his money bag. You sold him everything forever!" The lover whispers into her ear, accusing and conjuring: "until, moved, almost unconscious, she let go of his shoulders [the meaning is that she had been keeping him at arm's length], and sank into his arms." The two onlookers now prepare their weapons, pushing the bullets down the barrel. But the cossack has to confess that he feels unable to kill the young lady and that his tears are moistening the priming powder on the pan of his gun. "I will teach you to weep," says the voivode, "go ahead, light the powder . . . Higher . . . to the right . . . a little more . . . wait for my shot . . . first the young gentleman must get it in his head." And then the dramatic and unexpected ending: "The cossack turned, took aim, and without delay fired and hit the very head—of the voivode."

5. The Rescue

This third novel of the Lingard trilogy was conceived and begun in 1896, but never grew much beyond its first part at that time. Having written about one fifth of the novel, Conrad abandoned the attempt in 1900 to take up the task again only nineteen years later. *The Rescue* was finally finished in 1919. However, in conception and inspiration the story belongs to Conrad's Malayan period.

The Rescue begins with a magnificent prologue—a song of praise for the liberty loving Malays and the few whites who supported them in their valiant struggle for independence. The song is followed by an angry speech directed against the European powers whose imperialism divided and occupied the whole Malayan archipelago.

At first glance, it does not seem easy to explain Conrad's anti-European attitude and extreme emotional involvement, for this was written in 1896 when European colonialism was taken for granted. Moreover, Conrad never really lived among Malays, never mastered more than a few words of their language, and definitely did not know them well enough to appreciate their real motives.

Conrad's attitude becomes understandable if we realize that he was a Pole, belonging to the elite and descending from a well-known leader in what would now be called the Polish *résistance*. It is a son of Poland, the son of a great but occupied and divided nation, who speaks in this overture. Such pathos and righteous indignation only arise when you think of something near to your innermost heart, a cause with which you fully identify yourself. Just listen to this: "The vices and virtues of four nations have been displayed in the conquest of that region that even to this day has not been robbed of all the mystery and romance of its past—and the race of men who had fought against the [European powers] . . . has not been changed by the unavoidable defeat." Apart from the fact that only three instead of four nations took part in the partitioning of Poland, these lines apply perfectly to Conrad's native country. And the passage that follows gives a true description of the attitude of the unfortunate Polish people: "They have kept to this day their love of liberty, their fanatical devotion to their chiefs, their blind fidelity in friendship and hate—all their lawful and unlawful instincts. Their country . . . has fallen a prey [to the conquerors]—the reward of superior strength if not of superior virtue." In spite of their brilliant national qualities there is no hope for the vanquished, for "to-morrow the advancing civilization will obliterate the marks of a long struggle in the accomplishment of its inevitable victory"—*lasciate ogni speranza*!

Conrad has also a word of praise for the adventurers who, although belonging to the conquering race, helped the liberty loving natives in their fight against "progress." The Polish history of the nineteenth century is actually full of examples of high-minded Europeans who took the part of Poland, collecting money and arms, writing pamphlets and poetry exalting Poland's struggle for freedom, or volunteering to fight in the ranks of the Polish insurgents against the combined onslaught of German *Kultur*, Russian *Knoot*, and Austrian *Verwaltung* often giving all they had for a cause which had justice on its side, but not material superiority. In the end the fight proved too much and "their lives were thrown away for a cause that had no right to exist in the face of an irresistible and orderly progress . . . But the wasted lives, for the few who know, have tinged with romance the region . . . that lies far East . . ." If the fate of the Malay tribes and their native principalities had not struck a familiar chord in Conrad, those lines would never have been written.

No wonder Conrad loved and somewhat idealized those adventurers and rovers who "illegally" provided them with arms and helped them to build up their *résistance*. Tom Lingard is their prototype at this stage of Conrad's literary career—the Rajah Laut, friend and advocate of the Malays, the man who speaks their language, knows their internal quarrels, and above all, understands. At the same time, Lingard's real motives are misunderstood by the representatives of the West, a misunderstanding which is already expressed in a short passage of *An Outcast* (14) where the episode forming the subject of the book is seen through Western eyes: "After his first—and successful—fight with the sea robbers, when he rescued, as rumor had it, the yacht of some big-wig from home, somewhere down Carimata way, his popularity began."

After the magnificent pathos of its prologue, *The Rescue* unfortunately, but perhaps inevitably, falls short of its promise. This discrepancy between a magnificent promise of heroic deeds and the actual accomplishment seems to be a very Nałęcz Korzeniowski trait, if not a trait of the Polish gentry. The historical and sociological background—the struggle for independence of a noble people—becomes too remote. The action is almost completely within and fails to reflect the great political issues conjured up in the prologue. Conrad must have become aware of his inability to fulfill his promise. Moreover, his Malays, like the Poles, are divided into opposing factions even in their fight for independence, thus endangering their own cause. Be it as it may, the author became stuck after the completion of the first fifth of the novel and finished it only nineteen years later, when his acquired professional skill carried him over the inner contradictions of the story.

The foremost reason for this intriguing—and in Conrad's writing career: unique—blocking of inspiration is probably the following: During his Malayan phase, Conrad was preoccupied by the theme of loyalty versus treason. Betrayal in one form or another alienates the human from his fellow beings and finally destroys him by virtue of an inner necessity. The great exception to this rule is *The Rescue*, where the hero does not seem to be any worse for his betrayal. Conrad could not track Tom Lingard down to his inevitable end (as he pursues Lord Jim), since Lingard reappears in the *Outcast* as a man *sans peur et sans reproche*. This, I believe, is the real cause for Conrad's inability to finish the novel during his Malayan phase. The block occured at the very moment that Lingard decided to betray his brown friends in order to save the white intruders.

Compared with the brilliant inner consistence of *Almayer's Folly, An Outcast of the Islands*, and *Lord Jim, The Rescue* is a patchwork, a laboriously contrived piece of fiction lacking inspiration and devoid of that inner necessity of events which characterizes the other writings of the Malayan period. By Conrad's own standards, *The Rescue* may be a work of art but one conveying no real message—and therefore not much short of a failure. It finally becomes the story of an idealist betraying his own ideals, leaving an exiled princely couple to perish, contrary to his own solemn promises—all in order to save an uninteresting, unimaginative, but rich and sophisticated Western couple who do not want to be rescued by him at all. The theme, no doubt, bears some unmistakably Conradian traits, but the treatment of the subject is unsatisfactory as compared to the other writings of the Malayan period. The story very reluctantly drags to its happy-unhappy end, finishing on a note of truly Western moral compromise—the very kind of distasteful compromise which had sacrificed Poland. Not only does Lingard betray his better self and forfeit his word of honor in this "Romance of the Shallows," but the author himself appears to give up the fight and yield ultimately to the Western philosophy of money and opportunism by sacrificing the poor, simple, but noble, for the sake of the wealthy and selfish, and letting the hero Lingard get away with it.

Conrad's conflict connected with *The Rescue* is reflected in his letters. He began the novel on his honeymoon. He needed money and wanted the novel to be a success. In order to be successful, it had to be a love story. In April 1896, he told his prospective publisher: "If the virtues of Lingard please most of the critics, they

shall have more of them. The theme of it shall be the
rescue of a yacht from some Malay vagabonds [*sic*] and
there will be a gentleman and lady cut out according to
the regulation pattern."[83] That Conrad was ready to
make great concessions to the public is indicated also in
a letter to Edward Garnett (March 1896), where he
writes: "It will be on the lines indicated to you. I surrender to the infamous spirit which you have awakened within
me and, as I want my abasement to be very complete, I
am looking for a sensational title."[84]

Two years later, the abasement had obviously become too much, and Conrad felt unable to continue with
The Rescue. Just after he had sold the American serial
rights, he told R. B. Cunninghame Graham (March
1898), alluding to his inability: "Yes, we Poles are poor
specimens. The strain of national worry has weakened
the moral fibre—and no wonder, when you think of it.
It is not a fault, it is a misfortune. Forgive my
jeremiads. I don't repine at the nature of my inheritance but now and then it is too heavy not to let out a
groan!"[85] In the same month, he complained to Garnett:
"As to the serial, it must go anyhow. I would be thankful
to be able to write anything, anything, any trash, any
rotten thing."[86]

In a letter to Mrs. Bontine, of November 1898,
Conrad specifically mentioned two difficulties: "Attempt-
ing to tell romantically a love story in which the word
love is not to be pronounced seems to be courting disaster deliberately. Add to this that an inextricable confusion of sensations is of the very essence to the tale . . ."[87]
However one may interpret this passage (I myself would
put "feelings" for "sensations"), it shows at any rate that
the author was reaching an impasse. One gets the same
impression from a letter to H. G. Wells (December
1898): "I am eating my heart out over the rottenest book
that ever was or will be."[88]

It was only in 1916 that he took up the novel again,
apparently at the suggestion of his wife.[89] It was to be
finished three years later. Again, he considered it first
and foremost as a potential money-maker. In a letter to
his agent, J. B. Pinker, dated 30 January 1919, three
months before the completion of the novel, he expressed
the hope that it might become "a money hit," more so
than the reprinted *Outcast.* He based his hope on the
fact that *The Rescue* was "more picturesque and at the

same time more conventional" than the former.

In 1898, Conrad had obviously found the moral compromise unpalatable without which the novel—so he thought—could not be a success. This is the curse of being a persona: you are guided by your anticipation of what the critics might say and the public might feel. Both, so Conrad thought, would have objected to an ending which saved the noble Hassim and his tender sister at the expense of a conceited white couple. For the sake of the beloved dollar, it had to be the other way around.

One cannot read without astonishment the callous words Conrad wrote in an undated letter to Pinker, at the end of 1919: "You may however assure the representative of the *Cosmopolitan Magazine* that the story will end as romantically as it began, and that no one of particular importance will have to die. Hassim and Immada will be sacrificed, as in any case they were bound to be, but their fate is not the subject of the tale. All those yacht people will go on their way, leaving Lingard with the wreck of the greatest adventure of his life."[90]

We have read correctly: "Their fate is not the subject of the tale" (really!) and "no one of particular importance will have to die". Even if one takes these words in a sarcastic sense, it is incredible that a Nałęcz Korzeniowski should write this—the son of a man who had fought for a nation whose fate, indeed, was of no particular importance to anyone except themselves. Here Conrad clearly sacrificed his loyalty towards his Polish heritage to the build-up of a *persona*, the persona or image of the successful and talented English author. Moreover, he did not do this when he was poor, but when he was already famous. These are hard criticisms to make, but a study of the novel will bear out their truth.

Lingard's first mate is a Mr. Shaw, a primitive, conceited Englishman, who treats his Malay subordinates "with lofty toleration," feeling himself "immeasurably superior" to them. He thinks war is a bad and sinful affair. "unless with Chinamen or niggers, or such people as must be kept in order and won't listen to reason, having not sense enough to know what's good for them . . ." He is glad "Sir Thomas Cochrane swept along the Borneo coast with his squadron some years ago" to make the seas safe for British shipping, and he is annoyed to have "to make shift with" Malays, "them flatnosed chaps". He would much prefer "a proper crew of decent Christians." He is not at all impressed when Lingard tries to correct his notions about the "savages" by telling him how "pretty moral" they were, to the point that they would put a girl to death because she had thrown a flower to a white man and had thus forfeited her honor. Shaw very much reflects the attitude the Germans had toward the Poles.

Lingard himself is described as a man of "about thirty five, erect and supple," red-eyed, with a light chestnut beard that takes on a golden reflection in the sun. This man is proud of his brig which is "reckoned the swiftest vessel" in that part of the world. He had bought her with money he made in Australian goldfields. He was one with his vessel.

Lingard has taken the cause of the surviving Wajo warriors to heart. He plots to restore their power over their native land and to re-install their ex-ruler Prince Hassim. He is accumulating arms in the old schooner *Emma*, which he brought in to serve as a stronghold and storehouse, and which he purposely left stranded in the mud. A Dane called Jörgenson is in charge of this singular fort, while Lingard journeys around to prepare the uprising.

Much like Conrad's father, Lingard has been throwing himself "body and soul into the great enterprise," and living "in the long intoxication of slowly preparing success." And again like Apollo Korzeniowski, "no price appeared too heavy to pay for such a magnificent achievement." When talking to his freedom fighters he would shout, "We will stir them up! We will wake up the country," just as Conrad's father had no doubt exclaimed many a time when he had been the heart and soul of the revolutionary committee in Warsaw. "He would wake up the country! That was the fundamental and unconscious emotion on which were engrafted his need of action, the primitive sense of what was due to justice, to gratitude, to friendship, to sentimental pity for the hard lot of Immada," Hassim's sister and constant companion.

But as in the preparation of the Polish uprising of 1863, idealism alone did not suffice. "Money was wanted and men were wanted." Lingard needs the help of Belarab, the *de facto* ruler of this settlement of refugees. It is true that Belarab is now old, but, like the old men in Mickiewicz's poem, *Pan Tadeusz*, he still remembers the old days and how men fought then. "They have not forgotten the times of war." "There was no doubt that he could find men who would fight." Yet—one thinks of Poland again—he would also have to contend with the restless who, by "their folly, by their recklessness, by their impatience" might wreck the chances of the great patriotic enterprise. Among them Tenga and Daman will later emerge, and their discontent and impatience will contribute to precipitate the tragedy.

Lingard is particularly attached to Prince Hassim, the ex-ruler in exile, and to his sister Immada. Each time King Tom (as he is called) leaves the Shore of Refuge or returns to it, the two will stand "lonely on some sandbank of the Shallows, raising their arms in salutation, a weary and sad gesture like a sign of distress made by castaways in the vain hope of an impossible help," and this gesture "at each movement seemed to draw closer around his heart the bonds of protecting affection." Thus Lingard, like Apollo Korzeniowski in his time, acts under a "romantic necessity that had invaded his life." But unlike Apollo, Lingard is able to provide the money needed to defray the costs of preparing the romantic enterprise. Money runs "like water out of his hands."

And now, when Lingard is near his goal, with all the preparations practically finished, a British yacht blunders into the secrecy of their plot and threatens to jeopardize the carefully laid plan.

At this stage, Conrad's inspiration seems to have failed him. What follows is written fully nineteen years later, and in a different mood. What should have been a novel of action turns into a painful psychological study where intense hesitations, uncreative arguing and neurotic lack of willpower dominate the picture. Lingard, the man of action par excellence, finds his willpower paralyzed in a Hamlet-like fashion. For the first time in his life the King of the Sea is at a loss—he actually leaves the initiative almost completely to the youthful Carter (mate of the yacht), to Tengga, Daman, and Jörgenson. The happy-unhappy end does not come about through any decision of his own, but through his very indecision which forces Jörgenson to act, and through a betrayal on the part of Mrs. Travers who deliberately omits to transmit a message. As we hear in *An Outcast of the Islands*, this episode spreads Lingard's fame all over the Archipelago, for the ones who were betrayed will never be able to raise their voices. All of them, the noble, the heroes who once saved his life, and the bloodthirsty warriors alike, go down in history as a mere bunch of "sea pirates."

The greater part of *The Rescue* is a sort of psychological interplay between three or four personalities. There is the owner of the yacht, Mr. Travers, rich, conceited, unimaginative, despising and misunderstanding the bearded sea-rover who is going to save him. "I don't see my way of utilizing your services," he tries to dismiss Lingard. His wife is so different from him that their marriage could at best be described as "a successful mistake." She is attracted by Lingard who appeals to her still youthful imagination as a man who might have "stepped out from an engraving in a book about buccaneers." He just appears "picturesque" to her at first, then gradually her intuition makes her understand his motives. Then we have a guest-passenger on the yacht, Don Martin d'Alcacer. Being a Spanish nobleman, he is the first to recognize that Lingard's hesitations may be a matter of honor and of pledged word. The crew of the yacht is led by Carter, a youthful but unimaginative second officer, full of misdirected initiative. He suspects Lingard of mercenary motives. His explanation that this man is just "bent upon getting a lot of salvage money out of a stranded yacht" is only too eagerly accepted by the yacht-owner himself.

The unexpected appearance of Prince Hassim and his sister Immada on board the yacht (where they came to look for Lingard) gives Conrad another opportunity to expose the racial conceit of the white master race. Some members of the crew take the Prince for a fisherman, and the sailing-master bellows at him: "Hey! Johnnie! Hab got fish? Fish! Eh? *Savee?* Fish! Fish . . ." but without being able to "make them savages understand anything." To him it is obvious that it is sheer stupidity which prevents those "savages" from understanding his language, while it is racial superiority which does not allow him to understand theirs.

Then follows a scene where Mrs. Travers confronts Immada. The lady says: "I had no idea of anything so gentle." Lingard presents the girl to her rather rudely:

"What have you got to do with her? She knows war. Do you know anything about it? And hunger too, and thirst, and unhappiness; things that you have only heard about. She has been as near death as I am to you—and what is all that to any one of you here?" And to Mrs. Travers' question, "Who is she?" Lingard answers curtly, "a princess."

He then has to explain to Prince Hassim that it was not *he* who brought the yacht here, and that he had never seen "those people" before. Suddenly, Immada senses the danger and exclaims, "Let them die!", an outburst whose meaning the strangers fortunately do not understand. Worthy Mr. Travers, getting impatient at "this performance," requests Lingard to take "these natives away."

Mr. Travers is angry at Lingard. "The man wanted to force his services upon me, and then put in a heavy claim for salvage. That is the whole secret . . . I detected him at once, of course . . . he underrated my intelligence." He calls Lingard "a violent scoundrel" and says that "the existence of such a man is a scandal . . . a disgrace to civilization. . . ." He once more gives vent to his feelings of superiority as a white man by declaring dogmatically, "If the inferior race must perish, it is a gain, a step towards perfecting the society which is the aim of progress." He believes he has nothing to fear, and will not "admit the possibility of any violence being offered to people of our position."

Mr. Travers' unrealistic presumption is not shared by his wife and still less by d'Alcacer who has understood Lingard's real motives. However, Lingard, recognizing the necessity of informing someone on the yacht of the real situation, does not choose d'Alcacer, but Mrs. Travers as his confidante. He manages to see her alone and to tell her the story of the intended uprising. He explains to her that the presence of the yacht "may be death to some." To him, it may even "be worse than death," he may lose his honor in this affair. "A man who had saved my life once and that I passed my word to would think that I had thrown him over . . . and the girl would die of grief". (157-158) His vivid description conveys the visions and dreams of two years "into the night where Mrs. Travers could follow them as if outlined in words of fire." She is made the witness of "an exciting existence," seen through Lingard's "guileless en-

thusiasm." She senses a "heroic quality of . . . feelings" in
this adventurer, a "headlong fierceness of purpose," an
"obscure design of conquest" taking "the proportions of
a great enterprise." This man is truly inspired by a great
vision: "That simple soul was possessed by the greatness
of the idea; there was nothing sordid in its flaming impulses."

The shadow of Apollo Korzeniowski is present in
this scene: his fire, his pathos, his devotion to a romantic
political idea. Similarly, in Conrad's description of Immada, we find that combination of physical frailty, great
moral courage and absolute loyalty to a patriotic idea
which had characterized Ewelina Korzeniowska, née
Bobrowska.

Lingard now suggests that it may become necessary
for the people on the yacht to seek refuge on his brig.
Mrs. Travers believes him. She understands King Tom:
"There were in plain sight his desires, his perplexities,
affections, doubts, his violence, his folly, and the existence they made up was lawless, but not vile."

The same evening, after sunset, Mr. Travers and his
Spanish companion disappear from the sandbank. Mrs.
Travers orders her crew to transfer to Lingard's vessel.
King Tom himself takes her over in his little dinghy.

At this point, Lingard becomes aware of the fatal
fact that he no longer knows his own mind. "A new
power has entered his life and . . . cast over them all the
wavering gloom of a dark and inscrutable purpose." He
is stuck because he wants to save Mrs. Travers and Hassim alike. It is quite clear to him "that he [is] utterly lost,
unless he [lets] all these people [of the yacht] be wiped
off the face of the earth." It means either leaving these
representatives of high class Western society to their fate
or breaking his solemn oath to Hassim. So, when he is
moved by his infatuation for Mrs. Travers to say "Not a
hair of your head shall be touched as long as I live," the
die is cast. After those fatal words, events will take their
inevitable course. "The sadness of [moral] defeat [per-
vaded] the world." And when Lingard half-heartedly assures Mrs. Travers that "they" (Mr. Travers and d'Alcacer) "are to be saved," the sense of defeat is complete.
Conrad, taking up a simile already used in *An Outcast of
the Islands*, describes Lingard's situation as "that of a
swimmer who, in the midst of a superhuman effort to
reach the shore, perceives that the undertow is taking

him to sea. He would go with the mysterious current; he would go swiftly—and see the end, the fulfillment both blissful and terrible."[91]

It is interesting to watch how Conrad handles Lingard's distasteful volte-face. The crucial passage occurs in a declaration to Mrs. Travers·

> I suppose I didn't look enough of a gentleman. Yes! Yes! That's it! Yet I know what a gentleman is. I lived with them for years. I chummed with them—yes—on gold fields and in other places where a man has got to show the stuff that's in him. Some of them write from home to me here—such as you see me, because I—never mind! And I know what a gentleman would do. Come! Wouldn't he treat a stranger fairly? Wouldn't he remember that no man is a liar till you prove him so? Wouldn't he keep his word wherever given? Well, I'm going to do that. Not a hair of your head shall be touched as long as I live! (164)

Psychologically, this is one of the most awkward passages in the whole of Conrad. Lingard's life had once been saved by Prince Hassim and his friends. According to their code of honor (and the code of honor of the Polish gentry), Lingard was obliged to do the same for them now. If he acted otherwise, he would be a traitor deserving to die. Instead of explaining the real issue to Mrs. Travers, he drops the ancient code of honor (a code common to Hassim and Immada, Mickiewicz and Apollo) in favor of the English concept of "fairness." At the very moment when King Tom decides to break his solemn pledge to Hassim, this infatuated man has the cheek to talk about *keeping* his word—a word which, mind you, he has not yet given but which he subsequently concedes in the next sentence. Lingard hides behind the *persona* of the conventional English gentleman in order to justify what is actually a betrayal. Mrs. Travers is not even fooled by this subterfuge, for she considers King Tom as someone who "had no part" in her "social organization."

After Lingard's betrayal, one would expect events to move swiftly now, as in a Greek tragedy. But again Conrad lets fate linger almost intolerably. When the fatal decisions are made, we have but reached the middle of the book. The preparation for and the intricate description of the inevitable denouement will take another two hundred pages. Once more, Conrad appears as a master of the art of suspense. But is he? Is not this so-called suspense really the expression of his own Hamlet-like scruples and hesitations projected upon his heroes? Is not the author as much at a loss how to continue as King Tom?

Lingard is "unwilling to face facts." "He cannot bring his mind to the consideration of his position." And yet, "The world [is] waiting. The world full of hopes and fear." What should he do?

The situation has rapidly worsened. The two whites are kept as hostages by Daman, head of a tribe of warriors not much above sea robbers. Daman's intention is to force Lingard's hand. He wants to loot the yacht and desires a share of Lingard's store of arms and gunpowder, and he wants the uprising to be started here and now. On board his brig, Lingard is distrusted by his chief mate, Shaw. Mrs. Travers wants to save the life of her husband and his companion. In this plight, Lingard finally makes a half-hearted and dangerous move. After long palavers, he gets permission to install the two prisoners on the *Emma*. The understanding is that Lingard is to be their custodian, responsible not only for their confinement, but also guaranteeing that the whites will not attack anyone on shore. Lingard's move is unsuccessful because Carter, in command of the yacht, becomes nervous and fires at two Malayan boats. The two prisoners have to be returned to the shore, and are kept in Belarab's stockade. The excitement on shore is undescribable. Tengga and Daman, both impatient to fight, openly clamor for weapons and ammunition. They want the yacht as a prize and will not be held off very long. Belarab is wavering and considers giving in.

Finally, the Tengga warriors surround the *Emma*, threatening to take by force what is denied to them. Lingard and Mrs. Travers are in Belarab's stockade with the prisoners. In this dangerous situation, Jörgenson decides to blow up the ammunition store. The *Emma* is blown to pieces and Jörgenson, Hassim and Immada perish. A great number of Daman's warriors, the prospective revolutionary army, are killed or maimed. With this blast, the plans and hopes for which Lingard has devoted two years of his life are blown to shreds. In the ensuing confusion, the prisoners escape. The yacht, in the meantime, has been put afloat by the resourceful Carter. She sails off to the South. Lingard turns North. Mr. Travers will not have to pay any salvage money and will never know what price has been paid for his life, but at least Mrs. Travers and d'Alcacer will have understood. As for the princely couple whom Lingard was actually ready to betray, they live no longer, and through no direct fault of his own. Not that Lingard takes his moral defeat lightly. The Englishman Carter who, by his senseless shooting at two Malayan boats had contributed a good deal to the catastrophe, "gave all his sympathy to that man who had certainly rescued the white people but seemed to have lost his own soul in the attempt." (453) But Carter is too naive to understand. Nor does he know what Lingard lived through: "Reproachful spectres crowded the air, animated and vocal, not in the articulate language of mortals, but assailing him with faint sobs, deep sighs, and fateful gestures." (462) For Carter, these people had only been "cut-throats." (462) We do not know how Lingard settles the whole matter with his conscience. There is not a hint about it in the Lingard trilogy.

At first sight, Conrad's Malayan stories seem to take us far away from Poland. Yet nothing could be farther than the truth. Conrad knew the Malays only superficially. Sir Hugh Clifford, who knew them very well, even stated that Conrad had "no ideas of Malays," and that Karain, for instance, "could only be called Malay in Conrad's sense."[92]

Conrad was interested in the humanity of Malays, as people who had their own culture, language, and moral code but were considered "savages" and denied to work out their collective destiny. Feeling that they were treated by the colonial powers as Poland had been treated by three so-called civilized nations, he was wont to project into the Malays the feelings of the Polish people. He also exposed the ignorance, stupid superiority, and imperialistic arrogance of the ruling powers, and even of their uneducated representatives (Shaw). The whites in Conrad's first works form a gallery of adventurers, traitors, exploiters, dishonest businessmen (Hudig), untrustworthy and unpredictable. Many, like Mr. Travers, are unimaginative and suffer from an incurable superiority complex toward the "lower" race, which they do not even try to understand.

Only a Pole could have written the first chapter of *The Rescue* or described the aspirations and feelings of the Malays as Conrad did. There is a strong current of anti-colonialism running throughout the Lingard trilogy. Was not the partition of the East among the Western powers the partition of Poland all over again, and were not the same hypocritical arguments used to justify any amount of oppression?

The names chosen by Conrad are often symbolic; the choice, of course, being mostly an unconscious one. Lingard's *Lightning* has all the qualities of the owner: she is swift, efficient, decisive. She can strike. The schooner-yacht *Hermit* of Mr. Travers gets in the way of (*à travers*) Lingard's plans. Her name may well symbolize the actual loneliness of people of the highest society, and their desire to get away from it all. But what about the ship *Emma*, sitting in the mud and waiting to be blown up? Jessie Conrad's middle name was Emmeline (little Emma)—could it be that Conrad unconsciously vented his resentment against the demands of marriage and fatherhood by blowing up the *Emma*? (It is true that the name *Emma* also occurs in *Almayer's Folly*, but as the name of a Dutch girl). If we consider the evidence accumulated by Bernard Meyer in his psycho-analytical biography of Conrad, concerning the novelist's deep ambivalence towards his marriage, such an interpretation is possible. Then there is Jörgenson, the ghost-like figure in charge of the *Emma*: Jörgen means George, and George was Jessie Conrad's maiden name. The name George plays a singular role in Conrad's life anyhow: Mr. Georgeon in Cracow, Monsieur George in Marseilles, the marriage with Miss George, "George, jump" (*Lord Jim*), Don Jorge (*The Arrow of Gold*). All this may be dismissed as mere coincidence, but is it?

It has often been said that Conrad's female characters had a mysterious, unfinished, hazy quality. Mrs. Travers is no exception. What Conrad says about her is more in the nature of hints than of statements. A number of critics have found her unconvincing; a very few have called her the best female character in the whole of Conrad's works. But these critics were men. Women readers seem to be able to identify readily with Mrs. Travers—a kind of damsel in distress rescued by a romantic hero. Since this kind of approach is not satisfactory either, the need for a study written by a critical mind gifted with feminine intuition has always been obvious. Now the gap is closed with Mrs. S. B. Liljegren's valuable and detailed study entitled *Joseph Conrad as a Prober of Feminine Hearts—Notes on the novel "The Rescue'* (Stockholm, 1968).

Mrs. Liljegren considers the portrait of Mrs. Travers as Conrad's best description of a woman. She finds extremely convincing psychologically the love developing between the romantic captain and the emotionally frustrated lady cast in the wrong role of a society woman. According to her, the details and nuances of this slow-motion study of restrained feelings are just right.

Baines similarly finds that Mrs. Travers is one of Conrad's few convincing female portraits (*Conrad*, 418). This may be true, but even so Lingard's courtship to me is painfully boring and psychologically uninteresting.

According to Thomas Moser, Conrad was unable to write a convincing love story, and this was the reason for the blocking of his inspiration. Z. Dolecki wrote in 1958 that the subject of *The Rescue* was a conflict between ideal and heart, obligation (duty) and love. Miss Gaździkówna found that the conception of *The Rescue* was vitiated from the very start, and that very probably the crisis of "the Rescuer" coincided with a period of crisis and re-evaluation of Conrad's attitude to the problems of his own existence. It was only with the device of Marlow and the introduction of a complex and ironic manner of observation, that the author worked out an attitude of detachment allowing him to subdue the subjective element. Conrad could not get on with *The Rescue* as long as he had not himself resolved the complex of problems created by his decision of establishing himself as an Englishman and English writer. (*The Living Conrad* 171 to 180)

Jan Kott in 1946 wrote that *The Rescue* was "the most beautiful and at the same time the most tragic example of an escape to some happy islands, to an adolescent world." Behind the figure of the King of the Sea he detected a "longing for the fullness of life lost in the civilized world," and the "romantic myth of the outlaw or Rover who takes it in his own hand to correct the injustice of the world." (*Mythology and Realism*, 138)

V.

Lord Jim

Joseph Conrad's most famous novel has a rather unsatisfactory title. First, the author called it *Tuan Jim*, this being the form of address the natives would use to designate the hero of the novel. Before publication, Conrad changed the title to *Lord Jim*, which is supposed to be the English for *Tuan Jim*. But is it? Lord is a hereditary title of nobility which does not fit Jim, nor is it a proper translation of *tuan*. Almayer too was called *tuan*, but never *lord*. Conrad himself had serious doubts about the new title. Before the publication of the book, he wrote to his publisher Blackwood: "It seems to me that *Lord Jim* for the title of the book is meagre—perhaps misleading?" Blackwood submitted the question to his public relations agent, the Londoner Meldrum who replied, "Misleading it may be, but, commercially speaking, it is good."[93] So, for the sake of the pounds and dollars, *Lord Jim* it had to be.

Lord Jim belongs to the early period of Conrad's writing. The novel was terminated in 1900, eleven years after Conrad had written his first line of English fiction, and only five years after the publication of his first book. *Lord Jim* marks the end of Conrad's Malayan phase. With Patusan and its Malays we get the last glimpse of this race of people which must have fascinated Conrad because they reminded him in many ways of the simple Polish peasants he had known in his youth.

But if *Lord Jim* constituted the end of a period, it also marked the beginning of a new and powerful trend. With *The Nigger of the "Narcissus"* and *Lord Jim* Conrad became a depth psychologist. In his first writings, and especially in *Almayer's Folly* and *An Outcast of the Islands*, his psychology had been fairly conventional: the Malays are like this, the Arabs (who in the East played the role the Jews were playing in Poland) behave like that, the whites are conceited, corrupt, imperialistic. In the *Nigger* and *Lord Jim* the innermost, often unconscious motivations of man shape his fate and the external events are the consequence of what is going on inside of the main characters and not inversely.

At the same time, Conrad became the master of suspense. The heroes, all men, find themselves in what the German existentialists have called *Grenzsituation*, boundary situation. In the *Nigger* the ship is hovering for days, tilted at an angle of 45 degrees, on the brink of catastrophe. Similarly, the Negro James Wait is constantly between life and death. The crew never know whether his illness is real or a clever sham. The men themselves are on the border of despair, and on the border of mutiny as well. In *Lord Jim* the first boundary situation occurs on the *Patna*: this ship too is on the very brink of annihilation. As in Greek mythology, boundary situations are the supreme test of manhood. Jim fails this test for reasons which Marlow takes great pains to elucidate. After the *Patna* episode, it is the question of Jim's rehabilitation which remains constantly in a precarious balance.

The *Patna* episode in *Lord Jim* is based on a real event. In 1880, a ship named *Jeddah*, transporting 900 Moslem pilgrims from Malaysia to the Red Sea, was disabled after a severe storm. Water entered the boiler room through broken pipes and the coal fires went out. The white crew, believing the boat was sinking, abandoned the vessel during the night.[94] The first mate later said that he was thrown overboard by some pilgrims who rebelled at the behavior of the crew. In any case, he deserted with the rest. The ship did not sink. She was discovered the following morning by the British steamer *Antenor*[95] and towed to Aden. The captain of the *Jeddah* was an Englishman named Clark and the first mate also an Englishman by the name of Augustine Podmore Williams. They were picked up by another boat. There was a preliminary court inquiry at Aden and later a court trial in Singapore. Conrad was in London at the time and must have read the accounts of the London newspapers which wrote at length about this scandal at sea. The *Daily Chronicle* at the very first expressed the opinion that the deserters could not be Englishmen. Later,

Conrad must have heard more details during his frequent stays and stopovers at Singapore.

Conrad made important changes to the story, and the changes are significant. He dramatized the whole event considerably. The captain is not an Englishman, but an Australian German "renegade." He also describes the primary condition of the vessel as very bad, while the *Jeddah* was not at all an old decrepit boat, but only eight years old and well built.[96] Finally, and this is very important, it is not a British vessel which rescues the *Patna*, but a French gunboat.

There can be no doubt that the first mate of the *Jeddah*, Augustine Podmore Williams, served as a model for Conrad's third mate of the *Patna*, Jim.[97] Like Jim, Williams was the son of an English clergyman. The judge gave him a severe reprimand for his conduct, but refrained from cancelling his certificate. (We remember that Jim had his certificate cancelled) However, Augustine Podmore Williams never went back to sea. Captain Clark had his certificate suspended for two years. How did the prototype of Jim stick it out? For more than a decade the story of the desertion was talked about in Eastern ports, yet Williams decided to face the music and to settle down in the very port where his well publicized trial had taken place. Like Jim, he became a ship chandler's clerk. Later, he set up his own business and there can hardly be any doubt that Conrad must have met him in person. Whether he is identical with the person whom Conrad mentions in his Author's Note to *Lord Jim* is doubtful: "One sunny morning in the commonplace surroundings of an Eastern roadstead, I saw his form pass by—appealing—significant—under a cloud—perfectly silent. Which is all as it should be." There were many persons in those ports who were running away from their past. Williams had nothing appealing or pathetic about him. He was strongly built and tall, like Jim, but his personality was quite different. He married a sixteen-year-old Eurasian girl (a thing no Englishman did at that time), and she gave him sixteen children. After some time, this family father became a most respected businessman whom everybody in Singapore knew. Even those who still remembered that black page in his life, and there were many, did not discriminate against him.

The novel *Lord Jim* can be divided into four parts, as follows:

1. The moral failure
2. The haunting obsession: how to live it down?
3. The attempt at cure—Patusan
4. The cure fails.

Marlow, and through him Conrad, does everything to make Jim's desertion understandable. The way the boundary situation on the Patna is described, it was almost impossible for Jim to resist the temptation to jump to safety. Moreover, he only jumps on impulse, not by his own free will. Yet, despite these attenuating circumstances, Marlow refuses to *pardon* Jim. He tries to understand—and to make his hearers understand and "see," but not to excuse. "He was guilty and done for," says Marlow. He refuses to give Jim "an absolution which would have been no good to him." This astonishing refusal, however, is justified. One cannot but admire Conrad's psychological intuition, for fully 23 years later there appeared Freud's essay *The Ego and the Id* in which the Viennese master explained the mechanism of a guilt neurosis. This is what Freud wrote:

> In compulsive neuroses . . . the guilt feeling is overwhelming without being able to become acceptable to the ego. The patient's conscious personality resists the imposition of feeling guilty and wants the doctor's assistance to ward off those feelings. It would be foolish to give in to his ego, for it would be no use.[98]

In other words, in a guilt neurosis such as Jim's, the unconscious guilt feelings are so intense that the conscious mind has to ward them off in order to prevent immediate self-destruction. But keeping the conscious mind relatively free of guilt feelings does not help, and the doctor must not give in to the patient's urgent demand for hasty absolution. To give in would only increase the tension between the unconscious guilt feelings and death wishes on one hand, and the ego on the other.[99]

A French officer is called in to reaffirm Marlow's contention that Jim is "guilty and done for." We remember that it was, curiously enough, a French gunboat coming from Réunion which rescued the *Patna*. A

number of years later, Marlow meets a French lieutenant
who was connected with the affair. The French officer,
hearing Jim's story for the first time, explains that the
young man was under stress of "abominable funk" (*un
trac abominable*) and he adds, "The honor, that is real,
that is? And what may life be worth when . . . when the
honor is gone?—*ah, ça, par exemple*—I can offer no opinion . . . Because I know nothing of it."

After some years of fruitless attempts to settle down,
Jim is finally brought to Stein for a consultation. Stein
the trader acts like a psychiatrist: he makes a diagnosis,
and prescribes a cure.

Stein does not exonerate Jim from all blame. He
just explains that Jim's motives stem from his oversensi-
tive, overimaginative personality. Jim, Stein says, is a
romantic hero at heart. He is a born dreamer.[100] In imagination a hero, he failed when faced with a reality calling for heroism. "To follow the dream and again to follow the dream," Stein says to Marlow, and "It is not
good for you to find out you cannot make your dreams
come true." When such people have to face an unpleasant reality, "there comes the real trouble." And Stein
concludes with the following explanation which has puzzled many readers:

> A man that is born falls into the dream like a man
> who falls into the sea. If he tries to climb out into
> the air as inexperienced people do, he drowns
> . . . No, I tell you. The way is to the destructive
> element submit yourself, and with the exertions of
> your hands and feet in the water make the deep
> deep sea keep you up. So if you ask me—how to
> be? . . . I will tell you! . . . In the destructive element
> immerse.

Stein likens the sea to the dream, i.e. to the fantasies of
our unconscious, and to the unconscious itself from
which all dreams arise, but also all destructive impulses.
Both the sea and the unconscious can be destructive as
well as life-giving. Water is a life element, but if the sea
overwhelms us we drown. In the same way our unconscious is the substratum of our conscious life, but if certain unconscious obsessive fantasies flood our consciousness, we become psychotic, delusional, and/or criminal.
Only if we let ourselves be carried, be supported, by the
unconscious, keeping the head out of the water, will we

be able to exist normally. The head, of course, symbolizes the conscious mind, the willpower, the intellectual faculties. A romantic personality like Jim's cannot get out of the dream—he would perish. So the remedy is clear: let us feed him an everlasting dream. Let him live in an environment as romantic, as dreamlike as any ever described in Boys' adventure books—away from civilization, an environment where nobody will ever drag Jim out of his dream by mentioning his desertion.

What the reader of *Lord Jim* cannot know is that Stein's diagnosis of Jim's hereditary personality is a poetic version of what uncle Bobrowski had always said of Conrad, and of the whole Nałęcz Korzeniowski breed. "To follow the dream and again to follow the dream" certainly was the life principle of Conrad's father and grandfather, and of his two paternal uncles. And the real trouble always came when these men clashed with reality. Bobrowski never failed to oppose to these dreamers the realistic, hardworking "beavers" of Conrad's maternal family, the Bobrowski-Bibersteins.

Stein's theory sounds wonderful. It even seems to work. It might have been successful but for a scoundrel calling himself gentleman Brown who blunders into Jim's earthly paradise, Patusan.

Brown, who comes for easy plunder and is astonished to find a white man in charge, addresses Jim thus:

> What made you (come here)? . . . What do you deserve, you that I find skulking here with your mouth full of responsibility, of innocent lives, of your infernal duty? . . . I came here for food . . . and what did *you* come for? . . . I would let you shoot me and welcome . . . This is as good a jumping-off place for me as another. I am sick of my infernal luck. But it would be too easy. There are my men in the same boat—and, by God, I am not the sort to jump out of trouble and leave them in a damned lurch . . . Have we met to tell each other the story of our lives? Suppose you begin. No? Well, I am sure I don't want to hear. Keep it to yourself. I know it is no better than mine. I've lived—and so did you, though you talk as if you were one of those people that should have wings so as to go about without touching the dirty earth. Well, it is dirty. I haven't got any wings. I am here because I was afraid once in my life . . . I won't ask you what

scared you into this infernal hole, where you seem
to have found pretty pickings."

Brown's infernal flair makes him find exactly the
right words—"a jumping-off place," "my men are in
the same boat . . . I am not the sort to jump out of trouble and leave them in a damned lurch," "I am here because I was afraid once in my life," "what scared you
into this infernal hole?"—all these allusions touch Jim to
the quick and disarm him completely. So he lets Brown
and his criminals go away in possession of their arms.
This precipitates a tragedy ending with Jim's death. He
had been dragged out from his dream and had to
drown, in keeping with Stein's theory.

What would have become of Jim if Brown had not
interfered with his life? He would have most likely continued to live his dreamlike romantic existence of an eternal adolescent. An eternal adolescent is a person with
an adolescent mind and emotionality, but endowed with
the physical and mental powers of a man. Many adventurers, revolutionists, world travelers and explorers belonged to this type. Conrad's father Apollo was an outstanding example, and Conrad himself, as a 34-year-old
English captain, was called a "penniless dreamer" by his
uncle Bobrowski. But in a country where the political
situation was so hopeless and the oppression of the national spirit so complete, where the very ideas of independence, equality, justice, freedom of expression were
but beautiful dreams, what else could you expect? Very
little was left to the Poles of a hundred years ago but to
dream either of a better past, or of countries far away,
or of a better future. All this, they did abundantly in
their romantic literature. During the German occupation
of Poland from 1939 to 1945, *Lord Jim* was giving courage and endurance to many Poles. During the Warsaw
uprising of August, 1944, it was widely read and circulated by the partisans. The Polish army units which escaped to Rumania in 1939 and were being reorganized
in the Middle East had a cultural committee. They
printed some works, in Jerusalem, for the use of the
soldiers and officers, and the first volume which came
out was *Lord Jim*. In his introduction, the editor, Wit
Tarnawski, concluded that the Polish reader had no difficulty understanding Jim's psyche, contrary to the English reader. "No doubt," Mr. Tarnawski continued, "Jim
is one of us, he is a Pole."

There is a lot of symbolism in *Lord Jim*. The symbols are partly personal, partly of an archetypal nature. The latter aspect has been well described in Elliott B. Gose's (Jr.) *Imagination Indulged: the irrational in the 19th century Novel*, chapter 9. (McGill-Queen's University Press, Montreal and London, 1972) Already in my book *The Polish Heritage of Joseph Conrad*, I had expressed the conviction that what attracted Conrad to this kind of story was the guilt feelings he must have had for deserting Poland, at the age of 17. He had not just deserted Poland by leaving the country for ever, he had also deserted the Polish language which was as sacred to every Pole, as Hebrew is to a religious Jew. He had, by his own admission, been accused of desertion by his best friends, and when he left Cracow for Marseilles, on the 14 of October, 1874, the Polish writer Buszczyński told him, as we mentioned before, "Wherever you sail, you will sail back to Poland." Young Conrad also knew that his father, whose funeral had been the most imposing the Town of Cracow had seen for twenty years, would never have wanted his son to emigrate and become a foreigner. Later, when Conrad was just beginning to work on *Lord Jim,* he received a letter from the leading Polish novelist, Mrs. Orzeszkowa, accusing him of treason. The same writer also accused him publicly of having forsaken his homeland in order to earn foreign money by writing in a foreign language. No doubt that Conrad's conscience was sometimes troubled.

I said in my now forty-five-year-old book that the name *Patna* meant *Polska*, Poland. Later Czesław Miłosz added that it could just as well mean *Patria*. Since then, I have found more symbols. Patusan, for instance, sounds like the name of a medicine—names of medicines around 1900 often ended with -san (e.g., Salvarsan) so that Patusan could be translated as "the cure for Pat(na)."[101] Some critics found my interpretations "wild," "farfetched," etc. Mencken protested, saying that I had committed an autopsy on a dead genius. Norman Sherry wrote but a few years ago that "such speculations need not detail us long." As proof against my theory, he said that a ship called *Patna* really existed and that the ship was in the port of Singapore at the time when Conrad spent several weeks in a sailor's home there.[102] But what does this prove? Singapore is one of the greatest ports in the whole world. More than a hundred ships must be there at all times, and during the three weeks Conrad was at the Sailor's Home he might have seen as many as a thousand boats. Why then, out of so many hundreds of possible choices, did he pick the name *Patna*? Surely because it appealed to him, because it seemed particularly fitting. I would go even further. I can imagine Conrad Korzeniowski strolling along the waterside being struck by the name of a ship. The name seemed to be *Polska*. Coming nearer, it seemed rather like *Patria*. Finally, he made it out to be *Patna*. This is not as farfetched as it seems. I have often noticed, strolling along the St. Lawrence Seaway, strange names of ships passing by which I first mistook for something more familiar. The phenomenon could even be used as a projection test. You do not see what is there, but what is in you. If one splits the letter *n* into two slightly unequal parts, one gets the word *Patria*. Conrad himself may have been unconscious of this, but it does not matter. What is really significant is the fact that it would be difficult to find a word which would lend itself so easily to such a revealing transformation while at the same time being commonplace enough as to completely hide its real meaning. One may call this a mere coincidence, but modern depth psychology has shown beyond any doubt that such tricks are far too numerous and too clever to be due to chance. Furthermore, Conrad's father used the expression *Pro Patria* as a final greeting in many of his letters. As for the pilgrims, Poland was then inhabited by a great mass of peasants and laborers, mostly illiterate, devout Catholics, ready to make great sacrifices for just *one* pilgrimage to the shrine of Częstochowa.

The precarious condition of the *Patna* hardly needs an explanation when we think of the condition of Poland after the uprisings of 1831 and 1863. After the latter, all organized resistance came to an end. The leaders had either fled abroad, or, like Conrad's father, had been exiled.

The *Patna* is finally rescued by a French gunboat. This is rather astonishing, considering the extremely small number of French naval units in that part of the world. But the detail becomes quite natural when we remember that the Poles had always expected their salvation to come from France. Conrad's grandfather, Teodor, fought against Russia under Napoleon. The great Polish song and national anthem, "Poland is not yet lost," originated in one of the numerous Polish legions fighting for Napoleon not only in Europe, but as far away as San Domingo. The Poles thought that Napoleon would one day free Poland from the Russian yoke. In this, they were ultimately disappointed, but, during the uprisings of 1831 and 1863, Poland's eyes were turned towards France.

The hope in French help is expressed in a number of literary works of the period. In *Pan Tadeusz* (verses 493-498), Mickiewicz makes a Pole say, "Impatient men always assure us that the French are coming, but we look and look and our patience comes to an end." Victor Hugo, Alfred de Musset, Béranger, and others found moving words for Poland. Hugo wrote, "To France she slowly turns her glazing eyes, and humbly seeks for help before she dies." And Béranger told the French nation: "Now shouts a nation, o'er a gulf profound; a hand to save us, Frenchmen, but a hand!"

When Conrad makes Marlow insist on Jim's impossible return to England, he is actually thinking of himself, "I think it is the lonely, without a fire-side or an affection they may call their own, those who return not to a dwelling but to the land itself, to meet its disembodied, eternal, and unchangeable spirit—it is those who understand best its severity, its saving power, the grace of its secular right to our fidelity, to our obedience . . . *Each blade of grass has its spot on earth whence it draws its life, its strength; and so is man rooted to the land from which he draws his faith together with his life*." (222, My italics) Jim was one of those who could not face that spirit, for he had "straggled" and the fate of stragglers is to perish in a faraway country. He was a "straggler yearning inconsolably for his humble place in the ranks," for "we exist only insofar as we hang together."

In 1930, the theory that the pilgrim ship episode symbolized a fact in Conrad's own life, was almost universally rejected. Edward Garnett called it "very crude" and "farfetched." The newspaper *Manchester Guardian* said I was "treading on shaky ground." Richard Curle exclaimed, "Extremely ingenious and extremely wild." Nobody seemed to weigh the evidence. Only one intimate friend of Conrad's, R. B. Cunninghame Graham, wrote me a personal letter in which he said that he felt my interpretation was correct.

Today, more than forty years later, the theory appears to be more acceptable. Jean-Aubry, an intimate friend of Conrad's, accepted it (although without mentioning my name) in his "definitive biography" of Conrad, *The Sea-Dreamer* (239-240), while Adam Gillon, in his *Eternal Solitary* (54-56), calls it an oversimplification, exaggeration, etc. Polish critics, of course, had always more or less felt that the "shades" and "ghosts" that assail Jim had to do with Conrad's Polish heritage, even when they rejected the Patna-Patria interpretation as "Freudian." Mrs. Maria Dąbrowska, already in 1926, had written, "Poland seemed to Conrad a responsibility denied, a duty repudiated." In contrast to this, the famous Polish writer Jerzy Andrzejewski, in a "postface" to *Lord Jim*,[103] came out strongly against my interpretation. He did not think Conrad suffered from a "desertion complex." Stefan Żeromski had at the very beginning of Conrad's writing career also spoken of "treason," but after reading *Lord Jim* he had become Conrad's defender. He alluded to *Lord Jim* and its symbolism when, in his preface to the Polish translation of *Almayer's Folly* (1924), he compared Conrad's father to a "lonely stoker of a lost cause in his vessel doomed to destruction" who "does not even know whether the ship can still put up a fight, whether it has fired its last shot, or whether it is already sinking."

Żeromski was not the only one who compared a country to a ship. Alfred de Vigny, in his *Chatterton* (translated by Apollo), compared Great Britain to a huge ship. Conrad took up the symbol himself in the last pages of the *Nigger*, comparing the British Isles to a sturdy, well-anchored ship which no storm can overcome. But the most important influence may have come from Słowacki. In a well-known patriotic poem entitled *My Testament*, the Polish poet compares Poland to a ship in a storm:

> No inheritors did I leave behind
> Nor to my lute, nor to my name.
> This name like lightning once lit up
> To later generations it is just mere sound.
> But you, who know me well, will testify before them
> That for my country I wore out my younger years
> That, while the ship was fighting, up on the mast I
>   sat
> And when she sank, down I went with her.

Who else would, thus, despise the world's applause
Be so indifferent to ephemerous fame,
Content to be the pilot of a ship of ghosts
Then calmly disappear—such as a spirit?

Conrad knew Słowacki well. He was probably acquainted with these famous verses, as he may have also
known this prophecy from Słowacki's *Anhelli*: "Your
house shall be a sinking ship." In any case, it is just not
likely that a ship in distress and abandoned by its officers had no deeper meaning to him—especially after Orzeszkowa's letter. He had always been sensitive to
symbolism—a trait he shared not only with his father but
with the great Polish romantics. His writings often make
one think of Goethe's famous dictum *"Alles Vergängliche
ist nur ein Gleichnis"* (All things transient are by symbols).
Indeed, it is only when they become symbols that acci-
dental and passing events acquire their ultimate, archetypal, existential significance and continue to live in
the minds of men. Patna-Patria is no exception. Nor is
Jim—the man who, with his desertion, lost both his family name and his country forever.

Lord Jim is about a man who has lost his honor.
Consciously, he does not admit this. "It was plainly their
doing," he says, "as plainly as if they had reached up
with a boathook and pulled me over." According to
Freud, in such a case, when the guilt feeling is repressed
from the conscious mind, while the unconscious is
crammed full of it, you are bound to get an obsessive-
compulsive neurosis which I would label here a guilt
neurosis. It becomes a matter of utmost importance to
keep the conscious mind, the ego, clear of guilt feelings
in order to avoid the overwhelming danger of self-
punitive, self-destructive action. Indeed, the neurosis
protects the individual against all suicidal ideas and thus,
as Freud says, "the neurotic appears to be immune
against the danger of suicide." This is very true of Jim
also, but if he has no conscious desire to kill himself, the
unconscious desire for atonement by death is all the
stronger. Jim offers his throat liberally to fate. He is not
afraid of anything until Brown makes his guilt feelings
conscious. From now on, atonement by death is the only
way out.

In his Author's Note Conrad mentions a lady in
Italy who had found the book morbid. He comes to the

conclusion that the lady could not have been Italian, because "no Latin temperament would have perceived anything morbid in the acute consciousness of lost honor." And Conrad commented, "Such a consciousness may be wrong, or it may be right, or it may be condemned as artificial; and, perhaps, my Jim is not a type of wide commonness. But I can safely assure my readers that he is not the product of coldly perverted thinking. He's not a figure of Northern Mists either."

The allusion to the Latin temperament makes now understandable the role of the French lieutenant with his particular code of honor. *Boileau*, in his *Satires* (X, I, 167) wrote: "Honor is like a rugged island with steep cliffs, once you have left it, you can never return." For Jim, the ship *Patna* was exactly that island. "He had tumbled from a height he could never scale again."

Conrad's conception of honor is not only Latin, it is also that of the Polish gentry. It was a precious value which you could lose; and once lost, it could only be restored by bloodshed. In the Polish epic poem, *Pan Tadeusz*, one man expresses this very clearly, when he says (translation by Watson Kirkconnell):

I feel the blood of the Horeszkos running in my veins,
I know my debt to glory, my family—its name.
Yes! With Soplicas I'll talk no more as of today,
Let pistols speak, swords argue! That is honor's way.

Thinking of the many cases of vengeance, bloodshed, duels wiping out young, promising lives, one is tempted to exclaim "Oh honor, what crimes have been committed in thy name!" Yet originally, honor was what kept society together. People could rely on one another. When Conrad's father received permission, from the Russian authorities, to move from Vologda to Chernikov, a journey of about a week, he gave his word of honor that he would go there abiding by official instructions and the Russians let him travel without the usual police escort. They knew that a Nałęcz Korzeniowski would never break his word. Even today, when we release a prisoner on parole, we mean on *"parole d'honneur."*

Jim was not a descendant of the Polish landowning gentry, but he had the same exacting super-ego. Not just because ship's officers are bound by a code of honor which forbids any kind of desertion! Conrad informs us that Jim has a father with very exacting moral standards. This is expressed in a letter he writes Jim and in which we read, "who once gives way to temptation, in the very instant hazards his total depravity and everlasting ruin. Therefore resolve fixedly never, through any possible motives to do anything which you believe to be wrong." With these words, the worthy clergyman bars his son the only way out, namely the forgiveness of sins. Total depravity and everlasting ruin are the wages of sin. No wonder Jim must cling to the fiction that he was not responsible for what he was doing. No wonder he did not dare to contact his father after his "jump." It must be remembered that Conrad's father, too, was very rigid in his views and an uncompromising fanatical Polish patriot. The memory of his father lived in Conrad as a kind of exacting super-ego. We know that the boy, by going to sea, completely repudiated his father's philosophy. In Jim, however, the same uncompromising super-ego comes to the fore, and it is difficult not to see how much this has to do with the author's own father-image.

When Jan Parandowski wrote that Conrad was the "apostle" of "fidelity, honor, duty, courage, and perseverance," or when Zabłocki said that "Conrad differentiated himself from the contemporary trends of Western Europe" by his "uncompromising defense of romantic, idealistic values,"[103] they underlined that paternal heritage. Zbigniew Grabowski meant the same thing when he wrote that Conrad "put honor and dignity in the first place of his scale of values," and that this was "a foremost gift of Polish culture, of the heritage of J. K. Nałęcz Korzeniowski."[104]

Conrad was only too well aware that he had not always been true to that exacting father-image within himself. Had he not mentioned in *A Personal Record* that, before leaving Poland, he had been "charged with the want of patriotism, the want of sense, and the want of heart, too." In 1914, Aniela Zagórska notices that the great writer became troubled while meeting Polish visitors and afraid to be considered a deserter.

How can it be explained that Joseph Conrad was so interested in a clear case of obsessive-compulsive neurosis? How could he, as a layman, anticipate to such an astonishing degree, the findings of psychiatry on this subject? There is, I believe, only one answer to this: Conrad had gone through all this himself. Jim's story up to the Patusan episode is a dramatized, symbolized version of what happened to the author himself. Conrad's adult life was determined by his juvenile, fateful decision to break away from his Polish heritage. In *A Personal Record*, he calls his emigration "a standing jump,"[105] an expression strikingly reminiscent of Jim's famous "jump." Many Poles had spoken of Conrad as a deserter. Even more important, the French authorities too considered him as such, or as what we now call a draft dodger, and on this ground forbade him expressly to serve on any French ship. We should never forget that it was in consequence of this rejection that Conrad was forced to become a British sailor, a British citizen, and ultimately an English—instead of a French—writer.

As to the obsessive traits which characterize Jim, we find them in Conrad as well. Dr. Bernard Meyer, in his psychoanalytical biography of Joseph Conrad, has noted a great number of them. Jessie Conrad, too, has described his obsessive mannerisms. The record of Conrad's seafaring career tells an even more striking tale. On his first ship, the *Mavis*, he stayed only 54 days. Would any apprentice wanting to learn a job plus a language run away after less than two months? On his second boat, he lasted 72 days. On the sailboat *Sutherland* he makes his first long trip, to Australia and back, but leaves it as soon as the vessel is back in London. Yet later, he assured us how much he liked the ship, the crew, and the voyage. The following employment he kept just for fifty days, probably to the first payday. Does this not sound strangely reminiscent of Jim's work record after the Singapore trial? Apart from Marlow, Jim meets several father figures who try to help him[106] On wonders which of them were Conrad's models during his seafaring days, apart from Bobrowski and Dominic.

We find also in *Lord Jim* the already familiar theme of the pathos of exile. Exile as a last resort, exile as a desperate cure, exile as suffering without end, exile with its lure of success and its illusions, followed by bitter disappointments, exile with the impossibility of ever returning home—we find it all in Conrad's works, and especially in this novel where, before his doom, Jim becomes what he would never have become at home—a lord. When reading Conrad, one is reminded of his father who was an exile since 1861 and died in exile. One also thinks of so many famous Polish exiles, like Mickiewicz, Słowacki, Kościuszko (to mention only a few). Exile is a very Polish theme.

What effect did the writing of *Lord Jim* have on Conrad himself? Could he really unburden himself in this way? Did it provide him with the catharsis which he must have secretly been craving? And after the publication of the novel, did he get the conviction that the nature of the conflict had been "seen" and that the message had been understood? Did he succeed to make us understand not only Jim's plight, but with it implicitly also the plight of Joseph Konrad Korzeniowski? Do we not, by absolving Jim, also absolve the author of all blame? I think Conrad succeeded in all these aims. Thanks to *Lord Jim* Conrad has become one of the most beloved writers in his own homeland. In 1966, 50,000 copies of the Polish translation of *Lord Jim* were sold in Poland, probably as many as the book sold in the rest of the world at that time. Through *Lord Jim*, whose symbolical meaning and plea for forgiveness the Poles intuitively feel better than we do, the Polish homeland has generously forgiven her great son his historical jump from the *Patna-Patria*.

A painted glass window in the main auditorium of Nowodworski Liceum (formerly St. Anne's) honors its former student.

VI.

The Political Novels

After the Lingard trilogy and the Malayan stories, Conrad seemed to be looking around for new subjects. Between the first part of *The Rescue* (1896) and *Lord Jim* (1897-1900), he wrote a number of short stories, which comprise works as different as "The Lagoon" and "Karain" (already analyzed), "An Outpost of Progress" (1896), *Heart of Darkness* (1897), a misfit written in 1897 called "The Return" (where Conrad tried "to go modern"), and the masterpieces, "Youth" (1897) and "Typhoon" (1899/1900), where he again became his own self. Almost simultaneously with *Lord Jim*, three short stories of unequal merit were finished: "Falk" (1900), "Amy Foster" (1901), and "The End of the Tether" (1902).

This more or less experimental phase may be said to have come to an end with *Romance* (1902), for in this book a new trend affirms itself which becomes dominant from 1903 to 1910. Written in collaboration with Ford Madox Hueffer, *Romance* it is not much above a boy's book of adventure, but it is interesting because it marks the beginning of that not altogether new trend which we would call political.

Political intrigues already played their role in Conrad's first works. They become the main theme of what has been rightly called his political novels: *Nostromo* (written in 1903-1904), *The Secret Agent* (1905-1906), and *Under Western Eyes* (1908-1910). Each of these books reveals Conrad's keen interest in political power play, the nature of political dictatorship, the way, revolutions are made, the motivations of the different types of revolutionists, and the inhuman methods with which obsolete systems maintain themselves in power, and the often equally inhuman way with which new systems impose themselves. Throughout, Conrad's attitude is pessimistic: human nature being what it is, no change is really a change for the better, or, as a witty Frenchman put it, *"plus cela change, plus c'est la même chose."*

He perfectly describes the different kinds of politicians: the politician-psychopath for whom politics are a means of satisfying his thirst for power, the politician-sadist, the politician despite himself who would much rather prefer to look after his own business instead of taking responsibility for public affairs. We also find the genuine but impractical patriot resembling Apollo who loses everything in the game except his ideals. Then there is the Bobrowski-type of magistrate, a patriot in his own way, prudent and ready to compromise with the forces that be, partly because he dislikes risks, and partly for lack of imagination. Most of Conrad's politicians lack calibre and cannot deal with a real emergency, but then, the situation may be saved by an outsider such as Nostromo. We also find the lackeys of the aristocracy, the politicians from resentment, and finally the political *parvenu* motivated by jealousy and greed. To the political type of man also belong the numerous anarchists who derive a sinister satisfaction from the thought of making history by preparing the downfall of the existing order. The only really sympathetic politicians are some politically minded women (Antonia, Natalia Haldin) who are capable of inspiring others and who personify rather than preach a definite political ideal.

A. NOSTROMO

The legend according to which this novel was based mainly on Conrad's impression gained during a two days' visit to Venezuela in 1876—is erroneous. How did it really originate?

In a letter addressed to R. B. Cunninghame Graham and dated 8 July, 1903, (*LL*, I, 315), Conrad wrote: "I am dying over that cursed *Nostromo* thing. All my memories of Central America seem to slip away. I had just a glimpse twenty-five years ago[107]—a short glance. That is not enough *pour bâtir un roman dessus.* And yet one must live. When it's done I'll never dare look you in the face again."[108] Unfortunately this passage was misunderstood and the legend was taken up by John Galsworthy who wrote in his *Reminiscences of Conrad* (*Castles of Spain*, 93) that "in *Nostromo*, Conrad made a continent out of just a sailor's glimpse of a South American port, some twenty years before."

This view does not hold up to a closer examination of the facts. There are few details in the novel which can be called exclusively Latin American, and those Conrad got through his reading. All the really important events, and still more all the leading characters in the novel can be traced back to Conrad's Polish or Mediterranean days. The revolution theme itself, apparently so typical of Latin America, was of course familiar to a Pole of Conrad's generation. There are reminiscences of the struggles between the Poles and Russians and of the many "pacifications" Poland had to undergo. One must not forget either that young Conrad was at one time helping to smuggle arms to Spain for a revolution.

A close study of the main characters of this novel shows at once their un-American origin. Nostromo himself is an Italian and modeled on Dominic, Conrad's initiator to the sea: "But mainly Nostromo is what he is because [I] received the inspiration for him in [my] early days from a Mediterranean sailor ... Dominic, the padrone of the *Tremolino* might under given circumstances have been a Nostromo ... Many of Nostromo's speeches [I] have heard first in Dominic's voice ... he would utter the usual exordium of his remorseless wisdom: '*Vous autres gentilhommes!*' in a caustic tone that hangs on [my] ear yet. Like Nostromo! 'You *hombres finos!*' " Such is Conrad's own explanation in his "Author's Note" to *Nostromo*, dated 1917

In the same preface he reveals also the origin of Antonia Avellanos. She owes her existence to Conrad's first love, to that girl who, as we believe, called him a "traitor" when he left Poland. For this is what Antonia would have said to Decoud had he gone back to Paris instead of helping to build the new state she had in mind.

According to Baines, the girl was Janina Taube, who later married a Russian diplomat. But both Roman Taborski and Jarosław Iwaszkiewicz maintain that Janina Taube could not have been that patriotic girl. Iwaszkiewicz knew the family well since the Taube boys had lived with his parents in Riga, after having left Cracow. The family was much too cosmopolitan to be Polish patriots (the boys in Riga were taught in Russian), and it is not likely that Janina was an exception.

Moreover, Janina was only nine years old when Conrad' left.

I believe that Antonia Avellanos is modeled on Ofelia, the sister of Konstantyn Buszczyński. Konrad had known her "when she wore her hair in two plaits on her back . . . as a tall girl of sixteen, youthfully austere, and of a character already so formed that she ventured to treat slightingly his pose of disabused wisdom." Antonia's belief in the "cause" impresses Decoud as the Polish girl's patriotism must have impressed Konrad Korzeniowski. "You know you were a terrible person, a sort of Charlotte Corday in a schoolgirl's dress, a ferocious patriot" is what Conrad might have written Ofelia—*had* he written. The following scene is most probably an authentic remembrance: " 'Why should anyone of us think his aspirations unrealizable', she said rapidly. 'I am going to cling to mine to the end, Antonia', he answered, through clenched teeth."

Decoud is described as "a dilettante in life", an "adopted child of Western Europe", and "an idle boulevardier" with "a Frenchified—but most un-French—cosmopolitanism, in reality a mere barren indifferentism posing as an intellectual superiority." He imagined himself French to the tips of his fingers. Yet, far from being that he was in danger of remaining a sort of nondescript dilettante all his life. (153)

The whole description is closely modeled on Conrad's own life in Marseilles. He lived there between January 1874 and July 1876 under the name of Conrad de Korzeniowski or Monsieur Georges, often not working, wasting a lot of money, frequenting all sorts of *cafés, salons*. Conrad made only one journey to Central America, and the ship not only carried general cargo, but also smuggled arms to Mexico for some revolution.

Decoud originates from Costaguana, and is actually visiting his native country without intending to stay there. But he finds himself caught by the real political problems involving Sulaco. He is "moved in spite of himself by that note of passion and sorrow unknown on the more refined stage of European politics." (156) Passion and sorrow: the very feelings that characterized the Polish scene!

Apart from Decoud and Antonia, there is at least one other familiar figure in this novel—Giorgio Viola, the self-exiled freedom fighter from Italy. Viola had been a follower of Garibaldi who appears here as the hero who wanted his country to be free from Piedmontese kings and become a republic. There is a remark about Garibaldi which is almost a copy of a remark by Tadeusz Bobrowski concerning Apollo: "It was enough to look once at his face to see the divine force of faith in him and his great pity for all that was poor, suffering, oppressed in this world." (31). Besides, Garibaldi was a great admirer of Poland who in a manifesto had urged the Western peoples to come to the rescue of the Polish nation.

Giorgio Viola himself resembles Apollo in more than one way—first of all externally. He wears a "leonine mane". (The words leonine or mane occur no less than eight times). Beginning with his exile, Apollo was wearing his hair and his beard very long. The following character traits of Viola also apply to Apollo:

> This man . . . had all his life despised money. The leaders of his youth had lived poor. It had been a habit of his mind to disregard tomorrow. It was engendered partly by an existence of excitement, adventure, and wild warfare. But mostly it was a matter of principle . . . it was a puritanism of conduct, born of stern enthusiasm like the puritanism of religion.
> This stern devotion to a cause had cast a gloom upon Giorgio's old age. It cast a gloom because the cause seemed lost. (31)

Another interesting character is *José Avellanos*, one of the rare, true Latin Americans in this novel. His life story and portrait bear many traits borrowed from Stefan Buszczyński and Uncle Bobrowski. He is a real patriot who tries to transform his country, Costaguana, into a modern peaceful democracy. He is no revolutionary, for he uses peaceful, diplomatic means. He had been a well-known diplomat, ambassador to Great Britain and then to France. Under the dictatorial reign of Guzman Bento, he had undergone terrible ill treatment. Later, he had written a history of the country entitled *Fifty Years of Misrule*, which could not be published because too many people described in it were still alive. This, we believe, is a parallel to Bobrowski's *Memoirs* which was published in 1900, six years after his death—much too early, as it was said. Like Bobrowski, Avellanos also has a nephew to whom he writes many letters. Buszczyński, on the other hand, had written *La Décadence de l'Europe*, a book which would well deserve the title "Fifty Years of Misrule."

Avellanos is described as a very active patriot who "displayed in the service of the endangered Ribiera government an organizing activity and an eloquence of which the echoes even reached Europe." He was working for the "establishment of that national self-respect without which . . . 'we are a reproach and a by-word amongst the powers of the world' ". (137) Everybody had heard of his captivity and inhuman treatment under Guzman Bento. This sinister dictator, who preceded Ribiera, is described thus:

> Guzman had ruled the country with the sombre imbecility of political fanatism. The power of Supreme Government had become in his dull mind an object of strange worship, as if it were some sort of cruel deity. It was incarnated in himself, and his adversaries, the Federalists, were the supreme sinners, objects of hate, abhorrence, and fear, as heretics would be to a convinced Inquisitor (137).

It is not difficult to see how all this applies to the sinister "godgiven" rule of Russia (the Centralists) over the Poles, who at least wanted some sort of self-government (Federalists). What follows is closely modelled on Polish memories. Avellanos is made a prisoner by the "Army of Pacification," and driven along half-naked, and in chains. So terrible are his sufferings that he seems "only to exist in order to prove how much hunger, pain, degradation, and cruel torture a human body can stand without parting with the last spark of life." (137-138) Finally he is released "contemptuously" because the "Citizen Savior of the Country" thinks "this benighted aristocrat too broken in health and spirit to be any longer dangerous". Just like Apollo or Prince Roman!

Like many dictators, the tyrant is paranoid and believes in the existence of a sinister plot: "The whole story of the Great Conspiracy was hopelessly involved and obscure; it is admitted in Costaguana that there never had been a conspiracy except in the diseased imagination of the Tyrant;" but the distinguished Costaguaneros had been imprisoned and executed upon that accusation . . . the mere expression of sorrow for the fate of executed kinsmen had been punished by death" (312). Avellanos escaped with his bare life, but a "man possessed of passion is not bankrupt in life." (140)

The tyrant (Guzman Bento) is depicted as wearing a cocked hat. When describing him, Conrad was probably thinking of the Grand Duke, Constantine Pavlovitch, inspecting the soldiers of the so-called Kingdom of Poland. We read about this Duke in *A Personal Record* (53-54): "Sallow in complexion, with a Tartar physiognomy and fierce little eyes, he walked with his fists clenched, his body bent forward, darting suspicious glances from under an enormous cocked hat. His intelligence was limited and his sanity itself was doubtful. The hereditary taint expressed itself . . . by the fury of an uncontrollable temper which generally broke out in disgusting abuse on the parade ground." Guzman Bento has not only the same hat but also the same personality traits.

But there is even more Polish history to come. As we know, tyrants had always had methods of making prisoners admit their guilt. So we should not be too astonished to find, in *Nostromo*, a description of what we now call concentration camps and show processes:

> The old tyrant, maddened by one of his sudden accesses of suspicion, mingled spluttering appeals to their [his officers'] fidelity with imprecations and horrible menaces. The cells and casements of the castle on the hill had been already filled with prisoners. The commission was charged now with the task of discovering the iniquitous conspiracy against the Citizen-Savior of his country . . . The dread of the raving tyrant translated itself into a hasty ferocity of procedure . . . a conspiracy had to be discovered. The courtyards of the castle resounded with the clanking of leg-irons, sounds of blows, yells of pain: and the commission of high officers labored feverishly, concealing their distress and apprehensions from each other, and especially from their secretary, Father Berón, an army Chaplain, at that time very much in the confidence of the Citizen-Savior . . . (371).

Father Berón is a specialist for extorting false confessions. If a prisoner protested his innocence, he was taken away by Father Berón and tortured until he was ready to make a full confession. An English doctor named Monygham is one of the victims. He had been an

especially stubborn prisoner, therefore "his subjugation
had been very crushing and complete . . . His confessions, when they came at last, were very complete, too.
Sometimes . . . he wondered . . . at the fertility of his imagination when stimulated by a sort of pain which makes
truth, honor, self-respect, and life itself of little moment.
And he could not forget Father Berón with his
monotonous phrase, 'Will you confess now?' reaching
him in an awful iteration and lucidity of meaning
through the delirious incoherence of unbearable
pain . . ." (373)[109]

There is no need to say how surprisingly up to date
Conrad's description of Guzman Bento's methods sound
today. And so does the following reflection which Conrad puts into the mouth of Mr. Gould, the owner of the
silver mine: "The words one knows so well have a
nightmarish meaning in this country: Liberty, democracy, patriotism, government—all of them have a flavor of
folly and murder." (408)

The memory of his unfortunate country must have
haunted Conrad again when he described Mrs. Gould's
feelings while riding over Costaguana's countryside,
being received everywhere with truly Latin American
(read: Polish) hospitality:

> In all these households she could hear stories of
> political outrage: friends, relatives ruined, impris-
> oned, killed in the battles of senseless civil wars,
> barbarously executed in ferocious proscriptions, as
> though the government of the country had been a
> struggle of lust between the bands of absurd devils
> let loose upon the land with sabres and uniforms
> and grandiloquent phrases. And on all the lips she
> found a weary desire for peace, the dread of of-
> ficialdom with the nightmarish parody of administ-
> ration without law, without security, and without
> justice. (88)

Conrad may also have thought of his mother when
he says that Mrs. Gould "had that power of resistance to
fatigue which one discovers here and there in some
quite frail-looking women with surprise—like a state of
possession by a remarkably stubborn spirit."

Actually, there are so many hidden Polish memories
in this book that we must limit ourselves to only a few
more. There are the country residences with their blind

wall turned towards the windswept pastures (88), each
mansion with a heavy portal (the Polish *brama*) over the
entrance, a herd of horses dashing along the dusty road
(27), the servants falling on their knees at the passage of
their mistress (508). The landscape, too, at times resembles the Ukraine:

> It unrolled itself, with green young crops, plains,
> woodland, and gleams of water, park-like, from the
> blue vapor of the distant sierra to an immense quiv-
> ering horizon of grass and sky, where big white
> clouds seemed to fall slowly into the darkness of
> their own shadows—Men ploughed with wooden
> ploughs and yoked oxen, small on a boundless ex-
> panse, as if attacking immensity itself. (87)

Nothing could be more reminiscent of the Ukraine
than when Decoud, not wanting the coachman to understand what he said to Antonia, suddenly switches to
French. This is exactly what educated Poles used to do
in similar circumstances. Iwaszkiewicz has pointed out
this and a number of other Ukrainian reminiscences in
his essay, *Nostromo*.[110]

There is an association with Poland in Viola's diatribe: "It had been otherwise in his time when men
fought against tyranny . . . starving on half-raw beef
without salt, half-naked, with often a knife tied to a stick
for a weapon." (167) In Poland, it would not have been
a knife but a scythe.

When we hear of the two parties, the Whites (Blan-
cos) and the Reds (Rojos), we are instantly reminded of
Warsaw in Apollo's time; and we think of the same town
when we hear that Sulaco's main street was paved with
wooden blocks (475- 554). This kind of paving, less noisy
and easier on the hoofs of the carriage horses than
cobblestones, was characteristic of the Polish towns up to
about 1930. No South American city, as far as I know,
was ever paved with wooden blocks.

We also think of Poland when we read about the
warrior, Barrios, who is at the same time a great gambler who even stakes his sword; or Sotillo, who, "like
most of his countrymen", is "carried away by the sound
of fine words, especially if uttered by himself." (285)
And who would not think of Conrad's parents when
reading this remark: "A man haunted by a fixed idea is
insane. He is dangerous even if that idea is an idea of

justice; for may he not bring the heaven down pitilessly upon a loved head?" (379)

Finally, the name of Sulaco's main street, "Calle de la Constitución", reminds anyone familiar with Poland of the fact that every little town in Poland used to boast of a market place (Rynek), a Napoleon Square, and a "Street of the Third of May" (Street of the Constitution). In *Nostromo*, the "Third of May" marks the day of an important battle (479); on the same date in Polish history in 1791, Poland's first constitution was adopted by the Diet. At the end of the book, Captain Mitchell even serves "Third of May" coffee!   In Chapter seven of "The Isabels"[111] (*Nostromo*, 229), we find this curious detail: "Nothing was clearly visible but, on the end of the last flat car, a negro... swinging a blazing torch basket incessantly with a circular movement of his bare arm." The implement described here is quite familiar to the older generation of Poles. Conrad saw it used when living with his uncle, as a boy, and on his visit to the Kazimierówka in winter 1890. It is a so-called *kaganiec*. The word means literally muzzle, but it also designates an iron basket containing a torch. It was used outside, hanging at the end of a stick, mostly in order to show the way to a traveler, and it was especially impressive on a winter night.

In "Prince Roman," in a passage which is clearly a personal reminiscence, Conrad would write (italics mine):

> We children were aware that there was a guest staying in the house. He had arrived the night before just as we were driven off to bed. We broke back through the line of beaters to rush and flatten our noses against the dark window panes, but we were too late to see him alight. We had only watched in a ruddy glare the big traveling carriage on sleigh-runners harnessed with six horses, a black mass against the snow, going off to the stables, preceded by a horseman *carrying a blazing ball of tow and resin in an iron basket at the end of a long stick* swung from his saddle bow. (*Tales of Hearsay*, 32).

There is another Polish reminiscence on page 106, where Charles Gould speaks of Holroyd the financier, living in California and of the dangerous situation of Sulaco in face of a possible invasion. Gould says, "He is very far away, you know, and as they say in this country God is very high above." This, obviously, is an allusion to an old Polish saying "God is high above, and the friend is far away," meaning: when you really need somebody quickly, you will find nobody.

Nostromo is so full of reminiscences and impressions dating back to Conrad's Polish and Mediterranean days that the South American locale at times almost appears as a disguise, permitting the author to deal with the ghosts of his own past. But this must not lead to neglect the many details from Conrad's readings. The story of the stolen lighter has been identified by Halverson and Watts as taken from F. B. Williams' book of reminiscences, *On Many Seas* (New York, 1898). Further sources have been discovered by Rosemary Freeman: *Mémoires de Garibaldi* (Paris 1860), John Miers' *Travels*, and others. Eloise K. Hay pointed out that in G. F. Masterman's *Seven Eventful Years in Paraguay*, we find the names Decoud, Captain Mitchell, Monygham, General Barios, and a Simon Fidanza. Finally, a book of travel reminiscences, *Down the Orinoco*, by S. Perez Triana, was published in English just before Conrad began writing *Nostromo*. The book which had a preface by Cunninghame Graham, was used so freely by Conrad that he accused himself to Cunninghame Graham of being "a fraud" (*LL*, I. 33). Triana strongly believed in material progress and economic prosperity as the prerequisite for political stability in South America.

Despite the disparate sources of *Nostromo*, it says a lot for Conrad's creative genius that he was able—in an almost superhuman effort, it is true—to weld all these elements into a consistent portrait of a fictive state. Beyond that, he masterfully deals with boundary situations. Everyone except unimaginative, pompous Captain Mitchell is faced by an inner or outer crisis (the one often symbolizing the other) which confronts man with ultimate decisions, which in turn change him either for better or for worse, which make or break him.

The name Nostromo is senseless. It is a mispronunciation of the Italian *nuostro uomo* ("our man"). The corrupted name, launched by naive Captain Mitchell, is loathed by the Italians of the town: "a name that is properly no word," (23) "no name either for man or beast." (232) It sticks to an Italian immigrant whose peculiar physical and personal assets make him an ideal foreman of the "cargadores," or lightermen, of the harbor and an ideal caretaker of the jetty.

Sulaco is a port on the Pacific coast of Central America, where Conrad had never visited. The town is described as an historical site. Mrs. Gould says, "We are very proud of it. It used to be historically important. The highest ecclesiastical court, for two viceroyalties, sat here in olden times." (35) This reminds one of Cracow, once the capital of Poland.

The port is regularly serviced by the steamers of the Oceanic Steamship Navigation Company (based in New York). The company's representative, Captain Mitchell, is justly proud of their reputation for trustworthiness and quiet punctuality. He is all the more annoyed at the frequent revolutions sweeping Costaguana, endangering company property and the regularity of steamers' schedules. Politically, as its name perhaps implies[112], this is a dirty country. More than once, Mitchell had seen members of an overturned government running to Sulaco for shelter and a way out, entirely destitute, leaving the country in one of the company's boats. And more often than not he had seen them coming back on another boat well provided with arms and money to start another *coup*.

The most impressive event of this sort had happened some years ago when a defeated dictator called Ribiera tried to escape through Sulaco, was recognized there by his enemies and would have lost his life had it not been for Nostromo who, with the help of his port workers, saved him from the mob and brought him aboard an O.S.N. ship. This boat had just arrived in the gulf, but, having picked up Ribiera and his men, left hurriedly without discharging its cargo.

Nostromo, whose real name is Gian Battista Fidanza, lives with a countryman of his, old Giorgio Viola. This man had enticed him to leave a Genoese ship calling at Sulaco and to stay in town. Viola owns a small hotel and *café* not far from the jetty; his boarders are mostly Englishmen. His family consists of his wife Teresa and two daughters: fourteen-year-old, dark-haired Linda and twelve-year-old, red-haired Giselle. Both husband and wife are natives of Spezia (misspelled by Conrad as Spezzia). Some "China girls" and a mulatto boy serve as staff of the establishment. (The presence of the China girls is of course an error: seven pages later the girls suddenly become Indians, which is more credible).

Giorgio Viola, with his "white leonine mane," had been a great fighter for liberty in his earlier days. A fervent follower of Garibaldi, Viola was called the Garibaldino. As a matter of fact, Garibaldi's portrait hangs in the kitchen, as if presiding over Mrs. Viola's cooking activities. For Viola, "Liberty and Garibaldi were his divinities"; he did not believe in "priest Religion," but tolerated "superstition" in women. He had been a fighter for liberty: "In the Italian legion of the Republic struggling against the encroaching tyranny of Rosas, he had taken part, on great plains, on the banks of immense rivers, in the fiercest fighting perhaps the world had ever known. He had lived among men who had declaimed about liberty, suffered for liberty, died for liberty, with a desperate exaltation, and with their eyes turned towards an oppressed Italy. His own enthusiasm had been fed on scenes of carnage, on the example of lofty devotion, on the din of armed struggle, on the inflamed language of proclamations." (29)

This pathetic description of Viola's past has, of course, its parallel in Polish history. Replace Rosas with Russia, an oppressed Italy with Poland, think of the great Polish plains, the banks of the Vistula, and of the Polish legions fighting in distant countries—everything falls into place.

As the story progresses, the history of Sulaco, the capital of the Occidental Province of Costaguana, unfolds itself. It is dominated by an economic factor; the San Tomé silver mine. During the dictatorial reign of Don Vincente Ribiera, they begin to build a railway linking the interior of Costaguana (i.e. its capital Santa Marta) with Sulaco, the most important port of the Western province. The construction is difficult since the track has to cross a chain of mountains followed by a steep descent to the sea. Three leagues from the town, there is an abandoned silver mine. The dictatorial government, badly in need of money, forces a concession upon Mr. Gould, an English merchant living in Sulaco, and extorts large payments of advance royalties. The worries attached to the working of the mine finally kill Mr. Gould when his son Charles is a little over twenty years of age.

For ten full years, Charles Gould, being educated in Europe, is the recipient of periodical paternal letters, "twelve pages every month in ten years." Much like Conrad was kept *au courant* by letters from his uncle, so Charles shares all the worries of his father: and much like Conrad, young Charles takes lightly the paternal warnings. The more his father curses this mining business thrown into his lap by a greedy dictator, the more his son becomes romantically fascinated by this mysterious silver mine on the flank of a Central American mountain. He even chooses mining as the main branch of his engineering studies. He marries an English girl who is enthused about living in a strange country where a wonderful Casa Gould and a fabulous silver mine await them.

Charles Gould, who tackles the business of the silver mine in a spirit of enterprise and romantic adventure is lucky, as most adventurers are at the beginning. He finds his financier in an American named Holroyd, a resident of San Francisco, who invests his capital in mines and part of his profits in churches.

Holroyd is characterized by that mixture of materialism and idealism which appears so typical of many American businessmen. His philosophy of life is very American. Conrad eagerly seizes the occassion for drawing an ironic picture of the peculiar form imperialism takes in the U.S.A. He lets "the considerable personage" (Holroyd) declare, "Time itself has got to wait on the greatest country in God's Universe. We shall be giving the word for everything: industry, trade, law, journalism, art, politics, and religion, from Cape Horn clear over to Smith's Sound, and beyond, too, if anything worth taking hold of turns up at the North Pole. And then we shall have the leisure to take in hand the outlying islands and continents of the earth. We shall run the world's business whether the world likes it or not. The world can't help it—and neither can we, I guess." (77) It is in this spirit that Holroyd lends money for the modernization of the silver mine.

Two things about Charles Gould are noteworthy: his grandfather (Don Enrique) had already lived in South America, fighting valiantly under Bolivar. One of Charles' uncles had become president of the Sulaco province, before being shot by the dictator Guzman Bento as a traitor to the cause of unification and pacification. Both details are of course reminiscent of Conrad's ancestors.

As the story unfolds, more characters appear on the Sulaco scene. One of them is *Don Pepe* (misspelled Pépé by Conrad), the burly and energetic chief of the mine. Then there is *Don José Avellanos*, a very distinguished gentleman living near the Casa Gould with his daughter *Antonia*. Don José acts as a counselor to Charles Gould, a task for which he is perfectly suited. This elderly gentleman had always loved his country and worked in her interest, even had represented her in London before the dictator Bento had taken over more than a decade ago. He was then thrown into prison and treated so badly that it was almost a miracle that he survived.

Don José recuperates better than Apollo. He moves to his wife's estate in Sulaco, where he is "nursed back to life" by his devoted spouse and his daughter Antonia. His wife later dies, but Antonia stays with him. Backed by Charles Gould, Don José becomes quite an influential man. He not only looks after the interests of the mine, the prosperity of which becomes symbolic of the economic prosperity of the country itself. He also becomes a political influence. Thanks to him, Ribiera is elected president of Costaguana. The mandate gives the country an orderly government which honors its foreign obligations and bases itself upon law, justice, and peace. As we have seen, Don José also finds time to write the history of Costaguana.

Finally, there is Dr. Monygham, another Englishman, described as "old, ugly, learned and a little mad." He has one or two traits reminiscent of Apollo Korzeniowski: he can be bitterly taciturn like Apollo towards the end of his life, but when he speaks, people are afraid of the "open scornfulness of his tongue." (44) About a decade earlier, during the dictatorship of Guzman Bento, he had confessed things which had never happened and probably incriminated others; this was an "indelible blot which made him fit for dirty work." (453)

Antonia's and Decoud's patriotism are soon put to the test when Ribiera's honest and liberal government is overthrown by "General" Montero. In truly South American fashion, Ribiera escapes abroad and the people of the Occidental Province are faced with the possibility of an invasion by Montero. They despatch "General" Barrios (better known as a gambler and drunkard than a military hero) to the south to meet the expected invasion.

Decoud finds himself caught in the wave of events. His intention had been to return to France after a brief visit to Costaguana: but once in contact with the patriots of the place, and especially with Antonia (whom he had known as a schoolgirl), he becomes an altogether different person. He feels no longer "an idle cumberer of the earth," but is ready to take responsibility for the future of the country. With the pathetic exclamation "*Pro Patria!*"[113] he accepts the editorship of a new thrice-weekly newspaper called *El Porvenir* ("The Future"). The paper is Don Avellano's idea; he had bought the newsprint and the printing press abroad. As an experienced politician he realizes the importance of propaganda in the struggle that is being waged.

Yet Decoud is not convinced of the purity of local patriotism. He is periodically turning out the right catchwords, true, but in long conversations with Antonia, he expresses his conviction that the real motive behind the patriotic feelings of the Sulaco leaders are the material interests of the silver mine. He has no confidence in Sulaco's General Barrios. He has no great hope in the future and quotes Bolivar's disenchanted words: "America is ungovernable. Those who worked for her independence have ploughed the sea." (186) Decoud has no patriotic illusions. No one is a patriot by idealism. To this Antonia replies that they are going to change all that. Patriotism "had stood also for sacrifice, for courage, for constance, for suffering," and this is how it will be again.

Events are happening fast now. Barrios and his troops are about a hundred miles to the South and Sulaco is virtually undefended, protected only by the sea on one side and the high mountains on the other. Both barriers are overcome by the enemy. A turncoat named Sotillo, attracted by the fabulous wealth lying in Sulaco's storehouses, decides to invade the harbor from the sea. He sets out with a steamer and a handful of soldiers to rob the treasure. His intention is betrayed to the Sulaco notables, but apparently they can do nothing. Charles Gould decides to have the silver taken away by a lighter,

thus getting it out of reach. Nostromo is entrusted with
the task and Decoud offers to accompany him.

They leave at night and run into Sotillo's steamer
approaching without lights. There is a collision which
almost upsets the lighter but which is not even felt on
board of the steamer. During these fateful seconds, a
stowaway on board the lighter (the hide merchant
Hirsch) instinctively clings to the anchor of the steamboat sweeping over the smaller vessel. He is carried away
in this precarious position, discovered, brought to Sulaco
as a prisoner with a story to tell, tortured, and finally
hanged and shot by Sotillo who can get nothing out of
this confused fellow. Unseen by the steamer's watch,
Nostromo and Decoud escape with the silver and finally
bury their treasure on an uninhabited island. Nostromo
now returns to Sulaco under the cover of night. He is
immediately entrusted with another dangerous mission,
involving day-long horse rides, in order to establish contact with General Barrios and recall him to Sulaco. In
the meantime, Decoud, oppressed by his solitude, commits suicide by weighting himself with four silver bars
and shooting himself in a small boat in such a way that
he must fall overboard and go to the bottom. (In a similar way, Captain Whalley in *The End of the Tether* drowns
himself with metal in his pocket; in *The Mirror of the Sea*
Conrad tells the story of Cesar, the thief who is knocked
overboard with the loot of gold pieces in his belt and
promptly drowned).

On landing in Sulaco, Sotillo is, of course, furious to
find the silver gone. Everybody believes that the silver is
sunk, for Nostromo has not divulged the truth. Following a false tip, Sotillo is dredging for the loot at the harbor's entrance. In the meantime, a handful of Montero's
men come over the mountain range and the leaders of
Sulaco have to take refuge in the countryside where a
former criminal named Hernandez is raising a small
army for them.

Finally, Sulaco is liberated and the Occidental Province becomes an independent republic, prosperous
thanks to the silver mine and Mr. Holroyd. Economic
common sense has prevailed over political passion and
intrigue. Peace and order reign in the Occidental Republic whose economy expands by leaps and bounds.

Nostromo the "Incorruptible" (Viola) has decided to
keep the silver and to sell it by small amounts in distant

lands. He becomes the owner of a vessel, trading up and down the Pacific coast. He is getting "rich slowly." But one evening, when going to a clandestine meeting with Giselle, he is shot by old Viola who mistakes him for someone else. He is brought to the mainland where he makes a deathbed confession of his theft to Doña Antonia.

A great deal has been written about *Nostromo*. What made Conrad choose this location, these themes, these characters? As we have shown, this novel abounds with Mediterranean and Polish reminiscences. We believe that Conrad chose Latin America as the stage for *Nostromo* because this allowed him to make a freer use of his imagination. Central and South America are places we know little about, except that the people speak Spanish, that the governments are unstable, with periodical revolutions and power struggles involving "generals" and politicians. There are, indeed, quite a number of affinities between Latin America and the Poland that Conrad knew: the almost complete absence of a middle class, the presence of some fine aristocratic families, but with little political influence. And last but not least, the love of pathos and grandiloquent phrases on the part of the autocrats, contrasting with their total inability to manage the country for the good of everyone.

The novel is the story of a man with a ridiculous nickname, *Nostromo*, who finally succumbs to the great temptation of his life because of one inherent "fault" in his character. It is also the story of Decoud, the Frenchified cosmopolitan, and in many ways young Conrad's double. It is as if Conrad, when describing Decoud's vain attempt to become a son of his country again, had been reflecting of what would have become of "Monsieur Georges" had he integrated the ranks of the Polish nation again and taken an active part in its struggle for independence. The sad fate of Decoud may be interpreted as an alibi for Conrad who decided not to return to his homeland.

Nostromo is also the story of a mine and of the influence of "material interests" on power politics. Here, we find Conrad on the side of those who doubt that economic prosperity in itself is a guarantee of happiness and peace. But since he is equally sceptical of the idealists, there is really no solution. The whole political merry-go-round is to continue like a never-ending farce, whoever has the power. Even the most affluent society harbors within itself the seeds of its own destruction. The case of Costaguana is as hopeless as that of Poland.

In *Nostromo* an entire country comes alive, with its weaknesses and its potential greatness, its wonderful scenery, its riches, its poverty and dirt, inhabited by men who suffer, toil, or intrigue, exploit the earth as well as the people, who use others for the satisfaction of their own ends and desires. And in the midst of all this moral and physical squalor stands the serene figure of Antonia with her unselfish and unflinching belief in the future of the country and in the best of man. Surely, such an achievement is a *tour de force* such as few writers can accomplish. Even among Conrad's works, *Nostromo* stands out in this respect. It is written with that sarcasm which already characterized Apollo and which is an expression of a strong desire to "change all that" (Antonia), but a desire inhibited in action by a form of despair.

The main themes of this novel are already familiar to us from Conrad's preceding creations: the cruelty and utter futility of revolutions; the meanness of most people's purposes and motives; selfishness or impotence hiding behind some grandiose phraseology; the corruptibility of man. There is also that unmistakably Conradian pessimism. Even when all seems well in the Occidental Republic, there is a hint towards the end that this happiness and prosperity are already being undermined by subversive elements such as the photographer, and that people like Captain Mitchell or Charles Gould may be living in a fool's paradise.

It is ironical that Gian Battista Fidanza, the Trustworthy (Fidanza comes from *fidare*: to trust, to engage), steels a lighter full of silver and, thanks to his money, becomes all the more respected; that Don José Avellanos, an absolutely straight man, is the one who has to remit the bribes to the Central Government; that Captain Mitchell always becomes mixed up in "historical events" which for him are mere matter for table conversation; that Hirsch escapes death miraculously only to be hanged a little while later (as if in line with the Polish proverb "What is to be hanged, will not drown") etc. Finally, Conrad enjoys pointing out that so many dubious characters (most of them gamblers) in *Nostromo* take themselves so dead seriously.

B. The Secret Agent

Nostromo already contained the germ for both *The Secret Agent* and *Under Western Eyes*. The small, pale photographer, "frail, bloodthirsty, the hater of capitalists," who visits the dying Nostromo, might be a figure out of these novels. He belongs to that under-world of plotters, informers, potential terrorists, and anarchists planning to overthrow the existing order. What the photographer wants is money, money for the (anti-capitalistic) cause. "The rich must be fought with their own weapons," he explains to Comrade Nostromo. A slave of his own ideology, he suspects even Dr. Monygham of being "a dangerous enemy of the people." (*Nostromo*, 563)

Another stepping stone between *Nostromo* and *The Secret Agent* is the short story, *The Informer*, written in 1905, just before Conrad began *The Secret Agent*. The story, set in the same milieu of conspirators and anarch-ists, may be considered as a preliminary exercise in this kind of narration.

The Secret Agent is another story of betrayal. Verloc[114] betrays his own country in the interests of a foreign power, Russia. By doing so, he also betrays his wife, and her mentally deficient brother, as he also betrays his anarchist "friends." He is pushed to commit a stupid outrage by placing a time bomb near Greenwich Obser-vatory, that symbol of eternal order. Afraid to be caught with the bomb himself, he instructs his brother-in-law to place it in a certain spot, but in the park the boy stum-bles over a root, the bomb goes off, and blows him to pieces. Unknown to Verloc, the boy's name and address is sown inside his coat, and Verloc runs the risk of being arrested. But before that happens, Mrs. Verloc kills him with a knife and later drowns herself when she sees that she in turn has been betrayed and robbed by the "com-rade" who was to take her to France and to safety.

In this novel, Conrad shows two things: first the human stuff anarchists are made of, and second, that anarchism cannot possibly work. Anarchists not only bet-ray their country, they also betray each other.

In *The Secret Agent*, as well as in *Under Western Eyes*, Conrad reveals himself as a master of the psychology of man's motives. Quite a few become anarchists because they reject their fathers, and, thereby, any authority. Being profoundly dissatisfied with themselves, they project their dissatisfaction upon the existing society which they hold responsible for every evil. Most are estranged from their country of origin.

England, at that time, was a haven for revolutionists and anarchists of every kind, many of them Russians. A bomb outrage attributed to these refugees would force the British government to deal with these people. According to Conrad, the mind of the anarchist is essentially nihilistic, incapable of producing anything but disorder. But if he was so intensely interested in the mind of the anarchist, there must have been some common bond. Conrad was a man alienated from his own country, deeply dissatisfied, not yet accepted, and ever fighting that spirit of disorder which his uncle had equated with the Nałęcz heritage. By dealing with anarchists in his books, he probably dealt with his own inferior self, his own "shadow."

Some critics explained Conrad's interest in the anarchist mind by the fact that his father had played such a great part in the conspiracy preparing the uprising of 1863. In his Author's Note to *A Personal Record*, Conrad angrily rejected the implication:

> One of the most sympathetic of my critics tried to account for certain characteristics of my work by the fact of my being, in his own words, "the son of a Revolutionist." No epithet could be more inapplicable to a man with such a strong sense of responsibility in the region of ideas and action and so indifferent to the promptings of personal ambition as my father. Why the description "revolutionary" should have been applied all through Europe to the Polish risings of 1831 and 1863 I really cannot understand. These risings were purely revolts against foreign domination. The Russians themselves called them "rebellions," which, from their point of view, was the exact truth. Amongst the men concerned in the preliminaries of the 1863 movement my father was no more revolutionary than the others, in the sense of working for the subversion of any social or political scheme of existence. He was simply a patriot in the sense of a man who believing in the spirituality of a national existence could not bear to see that spirit enslaved. (IX-X).

After these words, Conrad describes his father's funeral, "the cleared streets, the hushed crowds," in short, "a manifestation of the national spirit seizing a worthy occasion." It was "a tribute not to the man, but to the idea."

Conrad probably protested too much. He was certainly right insofar as his father had no resemblance with the alienated political demi-monde of his political novels. Apollo never believed in political outrages of any kind. On the other hand, even as a patriot he was regarded as an extremist who, by his impatience and fanaticism, probably did more harm than good.

As Norman Sherry has shown[115], the story of *The Secret Agent* is based upon a real event. In 1894, an anarchist named Martial Bourdin tried to place a bomb near the Greenwich Observatory, but lost his life in the attempt. Conrad found the outrage utterly stupid, but he was interested in the real motives of the men behind the outrage. Like his model Bourdin, Verloc is a rather naive double agent, but contrary to the real story, the outrage is suggested to him by a Russian diplomat of whom we know only the first name.

In *The Secret Agent*, there are no direct Polish reminiscences. But Conrad's dislike of Russian officialdom is expressed in the way he brings in Mr. Vladimir (perhaps one more symbolic name, for it means "Ruler of the World"), and in his exposure of this gentleman's falsehood and abilities of political blackmail. This refined well dressed gentleman stands in contrast to a gallery of nihilistic and anarchistic characters, all as repulsive physically as mentally, dropouts of society, belonging nowhere. All are more or less at the end of the road, and all take themselves dead seriously, which makes them all the more ridiculous. Conrad's political irony actually feasts on these characters who are true caricatures. Only the woman, Mrs. Winnie Verloc, is really pathetic. But then, she is no anarchist.

If there are no Polish reminiscences in *The Secret Agent*, there is one episode in Conrad's life which is reflected in the novel. He had become a British subject in 1886, but it was only in May 1889 that he was officially released from Russian allegiance. Before leaving for the East, in February 1887, he must have called at the Russian Embassy in order to sign the appropriate demand. However, if he wanted to visit his uncle who was no

longer able to travel, he still needed an official certificate
from the governor of the province Podolia. After his return to London, in the summer of 1889, he once more
had to call at the Embassy in order to get that paper
without which he could not go to the Ukraine. He must
have gone to the Embassy once or twice during the second half of 1889, when he lived at Bessborough Gardens, near Vauxhall Bridge, London. The travel document must have arrived in January 1890, for in February of that year we find Conrad at last on his way to
the Ukraine.

Conrad has never mentioned his two or more visits
to the Russian Embassy. It was when waiting for the
travel document, that he began to write *Almayer's Folly*.
In *The Secret Agent*, we find what we believe to be the
exact description of Conrad's visits to the Embassy:

> Before reaching Knightsbridge, Mr. Verloc took a
> turn to the left out of the busy main thoroughfare,
> uproarious with the traffic of swaying omnibusses
> and trotting vans, in the almost silent, swift flow of
> hansoms . . . his business was with an Embassy. And
> Mr. Verloc . . . marched now along a street which
> could with every propriety be described as pri-
> vate . . . With a turn to the left Mr. Verloc pursued
> his way along a narrow street by the side of a yellow
> wall which, for some inscrutable reason, had No. 1
> Chesham Square written on it in black letters.
> Chesham Square was at least sixty yards away, and
> Mr. Verloc, cosmopolitan enough not to be de-
> ceived by London's topographical mysteries, held on
> steadily, without a sign of surprise or indignation.
> At last, with business-like persistency, he reached
> the square, and made diagonally for the number
> 10. This belonged to an imposing carriage gate in a
> high, clean wall between two houses of which one
> rationally enough bore the number 9 and the other
> was numbered 37; but the fact that this belonged to
> Porthill Street, a street well known in the neighbor-
> hood, was proclaimed by an inscription placed
> above the ground floor windows by whatever highly
> efficient authority is charged with the duty of keep-
> ing track of London's strayed houses.

Then Conrad describes the porter of the Embassy in
a red waistcoat and knee-breeches, and a lackey in
"brown trousers and clawhammer coat edged with thin

yellow cord," Privy Councillor Wurmt, Chancelier d'Ambassade, and finally Mr. Vladimir, First Secretary.

The Russian Imperial Embassy was located at 30/31 Chesham Place. It had been built by Thomas Cubbit in 1852/1853 as part of a row of houses (29-34 Chesham Place). Contrary to the other mansions (all with stately columns and shining door knockers), the Embassy had no entrance on Chesham Place. To enter the building one had to turn to Lyall Street, pass through a gate, across a wide courtyard, and enter 30/31 Chesham Place from behind. This arrangement allowed the visitors to be seen from a certain distance. They could "park" their horse-drawn vehicles in the well-sized yard. The building is still there; it now contains a number of luxurious apartments. As must have happened to Conrad, the visitor looks in vain for an entrance to 30/31 Chesham Place on the square of that name, but a small notice tells him that the entrance is on Lyall Street, where it adjoins No. 12. *(See plans pp. 265/266)*

Chesham Place is in Belgravia, one of the most aristocratic parts of London, undefiled by public transport and, as Conrad says, with streets that almost look private. Mr. Verloc's journey is probably identical with that of Conrad: coming from a district east or southeast of Victoria Station, he walked along Grosvenor Place, turned left into Halkin Street (still a very quiet street indeed), passed Belgrave Square, turned left again into Belgrave Mews (a narrow thoroughfare) which led him to Chesham Place. The Russian Embassy lay diagonally across Belgrave Mews, but a tablet must have indicated that "Chesham House" (as the Embassy building was called) was accessible through Lyall street. This must have considerably annoyed Captain Conrad Korzeniowski, who was accustomed to find his bearings without trouble. Belgravia, indeed, is full of "topographical mysteries," to mention only two examples: the entrance to 23 Belgrave Square is on Chesham Place, seventy yards away from the square, and 49 Belgrave Square is actually on Grosvenor Crescent.

There is no doubt that Conrad had the Russian Embassy in mind when writing about Verloc's fatal visit. We think also of Conrad rather than of poorly clad Verloc, when we read: "With his hat and stick held in one hand he glanced about"—a man like Verloc would hardly use a cane, while Conrad always did. I cannot understand what makes Osborn Andreas think this was the German Embassy.[116] The Germans at that time resided at Carlton House Terrace—not in Belgravia. That Russian diplomats had often German names is a well known fact. According to *Boyle's New Fashionable Court Guide of 1889*, the Russian ambassador was his Excellency de Staal, while the name of the Privy Councillor was Count Adlerberg. A. de Volberth was consul general, the vice-consul F. Knapp. There was of course no Privy Councillor Wurmt; here Conrad deliberately chose an ironic name (*Wurm* is German for *worm*).

The main purpose of *The Secret Agent*, however, was not so much to ridicule Czarism, but to expose the utter futility and sterility of international anarchism. Towards the end of the 19th century anarchism was very active in Britain which had become a haven for anarchists from the European continent. There were no less than four monthly anarchist publications: *The Torch, Freedom, Liberty*, and *The Anarchist*. Apart from that, 16 pamphlets written by well-known international anarchists were peddled on a great scale. One of these pamphlets, entitled *Anarchist Manifesto*, and issued by the "London Anarchist Communist Alliance" on 1 May 1895, expressed the aims of anarchism as follows:

> Thousands of our comrades are suffering in prison or are driven homeless from one country to another . . . Many consider the State a necessity. Is this so in reality? The State, being only a machine for the protection and preservation of property, can only obstruct freedom and free development . . . Patriotism and religion have always been the first and last refuges and strongholds of scoundrels . . . Religion is mankind's greatest curse. We are Atheists and believe that man cannot be free if he does not shake off the fetters of the authority of the absurd as well as those of any authority . . . Here we are met by the cry "Dynamiters," "Assassins," "Fiends," etc. The meanest and most repulsive "fiends" of the workers are the Teetotallers, Malthusianists, and the advocates of thrift and saving . . . Nature knows no outside laws, no external powers, and only follows her own inward forces of attraction or repulsion . . . [We advocate] communism where money and money cheques will have become equally useless.

As we can gather from *The Nigger of the "Narcissus"*, such pamphlets also found their way into the hands of sailors. Conrad who, in a way, had once been a rebel himself, knew of the deadly danger to a ship's crew (and to society which he tended to see much in the same way) of ideas which aimed at destroying authority, loyalty, and reliability. In *The Secret Agent*, under the cover of a crime story, he deals with the citizen saviors and their sham pretence of liberating the world. Conrad may have been a cosmopolitan, but he was never an internationalist. He firmly believed that every nation, as every individual, had to work out her own destiny and her own salvation by giving herself the political system best suited to her particular national genius. Writing *The Secret Agent* was obviously one way of freeing the nation of its false political apostles by exposing them to that utter ridicule which, according to the French saying, is deadly.

C. *Under Western Eyes*

Conrad never hated the Russian people; but he certainly hated the Czarist autocracy with its bureaucratic machinery, its censorship, its sinister way of administering justice, its imperialism and colonialism, especially towards Poland. *Under Western Eyes* is the one book where Conrad settles, once and for all, his accounts with sinister Russia. Here, the byzantine and cruel aspect of Czarism is exposed to a naive West.

The novel is narrated by an English language teacher residing in Geneva, Switzerland. It is through his English, i.e. his emotionally detached and rather unimaginative eyes, that the happenings in the Russian colony of Geneva, and the conflicts, hopes, and motives of the main characters are seen. This artifice gives the narrative an apparent objectivity it would have lacked if Conrad had given free rein to his indignation.

Under Western Eyes was written in 1908, one year after the last visit Conrad paid that Swiss town for treatment of his gout. During the first visit, in 1891, he stayed three and a half weeks at Champel near Geneva, recovering from a severe attack of gout and writing part of *Almayer's Folly*. The second visit was in 1895, when he spent two months in the same place. Roughly one third of *An Outcast of the Islands* was written then. He went there a third time, in 1906. Besides looking after his boy, Borys, who had whooping cough, and undergoing his own physiotherapy treatments, he finished *The Secret Agent* and wrote part of *Chance*.

Champel being only half an hour's walk from the centre of Geneva, Conrad became fairly familiar with the town and must have heard a lot about the then very notorious Russian émigrés. The Russian statesman, *von Plehve* had been assassinated by a terrorist in 1904 and the Russian exiles were still vividly discussing the event.

Conrad's knowledge of the town is very accurate. The description of the hexagonal island, named after Jean-Jacques Rousseau, where Razumov's "fine ear could detect the faintly accentuated murmur of the current breaking against the point of the island" (290-291), is certainly based on a personal impression. There is no doubt that it was his repeated sojourn in Geneva that provided Conrad with a fitting background for Razumov's story.[117]

This story is fairly simple: A Russian Minister of State, "President of the Repressive Commission," is killed by a bomb in St. Petersburg. The deadly weapon is thrown during a snowstorm by a young revolutionary, Victor Haldin[118], who manages to disappear after the deed. He seeks refuge with a casual acquaintance and a fellow student, Kirylo Razumov.

Razumov is far from delighted, since this makes him automatically an accomplice. The reason why Victor Haldin hides in Kirylo's room is clear; he wants to hide, not with a notorious friend and co-revolutionary, but with a relative stranger where the police are not likely to look for him. Moreover, he is not going to stay: at night he will leave the town. The arrangements for his escape are to be made by Razumov. Full of misgivings, the latter sets out on his errand, but finds the coachman drunk. Frightened to death at the thought that the police might already be searching his room, Razumov decides to save his skin and career by betraying the arrangement. He approaches a high official and discloses the whole story. The terrorist is arrested, tortured, and executed.

From now on, Razumov, who, like Jim, had acted under overwhelming moral pressure, remains a victim of his own deed. True, all seems to go well at first. He is promised a good education abroad and a job with the government on condition that he act as an informer spying on the revolutionary Russian students gathering in

European university towns. His first assignment leads him (via Dresden, Stuttgart, Munich, Zurich) to Geneva, where he meets Victor's mother and sister.

Victor Haldin's mother and sister are not politically dangerous, their only crime being their liberal views and the fact that they are the nearest relatives of a terrorist. They are no extremists. Their existence appears dreary: the daughter is just living for her mother. With the death of their beloved Victor (once more Conrad chose an ironical name), their lives are without purpose, but they do not realize it. Illusions replace realities. Who knows, perhaps Victor's death served a higher purpose? So when the "reasonable" Razumov (his name is derived from *razum*—"reason"), a man mentioned once with praise in one of Victor's letters, appears in Geneva, he takes the place, in their minds and in their hearts, of poor Victor himself. He has their affection before he even says a word. Thus, by a supreme irony of fate, the very person who was instrumental in the death of Victor is considered a fellow-fighter by the two unsuspecting women.

Razumov has to play a double role: on one hand, he is forced to live up to his unjustified reputation as late Victor's friend; on the other, he has to provide the Russian Secret Police with regular reports on the Russian émigrés in Geneva. Due to Razumov's activity as an informer, many more people will be arrested, tortured, sent to Siberia, or killed. Only incidentally, if at all, does he hear of these effects of his information.

In Geneva, everybody believes him to be a sincere revolutionary, despite his rather ambiguous statements. His reputation is all the safer as news from Russia reveal that the coachman who was supposed to drive Victor to safety had hanged himself after the latter's arrest, supposedly from remorse for having betrayed him. Razumov could not have found a better alibi, but it is no use. Entangled in a net of make-believe, he finally loses all self-respect and gives himself up to a group of fierce Russian extremists, after having sent his written confession to Natalia Haldin whom he secretly loves. Against his wish, he is not killed, but made deaf by two expert blows on his ears. After this, he runs into a street car he does not hear. Finally, he expiates his betrayal as a poor invalid in a Russian town, attended by a devoted woman.

The greatness of this novel derives from the

dynamics of three political systems: czarism, Western democracy, utopian revolutionism. Under czarism, "an opinion may be a legal crime visited by death." The Russian empire suffers from "the moral corruption of a society where the noble aspirations of humanity, the desire of freedom, an ardent patriotism, the love of justice, the sense of pity, and even the fidelity of simple minds are prostituted by the lusts of hate or fear, the inseparable companions of an unhappy despotism." (7)

The minister whose assassination leads to the events described by Conrad is seen as a man who had worked industriously at "extirpating from the land every vestige of anything that resembled freedom in the public institutions", who had aimed "at the destruction of the very hope of liberty itself," who had proclaimed that "the thought of liberty has never existed in the mind of the Creator. It was not Reason but Authority which expressed the Divine Intention," (8) and it was he who saw to it that "it was not always safe, for a student especially, to appear too much interested in certain kinds of whispers." (10) Conrad sums up the spirit of Russian autocracy thus: "In its pride of numbers, in its strange pretensions of sanctity, and in the secret readiness to abase itself in suffering, the spirit of Russia is the spirit of cynicism," which makes "freedom look like a form of debauch." (67)

The whole life of a Russian is determined by the autocratic system: "Whenever two Russians come together, the shadow of autocracy is with them, tinging their thoughts, their views, their most intimate feelings, their private life, their public utterances—haunting the secret of their silences." (107) Yet, autocracy is the rule of very few. Miss Haldin says, "they make only such a small handful, these miserable oppressors, before the unanimous will of our people." And again: "There is only a handful of cruel—perhaps blind—officials against a nation." (133)

When the novel was written, people in the West hardly realized what it meant to live under the boot of an autocrat. Western eyes were blind. The Western powers wanted good relations with Russian officialdom, as they later wanted good relations with Hitler or Stalin. For "Western ears . . . are not attuned to certain tones of cynicism and cruelty, of moral negation, and even of moral distress." (163-164) In this remarkable novel,

Conrad tried to make us understand. His analysis of the essence of Russian autocracy (and of any similar system) was not only meant to be penetrating, but also disturbing. Perhaps this aspect of the novel is better appreciated now than it was in 1909, when the book was published.

Nor was Conrad impressed by the Swiss democracy. Over and over again he pours his sarcasm on the Republic and Canton of Geneva. The narrator of the novel observes "a solitary Swiss couple, whose fate was made secure from the cradle to the grave by the perfected mechanism of democratic institutions in a republic that could almost be held in the palm of one's hand." (175) At the sight of a worker obviously enjoying a day off, Razumov exclaims, "Elector! Eligible! Enlightened!... A brute all the same!" (205-206) Shortly afterwards, he remarks: "Canton of Geneva, Commune of—what's the name of the Commune [municipality] this place belongs to?... Never mind—the heart of democracy, anyhow. A fit heart for it; no bigger than a parched pea and about as much value." (205-206) The narrator discovers in the quiet Boulevard des Philosophes "the very desolation of slumbering respectability." (335) Geneva is a "town of prosaic virtues and universal hospitality," (336) a "town indifferent and hospitable in its cold, almost scornful, toleration—a respectable town of refuge to which all these [Miss Haldin's] sorrows and hopes were nothing." (338) Towards the end of the novel, Geneva is defined as "the respectable and passionless abode of democratic liberty, the serious-minded town of dreary hotels, tendering the same indifferent hospitality to tourists of all nations and to international conspirators of every shade." (357) Despite his threefold stay in Geneva, Conrad evidently had not exactly lost his heart to a town which had produced a Calvin and a Jean Jacques Rousseau, and attracted Voltaire and Madame de Staël. Did he, with Razumov, find Geneva "odious" and "the very perfection of mediocrity attained at last after centuries of toil and culture"? (203)[119]

The ideal form of government is not a kind of British-style parliamentarism. Miss Haldin probably expresses Conrad's own conviction when she says: "We Russians shall find some better form of national freedom than an artificial conflict of parties—which is wrong because it is a conflict and contemptible because it is artificial." (106)

Conrad does not see the answer either as coming from the revolutionists. These are, as in *The Secret Agent*, a very mixed and mixed-up lot. Their answer, moreover, is too negative. In his Author's Note to *Under Western Eyes*, Conrad put this very clearly: "The ferocity and imbecility of an autocratic rule rejecting all legality and in fact basing itself upon complete moral anarchism provokes the no less imbecile and atrocious answer of a purely Utopian revolutionism encompassing destruction by the first means to hand, in the strange conviction that a fundamental change of heart must follow the downfall of any given human institutions. These people are unable to see that all they can effect is merely a change of names." He obviously expresses his own convictions when he makes the narrator say, "In a real revolution the best characters do not come to the front. A violent revolution falls into the hands of narrow-minded fanatics and of tyrannical hypocrites at first. Afterwards comes the turn of all the pretentious intellectual failures of the time. Such are the chiefs and the leaders. You will notice that I have left out the mere rogues." Then, possibly thinking of his parents, Conrad makes him continue: "The scrupulous and the just, the noble, humane, and devoted natures; the unselfish and the intelligent may begin a movement, but it passes away from them ... Hopes grotesquely betrayed, ideals caricatured—that is the definition of revolutionary success." (134-135)

Najder (*On Conrad*) had pointed out that Conrad's revolutionaries are mostly anarchists. This is right. Their exotic names and nihilistic backgrounds suggest that they are human flotsam, people without a country and therefore without any real loyalty. However, there is a second class of "revolutionaries" rejected by Conrad: the well-to-do society people posing as socialists. (The French used to call them "*socialistes de salon*"). Mme de S. in *Under Western Eyes* is only one prominent example. The short story "The Informer" (in *A Set of Six*) can be said to be a parody of this class of people. Conrad's conception of fidelity included absolute allegiance to one's native or adopted country, as it included loyalty to one's employer. His heart went out to the simple worker (such as the common sailor), and he strongly believed that society should not be governed by the material interests of a minority. But he was convinced that neither the foreign "apostles of change" nor the armchair socialists could bring about a better society. He doubted the purity of their motives and considered them as Utopians, if not as self-seeking freaks. The new world they would achieve at best would be a monotonous and regimented one, where every individuality, originality, creativity would be crushed in the interests of a smooth efficient administration of goods and men alike. While it would be wrong to say that Conrad was against socialism as such, he had good reasons to distrust the motives of the self-styled revolutionists in England of his time.

Razumov represents the pessimistic side of the author when he speaks of "the mental caverns where revolutionary thoughts should sit plotting the violent way of its dream of changes. As if anything could be changed!" (261)

Miss Haldin, who in many ways resembles Ewelina, represents the positive side: "I would take liberty from any hand as a hungry man would snatch at a piece of bread. The true progress must begin after. And for that the right men shall be found." (135)

She believes in a better future which "will be merciful to us all. Revolutionist and reactionary, victim and executioner, betrayer and betrayed, they shall all be pitied together when the light breaks on our black sky at last. Pitied and forgotten; for without that there can be no union and no love." (353) At the very end of the novel, when Natalia Haldin has heard the whole story, she makes this confession of political faith: "I shall never give up looking forward to the day when all discord shall be silenced. Try to imagine its dawn! The tempest of blows and execrations is over; all is still; the new sun is rising, and the weary men united at last, taking count in their conscience of the ended contest, feel saddened by their victory, because so many ideas have perished for the triumph of one, so many beliefs have abandoned them without support. They feel alone on the earth and gather close together. Yes, there must be many bitter hours! But at last the anguish of hearts shall be extinguished in love." (376-377)

It would be a mistake to identify Miss Haldin's political ideal with Conrad's political convictions. But one thing is certain: Conrad did not believe in the redeeming power of any system in itself, be it political or economic. He hated any form of autocracy, but he did not believe in the political machine of English parliamentarism either—a sort of never-ending football game fed by two artificial antagonisms. He knew that even a theoretically perfect system will not work unless it is based on concord, not discord; on love, not power play, or hate. He may have been too pessimistic to believe it could happen, but he certainly was convinced that, if a new world were possible at all, it would have to be along Miss Haldin's lines. As we know from *Nostromo*, he was against any political system based on "material interests." He believed in the primacy of the selfless man (like Garibaldi) and the selfless woman (like Miss Haldin or Antonia). His political credo seemed to be that of a nation where, as in a good ship's crew, the common man and the officers work together for the common good, freely accepting their obligations deriving from a higher purpose.

We have seen that the spirit of Ewelina is clearly to be traced in this political novel. Nor is Apollo's shadow absent. The way Victor Haldin refuses to answer the questions of the judge (91 and 93) is reminiscent of Apollo's "arrogant behavior" before the Russian court. Finally, when we read of Miss Haldin's youth: "a youth robbed arbitrarily of its natural lightness and joy, overshadowed by an un-European despotism"—who would not think of young Conrad himself?

Among the many things which have been said about *Under Western Eyes*, a few deserve our special attention. Hugh Walpole did not like the work, he called it "a book whose heart is cold." He also found that Turgeniev and Dostoievsky had too markedly their share in the creation of Razumov and the description of the cosmopolitan circle in Geneva. Ford Madox (Hueffer) Ford, on the other hand, was enthusiastic: "In *Under Western Eyes* you have all Russia forever alive in the background of a mass movement. In that book Conrad lets his Polish hatred for Russian czars make him almost kind, even to revolutionaries . . ." Another enthusiastic reader, but with some reserves, was André Gide: "A masterful book, but one that smells a bit too much of work and application, and overconsciousness . . . Even the latent irony . . .

might have been lighter and more amused. The book is perfectly done, but lacks ease."

Neither Hugh Walpole's nor Ford Madox Ford's ears were "attuned." Walpole seems to have overlooked what is the very essence of this tale: that Razumov's plight is similar to Lord Jim's, and just as pathetic. A young man is faced with an extraordinary situation and with superiors overtaxing his moral strength. The young man becomes a traitor and has to bear the consequences. Like Jim, Razumov is a basically honest young man, but he has no other choice than letting himself be corrupted by a corrupted environment, or to be ready to suffer, even to die, for his convictions.

To say that *Under Western Eyes* is inspired by "a Polish hatred for the Russian Czars" also misses the mark. This novel contains Conrad's political credo which is based on love of the victims much more than on hate of the tyrants. If Conrad had hated, he would have approved of Victor's terrorist act, instead of being sharply critical. What pervades everything, is sympathy for the Russian people. Even a drunkard like Ziemianitch, living in a cavern-like hole, is sympathetic. He is a man of the people, of the Russian soil. His name is not really Russian, but derived from the Polish *ziemia* (Russian *zemlja*) which means earth. These simple souls, also called "servants of God," are fundamentally wonderful people. Conrad had known them in the Ukraine and, like his uncle Bobrowski for whom they worked, had respected them very much. What Conrad reproached czarism was less the fact that these people remained poor and dependent, but that their human dignity was not respected. Despotism, says Conrad, always rules with fear, and Russia was no exception. As soon as a man from the people began to think, as soon as he had a son who wanted to go to a higher school, he was potentially dangerous. So, if Ziemianitch drinks it is because he is not allowed to think, and not even allowed to be a decent human being. The ruling powers have cast people like him in the role of "pigs", of underdogs.

In her book *The Political Novels of Joseph Conrad*, Eloise Knapp Hay gives a detailed account of the numerous sources probably used by Conrad in writing Razumov's story. But these sources concern only details, they have little to do with the inspiration of the book, nor with its purpose to show an insensitive West the cruelty, cynicism, and stupidity of a despotism which, having claimed to have God on its side, kept the Polish nation captive and denied its best citizens the possibility of developing their potential. Conrad took on an almost superhuman task, especially in view of the obtuseness of the West, and it is difficult to say how far he succeeded in his aim.

Polish critics, of course, have pointed out that this book could only have been written by a Pole. Wit Tarnawski called *Under Western Eyes* "a travesty of Dostoevsky's *Crime and Punishment.*" J. P. Dąbrowski pointed out that both the names Razumóv and Raskolnikov are symbolic, *raskol* meaning heretic. And the Great Inquisitor in *The Brothers Karamazov*, like Conrad's President of the Repressive Commission, sees God as the Autocrat of the Universe.

The Polish critics have also discovered some reminiscences from Mickiewicz. The well known sentence from *Forefathers' Eve*: "Someone, perhaps, seduced by gifts of state, betrays his free soul to the czar for hire" could even be the motto of the book.

In a passage in *Under Western Eyes*, Conrad uses a metaphor created by Mickiewicz, when he writes:

> Under the sumptuous immensity of the sky, the snow covered the endless forests, the frozen rivers, the plains of an immense country, obliterating the landmarks, the accidents of the ground, levelling everything under the uniform whiteness, like a monstrous blank page awaiting the record of an unconceivable history (33).

Mickiewicz said it more briefly and more poetically:

> This level plain lies open, waste and white,
> a wide-spread page prepared for God to write.[120]

The Archetypal Symbols in Conrad's Political Novels.

Claire Rosenfield's book, *Paradise of Snakes: An Archetypal Analysis of Conrad's Political Novels* (1967), is most valuable as representing the analytical approach—a method adding a new dimension to the art of criticism. We cannot go into the details of Miss Rosenfield's findings; we would only point out that Conrad's work, in a much greater degree that that of his English contemporaries, almost constantly evokes archetypal images.

This is not only true of his political novels, but perhaps even more, as we shall show, of his "shadow" stories. Some of the primordial images alluded to are related to the Polish heritage (e.g., the motifs of the ship, of the tomb, of exile), others are rooted in the biblical traditions (e.g., the snake, the symbolism of light and darkness as representing good and evil, and others), finally there are those primordial images which go back even further: to an age when nature was animated by spirits, when trees sighed in the wind, brooks babbled, and when the sea was foaming like an animal bent on destroying an adversary.

As I have shown, the Polish Romantics were masters in the use of such symbols, and Apollo the poet was steeped in this tradition. In this respect, Conrad is the direct descendant of his father. Miss Rosenfield could not see this, but she well sensed that the sources of Conrad's inspiration went very deep, far beyond the personal. She also saw that, in his best books at any rate, Conrad was always concerned about the state of the world, and about the decisive role which sinfulness, guilt, redemption, and corruption played in the destiny of individuals as well as in that of nations and of the world. Conrad never shared the easy optimism and the blind faith in everlasting progress and in "democracy" which prevailed in Western Europe up to the First World War. Thinking of the tomb of Polish liberty "triple sealed with the seals of three empires," he knew what man was capable of doing to man, whenever the powers of darkness got hold of him.

VII.

Shadows

I doubt whether there is any writer in the English language employing so often words like *sombre* (a term for which Conrad has a predilection), *gloomy, dark, ghosts and shades, shadows*. Conrad is fascinated by what happens in the twilight zone or boundary between the conscious and the unconscious—the latter being *inscrutable, mysterious, secret, incomprehensible, fathomless*. Conrad excelled in describing what goes on in that zone where the conscious personality tries to come to terms with the challenges and threats emanating from the unconscious. The actions, words, and conflicts of his heroes reflect the struggle between the conscious personality and the "ghosts and shades" which assail and haunt them. He most often lets different outsiders comment on the various aspects and incidents of that struggle, but leaves it to the reader to draw "rational" conclusions, if any.

Identification, as between Jim and Brown, has much to do with this twilight zone. The mysterious relationship by which a person recognizes himself (or his lower self) in another human being appeals to what C. G. Jung calls "our shadow." The term denotes the primitive, regressed and disreputable part of ourselves which, in a civilized being, is normally also the most repressed.

In Jung's psychology, the problem of how to deal with one's shadow plays a leading role. It is part of what Jung calls "individuation," i.e. the process of becoming oneself. The same process is at work in what we could call Conrad's "shadow stories," namely, in *The Nigger of the "Narcissus"*, "An Outpost of Progress," (both written in 1896), *Heart of Darkness* (1898/99), *The Secret Sharer* (1909), and *The Shadow Line* (1915). As a matter of fact, there is hardly a work written between 1896 and 1905 which does not at one time or another deal with the dark side of man, especially *Lord Jim*, "The Return," "Karain," "The Lagoon," "The Idiots." Only "Youth" (finished in 1898) keeps refreshingly clear of unconscious motivations, which makes it outstanding in a way. In "Typhoon" (1902), the unconscious is symbolized by the passengers deep down in the hold, belonging to an entirely different world than the skipper. However, there is no process of individuation here: the hero emerges unchanged from his experience, having learned nothing and forgotten nothing.

Conrad would have protested vehemently against the allegation that he was a writer of the unconscious. Indeed, any writer who deliberately sets out to write a "psychoanalytic novel" almost automatically becomes a pretentious bore; and Conrad was all but that. Yet when he wants us to "understand," that is, to identify with his heroes and their "shadowy ideals," he has to go beyond their *persona*, and to delve into the twilight zone of man.

The secret of the singular fascination of Conrad's earlier works lies in the fact that, in a hidden way, Conrad is always writing about his own "shades and ghosts." By leaving Poland, and again by leaving the Mediterranean (which in a way was an adopted home to him), by building up the *persona* of an English writer, he had to repress (or "forget") a good deal of his own self. He could not draw strength and self-confidence from his family and national heritage, as any creative person normally does. If he wanted to be successful, his Polish heritage had to be minimized, starved, repressed. He himself felt that this heritage was a liability. "We Poles are poor specimens," he wrote to Cunninghame Graham (*LL*. I, 230). To Blackwood, he mentioned his weakness for harboring illusions as a Polish trait (24 May, 1901). Garnett wrote: "The subject of Poland was then [1896-1900] visibly painful to him, and in those early years he would speak of it unwillingly, his attention being designed to warn off acquaintances from pressing on a painful nerve." (*Letters from Conrad*, 6)

Bobrowski's constant censure (from 1874 to 1895) of the Nałęcz Korzeniowski family heritage and the memory of his parents' fate had encouraged Conrad very early to reject a good deal of himself. Whoever has to repress so much, necessarily builds up a particularly strong shadow and the struggle to set these "shades and ghosts" at rest is reflected in Conrad's shadow stories. Like *Lord Jim*, they are in a way a confession, made in the hope of redemption. Since the reader has a shadow too, to "understand" (and to forgive) means to take part in the author's process of becoming himself and free. It is in *Chance* (1911), of all books, that Conrad could at last say it clearly: ". . . a confession, whatever it may be, stirs the secret depths of the hearer's character. Often depths that he himself is but dimly aware of." (212)

A. The Nigger of the "Narcissus"

In this story, the whole crew of a ship risks becoming the victim of a strange identification with the only Negro sailor aboard. This tall black man, of whom nothing is known, tyrannizes everyone with his mysterious chest ailment which may be imaginary but which, when the man suddenly dies of a pulmonary hemorrhage, turns out to have been authentic. Whole groups of sailors, as well as individuals, periodically fall under the spell of this identification, to become, at moments, more or less free again.

The way different members of the crew are affected is particularly well described. The psychological situation is intricate. On one side, the Negro represents the crew's "shadow," and specifically that repressed desire to have a good time, to be cared for instead of being mercilessly ordered around; in short, the desire of being a child again assured of the mother's tender care. This is why they become tender and motherly towards the poor, sick Negro and cease to behave like the rough sailors they are.

The identification with the Negro brings to the surface that repressed part of the male psyche which Jung called the *anima*, and which could be defined as the normally repressed feminine tendencies in man, responsible for the otherwise incomprehensible sentimental weaknesses of men which stand in such contrast to the matter of fact, hardened and realistic attitude of man's conscious personality. Confronted with this tall Negro, the sailors are turned into tender mothers and weeping grandmothers: their *anima*, this exact counterpart of their rough masculinity, has come to the fore.

There is still another symptom of regression: the men tend to become more superstitious, believing that the Negro will die once they approach land. This is exactly what happens, but even then they are not ready to give him up. At the funeral, the bag of sailcloth containing the corpse refuses to slide down the inclined plankway as if kept back magically by the wishes of all the men. In reality—a nice illustration to Freud's *Psychopathology of Everyday Life*—someone "forgot" to grease the slide and someone else let a nail stick out . . . Finally, having overcome these extra difficulties, the corpse disappears overboard and the spell is broken. From now on, a good breeze and smooth sailing to the home port are assured. The "shadow" is gone.

The singular fascination of *The Nigger* is not so much due to Conrad's talent as a story teller, remarkable as it is, but to the masterful way he handles the emergence and the ultimate resolution of several more or less simultaneous boundary situations of which the struggle between unconscious motifs and rational behavior is not the least.

B. *"An Outpost of Progress' (1896)*

This sarcastic tale may be called a forerunner to *Heart of Darkness*. Two young Belgians, Kayerts and Carlier, are sent as agents to an isolated trading post somewhere up in the Congo, where they are supposed to be visited every six months by a "sardine box steamer" belonging to their company. In the meantime, they have to attend to whatever trade there is—mostly exchanging cotton goods and brass wire for elephant tusks. There is a native employee, Makola, who serves as interpreter, storekeeper, and accountant.

Neither of the two men is in the least prepared, physically or mentally, for living in this geographical and psychological wilderness. Both were all right within their own environment: "they were two perfectly insignificant and incapable individuals, whose existence is only rendered possible through the high organization of civilized crowds." (*Tales of Unrest*, 89). "But few men realize that their life, the very essence of their character, their capabilities and their audacities, are only the expression of their belief in the safety of their surroundings." An outsider and cosmopolitan like Joseph Conrad could see this better than one who had never been thrown into a completely different environment and mentality: "The courage, the composure, the confidence, the emotions and principles, every great and every significant thought belongs not to the individual but to the crowd: to the crowd that believes blindly in the irresistible force of its institutions and of its morals, in the power of its police and of its opinions." (89) Anticipating his story, Conrad gives the description of the loss of security following the transplantation into a primitive environment: "But the contact with pure unmitigated savagery, with primitive nature and primitive man, brings sudden and profound trouble into the heart. To the sentiment of being alone of one's kind, to the clear perception of the loneliness of one's thoughts, of one's sensations—to the negation of the habitual, which is safe, there is added the affirmation of the unusual, which is dangerous; a suggestion of things vague, uncontrollable, and repulsive, whose discomposing intrusion excites the imagination and tries the civilized nerves of the foolish and the wise alike."[121] (89). After the departure of the steamer which brought them, the two Belgians feel very "much alone," "unassisted to face the wilderness" which is all the "more strange, more incomprehensible by the mysterious glimpses of the vigorous life" it contains.

At first everything seems to go well. Makola is invaluable, for he knows everything. There are ten watchmen under him looking after the safety of the people and the goods. And there are enough provisions. Thus, it is possible to live a civilized life.

One evening everything changes. A foreign tribe intrudes from out of nowhere, and, with the connivance of Makola, who makes his men drunk, they carry the ten watchmen away at night. As if by magic the natives living nearby vanish also. Despite the fact that the strangers leave some wonderful tusks behind, the situation is all but reassuring. The watchmen are gone; Makola can no longer be trusted; the normally friendly tribe has withdrawn into the bush. Kayerts and Carlier become scared, extremely irritable, and physically sick. They have nothing to eat but unsalted rice; the steamer is delayed and they are isolated and defenceless. Getting on each other's nerves, they quarrel about a lump of sugar. In the ensuing scuffle Kayerts accidentally shoots Carlier and then hangs himself at the very moment when the sardine box crawls up the last river bend in a mist "penetrating and silent . . . the mist that clings and kills;

the mist white and deadly, immaculate and poisonous;" in short, a mist symbolic of the debilitating, degrading, and blinding influence of the land upon the intruders.

We easily recognize here the theme of *Almayer's Folly* and of *An Outcast of the Islands*. But while Almayer and Willems only gradually sink into a state of moral degradation, Kayerts and Carlier are engulfed very quickly by the totally different and incomprehensible spiritual atmosphere for which they are not prepared, and which they have not had the time to assimilate in safe, small portions. In fact, it is their own shadow which, no longer being kept in check by the collective safeguards of civilization, devours them, for, as Conrad writes, "It was not the absolute and dumb solitude of the past that impressed them so much as the inarticulate feeling that something from within them was gone, something that worked for their safety, and had kept the wilderness from interfering with their hearts." (107)

Almayer, Lingard, and Willems lose their dignity as human beings and their liberty in an environment which is not devoid of culture. They live in a milieu they could understand and relate with. There are common points of reference between the Arabs and the Whites, and the Malays have a social structure and a civilization which can be understood by a white man. Such points of reference do not exist between the Belgian traders and the blacks.

The civilized way of life of the two Belgians protected by guards can be interpreted as our conscious life with its presumptions and defences, while the savages overwhelming the trading post represent the naked forces of darkness, of our "shadow." Ignorant of Jung, preceding him by 15 years, Conrad expresses an idea on which Jung very much insisted—namely, that our civilization is only skin deep, and no match for the forces of darkness, once they are mobilized.

C. *Heart of Darkness*

In this story, written immediately after the *Nigger*, we also find the shadow motive. This is so true that it even influences the style, for in this story of not much over one hundred pages, the words *dark* or *darkness* occur no less than forty times, the word *black(ness)* thirty one times. Other favorite expressions are *shade* or *shadow* (19), *sombre* (10), *gloom(y)* (10), and *ominous* or *sinister* (9), to say nothing of words like *tenebrous, sorrow, despair, inscrutable, mysterious.*

This is a story told by Marlow—a very thinly disguised Joseph Conrad. Like Konradek, the boy Marlow had pointed to a white spot covering the interior of Africa on a map and said: "When I grow up, I will go there." (*Youth*, etc. 52)

Captain Joseph Conrad Korzeniowski owed his short-lived job as commander of a Congo steamer (1890) to his aunt Marguerita Poradowska, née Gachet, a Belgian who had married a cousin of Apollo. This is exactly how Marlow gets his command on a little Congo steamer—through the protection of a good-hearted but somewhat naive female in Brussels. That town reminds him of a whitewashed sepulchre, an expression which may symbolize the hypocrisy of the whites bent on "civilizing" the natives of the Congo.

Marlow, like Conrad, fights his way up the Congo river and nearly loses his life there. But here, the similarity with Conrad ends and the real story begins. Marlow enters the heart of darkness and discovers the Belgian trader Kurtz. Conrad probably got the name from Cracow. Alexander Kurtz (pronounced *Coorts*) was a well-known Polish patriot who had settled in Cracow after the failure of the 1863 insurrection, and who became the president of the Galician Bank (with which Bobrowski did business). He also wrote articles in the Cracow daily *Time*. The name (German for "Short") fitted well a character whose prototype had been known as Klein (German for "Small").

Marlow is confronted with a boundary situation, with the absolute and ultimate. Kurtz has gone over the border while Marlow just manages to stay on the sane side. The Belgian has been engulfed by the darkness, both physically and mentally, while Marlow escapes, unscathed but not unscared, to tell the tale. Kurtz, having been exposed to the wilderness and to the natives' customs for some years, and who has become almost a deity to the natives, had finally identified himself with the uncanny dark powers lurking along the upper reaches of the Congo. His shadow (in the Jungian sense) and his social environment have become merged, much in the same way as Marlow, at one time, is no longer able to distinguish between the beat of the drum and that of his heart (*Youth*, etc, 142).

Kurtz has gone through the process of being hollowed out, of being emptied of whatever humanity he may have possessed. Instead of Kurtz civilizing the natives, the negroes uncivilize him. It is the same process which Conrad already described in *Almayer's Folly* and *An Outcast of the Islands*, but it goes further and deeper. "The wilderness had found him [Kurtz] out early and had taken on him a terrible vengeance for the fantastic invasion . . . it had whispered to him things . . . of which he had no conception till he took counsel with this great solitude—and the whisper had proved irresistibly fascinating." (131) When Marlow finally locates Kurtz, he finds a physical and mental wreck, a mere shadow, a "wandering and tormented thing," (143) of which he says, "The wastes of his weary brain were haunted by shadowy images . . . both the diabolic love and the unearthly hate of the mysteries it had penetrated fought for the possession of that soul satiated with primitive emotions. . . ," (147) Kurtz had become the victim of "the heavy, mute spell of the wilderness—that seemed to draw him to its pitiless breast by the awakening of forgotten and brutal instincts, by the memory of gratified and monstrous passions . . . beyond the bounds of permitted aspirations." (144) It was "an exalted and incredible degradation." "He had kicked himself loose of the earth . . . there was nothing either above or below him." His intelligence was perfectly clear, but his soul was in bondage: "Being alone in the wilderness, it had looked within itself, and, by heavens! . . . it had gone mad."

Marlow sees "the inconceivable mystery of a soul that knew no restraint, no faith, and no fear, yet struggling blindly with itself." (145) Marlow doubts whether his listeners will ever be able to understand the mysterious curse which befell Kurtz when his own shadow and perversity confronted him in the shape of the savage customs and rites of the Negroes. For the sake of being their leader, he identified himself with his shadow-projection at the price of surrendering his culture and humanity. As in *Lord Jim*, Marlow tries to make his listeners "see": "Do you see him? Do you see the story? Do you see anything? It seems to me I am trying to tell you a dream—making a vain attempt, because no relation of a dream can convey the dream-sensation, that comingling of absurdity, surprise, and bewilderment in a tremor of struggling revolt, that notion of being captured by the incredible which is of the very essence of dreams." (82)

What Marlow/Conrad tries to explain is a process of depersonalization as described by Lévy-Bruhl, a *participation mystique*, a term Conrad might have heard. At any rate, what happens to Kurtz is a mystical participation brought about by his identification with the natives. In other words, he becomes a Negro himself, a blood brother. This goes much farther than in the case of Jim who, although becoming a leader of a Malay community, always remains English. Even Marlow cannot quite escape the spell: at one time he feels a subtle bond with the black helmsman who has just been killed by a spear flying from the bush. But this identification is only a passing impression while the spell of the wilderness and the primitive seals the fate of poor Kurtz. The wilderness "had taken him, loved him, embraced him, got into his veins, consumed his flesh, and sealed his soul to its own by the inconceivable ceremonies of some devilish initiation." (115) It is only natural that he should die on the Congo before reaching the civilization which he betrayed.

In Jungian parlance, Kurtz had become the victim of his shadow-projection, had been absorbed or swallowed by it as it were, much in the same way that Nietzsche had become possessed, inflated, and precipitated to an early death by his shadow. Jung points out that the shadow, in dreams of whites at any rate, is often expressed symbolically by a dark man.

We do not wish to discuss here the literary merit of *Heart of Darkness*. According to Leavis, Conrad has failed to make the horror real. True, hardly any reader will be able to identify with the Belgian trader who becomes spiritually engulfed by his primitive surroundings. Has Conrad been able to make us visualize what really happened to Kurtz? The author does not tell us what kind of initiation rites deprived Kurtz of his dignity as a civilized person. We have to take Conrad's word for it that it was "horrible" as well as "unfathomable." As to Marlow, he undergoes a process of individuation, a descent into hell, a night journey into the unconscious (Guerard), a journey into the self from which he emerges a different man—as Conrad had actually done at the end of his Congo adventure. To Marlow, the whole experience appears like a dream (as many events in Conrad's books) and the decisive thing is now to find its meaning. In his excellent study of the archetypal meaning of Marlow's "quest for the grail, for illumination," Jerome Thale writes, "In Kurtz Marlow discovers not simply one man become evil, but a universal possibility."[122] Again, at the borderline separating civilized life from wilderness, and consciousness from the dark potentialities of the unconscious, we reach that boundary situation which forces man either to live according to new lights or to founder in darkness.

Conrad shared with C. G. Jung the idea that civilization is only a thin crust. Gentleman Brown's massacre of Dain's party is described as "a demonstration of some obscure and awful attribute of our nature which, I am afraid, is not so far under the surface as we like to think" (*Lord Jim*, 404) In Winnie Verloc's stabbing of her husband, Conrad sees "the simple ferocity of the age of caverns". Bertrand Russell wrote that Conrad "thought of civilized life and morally tolerable human life as a dangerous walk on a thin crust of barely cooled lava which at any moment might break."[123]

Of the several critics who have commented on *Heart of Darkness* (Collins, Commayer, Guerard, Ostaszewski, Spinner, Wilcox, and others), Stephen A. Reid was the first to pierce the mystery of the "unspeakable rites" mentioned by Conrad. Reid writes: "I suggest that Kurtz's unspeakable rites and secrets concern . . . human sacrifice and Kurtz's eating a portion of the sacrificial victim." Since Kurtz was considered a man-god by the natives, says Reid, his failing health must have filled them with immense fear. His death would have meant the end of the tribe. In such a case, the consumption of a symbolically important part of a young and healthy man killed for this purpose, was expected to magically restore the health of Mr. Kurtz.[124]

Reid's explanation is probably the right one. He bases himself on James G. Fraser's *The Golden Bough*, first published in 1890, eight years before Conrad began to write *Heart of Darkness*. Unfortunately, Conrad's Victorian discretion as to the nature of these "unspeakable" ceremonies only puzzles the reader and prevents him from fully understanding the story.

In *Heart of Darkness*, the word *pilgrim* is used in the same sense as in Mickiewicz's *The Book of Polish Pilgrims*. The Polish bard, of course, borrowed the term from

Bunyan. Like so many other time-hallowed terms, in Conrad it takes an ironical tinge which is, of course, absent in Mickiewicz.

Both Congo stories are stories of alienation, a subject dear to Conrad. Owing to the similarity of the Polish and the *méridionaux*, he had felt at home in Marseilles. In England, things were different: he was faced with an almost incomprehensible mentality, indifferent at best, but quite often markedly hostile towards any foreigner who had dropped in without being invited. Conrad's feelings in this respect are too clearly reflected in some of his works and in certain of his letters to be dismissed lightly.

He preferred to live in the English countryside which reminded him of the Ukraine, and to follow, on a small scale, the life pattern of a Polish country squire. (Both Bertrand Russell and Wells remarked on this). Yet, as far as his *polonitas* was concerned, he was being "hollowed out." He kept his Polish mannerisms to his very death and never forgot the language of his father. He also kept his father's attitude toward Czarism. But being completely separated from the mainstream of Polish life and generally starved of Polish influences, this attitude was static. His Polish soul withered. Dr. Górski, who met Conrad repeatedly in Zakopane (1914), sadly stated that Conrad's "Polish heart had stopped beating," explaining that although he could understand Polish problems intellectually, he had become unable to feel what was foremost in the Polish mind of that time.

D. The Secret Sharer (1909)

Conrad wrote this psychological masterpiece almost a dozen years after the Congo stories. It was one of the rare works he was satisfied with. "Every word fits and there is not a single uncertain note," he wrote to E. Garnett on 5 November 1912. Like the *Nigger* and the Congo stories, it is a story in an all-male world, "no damn tricks with girls there."

An unnamed (!) captain, during his first command, hides in his cabin a ship's officer called Legatt who, having killed a sailor during a storm, had deserted his vessel. The captain senses that the homicide may have been comprehensible owing to the most exceptional circumstances (one thinks of Jim's desertion), but he would still have had the duty to deliver the culprit to the authorities. Instead, he lets him escape, and to this purpose even endangers the safety of his vessel.

When Legatt justifies himself, we seem to hear Conrad replying to Orzeszkowa: "You don't see me coming back to explain such things to an old fellow in a wig and twelve respectable tradesmen, do you? What can they know whether I am guilty or not—nor of what I am guilty, either. That's my affair." (*Twixt Land and Sea* 131-132). Like Jim, Legatt wants very much to be understood: "As long as I know that you understand . . . But of course you do. It's a great satisfaction to have got somebody to understand." (132) And as in Jim's—and Conrad's—case, there are people at home, his father (a clergyman!) and others, including the very respectable skipper of the "Sephora" who had never left England spiritually, ready to condemn him. Their attitude makes a return impossible.

The Secret Sharer was written eight years after *Lord Jim*; it is interesting to note how much more tolerant Conrad appears to have become. For Jim, there had been no absolution. Marlow had been as definite about that as Jim's father. Legatt, whose crime is even more serious than Jim's and moreover committed by a more mature person, gets a much better deal: he has the full absolution of the captain and leaves with a clear hope of rehabilitation. The captain knows instinctively that, had he been in Legatt's place, he might have acted in the same way. His identification with the stranger is symbolized (and helped) by the fact that the latter is wearing his sleeping-suit and looks like his double.

It has been suggested that the end of the last sentence, "a free man, a proud swimmer striking out for a new destiny," proved that Conrad had at last overcome his own guilt feelings. There is much truth in this statement; but we should not forget that Legatt was a free man only as far as he felt free from guilt. This is certainly what Conrad had strived and hoped for. Yet, Legatt could neither go home nor go back to the sea. Once ashore, he was bound to run into great difficulties (including a change of name); and who knows whether this man, who had "lowered himself into the water to take his punishment," would not consider his exile and his struggles as a heavy price to pay for a deed that could not be undone?

The deserter represents the captain's shadow and

what happens is an attempt, on the part of the captain, to deal with this shadow become flesh. As to the reader, he is invited not only to identify with the captain and to share the latter's solicitude and risk, but to take part in the process of maturation which the young skipper is undergoing in this boundary situation. Herein lies the secret of the singular fascination of this unique short story.

E. The Shadow Line (1915)

This story was written shortly after the outbreak of the first World War, that is much later than the other tales analyzed in this chapter. Yet it belongs to the same group. Like them, it deals with the incomprehensible and the uncanny.

Here, the term "shadow line" has more than one meaning, but, first and foremost, it is symbolic of the line that divides the lighthearted youthful enthusiasm from mature sense of responsibility: "a shadow line . . . ahead . . . warning one that the region of early youth, too, must be left behind." (3) It is in the spirit of lighthearted youth that the hero of the story "chucked his berth" as a first mate of a sailing vessel in an Eastern port. But the new-found freedom from responsibility does not taste as sweet as our hero expected—rather the opposite. When, by a stroke of chance, he is offered the command of a sailing ship whose captain has suddenly died, he seizes the opportunity with the eagerness of youth. It is his first command!

When stepping into the shoes of his predecessor, he discovers some strange facts. The old captain has been a rather queer person. His spirit seems still to linger on board. He used to play the violin for hours on end, was hostile to the crew, and unmindful of the interests of the shipowners, keeping the vessel away from ports for weeks—even risking to run out of water. As described by the chief mate, Burns, the old man had been a paranoid and a sadist who deliberately toyed with the idea that his men should not outlive him. His last words were, "If I had my wish neither the ship nor any of you would ever reach a port and I hope you won't." (61) Thanks to Burns' watchfulness, this fate is averted. After the death of her (nameless) captain, the ship is safely brought to Bangkok where our hero takes over.

Burns seems to anticipate further troubles. The late

captain is buried at 8°20′ latitude North and the ship has to pass that line in order to gain the Indian Ocean. Burns tells the new captain, "You can't hope to slink past a cunning, wide-awake, evil brute like he was . . . he was just downright wicked . . . a thief and a murderer at heart. And do you think he is any different now because he's dead? Not he!" (118)

Events seem to justify these apprehensions. One sailor after another becomes the prey of some tropical disease, probably malaria. The disease appears as "an invisible monster ambushed in the air, in the mud of the river bank." Burns is its first victim—a fact which only confirms him in his idea. The whole crew is more or less sick with heavy bouts of fever every few days, but able to work somewhat in between. Only the captain and the cook, Ransome, are impervious to the epidemic. But it is known that Ransome has a heart defect and must be very careful—he might drop dead any moment, a fact that gives added feeling of suspense.

But illness is not the only trouble. The ship seems to be unable to approach the critical line. There is never a steady wind; just capricious light air currents getting the ship nowhere.

Our youthful captain feels keenly that the behavior of the late captain was a "complete act of treason." He realizes that "even at sea a man could become the victim of evil spirits," and he feels on his face "the breath of unknown powers that shape our destinies." (62) Much as he tries to keep clear of his chief mate's crazy ideas, he is under their spell all the same, for he feels unable to break through the magic line ahead, a line marked by the late captain's body. And he uses expressions like "the fever devil has got hold on board this ship." (103)

The fact that the captain has very little sleep favors a state of mind where dreams and reality merge and where all his youthful illusions just vanish. In such a mood, he begins to write a diary which contains this passage: "I feel as if all my sins had found me out . . . I have nothing to do to keep my imagination from running wild." Not unlike Jim, he feels he can no longer face the extraordinary responsibility thrown upon him: "I am shirking from it. From the mere vision. My first command. Now I understand that strange sense of insecurity in my past. I always suspected that I might be no good. And here is proof positive, I am shirking it, I am no good." (106-107) Fortunately, the "seaman's instinct alone survived whole in my moral dissolution." (109)

Finally, after two weeks which seem endless, the ship approaches the shadow line. Huge clouds are building up, the night gets pitch dark, the last star has disappeared. At this crucial moment of possible doom (for the captain is unable to foresee what is going to happen), Burns crawls on deck "to scare the bullying old rascal." The supreme contest with the captain's spirit is at hand. "You can't slink past the murderous old ruffian . . . you must go for him boldly . . . show him that you don't care for any of his damned tricks," (116) he says to the captain. These words, followed by a peal of laughter as insane as triumphant, form the climax of the story. After this, the spell is broken, the boundary situation overcome, the ship crosses the ominous line and finds good wind to get safely to Singapore.

The Shadow Line is not a story of the supernatural. Conrad was right when he protested against such an assertion made by some critics. It is a psychological novel involving the unconscious. We find the already familiar theme of treason versus fidelity (the old captain versus the crew), a man impervious to disease (like Lord Jim, Lingard, and others), a theme dear to Conrad who so often suffered from bad health, and the theme of an extraordinary task thrown upon a young man, a task that will either make him or break him. For Conrad, such boundary situations are the supreme test of manhood.

There is yet another meaning to the story. Burns has become the victim of a shadow-projection. By dealing with the behavior of the late captain he is actually grappling with his own (Jungian) shadow, that is, with the worst within himself. Kurtz is overwhelmed and defeated by his identification with his shadow, whose projection he finds in the savage customs of the primitives around him. Jim fights all his life to keep his shadow at bay, until his shadow appears in the shape of a completely amoral outcast and criminal. The hero of *The Shadow Line* has to face and overcome his shadow; but he has enough awareness of the worst within himself to say, "I am no good." His diary is an attempt at analyzing himself, facing his unconscious motivations—the whole being a process of *maturation*.

The fascination of Conrad's tale lies in the way

inner and outer events combine and interpenetrate each other. The stubbornness and negativism of the weather reflects the rigidity of the old man's paranoid character, the "fever-devil" his viciousness and hatred of mankind. The bad condition of the crew is due to physical illness, but at the same time, it is the condition the late captain wished them to have. This mutual reflection (the mental reflecting itself in the physical and vice-versa) is not un-common in literature, but not every writer succeeds in making it appear so compelling and fascinating. Once more, the transient is but a symbol. We find this truth in the great epic poems of all times where nature and natural phenomena often reflect what is happening to the souls of humans. But this also characterizes the so-called romantics who, for quite a different reason, loved to blend natural phenomena with psychological events, if not to imbue the first with psychological meaning. In this Conrad is a master. He combines utmost realism with the strangeness of unconscious influences without producing a discordant note.

The captain who so courageously faced his shadow and his shadow line was fortunate. In Jungian terms, his story is that of an important step in the process of mat-uration, i.e., of becoming himself, a step which (always according to Jung) necessarily involves absorption into consciousness (or growing awareness) of parts of our shadow.

In *The Shadow Line* (written shortly before Conrad's journey to Poland), we have Conrad's last attempt to free himself of the ghosts of his past. The memory of his father, the poet and patriot, and the paternal teach-ing that no Pole worthy of his name could be happy un-less he fought for the greatness and freedom of his country, had to be overcome if Conrad wanted to feel free in his career. The intolerable burden which his father had imposed on him ever since the day of his baptism, had to be shed. Conrad could not live all his life with the exacting super-ego which Apollo had created and to which Orzeszkowa had appealed. The crossing of his shadow line marked the passage from paternal dependency to fully self-responsible manhood and freedom.

It is interesting to note that the "shadow" also plays an important role in Dostoievsky's work. Conrad was al-

ways very angry when he was compared to Dostoievsky,
but, as Douglas Hewitt pointed out in 1952 (in *Conrad: a
Reassessment*, 126-127), there are striking resemblances
between the two authors, resemblances which we would
attribute to the importance of the "shadow" in the work
of both writers. Many of Dostoievsky's heroes are actually haunted by their shadow in much the same way as
Conrad's heroes are obsessed by theirs. The conflict is
between the manifest personality and the obsessive
shadow behind.

All the stories belonging to this period of creativity
have in common the confrontation of the man with his
shadow, much in the same way as Jim was confronted by
Brown. Conrad, here, was particularly preoccupied with
his own "shades and ghosts," including his own heredity
and childhood, and the scale of values in which he grew
up. Each of these stories can only be fully understood as
a reflection of the author's own conflicts. By leaving his
Polish past behind, Conrad had by necessity built up a
particularly strong shadow with which he had to deal.

In *The Nigger, The Secret Sharer*, and *The Shadow Line*,
the shadow is overcome after a long period of stress during which everything hangs in the balance. In "An Outpost of Progress" and *Heart of Darkness*, the shadow en-
gulfs the human being altogether. James Wait, the black
sailor of the *Narcissus*, represents the rebellious, mutin-
ous tendency that lurks in the heart of every man, and
which is especially dangerous on board a ship. We have
pointed out elsewhere Apollo's narcissism in wanting his
son to become a copy of himself. And we have shown
how much the boat symbolizes the collectivity, the country, the family, or national tradition. The opprobrium of
being a black sheep, a straggler, was what Conrad had to
overcome. This struggle for his justification, absolution,
and serenity is reflected in his shadow stories.

In the Congo stories, Conrad describes three whites
who go to the Congo without being the least prepared
for the completely different atmosphere in which they
intend to live. Would this reflect Conrad's problems on
his arrival in England? Of course, an Englishman may
find this comparison absurd; but when Conrad came to
England, he was quite unprepared. In London, he was
the loneliest man on earth. England was a jungle to him.
He did not understand the language nor the social rites

of the inhabitants, nor did they understand him. It took him years just to be accepted, a struggle which is best reflected in "Amy Foster."

Yet, there is even more behind the Congo stories. Here we find the nightmarish insight that if man were suddenly confronted with the worst of himself, he could only moan: The horror! The horror! Conrad's journey to the Congo also threw him into a boundary situation from which he barely managed to escape.

VIII.

Three Landmarks: Chance, Victory, and The Rover

A. Chance (1911/12)

According to general consensus, *Chance* is not among Conrad's best books. Yet, for reasons often speculated upon, it made Conrad popular. Was it the personality of the heroine, Flora—a figure sufficiently hazy to remain mysterious not only to the reader but to the chivalrous husband as well? Mysterious, and fatal in the end. Or is it the atmosphere of suspense created by Conrad's painstaking slowness of action which makes one wonder—here as elsewhere—whether the author himself did not suffer from that very indecisiveness which characterizes so many of his heroes?

As in a number of other books, Conrad wraps up his story in another one. First we hear Marlow telling us about a young mate called Powell who gets a berth by an extraordinary chance, and is thus able to witness part of the real story. Young Powell is a very convincing character, and the way he feels after receiving his mate's certificate ("I wouldn't have called the Queen my cousin") may well be a personal reminiscence of the author, including the swift disenchantment following the great day. There is the chance of Powell having the same family name as the shipping master, and of meeting this man just when the latter is informed that the *Ferndale*, owing to an emergency, needs a second mate for the very next day.

On the *Ferndale*, commanded by Captain Roderick Anthony, he runs into the real story which is the story of the captain's wife, Flora née de Barral, whose presence on board perturbs the officers. Her relationship with her husband-captain is obviously a very cool one. Captain's Anthony's personality is a bit vague, that of Flora still more so. The captain is a gentleman in the English sense. He has married Flora not from love, but from a sense of chivalry. He is never excited, knows no passion.

Then Flora's background unfolds itself. She is the only daughter of "financier" de Barral. Where Conrad got the name from, we don't know. Maybe he chose it only for the sake of the pun: "Suddenly the bottom fell out of the whole of the Barral concerns". De Barral's enterprise was even less serious than the Tropical Belt Company in *Victory*. He was a financier who, in good faith, could make the public believe that he would take care of their money. His "Thrift and Independence" company, his "Orb" bank and the "Sceptre" posed as Trust Companies. De Barral believed that he was helping people, while he was actually helping himself to their money. If his turnover grew, it was only due to the gullibility of the public. Then, as in all these snowballing businesses, the "bottom fell out" of the barrel one day, uncovering a stinking mess, and "Great de Barral" became a convict.

His only daughter was brought up in luxury by a governess who cruelly left her when the salary was no longer forthcoming. After the catastrophe, Flora found it difficult to believe in people, assumed a false name, and once attempted suicide. Then Captain Anthony picked her up, married her, and shielded her from the world by keeping her on board his ship. When her father was released from jail and had nowhere to go, he was also taken aboard the *Ferndale*.

He had become a taciturn and paranoid man who believed that his enemies had brought about his downfall, that everything would have been safe is they had only waited a little longer, and that Captain Anthony had taken advantage of the situation by appropriating his girl. He finally tries to poison his hated son-in-law. By a singular chance, his intention is discovered by Powell. Found out, de Barral swallows the poisoned drink himself and dies.

This event does not improve the captain's marriage. Some time later, the *Ferndale* collides in heavy fog with another ship and sinks. Everybody is rescued by the other vessel except the captain who, having lost all will to live, makes not the slightest effort to be taken off his rapidly sinking boat. Much like Captain Whalley in *The End of the Tether*, he goes down with his ship.

What are the main themes of this strange novel? Here, too, Conrad follows his usual pattern of leaving many questions unsolved. He wants to enlist the reader's sympathy, let him wonder and figure out the real motivations, especially of de Barral, Captain Anthony, and Flora. He just gives the facts as seen through the eyes of the problem-free Powell. Yet, the book was hardly written as an excercise in psychology and psychopathology. Conrad always has a message, describing something near to his heart.

We cannot help feeling that de Barral is a caricature of the Nałęcz, Conrad was haunted all his life by the ghosts of his youth (including his heredity), the ghosts and shades he tried to get rid of by leaving Poland for good, but which accompanied him wherever he went. He could not shake them off any more than Jim or Axel Heyst could shake off theirs.

As for Captain Anthony, the constant insistence that he is "the son of a poet" and the fact that this poet has an unusual Greek name (Carleon) is of course a reminiscence of Apollo the poet. Here we see Conrad dealing with his own father image, putting it in its place, as it were.

The main character, Flora, has very little individuality. She remains a riddle, like so many women in Conrad's works. Perhaps this has to do with Conrad's own mother who died very early, a victim more of her husband's reckless political speculations than of Russian oppression. For Conrad, the memory of her was always very hazy, but one thing was certain: she was an innocent victim of masculine power politics, devoted to her husband and child, and to an activity that she—being a Bobrowska—knew in advance would lead to disaster. Like Flora, she passed her short adult life moving from one place to another according to her husband's erratic plans, and finally had to accompany him to his exile where she slowly perished.

The reader does not have to know that in this story Conrad once more grapples with the ghosts of his history and prehistory. If he is fascinated by this pathetic novel, it is because he feels the pathos of this girl, whose life is shaped by the reckless speculation of her father.

B. *Victory* (1913/14)

The title of this "island tale" can be interpreted differently. We may call it ironic, for if anyone "wins" here, it is Schomberg,[125] the hotel keeper. From his point of view, at any rate, the victory is complete: he has revenged himself as fully as he could hope to. Most critics, such as Haugh and Tarnawski, see it differently: they interpret Lena's sacrificial death as the ultimate victory, as irrefutable proof of her invincible love for Heyst, whose deep-rooted scepticism is disproven by her sacrifice. This interpretation may be the right one, but we must not forget that the book was published in 1916, when "victory" was a magic word helping to sell any book.

The story is fairly simple. Axel Heyst, a Swedish baron by descent, is one of the many characters in Conrad who, once they have gone far away from home (and especially to the East), can never return. We do not know what kind of dream drove Heyst to the East; all we know that he is "enchanted" by "these islands", the Malay Archipelago. One day, "enchanted Heyst" finds himself in Timor where he runs into a stranger called Morrison who tells him his plight: unless Morrison can pay a fine imposed on him by the local Portugese authorities, he would lose his ship. Heyst, who always behaves like a gentleman, advances the money and thus gains Morrison's everlasting gratitude. Thanks to Morrison, Heyst becomes "Tropical Manager" of the newly founded "Tropical Belt Coal Company". This is one of those speculative businesses that start with a great flourish of a hundred thousand prospectuses, and then fold up after a few years in a way which Conrad defines as "evaporation precedes liquidation" In the meantime, Morrison had the imprudence of revisiting his native country, only to become the victim of the deadly English climate.

Conrad has described speculative ventures in more than one of his books: in *Nostromo*, where the operation of the San Tomé Silver Mine is linked with a political speculation; in *Chance*, in *Almayer's Folly*, etc. As we have shown, the roots of this interest in financial gambles are to be found in Conrad's Nałęcz heredity.

After the bankruptcy of the "Tropical Belt Coal Company", the now jobless Axel Heyst stays on the island with a Chinaman married to a native woman and who continues to serve his master faithfully. Apart from him, the Swede has no other company than the portrait and works of his father who is described as a nihilistic philosopher. There is quite a number of similarities between the son Axel Heyst and the son Joseph Conrad. Both remember their fathers who died when the sons were in their teens, but who remain in a way a haunting presence. Neither really remembers his mother. The father's works and portrait form a curious background for the son, who leaves his father's country at the age of sixteen, never to return.

This is what Captain Davidson says about the Swede: "Heyst said that his father had written a lot of books. He was a philosopher . . . he must have been something of a crank, too . . . Apparently, he had quarrelled with his people in Sweden. Just the sort of father you would expect Heyst to have. Isn't he a bit of a crank himself? He told me that directly his father died he lit out into the wide world on his own, and had been on the move till he fetched up against this famous coal business. Fits the son of his father somehow, don't you think?" (33)

It was Conrad's fate to be forced to relive, with minor variations, in one of his heroes, aspects of his own past. Axel Heyst belongs to the minor nobility; so did Joseph Conrad. He is a "baron" as Joseph Konrad Korzeniowski was a country gentleman by birth. In the wide world, of course, these titles mean absolutely nothing and are quietly dropped.

Captain Davidson regularly steams past Samburan (just in case he should be needed), but as a true Englishman he refrains from "intruding." It is through him that the world at large hears from Heyst. Then, to the surprise of everyone, Heyst arrives one day in Surabaya on Davidson's vessel in order to liquidate the last ties that connect him with the world outside. In his naivety he stays at Schomberg's hotel, unaware of the fact that this German innkeeper nourishes a senseless but profound hatred for all Scandinavians and particularly for the former manager of the Coal Company. We have to go into the details of this hatred, not only because it is the moving force behind the events to come, but also because of its psychological implications with regard to the author.

Poland's relationship with Germany was marked by the fact that Prussia had initiated the partitions. The Western part of Poland, from Upper Silesia to Danzig (Gdańsk), was a German colony, and the German rulers, with very rare exceptions, behaved like a master race looking down on its inferior subjects. Completely ignorant of Poland's glorious past and of the fact that Poland's cultural heritage was at least as old as that of the Germans, the German masters treated the Poles as semi-primitive, ignorant people incapable of keeping any order, speaking a barbaric language, the teaching of which was forbidden. The general opinion was that the Poles were dirty, disorderly, often drunk, false, cunning, etc., badly needing a strong paternal hand. One must have spoken with Poles who lived under German rule to understand how much of Schomberg's "lieutenant of reserve manners," senseless hatred, and ready abuse reminds one of the attitude of many Germans then living in Polish territory. The very word *Schweinhund* ("pig-dog") which occurs twice in *Victory* (46-47), was a favorite expression that a German would use when abusing a Pole, along with the expression "eins, zwei, march": imitating a military order.

Already in *Lord Jim*, Joseph Conrad had drawn the picture of a Teuton: the captain of the *Patna* with his "blood and iron air", who treacherously abandons his ship. Schomberg, the hotel keeper, with his totally subdued wife and his table d'hôte, is drawn much more in detail. His hatred of "that Swede" reaches new heights after Heyst has run away with a girl in order to save her from Schomberg's advances. After Heyst has taken her to Samburan, Schomberg brings up the subject again and again. According to him, Heyst is a cunning ruffian and swindler, who sent "poor Morrison home to die" and wrecked the company in order to put his money away. Schomberg believes in his own tale and deliberately sends two gangsters after him.[125]

Of the two gangsters, Mr. Jones is the boss, while Ricardo, alias Martin, is his henchman. Jones hates women, so the fact that Lena lives with Heyst on the island is carefully kept from him. In order to get rid of the gangsters, Schomberg hints at great wealth being hidden on the island by the dishonest Heyst. Since greed, like hate, creates blindness, the two gangsters believe Schomberg's wild tale and see in Heyst a sort of second self, much as "gentleman" Brown in *Lord Jim* expects the mysterious Jim to be like him in a way.

With Schomberg's help, the criminal pair are provided with boat, food, water, and the necessary instructions. By a singular mischance, one of the two barrels of water contains sea water and when the bandits are nearing the goal of their voyage, they are practically dying of thirst. Sighted by the Chinaman, Wang, who warns his master, they hide under the wooden jetty where Heyst discovers them. Not knowing that these men are planning his destruction, he revives them with water and invites them to stay in one of the bungalows left over from the Coal Company. Wang, who has a good instinct, decides to leave his master, but first steals his revolver in order to be able to defend himself. The disappearance of his only weapon comes as a shock to Heyst who is already alarmed by the mysterious remarks of the bandits. After Wang's departure, he is completely at their mercy.

From this moment on, the events quickly gain momentum. Ricardo gets in touch with the girl. Believing that Heyst is a scoundrel who will play her false, he thinks he can win her over to his side. He wants to know where all that money is and plans to elope with the girl and the riches. Curiously enough, the girl is impressed by him. She is not in love with the fiery Spaniard, but, not wanting to antagonize him, she withholds from Heyst the fact of his clandestine visit.

Ricardo is now sure that his scheme will work and that both his boss and Heyst will be his dupes. He arranges a meeting between Heyst and Mr. Jones in the latter's quarters. During this meeting, which takes place in an atmosphere of suspense and impending doom, Ricardo visits the girl again in order to carry out his plan. He tells her that Heyst is lost, that he has enough of being Mr. Jones' henchman and that he wants to go away with her. The girl listens intently, but her thoughts actually center around a deadly knife strapped to Ricardo's leg. She finally succeeds in getting it, for Ricardo thinks this is just a whim of hers that must be gratified.

In the meantime, Mr. Jones has, with indignation, learned from Heyst about the girl and he immediately senses that Ricardo is alone with her. For him, his faithful henchman is now a traitor, and he moves quickly to punish him. Accompanied by Heyst, he approaches the latter's quarters and there, in the light of eight candles, he sees Ricardo at the girl's feet. He shoots both and disappears. The rest of the story is told by Captain Davidson who visits the island soon afterwards. He finds Heyst alive but unwilling to leave. On his next voyage, he discovers that the bungalows have been burned down, that Heyst perished in the fire, and that Mr. Jones has drowned himself. Only Wang has survived

In this book we find several already familiar themes:

1. The lonely young man from a good continental family who loses his father too early and then goes out into the world where he becomes trapped.

2. Very Polish feelings against the conceited German master race, then personified in the presumptuous Kaiser William the Second. With the figure of Schomberg, Conrad revenges himself on the German masters so full of their assumed superiority and who, while actually satisfying their power drive, pretended to be the benefactors of mankind. The ironical remark concerning the "Teutonic sense of proportion and nice forgiving temper" is typical (27).

3. The reaction to English snobbery mirrored in Ricardo's insistence on the uniqueness of an English gentleman, as opposed to a "foreigner."

4. A tribute to the quiet, unassuming, unimaginative, matter-of-fact and extremely correct Englishman in the shape of Captain Davidson—a type very different from impulsive Captain Joseph Conrad Korzeniowski.

5. The psychopathic rogue who shuns honest work and lives at the expense of others.

Conrad knew the psychology of the psychopathic personality very well. Ruffians of every kind, swindlers, outcasts, gangsters, desperadoes of every shade abound in Conrad's works. Contrary to the mistiness of his women (Alma, alias Lena, in *Victory* is no exception), those sociopathic characters are well drawn, very convincing psychologically, actually more so than the type of unrealistic dreamer or idealist which one also finds in Conrad. Rogues like Ricardo, "gentleman" Mr. Jones, "gentleman" Mr. Brown (*Lord Jim*), the great financier and swindler, de Barral (*Chance*), and many others, strike one as real people, consistent in their aim, uncomplicated and primitive, and paradoxically enough, extremely straightforward in their crookedness, and honest about their dishonesty. Could it be that Conrad was so attracted to this type of man because it represented an inferior part of himself? That part of which Uncle Bobrowski had been so afraid? One way of sublimating them is to fight them in others (some of the best policemen are repressed criminals), to act them on the stage, or to describe them lovingly and fascinatingly as only a gifted author is capable of doing.

6. The theme of the wavering Hamlet-like man and of the woman who takes things in her own hands in order to save him. She makes the sacrifice of her own life, while Heyst commits suicide. Polish authors have pointed out how much the end of *Victory* resembles that of Mickiewicz's *Grażyna*.

In Mickiewicz's poem, Prince Litawor, faced with a dangerous situation, is wavering. His wife Grażyna decides to act in his stead. Clad in his garments and riding his horse, she leads his men to battle. The enemy is vanquished, but Grażyna is mortally wounded. Everybody thinks the Prince is dying, until the latter appears on the scene. Grażyna is burned on a funeral pyre. While the people lament her untimely but heroic death, the Prince jumps into the fire and perishes.

C. The Rover (1921)

Of all Conradian works, *The Rover* (together with *Romance*) probably comes closest to a boy's book of adventure. It takes place just after the French Revolution had spent itself in the Terror. The hero is an old rover who, having "knocked about the Eastern seas for forty-five years" (4) now longs for a peaceful retirement in his native land. At first it looks as if his wish is going to be fulfilled.

Peyrol the Rover, now Citizen Peyrol, does not arrive empty-handed at Toulon. He brings a prize, a foreign merchant ship captured at sea according to the customs of those times. He also has a treasure of foreign gold coins which he had once picked up and kept for himself, wearing his loot in a special waistcoat under his garments. He decides not to surrender it as the law would require him to do. Having attended to the legal matter with the port authorities at Toulon, Peyrol decides to go back to the very place where he grew up. Getting lifts on several farm carts, Peyrol finally arrives at Cap Esterel where he intends to stay at a lonely inn.

The inn is known as Escampobar farm. The owner, Scevola Bron, does the farming practically singlehandedly while his wife Catherine looks after the household, and occasional patrons. Being quite out of the way, but commanding a wonderful view of a bay of the Mediterranean, the place suits Peyrol.

However, he quickly finds out that this inn is not the peaceful haven it looked to him when he arrived. He learns that Scevola had been a killer during the Terror, hunting aristocrats and "enemies of the people" by the hundreds. He actually became known as the Blood-drinker. Now he appears subdued, but inwardly he still fumes and is ready to take his pitchfork and do away with all those new aristocrats he feels are cropping up everywhere. As for his wife Catherine, she is described as stolid, taciturn, almost wooden, but later we hear that she cannot sleep at night for fear something dreadful might happen.

Catherine is assisted by a girl called Arlette who is the daughter of an aristocrat killed by Scevola. She owes her life to the fact that she was only a small child then. Now she is grown up and pretty, and thus becomes more and more suspicious in the blooddrinker's eyes. Catherine took care of the orphan whose outlook on life is colored by her early childhood memories of violence and bloodshed. By order of Scevola, she is kept in strict seclusion.

Peyrol, who had never been nearer the scene of the French Revolution than a few thousand miles, becomes aware that this revolution which was fought in the name of liberty, equality, and brotherhood, had actually brought to the surface the worst instincts of man. Immortal Principles had become idols demanding lots of human sacrifices. Scevola's conviction that a republic is a holy institution which cannot do wrong, while a monarchy by definition means injustice and exploitation, strikes the Rover as simplistic. No more can he believe that a man of the people is by nature good while an aristocrat is necessarily a scoundrel. He has enough knowledge of human nature to see that it is not the system which makes man perfect or depraved, but in his discussions with the blooddrinker, he keeps his wisdom to himself. Nevertheless, his host already suspects him of being an aristocrat at heart, for Peyrol obviously does not share his revolutionary fanaticism.

Soon another guest arrives: Lieutenant Réal. Like Arlette, he is the son of an aristocrat killed during the Terror. But times have changed: Napoleon Bonaparte has just become first consul and needs an army. Good officers are too scarce to let considerations of origin interfere with enlistment and promotion. Réal is a naval officer in Toulon. Nobody knows whether he comes to Escampobar Farm on leave or on duty. The latter is not impossible, since the farm affords such a good view of nooks and corners of the Mediterranean used by units of the English fleet. Since Réal is not only a devoted officer but also a man, it is only natural that Arlette, so long deprived of congenital company, falls in love with him, and that he should once forget himself enough to kiss her hand.

Peyrol, finding the days long, decides to buy a sailboat of local make which had belonged to Arlette's parents and which is now lying ashore. Mending, painting, and outfitting this "tartane" provides a happy occupation for the Rover who finds a willing helper in a local man.

The French naval authorities decide to mislead the British fleet cruising in the Mediterranean. The stratagem to be used is making up a number of false letters and dispatches and letting them fall into the hands of the enemy. Réal had probably suggested the idea to the authorities, thinking of Peyrol as the most likely man to carry out the plan. He approaches the Rover obliquely and the latter pretends not to understand. Actually, Peyrol knows perfectly well that very few people could or would carry out the plan successfully and that Réal, at any rate, has no choice. Finally, in view of the Rover's reluctance, the lieutenant decides to carry out the mission himself and asks Peyrol for the tartane. Réal expects to lose his life in the attempt. Peyrol agrees and immediately prepares the boat. The false papers are put on board. The boat is to sail in the direction of Italy, and let itself get caught on the way. At the last moment, Arlette, who has sensed that something terrible may shatter her happiness, rushes down towards the boat, discovers the tartane being made ready to sail away with the lieutenant, faints, and is carried back to the farm by Réal himself. Taking advantage of Réal's absence, Peyrol sails away.

The last part of the novel is one of the best examples of Conradian craftsmanship, a well constructed and well written narrative full of suspense. Here Conrad has succeeded in expressing the pathos of this Rover who, having been not much more than a sea robber during most of his adult life, is moved by his deep sense of patriotism to sacrifice himself for France. Very cunningly, Peyrol manages to "act suspiciously," and once having attracted the attention of a British corvette, to put up a good fight. He could escape, but he allows himself to be captured just as the night sets in. He is not captured alive: to make sure that he does not get away under the cover of darkness, he is shot. The false documents are discovered the next morning and immediately passed on to the Admiral of the Fleet, Lord Nelson, who does not doubt their authenticity. It is true that the successful stratagem does not prevent the French navy from being beaten at Trafalgar. As for Lieutenant Réal, his is the happy end: he marries Arlette.

The Rover could only have been written by a man who knew the Mediterranean intimately[126], who loved France, and who had left his country as a youngster but had never ceased to love her in a hidden way. As we know from Mrs. Conrad, the author of *The Rover* sometimes cherished the thought (if not to say the illusion) of returning to Poland one day, thus closing the circle[127]. Peyrol does it for him. Also, Conrad's conviction of the futility of violent revolutions is once more expressed in this novel. Peyrol reflects Conrad in many ways but perhaps never better than when he is contrasted with Scevola, the fanatical patriot, revolutionary by principle, and a blooddrinker.

The Rover is the only novel by Conrad where the hero, after living abroad for the greater part of his life, succeeds in returning to his homeland, and where his return is meaningful in the sense that it leads to a higher fulfillment of life. We could interpret this as a sign that Conrad had overcome his own conflict of double allegiance. The Rover returns to a country very different from the one he had known. Such would have been the case if Conrad had returned to Poland after 1918. In more than one way, Peyrol is Conrad's double. With him and in him, Conrad symbolically goes back not only to the Mediterranean of his youth, but also to his native country.

IX.

Conrad's Polish Stories

. When (on Christmas Eve of 1896) Conrad protested that he would lose his public if he took up Polish subjects in his writing, he was perfectly sincere. Moreover, he was probably quite right in his judgement of what the English public wanted. Yet, Joseph Spiridion's remark must have sunk into his unconscious, for in June 1901, one year after completing *Lord Jim*, he wrote the story of a young Polish peasant shipwrecked on the English coast. He may also have been inspired by a well-known passage from Mickiewicz's *Books of the Polish Pilgrims*, paragraph XI: "You are among strangers as shipwrecked men on a strange shore. Once upon a time a ship [Poland] was wrecked; part of her people, however, swam forth to a strange shore."

Conrad was cautious. He called his story "Amy Foster" despite the fact that this is less the tale of a simple-minded English country girl marrying a foreign peasant boy shipwrecked on the nearby shore, than a study of the man himself, "cast out mysteriously by the sea to perish in the supreme disaster of loneliness and despair" (*Typhoon*, 142). Nowhere does Conrad state that this is a Pole. Yanko's Polish is degraded to "a dialect" which sounds "disturbing," "passionate," "bizarre." Conrad says only that this man comes from the "Eastern range of the Carpathians" and calls him a descendant of the "Sclavonian (!) peasantry" in "the more remote provinces of Austria." Yet, Conrad knew perfectly well that the *górale* live in the *Western* part of the Carpathians, namely in the Tatra mountains south of Cracow. Many Poles, when reading the story of Yanko Goorall, were hurt by Conrad's reticence. Perłowski gave vent to their indignation when he wrote[128]:

225

The Polish reader puts the book away with a feeling of bitterness. What does this story really mean? In the soul of the author there is obviously some struggle: something draws him back to the country, yet something keeps him away from it. He would like to bury the past, but its visions pursue him.

Another Pole, Wacław Borowy, in his article "Did Conrad Describe a Polish Mountain Dweller?" expressed his discontent with Conrad's vagueness concerning the *góral*[129]. A third Pole, Witold Turno, also took part in the discussion[130]. What irritated the Poles so much was the fact that Conrad, against his better judgement, consistently represented his poor compatriot—and in a way his other self—as seen through strictly English eyes, with the corresponding distorting effect.

Since Yanko's story will be treated in the next chapter, not much more need to be said here. But it is interesting to note that, like Yanko, Conrad used to rave in Polish when in fever[131] and that at first his wife was scared when he was in a delirious condition.

Another camouflaged Polish story is "Il Conde." The title should, of course, be *Il Conte* for *Conde* is Spanish, while *Il* is Italian. Since Conrad himself spoke twice of a misspelling[132], and ordered that *Conte* be written for *Conde* in the Polish translation, the mistake should be corrected at the first opportunity.

Conrad got the story from a Polish gentleman, Count Szembek, whom he met at Capri, in the spring of 1905. The story itself was written towards the end of 1907 and published in *A Set of Six* (1908). Jean-Aubry, who gives this information (*LL*, II, 2 and 6), does not say whether this was the count's own adventure, but this is likely. In his story, Conrad is very secretive about the origin and name of "il conte." All we hear is the following—misleading—information:

> He told me [his married daughter's] name. It was that of an aristocratic family. She had a castle—in Bohemia, I think. This was as near as I ever came to ascertain his nationality. His own name, strangely enough, he never mentioned . . . he was a good European—he spoke four languages to my certain knowledge (*A Set of Six*, 272).

In fact, Conrad spoke Polish or French with Count

Szembek. Even in the story, the count seems to take the road to Poland, not Bohemia, traveling via Trieste and Vienna—the very route Conrad traveled when he returned from Italy to Cracow in 1873. The end of this "pathetic tale" (as Conrad called it) is very probably fictitious. For this elderly man, exchanging the sunny South for the Northern mists of his native country was tantamount to suicide. In the same way in *Victory*, Morrison's return to wet and damp Dorsetshire seals his fate. One may ask oneself whether this deadly effect of returning to one's native country after a very long absence has not a symbolic meaning with regard to Conrad himself.

The only frankly Polish tale published by Conrad is "Prince Roman." It was written in 1911, printed in the *Oxford and Cambridge Review*, then included in *Tales of Hearsay*. Here, Conrad finally did what Joseph Spiridion (Kliszczewski) had wanted him to do in 1896; he wrote a story telling the English about Poland's misery and grandeur.

Two elements contributed to the making of this story. At the age of seven, Konradek had met Prince Roman in person (in 1869, at his uncle's home in the Ukraine). The youngster, imbued with Grimm's and Krylov's fairy tales, had been astonished to meet a prince who was old and deaf instead of young and charming. As for the Prince's life story, Conrad took it from his uncle's *Memoirs* which he had received in 1901. He changed only one significant detail, thus making it a story of an involuntary betrayal. Conrad saw the events with the eyes of a poet and his narration stands in strange contrast to the matter-of-fact relation of his uncle. He also added the figure of the patriotic Jew, Yankel, which he took from Mickiewicz's *Pan Tadeusz*.[133]

In his *Memoirs*, Bobrowski mentions Prince Roman no less than twelve times.[134] Using his imagination and availing himself of his poetic license, Conrad draws a wonderful picture of Prince Roman's happy marriage and of the tragic early death of his wife. The Prince's momentous decision to join the insurgents is described in detail. Conrad also brings in his grandfather, Teodor, whom he describes as the Prince's nearest friend which in fact he was not. The inevitable sad end is described with great power: Instead of seeking asylum in Prussia, the Prince fights his way through to a Polish fortress, the last to fall before the Russian onslaught. Finally, he becomes a prisoner and is tried in much the same way as Apollo was tried in the Warsaw Citadel.[135]

Up to this point, the narrative follows the pattern of Apollo's trial. Then Roman's story, as told by Bobrowski, takes over. There is an obvious inconsistency (which Conrad felt and tried to explain) in the fact that the same men whom Conrad had just called the Prince's "enemies" now try to save him.[136]

We have said that *Prince Roman* is also the story of an involuntary betrayal. The Prince had been serving under an assumed name[137], but his real identity had come to be known. In fact, he had never intended to hide it, yet one of his friends believed that he had betrayed the Prince. The relevant passage in Bobrowski's *Memoirs* reads as follows:

> Florian Rzewuski lived under the most terrible self-reproach that he had given away the real name of his contemporary and childhood friend Prince Roman Sanguszko, when the latter had been arrested during the rising of 1831 . . . Prince Roman returned [from exile] only in 1842, when Rzewuski already lived in Lithuania. He most categorically denied the version about a betrayal by Rzewuski (so he told me himself in 1869), explaining the whole incident very simply. When, with a number of other prisoners, he was brought into the quarters where Rzewuski was serving as a clerk, the latter, at the sight of the Prince, got so upset that he exclaimed, "Roman, that's you!" But this could not be a betrayal, since Prince Roman's co-prisoners knew who he was. Nonetheless, Florian Rzewuski remained the rest of his life under this terrible self-accusation and it is quite possible that his entire later life was marred because of this. May the present statement be a relief to his memory! (I, 132)

In Conrad's version, the involuntary betrayal is taken for granted:

> The position of the fortress being central, new parties, captured in the open in the course of a thorough pacification, were being sent in frequently. Amongst such newcomers there happened to be a young man, a personal friend of the Prince from

his school days. He recognized him, and in the extremity of his dismay cried aloud: "My God! Roman, you here!"
It is said that years of life embittered by remorse paid for this momentary lack of self-control. All this happened in the main quadrangle of the citadel. The warning gesture of the Prince came too late. An officer of the gendarmes on guard had heard the exclamation. The incident appeared to him worth inquiring into. The investigation which followed was not very arduous because the Prince, asked categorically for his real name, owned up at once. (*Tales of Hearsay*, 49-50).

One of the most pathetic features of the case was the Czar's order that Prince Roman should walk all the way to Siberia chained to some criminals. Bobrowski's account is as follows:

Below, it was done with money—at the top with protection. The very great were perhaps in a worse position, for their estates invited confiscation, moreover their names were known to the emperor Nicholas, who had a good memory and personally confirmed the sentences involving the nobility. So, having confirmed Prince Roman Sanguszko's exile to Siberia, he thought that perhaps his parents might obtain from the authorities that he could travel by carriage—he therefore sent an express messenger with an order in his own handwriting that not the slightest indulgence be granted to him—and the Prince walked for about a year to the designed place, chained to a rod with criminals. (*Memoirs*, I, 30).

Conrad is less explicit:

He was condemned for life to Siberian mines. Emperor Nicholas, who always took personal cognizance of all sentences on Polish nobility, wrote with his own hand in the margin: "The authorities are severely warned to take care that this convict walks in chains like any other criminal every step of the way." (*Tales of Hearsay*, 53)

The end of *Prince Roman* is also based on Bobrowski's *Memoirs*:

[Prince Roman asked Bobrowski to recommend a certain Zmijowski to Roman's son-in-law Count Alfred Potocki] stating that my recommendation would be more successful—"for you see, they have the opinion that I do not know much about people" the Prince told me. (II, 367).

Conrad rendered his uncle's statement thus:

They moved on and forgot that little boy . . . They moved very slowly across the room. Before reaching the other door the Prince stopped, and I heard him—I seem to hear him now—saying: "I wish you would write to Vienna about filling up that post. He's a most deserving fellow—and your recommendation would be decisive."
My uncle's face turned to him expressed genuine wonder. It said as plainly as any speech could say: What better recommendation than a father's can be needed? The Prince was quick at reading expressions. Again he spoke with the toneless accent of a man who has not heard his own voice for years, for whom the soundless world is like an abode of silent shades.
And to this day I remember the very words: "I ask you because, you see, my daughter and my son-in-law don't believe me to be a good judge of men. They think that I let myself be guided too much by mere sentiment." (*Tales of Hearsay*, 54-55)

Conrad's story deviates from the facts in some other respects. Roman's wife died eighteen months after her marriage, not when her daughter was two. And Konradek was not eight but eleven years old when he met the Prince at Bobrowski's mansion. The Prince's exile lasted 14 years, not 24 as in Conrad's story. Finally, it must be pointed out that in all current editions two Latin words are misprinted: *patride* should be *patriae* (42), and *cripit verba dolor* should read *eripit verba dolor* (43). In the first printing, in the *Oxford and Cambridge Review*, these words were rendered correctly.

In "Prince Roman" Conrad undoubtedly intended to set up a memorial to his parents and to all fighters for Poland's freedom. But it is noteworthy that even here he suppressed the Polish surname.

It is a sad story dealing with people dead and gone,

a wreath laid upon the tomb of Poland's past greatness and glory. It was again Jan Peplowski who expressed the feelings of many Poles when he said, "He remembers her [Poland] with the deep feeling one has for a dear departed one. It is a love without obligations. Conrad most obviously does not believe in the future of Poland, while hating her oppressors from the depth of his heart."[138]

Obviously, it was not easy to satisfy both the English public and the Poles at the same time. Yet Conrad, for the first time in his writing career, had openly written a Polish story and he had found these words for his nation: ". . . that nationality not so much alive as surviving, which persists in thinking, breathing, speaking, hoping, and suffering in its grave, railed by the million of bayonets and triple-sealed with the seals of three great empires." (29) He made his narrator (the man, who, as a boy had met Prince Roman at his uncle's house) talk of Poland as "that country which demands to be loved as no other country has ever been loved." This would have been fine, if he had not continued, ". . . loved with the mournful affection one bears to the unforgotten dead and with the unextinguishable fire of a hopeless passion which only a living, breathing, warm ideal can kindle in our breast for our pride, for our weariness, for our exultation, for our undoing." (51) One wonders whether Conrad would have written these lines had he known that less than ten years later Poland would be independent.

The Sisters

A fragment by Conrad also belongs here, namely, *The Sisters*. Published privately in America in only 926 copies, it was translated into Polish and published first in the periodical *Creativity*, 1964, No. 6, and in book form in 1967 by the Polish State Publishing Institute in Warsaw. In 1968, Mursia in Milan published another English edition of 950 copies, with a preface by Ford M. Hueffer). The Poles, on the other hand, have published 10,000 copies—a lot for a country of 30 million. Wit Tarnawski explains this as follows in his preface:

> It is as if *The Sisters* had only waited for a Polish translation. The fragment belongs more to Polish than to English literature. This not only because of

the reflection of his family heritage unique in Conrad (excepting "Prince Roman") but also because of its emotional involvement, its stress on immaterial values and its vivid romantic undertones. When working at this translation, I had at times the impression of translating a text transposed into English back into the original. Who can know whether the feeling that he was writing for a deaf·public [the English] was not one of the reasons why Conrad finally gave up writing *The Sisters*?

Indeed, had *The Sisters* been completed, we would have had a strongly autobiographical book. The hero, Stephen (Stefan), comes from the Ukraine. Having gone abroad, he finds he cannot return any more. Not that he is enthusiastic about the West! He is "lonely" and "without a star." Instead of finding the truth, he sees that the West has nothing to offer but "vociferations of idle fanatics" and "disconnected mutterings." He tries to find the answer in the master works of art galleries from Rome to Cologne, "The Western life captivated him by the amplitude of its complicated surface, horrified him by the interior jumble of its variegated littleness." The sentence is not only remarkable because of its obviously autobiographical contents, but also because it sounds like a too literal translation from a Polish author of the last century.

Stephen's father, a freed peasant become prosperous, could never understand why his oldest son wanted to become an artist-painter, nor why he decided to emigrate. Actually, the son is disappointed by the West. His reaction reminds us of Apollo's poem concerning falsehood quoted by us on page 9:   "He wanted to shout at immortal achievements, 'You have no heart.' To his lofty aspirations he said, 'You have no conscience.' To Beauty, 'Thou art a lie!' To Inspiration, 'Go!' . . ." (51)

The parents die, and letters reach him from the Ukraine, begging him to return. Despite real nostalgia, he stays in the West. The ghosts of the past visit him in his daydreams. Like Jim, he suddenly disappears, without taking leave from anyone. He turns up at the sea shore, then in Paris where he had once lived with a Bohemian crowd of artists. He avoids them completely and lives a lonely, joyless life, trying to paint a little.

Some call him a "dreamer," for others he is a fool. We are reminded of Conrad's French years.

Now the story switches to the "sisters," Rita and Teresa, daughters of a mountain peasant (not from Poland but from the Pyrenees) who is shot in a smuggling expedition. Rita is adopted by an uncle residing in Paris, but soon lives with a French family who give her a good education. She has to visit her uncle José and his awful wife from time to time. As she grows up she becomes aware that her uncle has deeper feelings for her than he should have. At this point the fragment ends.

The most beautiful, and at the same time, the most Polish passages in *The Sisters* describe Stephen's father and his family, the Ukrainian landscape, and the young emigrant's feelings towards the West, whose "jumble" of values he cannot accept. In "Prince Roman," too, we have a few sentences about the landscape, but in *The Sisters*, the landscape is described as it unfolds itself when one travels for days along a winding and dusty Ukrainian road. Only someone who loved this country could describe it with such inner warmth. Of course, Mickiewicz had given the precedent. It is remarkable that Conrad should dare to do the same thing in English at the beginning of his writing career. Stephen's nostalgia—mixed with remorse but counterbalanced by the stubborn resolution never to return home again, but rather to become somebody abroad—probably reflect Conrad's own feelings.

We know that it was Edward Garnett who persuaded Conrad to drop *The Sisters* in favor of some better selling sea story—namely *The Nigger*. Ford Madox Ford, who later edited the fragment of *The Sisters* blamed Garnett for his interference. Yet, it is doubtful whether *The Sisters* would have become a masterpiece. The subject—a story of incest and murder—could well have defeated the author.

X.

The English Shock

For three and a half years, young Conrad lived in Marseilles. During this time, he made two journeys to the West Indies, each of five to six months duration. The first voyage was on the four hundred ton barque, *Mont Blanc*, where he was listed as an apprentice (which meant that he was not paid); the second on the more elegant, but hardly bigger *St. Antoine*, where he was listed as a steward and got a small pay. The captain of the *St. Antoine*, Mr. Escarras, liked him very much and Conrad wanted to make a third journey with him, but apparently was prevented from doing so by some illness. The ship sailed without him, but it was understood that Conrad would make his naval apprenticeship on her after her return. The *St. Antoine* then was to make a journey around the world, not in eighty days, but in one year and a half, a prospect that fired even Bobrowski's sluggish imagination. Conrad made his uncle believe that he needed 3000 French francs in order to prepare for that voyage; in fact, the young man, in the best Nałęcz manner, invested the money in the Tremolino adventure, hoping to make enormous profits smuggling arms to Spain. After the shipwreck of that boat, Conrad was back in Marseilles, *sans le sou*, but borrowing freely from different friends to bridge the gap until more money would be forthcoming from Poland and until the voyage around the world would begin. The *St. Antoine*, under captain Escarras, was to leave in February 1887. Conrad's name was on the list of the crew members. Almost at the last moment, the French naval authorities, considering Conrad a draft dodger from Russia,[139] prevented him from joining the ship, and thus radically altered his life. Had he been able to go, he would most probably never have written a book in the English language.

After another financial debacle with a suicidal attempt[140], straightened out by his uncle, no other course was left open but to serve on the first British ship that came along. It happened to be the *Mavis*, bound for a Russian port—the last country Conrad really wanted to see, and where he did not dare to put foot on shore. From Russia, the vessel brought him straight to Lowestoft, England.

We do not know what made Conrad leave this vessel to be stranded in a country where he knew absolutely nobody. In a letter to his uncle, he explained that he did not have the money to pay the premium, but Bobrowski doubted this, for Conrad also mentioned that he had quarrelled with the captain.

Conrad was twenty. He knew only a few words of English. He had some money left which he used to travel to London from where he wrote his uncle for help. In the meantime, he had to live, so after three weeks he took a job on a coaster, making six voyages from Lowestoft to Newcastle and back. Bobrowski commented on Conrad's behavior in the following words: "Having collected your allowance [$250] from Mr. Fecht you set off on an English ship for Lowestoft and there again you committed another absurdity—having quarrelled with the Captain, which you might have been justified in doing, you went to London and there squandered prematurely the remainder of your allowance." Undisturbed by his uncle's admonitions, Conrad once more went from Lowestoft to London, pinning his hope on a cutting from a newspaper containing one address. In London, he collected £25 from his uncle and set out to find a job. He was more lucky than he deserved, for he got a berth on the *Duke of Sutherland* sailing for Australia. One year later he was back. Common sense, backed by Bobrowski wisdom, would have demanded that he stay with the vessel, but the Nałęcz blood decided otherwise. From October 1879 to the end of August 1880, with the exception of a six-week voyage to the Mediterranean on the *Europa*, the young sailor lived in London.

We have seen that Conrad quarrelled with the captain of his first English ship. With the commander of the *Europa*, he must have had violent rows. This is at least the reason he gave to Bobrowski for not staying on his fourth English ship. However, there was one redeeming

feature during this long period of unemployment: in
June 1880 Conrad passed his examination as second
mate. But to do this, it was hardly necessary to sit
around in London a full half year. It was only on 21
August 1880 that Conrad got his first berth as second
mate. He sailed to Australia and back on the *Loch Etive*,
a voyage lasting ¾ of a year. Again common sense
would have demanded he stay on, but the Nałęcz blood
was stronger. From April to September 1881, he was
again unemployed. He finally had to accept a berth on a
miserable little barque called *Palestine*, bound for
Bangkok with a cargo of coal. The vessel was hardly
seaworthy and for a full nine months was in repair at
Falmouth, before she could leave. Finally well on her
way, the barque caught fire néar Java and sank. To this
misfortune we owe one of Conrad's best short stories,
"Youth."

One may wonder what Conrad was doing in London and Falmouth during his long months of unemployment. He probably lived in sailor's homes or in
cheap boarding houses. Apart from seamen and teamak-
ing and money-cashing landladies, he hardly knew anyone. He spent a three-months-salary from the *Palestine*
in one day in London.

England must have been quite a shock to Conrad.
In Marseilles, he had felt thoroughly at home, even to
the point of acquiring the provençal accent. He had
been accepted by everyone, had easy access to the homes
of well-to-do people, had been popular. The mentality
of the *méridionaux* is very much akin to that of the Poles:
easygoing, very sociable, extremely hospitable. They are
often good story tellers, and very generous both in borrowing and in lending. On board the *St. Antoine*, his
polished manners had earned him the nickname, "The
Count." He was always very conscious of the fact that he
was a descendant of the Polish landed gentry.

England was neither tolerant nor generous towards
foreigners. Stranded on the quay of Lowestoft, Conrad
was a nobody. Not knowing the language and trying to
supplement his failing speech with violent gestures, he
did not appear as a count, but as a Dago. When he told
his good Polish name to somebody, they would not say:
"*Enchanté de faire votre connaissance*," but: "What's that?"
In Marseilles, Conrad had letters of introduction to at
least two well-known people; in England, he knew no-

body. As a matter of fact, he had so little to recommend him that in our more enlightened age of immigration laws he most certainly would have been turned away.

During his long stays ashore, Conrad, for a number of years, made no friends. He probably was never invited to an English home until 1885 (seven years after his arrival in Lowestoft) and this home, typically enough, was the home of a Pole living in Cardiff. He made two more visits there, in 1889 and 1895. In the course of years, he also acquired some English friends: Mr. Krieger and Captain Hope, who put him on the track of the gold mining speculation. It was only after he had had *Almayer's Folly* accepted, and when he was married and could practice Polish hospitality, that the number of his friends grew.

During his whole life, Conrad kept a strong foreign accent. His manners also remained quite Polish; Hueffer writes that "he was Oriental even to his grocer," oriental to the point of expecting this man to give him several months—if not years—credit. Everyone noticed Conrad's polished manners. In the East, he got the nickname "Russian Count." Jessie Conrad has described his outlandish ways in her *Joseph Conrad and His Circle*.

Conrad always tried to live like a Polish country squire. Despite the fact that he was constantly hard up (to the point of asking for advances and loans of £20 or £50), he always needed a house in the country, a horse and carriage, a maid, and a coachman who doubled as a gardener. True, all these people were paid very little, but it all added up. For his six-month (!) honeymoon, he rented a house, complete with a maid, and a sailing yacht which had to be looked after by a local man. This happened at the very moment when he lost most of his inheritance in his South African speculation. He was one of the first in Kent to have an automobile and a chauffeur[141]. He always traveled first class by train.

Once, when his older boy ran a temperature, he wired for a nurse. When his wife was due for her first operation, he invited twenty people for dinner the evening before, regardless of the fact that he was already heavily in debt. Perhaps the most extravagant feat was the journey to Capri, in 1905, which Conrad himself later called "a mad thing really."[142] He was accompanied by his wife (who was unable to walk), the little boy, and a nurse. Twice Mrs. Conrad had to be carried from shore to ship and vice-versa. On the train, they had a first class compartment for themselves. It must have been a pretty nerve-wrecking affair, and costly too, especially as these holidays produced little more than the short story "Il Conde." Many other instances of Conrad's extravagance could be mentioned. If his books had not sold extremely well beginning in 1914 (a fact he could not possibly foresee), he would have died heavily in debt. One may well say that his decision to invest everything in his yet unknown writing talent was the most daring speculation of his life—and the only successful one.

In Conrad's works, we find many reflections of his English shock. Curiously enough, this aspect of his writings has never received much attention.

From his often one-sided and extremely personal remarks, we can deduce that it was the following traits he disliked most in the English character: 1. Snobbery of any kind, including the feeling of national superiority. 2. Intolerance towards the "different." 3. A deplorable lack of imagination. 4. The pompous role played by trade and commerce on the English scene, and the gullibility of the people. 5. Imperialism and colonialism. 6. Sentimentalism.

Already in "Amy Foster" (published in 1901), Conrad, to use the Freudian term, "abreacted" his feelings towards the English. This is the story of a Polish emigrant who, on his way from Germany to America, becomes the only survivor in a shipwreck off England's coast. He swims ashore and faces a reality as grim as if he had landed amid savages. Apart from the girl Amy Foster (who is a bizarre person), everybody rejects him for no other reason than that he is too different and cannot communicate with them. What the author actually describes is an experiment—throwing an illiterate Polish peasant into the test tube of an average English country village to see what happens. The utter bewilderment and deadly anxiety of the poor man are well depicted. He is in every way different from the people around him, for, while these are "uncouth in body and as leaden of gait as if their very hearts were loaded with chains," he is "lithe, supple and strong-limbed, straight like a pine[143], with something striving upwards in his appearance as though the heart within him had been buoyant . . . the soles of his feet did not seem . . . to touch the dust of the road." "He vaulted over the stiles, paced 'along these slopes with a long elastic stride that made him noticeable at a great distance, and had lustrous black eyes." (111) This description, of course, would just as well apply to a representative of the Latin races, a *méridional* or an Italian, for instance. And the same would also be true of his language which is described as sounding very fierce and passionate.

After his arrival on English soil, Yanko is not exactly well received. The milkman hits him across the face with the whip to make him go away. The schoolmistress considers him a tramp and calls him a "horrid-looking" man who frightens her schoolchildren. Others talk of a madman and lock him up without noticing that he is almost dying of hunger and thirst. He is "odious" to the countryside. Finally, a man called Swaffer, moved by a curious weakness for things outlandish and bizarre, gives him food and work. Yanko tries to be friendly; he is rejected. When he wants to entertain them by dancing for them at the village inn, he is thrown out. Only Amy seems to understand him, so he marries her. They have a boy to whom Yanko speaks in Polish. He looks forward to the day when little Johnny will be able to speak to him in his own language. But fate wills it otherwise. Yanko falls very ill (either with pneumonia or tuberculosis), and in his fever utters strange sounds which frighten his wife. When he demands water, she runs away with the child as if he were a madman. He runs after her and dies. Thereafter, Amy Foster never even mentions him. Johnny grows up oblivious of his father. The village is at peace again. Father Foster expresses the general feeling when he says, "I don't know that it isn't for the best."

In this tale, told by the village doctor, Conrad tries to be fair to both sides. But one feels that his real sympathy goes to his countryman, Yanko, who, having been thrust in an English environment against his will, fails to adjust. The village reacts to his presence as the human flesh does to a foreign body: irritation, heat, and if possible, rejection. Yanko is being punished for being ignorant of the language and the conventions of the country.

But there is more. Conrad does everything to stress the incredible lack of imagination of the population, including the doctor. There had been a fierce gale and a shipwreck nearby, with hundreds of corpses washed ashore; yet "for days, nay, for weeks—it didn't enter our heads that we had amongst us the only living soul that had escaped from that disaster." (128) Yanko's Polish speech is taken as the speech of a lunatic, for it is "senseless." As always when Conrad wants to make a point, he really piles it on. A man called Smith is "not imaginative enough to ask himself whether the man might not be perishing with cold and hunger," for he "had room in his brain only for that idea of lunacy." (121) Some think that Yanko is a "Hindoo." (126) Dr. Kennedy himself believes that he might a "Basque." Everything he does is "a cause of scorn and offense to the inhabitants of the village," (132) some call him a "Jack-in-the-box." (137) The ladies of the rectory try to wean him from his habit of crossing himself before meals. Even his wife does not understand him. Her attachment seems to be a neurotic one and it breaks apart when he appears to talk irrationally in his fever. In short, no one seems to have enough imagination or intuition to understand the needs of this stranger.

Of course, Yanko is not Conrad, but it is safe to maintain that young Conrad, after his arrival in England and for many years afterwards, must have run into that insular attitude of the average Englishman who considers every foreigner as funny and interior, if not a downright freak. As late as 1907, some journalist called him "a man without country and language"![144] Coming from a very good family, he must have experienced quite a shock to meet this attitude, for neither in Poland nor in the South of France is a foreigner *eo ipso* considered inferior—rather the opposite. The pathetic tale, "Amy Foster," may be considered as the expression of this shock: one has the feeling that Conrad wants to hold up a mirror to the average self-satisfied unimaginative Englishman to try and make him "see" what the author experienced.

Yanko is another of Conrad's characters whose surnames remain unknown. It is true that the Rector marries him as *Yanko Goorall*, but, as the author points out, the second name only means "mountain dweller" (Polish *góral*, the name given to the peasants living in the Tatra mountains south of Cracow). Was Conrad afraid that an authentic Polish name might be distorted, as his own so often had been disfigured?

There is, in Conrad's works, one case where a family name is distorted "by the English" much in the same way as *nuostro uomo* becomes *Nostromo* in Captain Mitchell's pronunciation. In the tale "Freya of the Seven Isles" (published in 1912), the Danish name of Freya's father is anglicized. "Remember old Nelson! Certainly. And to begin with, his name was not Nelson. The Englishmen in the Archipelago called him Nelson because it was more convenient, I suppose, and he never protested. It would have been mere pedantry. The true form of the name was Nielsen." (*'Twixt Land and Sea Tales*, 147)

But despite the remark concerning pedantry, Conrad cannot help correcting the Englishmen's error not less than sixteen times in the course of the story by using the term "Nelson (or Nielsen)", and once he actually writes "Nielsen." It is difficult not to see in this obsessively repeated detail a subtle revenge for the constant and irritating distortion of Conrad's own honorable family name at the hands of the English.

The arbitrariness of English spelling and pronunciation is more than once alluded to in Conrad's works. Thus, at the beginning of "Youth" (3) he writes: "Marlow (at least that is how he spelt his name)"—a remark a storyteller would hardly make. The following remark, in the same book, would easily be made by a Frenchman, but hardly by an Englishman: [The mate's] "name was Mahon, but he insisted that it should be pronounced Mann" (5). The *Judea* belongs "to a man Wilmer, Wilcox—some name like that" (5). In *Heart of Darkness*, Marlow finds a book in an abandoned hut, written by "a man Tower, Towson—some such name" (99). Finally, in *The Secret Sharer*, there is an uncertainty about the name Archbold.

In a few instances, Conrad wanted to make sure a name was not distorted but pronounced correctly; thus, he wrote *Yanko Goorall* for the Polish *Janko Góral*, or *Don Pépé* (in *Nostromo*) for the Spanish *Don Pepe*.

The fear of having a name distorted even guided Conrad in the choice of his first boy's Christian name. As he told his aunt, Mrs. Aniela Zagórska, in a letter dated 21 January 1898, he decided that the child should have an Anglo-Saxon as well as a Slavonic name. But the latter gave him trouble, for good Polish names such as "Władysław, Bogusław, Wienczysław and similar ones" could "not be pronounced by the English." So finally he decided to call him *Borys*. Unfortunately, the only thing

Polish about this name is the *y* (the Russians spell it *Boris*) and, as Miss Aniela Zagórska remarked[145], the name is only exceptionally used in Poland, and Conrad's choice "led to a great many misunderstandings." Since in Poland the choice of a first name is practically a confession of political faith (as we have already seen regarding the name Conrad), "many [Poles] believed that Conrad was a russophile!"

Jean-Aubry, in his "definitive biography of Joseph Conrad," *The Sea Dreamer*, has listed all the distortions of Conrad's honest Polish surname, as found on his certificates from the different English ships he served on (288-289): Kokenowski, Koreinowski, Korzen, Kerzeniowski, Korzewienski, Kokeniokth, Korzniowskir, Korzewowin (on the *Torrens!*). On the last ship, the *Adowa*, Conrad had given up and listed his name simply as Joseph Conrad. To the librarian at Cracow's Jagiellonian Library, Józef Korzeniowski Conrad explained already in February 1901 that he had dropped his Polish surname because he could not stand hearing it distorted by the English.

The "Gentleman" Complex

Conrad came from a distinguished family of landowning gentry and had a good formation, especially in his native language, but also in French. As an adult, he had very polite manners and was very conscientious about his appearance. He developed a strong sense of duty, justice, and honor. Yet, he must have come across Englishmen who told him bluntly that to be a *real* gentleman one must be born and raised in England, but also have happened to Conrad not only because it happens to every educated foreigner living in England, but also because the reflection of this experience can be clearly seen in some of Conrad's works.

The term "gentleman" is used in seven works of Conrad. It occurs three times in *The Rescue*. Once it is applied to Shaw's father ("the old gentleman," 22), then to Prince Hassim (138). Finally we meet the term in that crucial passage written in 1918, which we already quoted in chapter IV.

In *Suspense*, an English doctor, speaking of the noisy British naval officers seated in an Italian inn makes this remark: "All heroes, no doubt, but not a single gentleman." (58) Obviously, an English gentleman can be recognized at one glance!

In his short story, "Il Conde," the (Polish) count is described as "a fairly intelligent man of the world, a perfectly unaffected gentleman." (*A Set of Six*, 269)

In four books, however, Conrad uses the term "gentleman" in an ironic sense, and in the short story "The Return" he draws the caricature of another English gentleman, Alan Harvey.

In *The Nigger of the 'Narcissus,'* Conrad had first brought up the subject of the gentleman in a jocular way:

> By the foremast a few discussed in a circle the characteristics of a gentleman. One said: "It's money as does it." Another maintained: "No, it's the way they speak." Lame Knowles . . . explained craftily that "he had seen some of their pants." The backsides of them—he had observed—were thinner than paper from constant sitting down in offices, yet otherwise they looked first-rate and would last for years. It was all appearance. "It was," he said, "bloomin easy to be a gentleman when you had a clean job for life" . . . From a distance Charley screamed at the ring: "I know about gentlemen more'n any of you. I've been intermit with 'em— I've blacked their boots."
>
> (32-33).

In *Lord Jim* we meet "gentleman" Brown whom we do not have to describe again. In *The Shadow Line*, another self-styled gentleman bears the name of Hamilton. He hardly condescends to speak, except to say that "the food [is] not fit to be set before a gentleman." (15) This distinguished person has not been working for months, nor has he paid his bills at the officer's home. He is in no hurry to get a job, for "they will be glad enough to get a gentleman, I imagine." (17) In fact our gentleman is a "fool . . . an overbearing, impudent loafer."

But it is in *Victory* that Conrad most vehemently exposes that typical English snobbery into which he must have run more than once. He makes Mr. Jones' henchman Ricardo say, "A foreigner can't be expected to know any better. I am an Englishman and I know a gentleman at sight. I should know one drunk, in the

gutter, in jail, under the gallows. There's a something . . . no use me trying to tell you. You ain't an Englishman; and if you were, you wouldn't need to be
told." (125) Later, Ricardo describes Mr. Jones, the
"gentleman," in this way: "Up he comes, and in his
quiet, tired way of speaking—you can tell a gentleman
by that as much as by anything else almost . . ." (128)
Ricardo then assures us that "with a gentleman you
know at once where you are." (132) Again and again,
Conrad comes back to the subject, and always in the
same ironic vein. Later, Ricardo says, "You can't tell how
a gentleman takes that sort of thing. They don't lose
their temper. It's bad form . . . Ferocity ain't good form
either." (136) Then Ricardo elaborates: "The governor
[Jones] hadn't turned a hair. That's where a gentleman
has the pull of you. He don't get excited. No gentleman
does—or hardly ever." This passage will be best understood if we remember that Conrad himself was a very
excitable person easily subject to fits of anger. (He did
his best to keep his temper, though, and it is quite possible that his attacks of gout were a substitute for those
fits of temper which he suppressed). In another passage,
Ricardo says: "A dog knows a gentleman—any dog. It's
only some foreigners that don't know; and nothing can
teach them either." And: "That's another thing you can
tell a gentleman by—his freakishness. A gentleman ain't
accountable to nobody, any more than a tramp on the
roads." (150)

Another caricature of a gentleman is Alvan Hervey,
the husband in "The Return" (*Tales of Unrest*). There is
so much sarcasm heaped upon this fine product of English social conventions that one strongly suspects Conrad wanted to expose this type of Englishman. As usual,
Conrad cannot stop underlining the shallowness and the
hollowness of the Alvan Herveys:

> [The bride] strode like a grenadier, was strong and
> upright like an obelisk, had a beautiful face, a can-
> did brow, pure eyes, and not a thought of her own
> in her head. He surrendered quickly to all those
> charms. (*Tales of Unrest*, 120).
> [The proposal]. He was very dull and solemn about
> it—for no earthly reason, unless to conceal his
> feelings—which is an eminently proper thing to do.
> (120)

[Society]. After their marriage they busied themselves, with marked success, in enlarging the circle
of their acquaintance . . . they moved in their en-
larged world amongst perfectly delightful men and
women who feared emotion, enthusiasm, or failure,
more than fire, war, or mortal disease; who tolerated only the commonest formulas of commonest
thoughts, and recognized only profitable facts. It
was an extremely charming sphere, the abode of all
virtues, where nothing is realized and where all joys
and sorrows are cautiously toned down into plea-
sures and annoyances. In that serene region, then,
where noble sentiments are cultivated in sufficient
profusion to conceal the pitiless materialism of
thoughts and aspirations Alvan Hervey and his wife
spent five years of prudent bliss unclouded by any
doubt as to the moral propriety of their existence.
She, to give her individuality fair play, took up all
manner of philanthropic work and became a
member of various rescuing and reforming societies
patronized or presided over by ladies of title. (120-
121)

As for the husband, he takes over "a moribund society paper." This publication is "semi-political" and
"scandalous," but "redeemed by extreme dullness";
moreover, "it contained no new thought," had "never by
any chance . . . a flash of wit, satire or indignation" and,
therefore, is judged by him to be entirely "respectable."
This all the more so when it brought pecuniary awards:
"Afterwards, when it paid, he promptly perceived that
upon the whole it was a virtuous undertaking." (121)
During five prosperous years, the Herveys lived side
by side, "but were no more capable of real intimacy than
two animals feeding at the same manger, under the
same roof, in a luxurious stable." (122) "They skimmed
over the surface of life hand in hand, in a pure and
frosty atmosphere . . . disdainfully ignoring the hidden
stream, the stream restless and dark; the stream of life,
profound and unfrozen" (123)—a typically Conradian
passage.
Unlike Conrad, Alvan Hervey makes restrained and
rare gestures (124), he "could be trusted to do nothing
individual, original or startling—nothing unforeseen and
nothing improper." (125) Under these circumstances,
any "odd action" was "essentially an indecent thing in it-

self." (125) Precisely such an action takes place. Conrad, the son of a passionate race and of a passionate patriot, then makes this ironical comment: "Passion is the unpardonable and secret infamy of our hearts, a thing to curse, to hide and to deny; a shameless and forlorn thing that tramples upon the smiling promises, that tears off the placid mask, that strips the body of life." (130) Owing to the unconventional act of his wife, "he ceased to be a member of society with a position, a career, and a name attached to all this, like the descriptive label of some complicated compound." (133-134) Stripped of his conventional reputation, "he was a simple human being removed from the delightful world of crescents and squares. He stood alone, naked and afraid, like the first man on the first day of evil." (134) He would have wept now "if it had not been for his conviction that men do not weep. Foreigners do; they also kill sometimes in such circumstances." (135) Never does Alvan Hervey lose his English composure; "his aspect, at any rate, would let no one into the secret of his pain," (136) for "self-restraint is everything in life . . . it's happiness, it's dignity . . . it's everything." (155) People like Hervey are the high priests of English society, "the severe guardians of formulas, of rites, of the pure ceremonial concealing the black doubts of life." (156) It was a "profitable persuasion" reigning over "the crowd of houses outside, all the flimsy and inscrutable graves of the living, with their doors numbered like the doors of prison cells, and as impenetrable as the granite of tombstones." (156)

Conrad also exposes the collective nature of Hervey's conscience: "Nothing that outrages received beliefs can be right. Your conscience tells you that. They are received beliefs because they are the best, the noblest, the only possible." (157) He admonishes his repentant wife by telling her "I'll have no scandal in my life . . . for a scandal amongst people of our position is disastrous for the morality—a fatal influence . . . upon the general tone of the class . . . the most important . . . in the community." (163-164) He believes in the "ugliness" of certain truths and in the necessity of keeping them "out of daily life by unremitting care for appearances." (167)

But finally Hervey's *persona* breaks down. He experiences "divine wisdom," a "revelation" that conventional "morality is not a method of happiness," that "nothing of what he knew mattered in the least," it was all "a question of truth or falsehood—it was a question of life and death." (183) Not being able to stand his former way of life any more, finding himself in a boundary situation, he leaves the house, never to return.

Conrad, who had the great "power of picturesque exaggeration" (Jessie Conrad), loved to depict English unimaginativeness. Most of his English captains lack imagination. Apart from those who are mentally sick (as the late captain in *The Shadow Line*), they are a placid lot, abiding by the rules of navigation, acting with a strong sense of duty: Captain Mitchell in *Nostromo*, Captain Whalley in "The End of the Tether," Captain Anthony in *Chance*, Captain Davidson in *Victory* etc., but above all, Captain MacWhirr of the steamer *Nan-Shan* ("Typhoon").MacWhirr's lack of imagination which prevents him from circumventing a typhoon stands out because he finds himself in a situation which would call for a little imagination. He has the defect of his virtues and vice versa: his absence of imagination makes for stolidity and stubborn courage which, while it cannot imagine the worst before it comes, can stand it once it is there. The only touch of imagination he experienced in his life was at the age of eighteen when he decided to run away to sea. Conrad perpetually comes back to this point: MacWhirr, "having just enough imagination to carry him through each successive day, and no more . . . was tranquilly sure of himself." It was "as impossible for him to take a flight of fancy as it would be for a watchmaker to put together a chronometer with nothing except a two-pound hammer and a whip-saw in the way of tools." (4) His reaction to an extraordinary fall of the barometer is typical: "The fall . . . was of a nature ominously prophetic; but the red face of the man betrayed no . . . inward disturbance. Omens were as nothing to him, and he was unable to discover the message of a prophecy till the fulfillment had brought it home to his very door." (6) All he can think of is of "some dirty weather knocking about," for to him "the view of a distant eventuality could appeal no more than the beauty of a wide landscape to a purblind tourist." (8) MacWhirr's honesty "had the very obviousness of a lump of clay." (16) He is "against the use of images in speech" because he always tends to take them literally. (25) Owing to his absence of imagination, he cannot understand the theory of storms (32) and speaks contemptuously of what other captains call "dodging the storm." This is his opinion: "A gale is a gale . . . a full-powered steamship has got to face it . . . with none of what old Captain Wilson . . . calls 'storm strategy.' The other day ashore I heard him hold forth about it to a lot of shipmasters who came in and sat at a table next to mine. It seemed to me the greatest nonsense. He was telling them how he outmanoeuvred, I think he said, a terrific gale, so that it never came nearer than fifty miles to him. A neat piece of headwork he called it. How he knew there was a terrific gale fifty miles off beats me altogether. It was like listening to a crazy man." (34-35) During the storm, Captain MacWhirr sends several men down to find out what happened to the passengers in the 'tween deck without realizing that "if most of them [the passengers] hadn't been half dead with seasickness and fright" not one of these crewmen "would have come out . . . alive." (81) Even while the storm is on, the captain does not think that some storm strategy, such as described in books, might have been useful: "These books are only good to muddle your head and make you jumpy." (87) and "we must trust her to go through it and come out on the other side. That's plain and straight. There's no room for Captain Wilson's storm strategy here." (88)

The ship finally makes it to port. MacWhirr writes a letter to his wife telling her about his latest experience. He is not the only unimaginative person. His wife does not grasp the meaning of her husband's cautious statements and only yawns. Lack of imagination can be bliss! *Gorze ot uma!*

"Typhoon" is a story of a small steamer going right through the centre of a typhoon because her captain had not enough imagination to foresee what was going to happen. The story was terminated in January 1901, and published together with "Amy Foster" in the same year. captain in "A Smile of Fortune" has a narrow escape). 1918, a ship called *Great Britain*, under the command of a political MacWhirr went exactly through the centre of a storm (which could have been foreseen) much in the same way as the *Nan-Shan* steamed through a typhoon. That was bad enough, but the incredible happened: the same lack of storm strategy was evident twenty-five years later. Had Conrad lived he would have probably repeated what he wrote on 1899 to Joseph Spiridion: "I am simply sick to see the blind and timid bungling of the man at the head of [foreign] affairs." (*LL*, I, 74)

That the similarity of MacWhirr and—say— Chamberlain is not far-fetched is borne out by Conrad's description of Sir Ethelred in *The Secret Agent*. This excellent functionary does not believe in knowledge and theory, but only in so-called experience. He is characterized as an unimaginative fellow who would like to see all his problems (and life) reduced to a sort of game with a few simple rules. He just cannot see the really relevant, still less is he able to foresee anything. His dullness is only matched by that of police inspector Heat who might have stepped out of a Sherlock Holmes book.

Captain MacWhirr, Captain Anthony, Sir Ethelred are all suffering from lack of imagination, but there is one character in Conrad's works who manages to beat them all: the English imperialist and capitalist, Mr. Travers. When he wants to emphasize, Conrad easily exaggerates beyond the limits of credibility. He describes Mr. Travers, the yacht-owner, as a conceited, hopeless blockhead who completely fails to understand anything and who never realizes that his life is hanging by a thread. Travers believes that Lingard is interfering needlessly in order to claim a huge amount of salvage money. He lets himself be saved without noticing that his rescue is dearly paid for by the betrayal of the people whom, as contemptuously as inaccurately, he calls "Moors" but who, in the eyes of Lingard (and of Conrad himself) must be worth more than he is. In fact, the Englishman owes his life only to the fact that Lingard is sentimentally attached to Mrs. Travers and in a moment of weakness promises her to save them *all*.

Conrad goes still further. Several times, in his books, people are severely punished for showing imagination once in their lives. The lesson seems to be: if you are born unimaginative, let imagination alone. One example is Amy Foster, of whom Dr. Kennedy says: "She is very passive. It's enough to look . . . to know the inertness of her mind—an inertness that one would think made it everlastingly safe from all the surprises of imagination. And yet which one of us is safe?"

There is de Barral in *Chance* whose career as a "financier" is wholly based on too much imagination, while the Fynes remain blissfully dull and unimaginative. To develop some sudden imagination, in Conrad, is almost tantamount to becoming the victim of illusions, an accident which often includes falling in love: Willems, Lingard, Captain Anthony, Amy Foster, Heyst. (The captain in *A Smile of Fortune* has a narrow escape). "Lord" Jim may also be mentioned among the victims of too much imagination, in contrast to his utterly unimaginative father, in contrast also to Marlow's English listeners whom this worthy teller of yarns once apostrophies thus: "I would be eloquent were I not afraid that you fellows had starved your imaginations to feed your bodies." (*Lord Jim*, 225)

In this connection we should also mention the English reluctance (or inability?) to think problems to their logical end. Decoud expresses this thought when he says of Charles Gould: "It's part of English solid sense not to think too much; to see only what may be of practical use at the moment." (*Nostromo*, 209) Decoud once explains that the lack of imagination and logic in the English is replaced by illusions (meaning: happy prejudices). With the exception of Marlow, most Englishmen in Conrad show these traits; not only most of his captains, the Fynes in *Chance*, the doctor in "Amy Foster," Mr. Travers in *The Rescue*, etc. Lack of logic, like lack of imagination, is bliss, but Conrad displays a particular determination to expose if not to destroy this artificial paradise by confronting his unsuspecting heroes with some facts of raw life. He places them in boundary situations where they stand face to face before the ultimate—a notion that does not exist for the Anglo-Saxon pragmatist and empiricist who believes in the law of averages and not in extremes.

Conrad as a Critic of the Anglo-Saxon Society

One of the most devastating and Apollo-like articles by Conrad was his essay "The Censor of Plays" (1907). The venerable English institution is described as "outandish," as "a memorial to our forefathers' mental aberration," as "a monster . . . hatched in Pekin" and probably "come to us by way of Moscow." (*Notes on Life and Letters*, 80) The un-English virulence of Conrad's attack horrified Conrad's friends all the more as it was most unfair to the distinguished gentleman who held the office, and whom Conrad accused of stifling artistic creativity! The attack could only do harm.

Conrad never hid his sympathies or antipathies. He expressed his political and social convictions forcefully.

Like his father, he was an aristocrat at heart who did not believe in any automatic virtues of democratic institutions, nor in equality, but rather in the personal merit of the creative individual. At the same time (again like his father), he had a special sympathy for the humble and a strong distrust for the rich and powerful of this earth. Like many who were brought up under financial strain and for many years had to fight hard for a living, he often showed the greatest contempt for those who struck it rich, whether by personal merit or by luck. The sarcasm with which Conrad describes old Hudig, the ship-chandler, the financier Holroyd (*Nostromo*), Charles Gould, Mr. Travers the millionaire and yacht-owner (*The Rescue*), and those "whom an unerring providence enables to live in mansions" (*Lord Jim*, 5), is typical. Those who work hard and do their duty to the utmost never get anywhere: Nostromo (until he steals the silver), Captain Whalley, Captain Anthony, Captain MacWhirr, not to speak of their crew. More often than not, they even lose the little they have through some misfortune or through the greed of others.

Throughout *Nostromo*, Conrad makes ironic statements about the most esteemed twin institution of Anglo-Saxon countries, namely commerce and finance. The irony is often so subtle that it is hard to say where Conrad is talking tongue-in-cheek and where he is not. Sometimes, however, he is quite outspoken. In a letter dated 7 October 1907, he mentioned to Cunninghame Graham "the true anarchist which is the millionaire." (*LL*, II, 60) In *Chance*, he pokes fun at the gullibility of people who think they can get something for nothing and invest their hard-earned savings in de Barral's enterprise. At the beginning of the tale "An Anarchist," we find this diatribe:

> Of course everybody knows the B.O.S. Ltd., with its unrivalled products: Vinobos, Jellybos, and the latest unequalled perfection, Tribos, whose nourishment is offered to you not only highly concentrated, but already half digested. Such apparently is the love that Limited Company bears to its fellowmen—even as the love of the father and mother penguin for their hungry fledglings.

> Of course the capital of a country must be productively employed. I have nothing to say against the

company. But being myself animated by feelings of affection towards my fellowmen, I am saddened by the modern system of advertising. Whatever evidence it offers of enterprise, ingenuity, impudence, and resource in certain individuals, it proves to my mind the wide prevalence of that form of mental degradation which is called gullibility (*A Set of Six*, 135-136).

Most people with anti-capitalist tendencies turn to socialism. Not so Conrad. Contrary to Bernard Shaw whose background resembled his, Conrad was convinced that socialism could only lead to the abolition of individual responsibility and to "caesarism." Moreover, it was in Germany and in Russia that socialism was bred, and he distrusted both countries intensely. He was sure that nothing good could come from these two powers who had been responsible for the crime of the partition of Poland. During the war he spoke of the *German learned pig* and of the *Russian mangy dog*. He intensely hated not only the autocrats, but also their adversaries, the demimonde of revolutionists, informers, spies, and anarchists who, he thought, were not better than the people they opposed. At a time when English intellectuals and writers increasingly developed a weakness for socialist philosophers, Conrad remained as firm as a rock.

Coming from a country subjugated by three imperialistic powers (of which Austria was the only benign one), Conrad could not share the belief in the greatness of the imperialistic idea. He was loyal as a British subject[146] and once even tried to justify the Boer war (in a letter to Mrs. Poradowska who was in favor of the Boers), but he was always very ironic about the alleged merits of colonialism and imperialism. The beginning of *The Rescue* (written in 1896) may be taken as typical of this attitude. In the two Congo tales, "An Outpost of Progress" and *Heart of Darkness*, Conrad's ironical treatment of progress, civilization ("civilization follows trade"), and of the paternalism of the whites towards the natives, is very much in evidence. This happened at a time when imperialism was still very much accepted.

Conrad did not believe in "the white man's burden," neither in the Congo where colonialists behaved like savages, nor in the colonies of the Dutch and the British.

One more thing that irritated Conrad in the English was their "sentimentality." What he meant was the

Anglo-Saxon trait of mistaking sentimentality for feelings. He was critical of the way the British clung to—almost cherished—an obsolete spelling, time-honored Parliamentary traditions, an antique measuring and monetary system. He saw that flaw in the character which (the example is mine) would make an English neighborhood shed tears about a young cat that had climbed a pole and now was afraid to come down, while the same people would treat a Yanko Goorall like a man who had no right to exist. (The historian Toynbee too has pointed out the curious contradiction in the Anglo-Saxon character which makes them cherish sentimental values such as "charity" but which did not prevent them from practically exterminating the Red Indians and organizing a most profitable traffic of slaves for the benefit of the English settlers in North America).

In Conrad's works, we find several sarcastic descriptions of Anglo-Saxon sentimentality. Already in his first two novels, Lingard emerges as a sentimental fool, who, out of his good heart, "makes" Almayer and saves Willems twice. Both Almayer and Willems actually betray him, but the incorrigibly sentimental Lingard spends one hundred and fifty dollars on a tombstone for Willems. In *The Rescue*, too, Lingard's sentimentality takes its toll.

In *Nostromo*, Decoud (very much a double of young Conrad) talks disparagingly of the Costaguanero politicians who are "all great politicians here—on the English model." (238) He calls Charles Gould a "sentimental Englishman." He is the "King of Sulaco" as Lingard was the "King of the Sea," and like the latter is guided by sentiment, contrary to the Garibaldians and the Polish freedom fighters who were inspired by a noble passion. Decoud, who wants the Oriental Province to become an independent republic, knows that he has to win Charles Gould's and his wife's approval. This he can only do by appealing to their sentiment: "Their sentiment was necessary to the very life of my plan; the sentimentalism of the people that will never do anything for the sake of their passionate desires, unless it comes to them clothed in the fair robes of an idea." (239) What these ideas are, we hear later: "Those Englishmen live on illusions which somehow or other help them to get a firm hold of the substance. When he speaks it is by a rare 'yes' or 'no' that seems as impersonal as the words of an oracle." (239) As for the American Holroyd, financier of the mine, he is "an utter sentimentalist" who pursues his financial interests together with "that pet dream of his of a purer form of Christianity." (240)

Nowhere does Conrad imply that the English are hypocrites. They sincerely believe in their "illusions," i.e. in their sentimental social and national prejudices. Here Conrad was only following Dickens who was so excellent at describing the curious dichotomy of the English character which explains that industrialists who exploited their workers were convinced of being their benefactors, or the colonialists who seemed to think that the British flag somehow had the supernatural power of curing the ills of "inferior" races.

In *The Nigger of the "Narcissus"*, one of the sailors, a Russian Finn, gets into trouble because he does not understand English well enough. He is called Dutchy, "a squarehead," and "a blanked deaf and dumb fool." Donkin comments: "These damned furriners should be kept under . . . If you don't teach 'em their place they put on you like anythink." (13) Later, Donkin declares that he "didn't want to 'ave no truck with 'em dirty furriners . . . Wish you Dutchmen were all dead—'stead comin' takin' our money into your starvin' country." (43) I think we are on safe ground when we believe that these are echoes of what the sailor Joseph Conrad Korzeniowski himself had to put up with on his first English ships.

In *The Secret Agent*, we find several passages where Conrad vents his dislike of the capital of Great Britain. London is "slumbering monstrously on a carpet of mud under a veil of mist." (300) It has "darkness enough to bury five millions of lives." (Author's Note). In a passage already quoted in Chapter VI, Conrad, speaking of "London's strayed houses" is irritated with the English lack of logic which makes the English unable to properly number their houses.

XI.

Conrad's works in Poland

What reception did Conrad's writings get in Poland? Things began to stir early there. Already on 16 November 1896, Conrad wrote to Edward Garnett that they had heard of him in Poland through Chicago[147], and that there was some talk about translating *Almayer's Folly* and the *Outcast*. At the same time, in November 1896, the *Literary Review* (Cracow) reviewed Conrad's first two novels, mentioning that the author was a Ukrainian born Pole whose real name was Konrad Korzeniowski, son of the poet, Apollo, and of a Bobrowska.

It was the *Outcast of the Islands* which was to be the first translation of a book by Conrad. Beginning in January 1897, the Polish version was serialized in the *Fashion and Fiction Weekly*, a Warsaw illustrated periodical mainly read by women. The novel, presented as a story of adventure, did not attract much attention. The translation, by Maria Gasiorowska, was fair; it is now replaced by Aniela Zagórska's.

In spring, 1899, the attack by Orzeszkowa took place. It had no lasting influence, for already in January and February 1904, a Polish journalist living in Paris, Kazimierz Waliszewski, published an article in the same *Homeland* (Kraj) which had been the scene of that attack. This article "A Polish Novelist in English Literature," very politely overlooks the former bitter dispute.[148] It is an honest attempt to present Conrad to the Polish nation and it is based on an exchange of letters (mostly in French) between Waliszewski and Conrad, letters which have been published in *Joseph Conrad: Lettres françaises*. Among other things, Conrad told Waliszewski: "If you will accept my word, you may say that during all my travels over the globe, I have never been far away from my native country, neither in spirit nor feeling, and I hope to be accepted there as a compatriot despite my anglicism." (15 November 1903)

In another letter to Waliszewski, Conrad called himself a *homo duplex*: "My point of view, on land as on the sea, is English, but one should not conclude from this that I have become an Englishman. This is not the case. The expression *homo duplex*, in my case, has more than one meaning. I cannot go into this question." (*Joseph Conrad: Lettres françaises*, 61). It is probable that Conrad, besides speaking of the Polish-English dichotomy, was also alluding to his two careers as seaman and writer.

The second novel to be translated into Polish was not *Almayer's Folly*, but *Lord Jim*. The translator was again a lady, Emilia Węsławska. The novel appeared in book form in 1904. The translation was adequate, but was later superseded by Aniela Zagórska's superior version. Ever since 1904, *Lord Jim* has been popular with the Poles, who still consider Conrad mainly as the compatriot who wrote *Lord Jim*.

It is of some interest to hear how Emilia Węsławska introduced *Lord Jim* to the Polish reader. In her preface, she wrote: "The theme of *Lord Jim* is the spiritual conflict and the story of the hero who, once carried off the way of duty by an incomprehensible force undergoes hellish torments, for the image of his misdeed is constantly before his eyes . . . One wonders whether a born Englishman would create a Jim imbued with such romanticism and sensibility. For that, one must have the dreamish Slavonic blood." As for Conrad's style and method she had this to say, "The work of our compatriot is like a capricious and unruly torrent, with a thousand leisurely bends followed by abrupt waterfalls. Conrad practically never goes straight to his goal, he rather approaches it in a random and subtle way. He does not mind to tire the reader or to lure him off the track." Finally, she concludes, "Although writing in a foreign language, too much in Conrad betrays feelings akin to ours to consider him as a foreigner."[149]

This Polish version of *Lord Jim* did not attract much attention. But one review, by Wiktor Gomulicki, again in *Homeland* (no. 1, 1905), stands out. For the first time, the symbolism of Jim's story was pointed out (and, of course, by a Pole). The following passage is particularly representative:

I had already closed Conrad's book with great antipathy, I had already told myself, No! This writer did not tear himself away from Poland, he had never belonged to her—when suddenly something within me shouted: But perhaps all this is just a symbol? This boat condemned to sink—these passengers overcome by sleep, their nerves exhausted by religious fervor—these egoists whose life instinct tells them to escape from the boat under their care—and especially this fundamentally chivalrous youngster who had blundered amongst these villains—this youngster whose Promethean heart for the rest of his life will be torn by the vulture of remorse—this "noble man" finds on foreign soil prosperity, love, confidence but all the same seeks his last relief in a voluntary death. Should all this in its deepest sense be nothing more than what it appears to the English reader? Sometimes at night, a loud shout awakes us. We rub our eyes and look around: besides ourselves nobody is in the room. This shout came from our own breast. We had slept quietly, having made beautiful plans; we may even have had agreeable dreams. Then our soul, lulled to sleep, after a while became conscious and manifested itself by a shriek. It was such a shriek that reached me from Conrad's novel: a shriek uttered perhaps unconsciously. Therefore: a symbol? Only Konrad Korzeniowski could answer this question.

Konrad Korzeniowski never answered. Yet, already in 1900, he had sent the English version of *Lord Jim* to three people in Poland, one to Mrs. Aniela Zagórska, another to a second friend, and a third to the editor of *Chimera*, a literary paper representing the most avant-garde literature. Conrad expected to be torn to pieces there[150], but there was no echo until the Polish translation had appeared a few years later. The review was by Maria Komornicka and highly laudatory. The reviewer discussed mainly the artistic qualities of the book, not its symbolism. To be accepted by *Chimera* meant to be accepted by the literary movement "Young Poland," to which many writers of Conrad's generation belonged. The general tendency of "Young Poland" was away from stark realism and towards symbolism. Moreover, the peasants (Reymont) or the mountain dwellers or *górale* (Tetmajer) became popular subjects. *Lord Jim*, with its exotic atmosphere, its pathos, and its preoccupation with unconscious motives, fitted the mood of the modern Polish *literati*.

After *Lord Jim*, the next book to become available in Polish was *The Secret Agent*. The translation, by Maria Gasiorowska, appeared in 1908, the year when Maria Rakowska drew attention to Conrad as a writer in *Warsaw Library*. In 1911 followed "Il Conde," not a surprising choice, since the count was obviously a Pole. Then all remained quiet until 1914. At the beginning of that year, "Amy Foster," under the more appropriate title "Janko Góral," appeared in Lwów, in a popular edition costing 15 cents. In April of the same year, Marian Dąbrowski told the Polish public of the interview he had with Conrad in January. In this interview, Conrad had also complained about the quality of the Polish translations: One translation of the *Outcast* which had appeared as a serial in the *Lwów Courrier* under the title *Banita* made him particularly furious because the word "Malay" had been rendered as "Negro."

It was part of Conrad's Polish-English dichotomy that while he did everything to hide his Polish origin from the English, he at the same time made great efforts to have his first works published in Poland. He even tried to find a suitable translator, and it was he who finally persuaded his niece, Aniela Zagórska, to tackle the job. This was not easy, since she had no knowledge of nautical terminology.

Aniela Zagórska met Conrad for the first time in August 1914, in Zakopane. This contact was very helpful, and after the end of the war, she began to translate Conrad's works. The standard Polish versions of *Almayer's Folly, An Outcast of the Islands, Lord Jim*, "An Outpost of Progress," and *Victory*, are due to her, For these outstanding ing translations, she got a reward from the Polish PEN-Club. She visited England a few weeks after Conrad's death. She herself died in 1943, at the age of 62, owing to wartime hardships. She cherished too much the many letters in Polish which Conrad'had sent her to have them published. Unfortunately, they were lost during the war, but a French translation of them (probably made for the benefit of Jean-Aubry) has survived.

In 1922, the first volume of *Selected Works of Joseph Conrad, Almayer's Folly*, was published in Warsaw with a preface by Żeromski who sent Conrad a copy. On 25 March, 1923, Conrad answered Żeromski with a letter in

Polish, signed "J. K. Korzeniowski." This interesting letter was published in English in LL, II, 289, together with a facsimile of the original.[151]

Conrad writes very good Polish here. His extreme politeness, too, is characteristic of the way one famous Pole would write to another famous Pole. Jean-Aubry's translation is faithful enough, but it does not render the fact that Conrad wrote "my country" and "master" with capitals. The second and third paragraphs of the letter are particularly important; this is how we would render it:

> Directly after having read, beloved Sir, your magnificent preface to *Almayer's Folly*, I asked Aniela to express to you my gratitude for the favor you had bestowed on me. I must admit that I cannot find words to describe my deep emotion in reading this testimony honoring me, testimony coming from my Fatherland and expressed through your voice, beloved Sir, through the greatest Master of her literature!
>
> Please accept, gracious Sir, my most affectionate thanks for the time, thought and work you devoted to me and for your sympathetic appraisal which discovered the compatriot behind the author.

Alluding to this letter, Żeromski wrote an article entitled "The Compatriot behind the Author" which appeared in the magazine *Around the World* in March 1925, shortly before Żeromski's death.

Lord Jim seems even to have inspired one of Żeromski's works, namely, *History of a Sin* (Dzieje Grzechu), Warsaw 1908. It is the story of Eve Pobratyńska, who has just turned twenty when she becomes trapped by fate. She is a naive office girl who, one day, meets Luke Niepołomski, anthropologist and philosopher. The fact that he has an unhappy marriage and tries to get a divorce rouses her sympathy and she falls in love. But one day, Niepołomski disappears and Eve is a "lost and lonely soul" who says: "Fate threw the dice and I got my destiny." Many months later she hears he has been wounded in a duel. She disappears from Warsaw, rushes to his bedside, nurses him back to life, and then lives with him in the country. Suddenly, he leaves for Rome and she loses track of him. She lives in misery, deep in the country, lonely and pregnant. When

the child is born in an outhouse, she throws it into the
stinking pit. (The last phase of pregnancy, the delivery
and the murder are described with a repulsively stark
naturalism reminiscent of Zola). After stealing six roubles she disappears. Back in Warsaw, she works as a
cashier. In her thoughts, she is haunted by the murder
of her child. She again disappears, travels to Rome, trying to find Niepołomski, then to the French Riviera. She
cannot find him and suddenly appears in Corsica. Her
fifth disappearance brings her to Montreux, her sixth to
Vienna where she comes across the head of a gang of
robbers who take her money and then force her to kill a
man with an injection. She again disappears and turns
up under a false name on a cooperative farm, a kind of
kibbutz devoted to the rehabilitation of prostitutes. This
is her Patusan where she hopes to bury her past. But
one day the gangster appears with a letter from
Niepołomski. Out of weakness for her former lover, she
follows her Gentleman Brown to Warsaw. He blackmails
her into ringing at Niepołomski's door. When she an-
nounces herself and the door is opened, the gangsters
rush in. In the ensuing scuffle she is shot. She dies feeling that she has at last expiated her sin.

    Conrad got the novel from Poland and was asked by
Garnett whether it should be translated. Conrad's reaction, dated September 1921, was negative:

> I have just read through the novel you mean: *His-
> tory of a Sin*. Honestly I do not think it will do for a
> translation . . . The whole thing is disagreeable and
> often incomprehensible in comment and psycholo-
> gy. You know I am not squeamish. The other work
> [by Żeromski], the great historical machine, is called
> *Ashes*. Both of course have a certain greatness—the
> greatness of a wild landscape—and both take too
> much for granted in the way of receptivity and to-
> lerance.[152]

    As can be seen, Conrad did not comment on any
similarities with *Lord Jim*; it is obvious that he placed his
own work at a different level altogether.

    The first Polish critic of Conrad's art was Maria
Rakowska. Her study appeared in *Warsaw Library* in
1908, the same collection of small books in which had
been published *A Comedy* and a study on Shakespeare by

Apollo Korzeniowski, in 1854-55 and 1868 respectively.

In her essay, "Joseph Conrad" (Konrad Korzeniowski)", Maria Rakowska states that Conrad is far from being a popular writer and probably never will be, for he is in a class by himself, writes very personally, and does not belong to any school. "It is easy," she wrote, "to see the reflection of his family heritage in his melancholic irony and his pessimism, but his most brilliant asset is his power of visualisation. He sees men and nature always as part of the universe. On the sea, the life of the men and the doings of the elements are intertwined. His heroes do not ask for pity, nor does the author show any towards them."

Immediately after Conrad's death, Żeromski wrote an article in *Literary News* (Warsaw, 17 August, 1924), from which the following passages seem particularly interesting:

> The most beautiful and the most intriguing, in my mind, of Conrad's works will always be *Lord Jim* . . . a gigantic work! One of the most penetrating and subtle of all our critics, Wilam Horzyca . . . once drew my attention to the secret of *Lord Jim*, raising the question whether this work is not perhaps a symbolic confession? . . . Whether it is not an ingeniously contrived story of another but the described inner process: the story of forgotten, rejected and repressed obligations of quite a different kind?

> Now that this productive, rich and brilliant life has come to its close . . . the time has perhaps come to recognize the hidden factor in that life—his Polish origin. I believe that throwing light on it, to point out the extraordinary nobility, dignity and beauty of this life, would explain not a little . . . His life is known on the whole and will certainly be described more than once. No doubt, the sources of his creativity will be uncovered as well as the influences to which he was exposed. But for the West, his Polish roots will always be shrouded in mystery, since Joseph Conrad himself, apart from some articles of a journalistic nature, kept them in the dark.

In the same article, Żeromski saw the influence of Conrad's Polish heritage in his style which he found "sublimely different;" Conrad's choice of expressions, the rhythm of his prose, its imagery, forcefulness and "abundance" are all attributed to Polish influence.

As we know from Grabowski,[153] Żeromski intended to write an essay on Conrad's *polonitas*, but died before he could carry out his plan.

The first Polish book on Joseph Conrad appeared in 1927, in Poznan. It contained a series of essays by Zbigniew Grabowski, who based himself on English sources and who was interested in Conrad's *polonitas*. Curiously enough, he found hardly any Polish influences in Conrad's works which he considered to be perfectly within the tradition of the English novel. Grabowski, in a further study published in 1930, also commented on my *Polish Heritage of Joseph Conrad*, concluding: "Personally I am deeply convinced that the author of a really exhaustive and profound monography on Joseph Conrad can only be a Pole."

In 1934, Ujejski published the second Polish book on Joseph Conrad. It was never translated into English, but a French translation appeared in 1939. In a preface to the latter, the translator, Z. L. Zaleski, explains that Conrad's *polonisme* betrays itself in two ways: in isolated gestures and through a constant peculiar nuance of his inspiration. It was the latter that Ujejski tried to define.

Like every Pole, Ujejski was particularly attracted by *Lord Jim*. From certain confidences in *A Personal Record*, from Marlow's reflection that returning to one's homeland was like rendering an account, and from what "pierces" through the novel, Ujejski drew the conclusion that "the action which troubled Conrad's patriotic conscience, seems to be his voluntary emigration from Poland and his rejection of the obligation to fight in his place in the rank".[154]

The death of Conrad, in August 1924, was followed by an upsurge of articles and essays in the Polish press. Most articles were highly laudatory and expressed pride that a son of Poland had become world famous. The Polish edition, *Selected Works of Joseph Conrad*, was terminated in 1936; the volumes were widely read. As a measure of Conrad's popularity in Poland, one may mention Professor Ujejski's lectures on Conrad, at Warsaw University, in 1933 and 1934. The great aula in which those lectures took place, was filled to capacity; even the window sills were occupied. "Conrad lived in my thoughts that whole academic year", one of these students was to write later.[155]

Great Polish writers had always been considered as the mouthpieces of the collective soul of the nation. Mickiewicz, Słowacki, and Krasiński were called "wieszcze", a word which has been rendered as "bards" A *wieszcz* is not only a poet; but also a national prophet, who not only expresses the sufferings and the joys of the nation, but also inspires and guides her. During the war of 1939 and the German occupation, Conrad almost became a "wieszcz". His writings inspired many Poles.[156] As mentioned before, *Lord Jim* was printed in Jerusalem for the Polish soldiers in the Middle East. Other popular books were "Typhoon," "Youth," *The Rover, Heart of Darkness*. In the first years after the war, a great number of articles on Conrad appeared. Conrad's *polonitas*, which had been the main theme during the twenties and part of the thirties, was no longer discussed, it was taken for granted. Poland had adopted her son.

The only negative note was sounded by Jan Kott who represented the marxist viewpoint. In 1945, he compared Conrad's heroes with "the heroes of the Soviet Union" and found that contrary to the latter, his men do not know what they are dying for. The heroism of Conrad's heroes is useless; it only serves to increase the profits of the shipping companies "who make money out of the others' contempt for death". Kott attacked Conrad's concept of fidelity, which is "the fidelity of slaves": "for it is a slave who listens to a master whom he despises and cares only for his inner righteousness". Conrad's heroes have thrown away "their right to revolt". In *Nostromo*, the marxist critic discovered "a constant aversion of Conrad against all efforts to improve the social order, an enmity against socialism, a disgust for revolutionaries and a frank horror of those who believe in progress in the light of scientific ideology." Kott also opposes a quotation from Lenin to one from Conrad: Lenin once prophesied that "a time will come when the community will build apartments of gold" while Conrad wrote "the stodgy sun of the future . . . will rise . . . to throw its sanitary light upon a dull world of perfected municipalities and WC *sans peur et sans reproche*."[157]

Referring to "Typhoon," and to Ujejski's definition of Conrad's philosophy as "pessimistic heroism," Kott exclaims, "Pessimistic heroism? No! Stupid heroism. The heroism of an ass pulling a cart over a mined bridge. A heroism without words, without pathos, not even conscious of itself, a heroism that is just fidelity." Finally Kott characterizes Conrad as "the last bourgeois moralist."

It is typical for the measure of tolerance reigning in Poland, at that time, that several other critics were allowed to contradict Kott. Thus, Jerzy Dziewicki, in the *Baltic Daily* ("In Defence of Conrad", No. 134, 1945), Antoni Gołubiew in *Today and Tomorrow* ("I correct Kott", No. 3, 1945), and the well-known author and critic, Maria Dąbrowska ("Conrad's concept of Fidelity" in No. 1 of the periodical *Warszawa*, 1946). Maria Dąbrowska saw in Conrad's novels "an artistic attempt to discover whether and how a human being can save his moral integrity in a world of immoral material interests." Despite Kott's reservations, the State Editorial Office in Warsaw republished *Lord Jim* in Aniela Zagórska's translation (1949), followed by *The Mirror of the Sea* and *The Shadow Line* in 1950.

In 1949 there began in Poland (as in Russia) the era of "socialist realism", and Conrad became one of its many victims. In 1950 a note signed *lbg* appeared in the official literary weekly *Nowa Kultura* in which the writer asked how it was possible to release for the book market an author as suspect as Conrad without at least providing an appropriate commentary. This article was a signal for what was going to happen. Conrad's books were no longer printed by the State Editorial Institute and the old copies fetched fabulous prices on the used book market. The ban was finally lifted in 1955. *Chance* was the first book by Conrad to be reprinted, accompanied by a commentary by Róża Jabłkowska. Ever since, the State Editorial Institute has printed huge editions of Conrad's most popular books. In 1966, the Institute published the seventh edition of *Lord Jim*, 50,000 copies, and the second edition of "Typhoon," 30,000 copies. *Lord Jim* is still by far the best selling book. Of the political novels, only *Nostromo* has been reprinted since the war. In 1974, the *Complete Works of Joseph Conrad* in Polish were published.

In 1947, the newly founded *Rhapsody Theatre* of Cracow presented a dramatic version of the *Patna* episode of *Lord Jim*. This is the only instance where a work by Conrad ever met with success on the stage, for

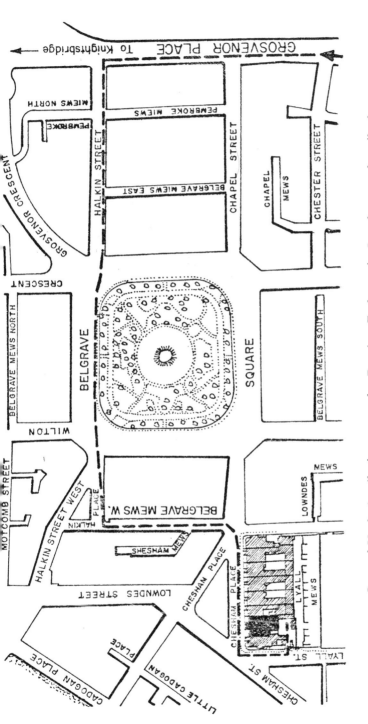

Conrad-Verloc's pilgrimage to the Russian Embassy in London, as described in the second chapter of *The Secret Agent*. The itinerary (- - - -) is actually a detour, but no other interpretation is possible. The "narrow street" with its "yellow wall" could only be Belgrave Mews West, from which he crossed Chesham Place "diagonally" indeed. (London Ordnance Survey, 1895)

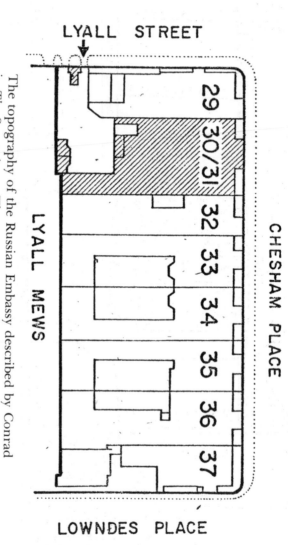

LYALL STREET

LYALL MEWS

CHESHAM PLACE

LOWNDES PLACE

29 | 30/31 | 32 | 33 | 34 | 35 | 36 | 37

The topography of the Russian Embassy described by Conrad in *The Secret Agent*. The entrance to 30/31 Chesham Place was through a carriage gate on Lyall Street, past a porter's lodge. (London Ordnance Survey, 1895) the play ran for 88 performances, placing it in the 13th position of the 65 works played between 1945 and 1966. The play was also brought to Warsaw in October 1948. It was a most modern and original piece, somewhat in the style of Reinhardt, representing Jim's inner struggle for moral survival against the background of a boat fighting for its material survival. Jim was played by the founder and director of the company himself, Mieczys-/aw Kotlarczyk. The hero's conflicts were commented upon by a chorus in the ancient Greek style. Most reviews were enthusiastic. 88 performances in a town of half a million people was a smashing success for a modern work; only Polish classics used to go beyond. Goethe's *Faust* only made 35 performances!

Beginning in September 1966, Conrad's short story, "To-morrow," was presented at the Warsaw Opera in the form of one hour opera by the well-known Polish composer Tadeusz Baird. Again, the success was great and the opera was still being played during the 1967-68 season. I saw it in 1972. (One remembers that Conrad dramatized the same story in 1904, but that drama was only played privately and met with no success).

"To-morrow" is indeed a story that contains a number of Polish associations. There is the theme of the young man running away to sea (and whose return leads to a catastrophe), the theme of the father whose thinking and feeling have drifted further and further away from reality, a father who harbors a delusional vision of his son and of the future, and who denies and destroys his real son rather than to give up his belief in a wonderful to-morrow and in a fictional son to his liking.

The contemporary Poles tend to consider Conrad a Polish author who happened to write in English while feeling in Polish. He is seen as a neo-romantic author who perfectly fits into the trends of Polish literature at the beginning of the century. Since the romantic period of Polish literature produced the most brilliant as well as the most Polish of all writers, it was not easy to be a neo-romantic. Owing to the fact that Poland was divided and ruled by three foreign powers who did not allow any writing that would express what was nearest to the heart of every Pole, namely the intolerable burden of foreign occupation, literature before 1918 was often characterized by a form of escapism: the writers had to turn to historical, or folkloristic, or exotic subjects. Conrad, with his Far Eastern stories and his concern with the alienated, lonely man separated from his homeland by an invisible barrier, fitted perfectly into this pattern. His life story, too, so typically Polish in many ways, so comprehensible considering the political conditions of a divided Poland, attracted the Polish public. Conrad was not the first Pole who had found opportunities abroad which would have been denied to him under the political conditions at home.

In the modern Polish view, Conrad is, of course, seen as a representative of his age and a descendant of the landed gentry, a man whose rather conservative outlook is redeemed by some progressive insights. His russophobia is explained as a heritage from his father which should not detract from the original beauty of his works.

The peculiar esteem in which Conrad is held also by the Poles abroad, expresses itself in many ways. In London, there is a Polish Conrad Club which has quite a collection of Conradiana and which tried, unsuccessfully, to acquire Conrad's last abode, the Oswald's, in order to transform it into a Conrad museum. In Tasmania, a Polish club watches over the remains of the *Otago*, the only ship where Conrad served as a captain. The stern of this boat is now in San Francisco. In America, the *Polish Review* (New York) frequently publishes articles on Conrad. A collection of essays by Polish writers abroad was published in London under the title *The Living Conrad* (Conrad Żywy). The Polish monthly *Kultura* in Paris also printed a number of essays on Conrad. Altogether, the number of studies on Conradian subjects published by Poles abroad since 1945 is considerably higher than the number of publications in Poland: the source book *Polish Writers Abroad* for the years 1945 to 1962 lists 38 essays on Conrad.

Since the second world war, and up to 1974, six books on Conrad have been published in Poland.

The first was *Joseph Conrad* by Róża Jabłowska, (Wrocław 1961). This is a biography seen through Polish eyes, followed by a study of some of Conrad's works, especially *Lord Jim* and *Nostromo*. The author points out that Jim very much resembles one of Sienkiewicz's heroes, Andrzej, a Polish gentleman who expiates his mistake with his own blood. But she does not believe that the theme of cowardice in *Lord Jim* has anything to do with guilt feelings on the part of Conrad. She finds the arguments not sufficient "to build upon them a problem of guilt and desertion." Jim's weakness towards Brown is interpreted as "naive goodness."

In 1965, Zdzisław Najder published a book simply entitled *On Conrad* (Warsaw 1965). Here we find two curious biographical details: Najder does not believe that Conrad ever went to St. Anne's junior college, and he maintains that he suffered from epilepsy. Both points had been taken up by us in an earlier chapter.

According to Najder, Jim is a romantic hero and as such resembles both Priest Robak in Mickiewicz's *Pan Tadeusz* and Konrad in *Forefather's Eve*. Mickiewicz—says Najder—describes a hero who starts as an individualistic dreamer to finally become a patriotic hero. Jim's weakness towards Brown is due to the fact that this gangster reminds him of his own downfall. He cannot deny Brown that pardon which he so badly desires for himself. The question of a possible guilt complex on the part of Conrad is not discussed. Najder is especially attracted by Conrad's political novels and ideas.

A third book, by the editor of *Reminiscences and Studies on Conrad*, Barbara Kocówna, is entitled *Conrad's Polonitas* (Cracow 1967). Here again, we have a Polish biography of Conrad and an appraisal of some of his works. One chapter, of course, is dedicated to *Lord Jim*. Miss Kocówna mentions that this novel "up to this day raises hot arguments as no other novel does. These discussions have to do with Conrad's Polish origin, with cowardice, irresponsibility, daydreaming, false romanticism, and such like." The author finds Jim "a straightforward, uncomplicated man." His chivalry and belief that Brown will honor his word and clear out lead to his downfall.

In a last paragraph, Barbara Kocówna concludes:

> The faithfulness towards the tradition with which man is forever connected—whether he wants it or not—permeates the whole work of Conrad. Beginning with *Almayer's Folly*, continuing with *Heart of Darkness* and *Lord Jim*, and up to *The Rover*—everywhere we find that same idea that a man belongs to the soil from which he sprang before he went out into the world.

Maria Dąbrowska, on the other hand, has published

her different essays on Conrad, from 1924 to 1959, in a volume entitled *Sketches on Conrad* (PIW 1959).

In 1971, Stefan Zabierowski, professor of Polish literature at Katowice, published a book entitled *Conrad in Poland*. The first half of the book deals with "The Polish Conrad Legend," the second with Conrad's place in world literature and especially in Polish and Western romanticism.

Jessie Conrad's *Joseph Conrad and his circle*, Jean-Aubry's *The Sea Dreamer*, and Borys Conrad's *My Father: Joseph Conrad* are available in Polish translations. Z. Najder published 400 letters by Joseph Conrad (*Conrad: Listy*) translated by Halina Carroll-Najder. Finally, the Polish writer Andrzej Braun published a very fine album *Contact with the East* (Warsaw 1970) illustrating different passages from Conrad's early writings and in 1972 a book entitled *In Conrad's Footsteps*, the fruit of one year's cruising amongst the settings of Conrad's Malayan stories. There is even a picture of Almayer's tomb, and there are detailed descriptions of "Sambir," "Patusan," etc.

XII.

Man of Three Languages

Joseph Conrad was able to read and write in three languages, Polish, French, English, but his relationship to each of these idioms was different, each meant something else for him.

Polish, of course, occupied a special place in Conrad's life. It was the language of his childhood and youth, the inherited language. It was the language which, during the oppression of Poland, was holy to every Pole. It was because of her national language and literature that Poland survived spiritually. The Germans knew this well. Until the first world war, speaking Polish on the school premises in Eastern Germany was severely punished, and any formal teaching of Polish to young Poles was illegal. Under these conditions, giving up Polish for another language was widely considered as treachery. This explains why the Poles, when meeting Conrad, always made a mental note of the condition of his Polish. It might be all right to emigrate to England and even to write in English, but to *forget* the Polish language would have been the ultimate treachery. The Poles, from Bobrowski, Lutosławski and Dąbrowski to Żeromski and Borowy, were glad to be able to report that, in this respect, Conrad was blameless. Only Perłowski, as we have seen, had some reservations.

Conrad had been taught Polish with the greatest care and there is no doubt that when he left Poland at the age of nearly seventeen, his Polish was better than average. He took with him a number of Polish books, among them Mickiewicz's epic poem *Pan Tadeusz*. We know how upset Uncle Bobrowski got when Conrad lost them through carelessness.

Four years after Conrad's departure from Poland,

in March 1879, Bobrowski met him in Marseilles and
noted with satisfaction that his nephew had "forgotten
nothing of his Polish".[158] In May of the same year, Bobrowski stated that the Polish in Conrad's letters was "as
good as if he had never left Poland."[159] Only once, in his
extensive correspondence with Conrad, did Uncle Bobrowski have to point out a grammatical error. In the
winter of 1890, fifteen years after Conrad's emigration,
Perłowski noted that he sometimes had to help Conrad
out with a Polish expression and he added: "What struck
us in his speech was a somewhat foreign accent, with our
borderland intonation breaking through at times."[160] Retinger himself, brought up in Austrian-governed
Cracow, met Conrad for the first time in 1912, 38 years
after Conrad's departure from Poland. He was to write
later: "He greeted me in Polish in what surely must have
been the most drawling singing voice that ever came out
of the Ukraine."[161]

Zeromski's impression was different: "I convinced
myself [in 1914, in Zakopane] with a certain surprise
how perfectly he masters our language. In the course of
forty years . . . he lost not one expression, nor did he
lose his Cracovian accent."[162] In this statement we must
allow for the Polish propensity of paying exaggerated
compliments. We know from Aniela Zagórska that Conrad had been unnatural in the presence of the leading
Polish novelist.[163] Dr. Casimir Górski in Zakopane, with
whom Conrad had a number of conversations (mostly on
political affairs) in August and September 1914, stated
that Conrad spoke a pure Polish, free of anglicisms.[164]

Wacław Borowy (1860-1950), professor of Polish
and English literature at the University of Warsaw,
wrote a study of Conrad's knowledge of Polish during
the last years of his life.[165] In November 1933, the *Warsaw Review* had printed a Polish translation of "Il Conde." The translator was not familiar with modern English and made a number of mistakes. Aniela Zagórska
sent a copy to Conrad who, in his reply, pointed out
these obvious misinterpretations. She then asked him to
completely revise the Polish text. Conrad sent an extensive answer which is now deposited at the Warsaw University Library. After pointing out that the title should
read "Il Conte" instead of "Il Conde", he proposed 22
changes, some of them followed by a question mark.
About half of the corrections concern obvious mistakes,

„100-LECIE URODZIN JÓZEFA CONRADA-KORZENIOWSKIEGO"
„PIERWSZY DZIEŃ OBIEGU — F. D. C."

Two postage stamps issued by the Polish Post Office for the 100th anniversary of Conrad's birth. The ship is the "Torrens". (First Day Cover)

the others deal with nuances of expressions. Conrad's detailed revision of this translation (the only known instance when he dealt with a translation in this way) not only shows his interest in being translated into Polish, but also his well retained knowledge of his native language. However, as Borowy pointed out in his study, some of Conrad's corrections betray uncertainty. Moreover, Conrad overlooked quite a number of bad expressions. Borowy concluded that while Conrad could read Polish without difficulty and possessed quite a good vocabulary, he would have been unable to write literary Polish at that time.

Even the question of how far Conrad was thinking in Polish has been debated. Żeromski had not only talked with Conrad in 1914, but also got a letter written in elaborate Polish from him a number of years later. He explained Conrad's persisting mastery of the language in a very straightforward way. Conrad, he wrote, must have been thinking in Polish all his life," especially in moments of stress or elation, that is during his creative periods."[166] This is in contradiction to what Perłowski had observed already in 1890 and to what Conrad told Dr. Górski, namely, that he was practically always thinking in English and would have to translate from the English, if he wanted to write in Polish.[167] On the other hand, it is well-known that Conrad spoke (and thought) Polish when in high fever. He also may have thought in Polish during his frequent bouts of absentmindedness and rumination. There are a few obvious polonisms and even a well-known Polish proverb in his fragment *The Sisters* (1896), which seems to prove that when writing about the Ukraine he must have been thinking in Polish. This would explain why the translator of this fragment had often the impression of translating certain passages "back" into Polish. In "Amy Foster," too, when describing Yanko Goorall, a number of expressions are actually taken from the Polish, and the same is, of course, true of "Prince Roman," but in those two stories, the "loans" were made purposely, for the sake of local color.

Apart from the Polish letters which he received very frequently, Conrad read very little Polish till 1914. This changed in Zakopane where he read and spoke Polish indefatigably for two months. After 1918, Aniela Zagórska often sent him Polish books or articles. But it is not likely that he ever read his father's comedies which were then practically forgotten.

Conrad became fully recognized in Poland after the first World War. The attempts to repolonize him ceased. This in turn made him feel at greater ease with the Poles. As one Polish critic joked, Conrad was now accepted as a "Cosmopole."

Conrad's Polish letters are generally in very good Polish and the spelling is perfect down to every accent. Yet already in 1890, Conrad wrote in a letter that he must "see" his relatives in Radom. "See" a family, or "see" a doctor is a typical anglicism for "visit" respectively "consult" which the Poles would use. Gillon has pointed out a similar obvious anglicism in another letter of the same year.[168] Conrad was awkward when he did not write conversational language, and his political "Memorandum" (1914) reads as if it had been translated from English. The same thing must be said of his letter to Consul Marynowski in Milan, dated 8 September 1921. This is a business letter on behalf of his cousin Karola Zagórska. It was published by Alexander Janta in *The Living Conrad* (1957) and, as Janta pointed out, is written in a most awkward style and contains three glaring anglicisms, but no spelling mistakes.

The obvious question: are there any polonisms in Conrad's prose? has already been answered. But to go fishing for polonisms is an unprofitable business. There are perhaps two dozen of them in the 22 volumes of Kent's (respectively Dent's) edition of *Conrad's Complete Works*.

Retinger stated: "Although Conrad's style is very idiomatic, yet one comes up against expressions which are wholly foreign, mostly Polish. I pointed out a few to him, in particular the following two which occur fairly frequently: 'under the angle of eternity' and 'civic valour'. Conrad picked them up bodily from the Polish. He agreed with me."[169]

To me this seems nonsense. These expressions are quite rare in Conrad's works. The first one is a translation of the Latin *sub specie aeternitas*, while *civic valor* is the equivalent of the French *civisme*.

A more serious study of the problem has been published by *A. P. Coleman* in *Modern Language Notes* (November 1931), entitled "Polonisms in the English of Conrad's *Chance*". Coleman mentioned the following examples:

I have never seen so many fine things assembled together out of a collection [meaning: outside of a collection] (76).

She no longer looked a child (132).

The tiger prepared to drag her away for a prey to his cubs (177).

Almost at once Fyne caught me up (229).

She felt the desire of tears [a construction imitating a Polish genitive case] (371).

It has been pointed out by several authors (Coleman, Gillon, Najder, and others) that the Polish language is built like Latin. It has no articles and many prepositions are replaced by inflection. This probably explains sentences like the following, equally found in *Chance*:

She raged *at him* with contradictory reproaches *for* regretting the girl (3), [a sentence that would sound very good in Polish].

I got irresistible conviction (5).

Extraordinary stiffbacked figure all in black (94).

Followed complete silence (443) [a very Polish phrase!]

The uncertainty about the proper use of the article is very visible in this famous sentence from *A Personal Record* (110): "I have been charged with *the* want of patriotism, *the* want of sense, and *the* want of heart too," where the article is perfectly unnecessary.

As we would expect, Polish influences are comparatively frequent in Conrad's first books, but as we have seen from these examples they are not absent from his later novels.

The following phrases from *Almayer's Folly* can be interpreted as an attempt to render Polish inflections (italics mine):

Great floods making the river almost *impossible of ascent for* native canoes (73).

His untamed soul *longed in an intensity of desire* (83).

Catching himself up in a great fright with a few quick turns of the handle (88).

Nature slept *in an* exhausted repose (88).

Groups of children brought up the rear, warbling joyously *in* the delight *of* unexpected excitement (93).

The loose planks rattled rhythmically *under* their steps *with obtrusive dry sound in* the perfect silence *of* the night (146).

The chairs ... lay about the verandah *with* a lamentable aspect *of* inebriety *in* their helpless attitudes (157).

Almayer's head rolled from shoulder to shoulder *in* the oppression *of* his dream (158).

... bringing terrible defeat *in* the delirious uplifting *of* accomplished conquest (171).

He is grieving—*as who should not* grieve at losing
thee! (177).

Long time ago, a very long time (199).

A few of Nina's dresses hung *on* wooden pegs, stif-
fened *in* a look *of* offended dignity *at* their aban-
donment (198).

In Polish, such turns of phrases, thanks to the
judicious use of the right case, are much less clumsy,
especially the sentences held together by "In an attitude
of . . ." and "in an aspect of . . .".

In Conrad's second book, *An Outcast of the Islands*,
we find no less than 27 instances of Polish turns of
phrases. On page 12, we read of the sea as "the element
that gave *the* life and dealt *the* death (italics mine, as in
the following examples), a good instance of the wrong
use of the article typical of many Poles speaking English.
On page 59, we come across the expression "Balabatchi
noted the arrival of Willems *with* alarm *at* this new acces-
sion *to* the white men's strength", a sentence which
would be shorter and more elegant in Polish.

Other instances where the Polish use of the different cases is reflected are: "This feeling of repulsion
overmastered his reason *in* a clear conviction *of* the impossibility *for* him to live *with* her people" (152); "He sat
silent for a while *in* dejected meditation" (178); or "She
stopped with one foot advanced *in* an appearance *of*
sudden terror." (243) On page 251, Aissa explodes "*into*
pained fury," and on page 274, we read "His
laugh . . . seemed to be brought violently *on* the surface
from under his bitterness, his self-contempt, *from under* his
despairing wonder at his own nature" where the use of
from under, a favorite expression in Conrad, is very
Polish. It is only one syllable in that language: *zpod*.

It is a peculiarity of the Slavonic languages to use
different verbs, or verbs with different prefixes,
whenever an action is expressed. In Polish, one always
makes a distinction between "writing", "writing down",
or "writing as a profession." "To fall" is expressed differently according to what is meant: to start falling, to fall
continuously, to fall down, etc. Conrad tried to render
this precision, which does not exist in English, by using
abundantly such expressions as *from under, from amongst,*

from beside, etc. Of Almayer sitting down at a lamp-lit table, Conrad says: "His anxious visage dropped *from above into* the light thrown *down* by the lamp-shade." (*Almayer's Folly*, 294). In *The Outcast*, we find sentences like the following:

> All expression disappeared from his face *in an aspect of* staring vacancy. (297)

> He lost his old point in *the saner appreciation* of his situation (300).

> The water [flowed] ceaseless and fresh *in a soft cool murmur of* ripples *at* his feet (329).

> Aissa rose *from before* the fire (335).

> The sombre line of the great forests bounded that smooth sea of white vapours *with an appearance* of a fantastic and unattainable shore (339).

> *In* an exaggerated sense *of* his great bodily weakness he felt somewhat *apprehensive of* possible assault (344).

> She sobbed *out in* a fresh *out*burst of grief (346).

> Why does she not *go from before* my face? (358).

> The blue smoke had drifted *from before* his eyes (360).

I do not mean to say that this is not English, but Conrad's exaggerated care of distinguishing the exact spot and the exact movement follows a Polish pattern.

There is also a passage in the *Outcast* which has a direct bearing on Conrad's Polish. "[Willems] was tormented by things that made him speak in the words of his own people. Speaking to himself—not to me . . . I followed him anywhere, watching for some word I could understand; but his mind was in the land of his people—away from me." (252)

Both the Polish and the French languages have the peculiarity of putting the adjective behind the noun for greater emphasis: *Une grande maison, une maison immense*. Conrad hardly used this stylistic means in *Almayer's Folly*; he became fond of it while writing *An Outcast*. In *Almayer's Folly*, we read "this sunny and smiling sea," (8) "a faint and sickly perfume," (16) "a brutal and merciless force," (19) "the grey-headed and foolish dreamer," (35) etc. In the *Outcast*, the post-positioning of adjectives becomes frequent, as if Conrad had discovered the trick while writing that novel: "A silence, cold, mournful, profound," (143) "a man angry, powerless, empty-handed," (215) "sounds surprising, unknown and strange," (264) "rags yellow, pink, blue: rags limp, brilliant and soiled," (301) "a ray merciless and crude," (301) "the night cool and merciful," (302) "men shivering and sleepy," (321) "the scent charming, penetrating, and violent," (337) "a gesture careless and tragic," (340) "an apparition unexpected, familiar and odd." (343) As can be seen, Conrad adopted the habit *while* writing the novel. There are only twelve examples in the first two hundred pages, but in the second half, 34 of them are on pages 300 to 357 alone.

In his following writings, there are not so many examples. In the tale "Karain," we read: "faces dark, truculent, and smiling; the frank audacious faces of men barefooted, well armed and noiseless." (*Tales of Unrest*, 3) But nowhere is there such an accumulation of post-positioned double or triple adjectives as in the last quarter of *An Outcast*.

This sentence from *Lord Jim* seems to follow a Polish pattern: "He pelted straight on his socks, beplastered with filth *out of all semblance to* a human being." (254)

Róża Jabłowska pointed out the following expressions as Polish-inspired:

The sloe-black eyes [Polish: oczy jak tarki] (*Romance*, 518).

I am like a pig at a trough (*Under Western Eyes*, 314).

The oldest bird can be caught with chaff (*The Rover*, 110) [a well-known Polish proverb]

Simple servants of God [meaning peasants] (*The Warrior's Soul*, 42).

Made me forget my tongue in my head (*Arrow of Gold*, 15).

The superterrestrial nature of my misery (*Ibid.*, 247).

Róża Jabłkowska also points out that in *Prince Roman*, Conrad has tried to render typically Polish forms of address, such as "Your Serenity" (116), "Master of the Horse," (121) (one word in Polish), "Master Francis," (124) and "Princely Mightiness." (126)

In *A Personal Record*, 21, Conrad literally translates Polish speech, when he reports that V. S., Bobrowski's confidential servant and major-domo, addressed him thus: "[The coachman] is the son of that Joseph that I suppose the Captain remembers. He who used to drive the Captain's [i.e. your] late grandmother of holy memory."

Yanko's speech in "Amy Foster" contains a number of wilful polonisms. Thus, when Yanko says *iron track* for railway, he is translating the Polish *kolej żelazna*. His *steam machines* (locomotives) derive from the Polish *maszyna parowa*. Conrad also makes Yanko imitate the Polish instrumental case in the sentence "a land that wearied his eyes *by its flatness*" (*Typhoon and other stories*, 115). He also makes him say "and the Miss too", aware of the fact that a Pole never uses the word *Miss* together with her family name, but uses it either by itself or followed by a Christian name.

When, in *Under Western Eyes*, the student Kostia asks: "may one come in?", he uses the common Russian or Polish phrase, to which the answer is not "yes" but "Come in!" Another Slavonic expression used by Conrad is "God's creation" for "living being."

Richard Curle pointed out that Conrad's style has a peculiar "musicality." Żeromski agreed with this and put it down as being due to Conrad's Polish heritage. He found in Conrad's prose a cadence or resonance which reminded him of Polish romantic poetry. He was thinking of sentences like the following: "His saved life was over for want of ground under his feet, for want of sights for his eyes, for want of voices in his ears" (*Lord Jim*, 115), or "The perforated pipe gurgled, choked, spat, and splashed in odious ridicule of a swimmer fighting for his life" (*Lord Jim*, 181). "Tell the brook not to run to the river, tell the river not to run to the sea" (as in *An Outcast*, 254). The post-positioning of adjectives which we already mentioned, also has this musical effect. We must not forget that in his youth, Conrad's ears were trained to hear Polish verse.

Another very Polish trait is Conrad's love for picturesque expressions and original similes. Polish speech, expecially that of the country people, indulges in proverbial expressions to an extent quite unknown in English speaking countries. New proverbial sayings are constantly invented and a few of them become established proverbs. One must have lived in the Polish countryside to appreciate the expressiveness of proverbial sayings used in everyday speech. I have heard Polish children of ten or twelve using quite intelligently sayings which are current, no doubt, but the use of which needs not a little imagination.

When, after a severe winter, I remarked to a boy how much warmer it was getting, he simply replied with two words: *Marzec, starzec*, "[In] March [winter is an] old man". I also remember a Polish schoolboy who wrote his name in beautiful letters on a copy book. When complimented on his achievement, he replied: "Every fox praises his own tail." A Polish peasant who broke a tool used to say: "This is as necessary as a hole in a bridge." If somebody looks pale: "He looks as a mouse who has come out of the flour." To characterize an overly curious person: "Eve herself could not have been more curious." Somebody looks at you in utter astonishment: "He stares like a wolf at his butcher." Two unsimilar things are "as similar as a dog and a bundle of straw." Something gets lost without a trace: "It fell through like a stone in the water". Something very funny "might make a horse laugh."

No doubt, Conrad's keen sense of picturesque expression is a Polish trait. In his work, he uses a great number of English proverbs (often accompanied by an apologetic "as the saying is"), but he also smuggles into his writings at least six Polish proverbs or proverbial expressions—three of them under a Russian flag! "Man discharges the piece, but God carries the bullet" (*A Set of Six*, 18), "When a guest enters the house, God enters the house" (*Victory*, 358), "One can do everything, but cautiously" (*The Sisters*, ed. Mursia, 45). In *Nostromo* (206), Charles Gould alludes to the Polish saying "God is very high above and the friend is far away." In *A Personal Record* (52), we find a Polish gentleman "stripped naked as a Turkish saint." This is an old Polish expression which has been used by almost every leading Polish novelist. Conrad took it from his uncle's *Memoirs*, together with the whole episode. Finally, a Polish saying underlies the lieutenant's exclamation in "The Duel" (*A Set of Six*, 197): "There's some milk yet about that moustache of yours, my boy," and the old warrior's indignant remark in "The Warrior's Soul" (*Tales of Hearsay*, 1): "Some of you had better wipe the milk off your upper lip before you start passing judgment." In Europe, no adult person would drink milk at that time.

Schomberg's statement: "He [Heyst] has turned hermit from shame. That's what the devil does when he's found out" (*Victory*, 31) is an allusion to two Polish proverbs which say that, when the devil is in a bad spot, he poses as a saint or a monk.

When Conrad does not find a fitting proverb, he occasionally fashions one: "The conveyance that was awaiting them would have illustrated the proverb that 'Truth can be more cruel than caricature', if such a proverb existed." (*The Secret Agent*, 155)

In "The Warrior's Soul," (*Tales of Hearsay*, 5), Conrad describes Tomassov's eyes as "blue . . . like the blue of autumn skies," obviously alluding to the customary serenity of the Polish and Ukrainian autumn. And when James Wait (*The Nigger of the "Narcissus"*, 23) says to the too familiar Donkin "We haven't kept pigs together," he uses a phrase well known in Central and Eastern Europe.

A few of Conrad's picturesque expressions allude to archetypal images: "Captain Giles . . . began to haul at his gorgeous gold chain till at last the watch came up from the deep pocket like a solid truth from a well" (*The Shadow Line*, 27) and, a big wave "made for the ship, roaring wildly, and in its rush it looked as mischievous and discomposing as a madman with an axe" (*The Nigger of the "Narcissus"*, 57).

The following expressions seem to be taken from Oriental speech: "Even a lizard will give a fly time to say its prayers" (Tengga in *The Rescue*, 174); and, "But even a spider will give the fly time to say its prayers" (Jörgenson in *The Rescue*, 446).

Other picturesque sayings are taken from daily experiences. Only a sailor would say of the fixed idea of his captain that "a steam windlass couldn't drag it out of him." ("Typhoon," 98) Some are definitely too sophisticated and remind one not of the picturesque speech of the Polish peasant, but rather of the mannerisms of modern writers: "He picked up the thread of his fixed idea" (*The Arrow of Gold*, 319), or, "[Morrison's] mind was like a white walled, pure chamber furnished with, say, six straw-bottomed chairs, and he was always placing and replacing them in various combinations," (*Victory*, 202)

To give an idea of the incredible wealth of Conrad's picturesque sayings, we will quote those to be found in the first four chapters of *Lord Jim*:

his incognito had as many holes as a sieve (4)

[the lighthouse] seemed to wink at her its eye of flame (15).

a throat bared and stretched as if offering itself to the knife (18).

he felt a pleasurable languor running through every limb as though all the blood in his body had turned to warm milk (21).

His breast glistened soft and greasy as though he had sweated out his fat in his sleep (21).

a voice harsh and dead, resembling the rasping sound of a wood file on the edge of a plank (21).

the fold of his double chin hung like a bag triced up close under the hinge of his jaw (21).

the thin gold shaving of the moon (21).

[The ship resembled] a crowded planet speeding through the dark spaces of ether behind the swarm of suns, in the appalling and calm solitudes awaiting the breath of future creations (22).

[The skipper] let loose a torrent of foamy, abusive jargon that came like a gush from a sewer (22).

[The skipper] a clumsy effigy of a man cut out of a block of fat (23).

From the thick throat of the commander of the *Patna* came a low rumble, on which the sound of the word *Schwein* fluttered high and low like a capricious feather in a faint stir of air (23).

He puffed like an exhaust pipe (24).

When [the chief engineer] moved, a skeleton seemed to sway in his clothes . . . [he was] smoking . . . with the imbecile gravity of a thinker evolving a system of philosophy from the hazy glimpse of a truth (24.

The last ten minutes of the watch were irritating like a gun that hangs fire (24).

The line dividing his meditation from a surreptitious doze on his feet was thinner than a thread in a spider's web (25).

She went over whatever it was as easy as a snake crawling over a stick (28).

His mouth was tastelessly dry, as though he had been eating dust (32).

The court peons . . . flitted rapidly to and fro . . . as noiseless as ghosts, and on the alert as so many retrievers (32).

Marlow's body . . . would become very still, as though his spirit had winged its way back into the lapse of time and were speaking through his lips from the past (33).

As can be seen from this collection, Conrad's picturesque similes are of very different value. Some of them, like "smoking like an exhaust pipe" are weak. Others, (like the one on page 33) are pseudo-profound. Some comparisons are out of proportion, as when Conrad writes in *Lord Jim*, "The tugs, smoking like the pits of perdition, get hold and churn the old river into fury" (45); the "pit of perdition," being an archetypal Biblical idea, is out of proportion here because the tugs have absolutely nothing devilish about them. "A fist as dumpy and red as a lump of raw meat" (*Lord Jim*, 47) is an adequate simile because it expresses the coarse and disgusting appearance of a hand incapable of delicate differentiated action. But when the owner of the hand disappears with his gharry as if "he had flown into space like a witch on a broomstick," the simile is incongruously applied to a man who, just before, had been called an "elephant" and "probably the heaviest man in the tropics."

Conrad and the French Language

Traditionally, French had always been the language of adoption of the Poles. It was learned from childhood and without tears. Konrad, too, had learned it naturally and with alacrity, while he had refused to learn English and had absorbed some German and Latin with obvious reluctance. During the last century, French words were adopted into the Polish language by droves. The language of the educated Pole was larded with French expressions, some used *tel quel*, others in polonized form. This is well reflected in the literature of the period, and even, to a moderate extent, in Bobrowski's letters. Apollo was rather an exception; but even his *Comedy* contains ten French expressions (apart from three Russianisms and 22 archaic Polish expressions).[170]

In his Polish letters, Conrad himself kept the Polish habit of switching to a French phrase whenever he wanted to emphasize something, but followed the trend of the younger generation to discard unnecessary gallicisms in Polish speech.

Contrary to the Anglo-Saxons who just lean back and wait for the rest of the world to learn their idiom (including its grotesquely archaic spelling), the Poles knew that the mastery of the French language was their key to that Western civilization of which they considered themselves—with good justification—to be the defenders and representatives in the East. Were they not called "the French of the East?"

Every well-to-do family had a *mademoiselle* for their children; the Bobrowskis being no exception. Conrad mentions her name as Mlle Durand (*A Personal Record*, 64). Her recommendation, "n'oublie pas ton français, mon chéri," uttered when he left Novofastov for Chernikov at the age of seven, remained forever engraved in his memory.

For the girls, French was a particularly important subject (as was playing the piano). Most young, intelligent women of the educated classes spoke French with ease. Ewelina was no exception, nor—a full generation later—Janina Taube. We know that Apollo (and probably also his mother as long as she was able to do so) taught the small boy French in exile. At St. Anne's, there was no French, but during the year preceding Konrad's departure for France, he lived in a house where the use of French was mandatory.

When the boy arrived in Marseilles, he found himself well rewarded. He very quickly became Monsieur Georges, "one of us," and a real *méridional*, even in the way he rolled his r's. Within a few months, he made more friends than he would make during his first years among the distant English. Had the petty bureaucracy of the *grande nation* not prevented his serving on any French vessel, the life of Conrad would have been forever linked with France and—so Jean-Aubry believed—with French literature.[171]

There can be no doubt that Conrad loved to speak and think in French. In his letters, he often falls back on a French phrase. He spoke French with a strong meridional accent, as we know from such a good judge as Paul Valéry.[172] While many people found his spoken English difficult to understand (Doubleday's New York secretaries even declared themselves unable to take his dictation),[173] nobody ever questioned the clarity of his French. As we can see from his many French letters, he mastered the language.

The influence of the French language on Conrad's English prose is quite visible. It is well-known that his masters were Flaubert, Maupassant, Balzac, Daudet, and others. It is not without significance that his one-time collaborator was Ford Madox Hueffer who knew French extremely well and whose book of reminiscences is a typical display of fireworks in the best French manner.

Conrad had a partiality for French-derived words, such as *ascend, descend, immense* for "big," *augment* for "increase," *access* (French accès) for "fit," *commence* for "to begin," *traverse* for "to cross," *visage* for "face," *a bound* (un bond), *a pace* (un pas) for "step," *arrest* (arrêter) for "to stop," *famous* for the colloquial French "fameux" in the sense of "excellent." The following are examples from Conrad's first books (italics mine):

The younger men *in an access* of good fellowship made their host talk (*Almayer's Folly*, 35).

A Malay girl whom the old seaman had adopted *in one of his accesses* of unreasoning benevolence (*Outcast*, 64).

. . . *in an access* of despair (*Ibid.*, 337).

. . . *in an access* of trembling pain (*Ibid.*, 342).

. . . in an access of insane terror *(Ibid.,* 359).

. . . traversing in all directions the field of his operations *(Ibid.,* 111).

Almayer . . . picked up his hat and . . . *commenced* to fan himself with *(Ibid.,* 207).

. . . it drove Lingard back a *pace (Ibid.,* 251).

That old business was good. Famous! *(Ibid.,* 251).

Conrad also had quite a weakness for the French-derived word *sombre* in preference to *dark. Sombre* (the usual French word for *dark*) occurs no less than 36 times in the *Outcast,* 29 times in *Lord Jim,* 17 times in *Nostromo.* In the same works, *dark* and even *gloomy* are comparatively rare.

A wilful gallicism, of course, is the phrase "deranged in his head" *(dérangé:* mentally disturbed) in *The Idiots,* written in 1896 in France *(Tales of Unrest,* 74). Another gallicism occurs in *A Personal Record,* where Conrad writes on page 88: "I have *essayed* (J'ai essayé) to put into the hollow sound the very anguish of paternity."

In *Almayer's Folly,* we find the expression *tranquilized* for *reassured* three times (54, 67, and 81). Conrad often uses the word *sentiment* in the French sense (i.e. for "feeling"). In *Nostromo* (201), the hide merchant, Hirsch, "had seen three men on the road arrested suspiciously," meaning the three men had stopped. In *The Secret Agent* (282), Winnie Verloc, speaking to Ossipon, "had no *conscience* of how little she had audibly said". In the same work (222), we find this expression: "A youngish composer *in pass* of becoming famous." In *Under Western Eyes,* the explosive device is called "an engine." This is not Russian but French: *engin* being the current French word for "device." In *Lord Jim,* there is at times quite a mix-up of languages, as on page 148 where the French officer is made to say: "And what life may be worth when . . . the honor is gone—ah ça, par exemple—I can offer no opinion. I can offer no opinion—because— monsieur—I know nothing of it." In this sentence, the expression "what life may be worth when the honor is gone" is very English. A Frenchman would have said it more forcibly: "What life is worth once the honour is lost." Also, there is no expression more English than, "I offer no opinion." A Frenchman may offer you anything from a cigarette to the hospitality of his home, but never an opinion! On the other hand, the last part ("I know nothing of it") is idiomatic French: *Je n'en sais rien*.

The formative influence of French style is strong in Conrad's works, as has been pointed out by several critics. The fact that he chose French rather than English authors as his models seems to betray a certain regret of not being able to write in French altogether. He had a great admiration for French literature, and if he let himself be influenced by his French readings, he only followed the tradition of his father's generation which, like the French, attached great importance to the formal aspects of their language.

Conrad's English

Conrad had learned Polish as his mother tongue, and better than the average Pole. In the Polish tradition, he had also acquired French as the language that would open the gate to the West. Learning English was a different matter, not a labor of love, but a sheer practical necessity. Moreover, nobody learns a language at 21 the same way a child does, or even an adolescent. Conrad learned English in two ways, colloquial English from the men around him, literary English from books. In his first works, the two kinds of English are curiously mixed. When he read some passages from the *Outcast* to Garnett, he mispronounced quite a number of words—he knew them only from books. In other passages (as in *The Nigger of the "Narcissus"*), he renders the speech of people as he had heard it. The introduction of Marlow also helped Conrad to get away from a stilted literary style. Yet even Marlow can fall into that very style, and not only when he tries to philosophize or be too clever. I doubt whether a captain telling a story would express himself as follows: " 'It is unfortunate you didn't know beforehand!' I said with every unkind intention; but the perfidious shaft fell harmless—dropped at his feet like a spent arrow, as it were, and he did not pick it up" (*Lord Jim*, 84).

In his first books, Conrad was not sure how well he was understood. There is quite often an overemphasis which reinforced the "exotic" (Polish) factor he had inherited. This overemphasis, among other things, led to unconvincing similes, often introduced by "as if." They are particularly frequent in *Nostromo* (italics ours, as in all the following quotations):

> [The Isabel Islands in the darkness] There was not a hint of them to be seen, *as if* they had sunk to the bottom of the gulf (263).

> Giselle . . . raised the altar cloth from time to time to hide nervous yawns, *as of* a young panther (533).

> [Nostromo saw] the fascination of her person in the night of the gulf *as in* the blaze of noonday (540).

> She seemed to skim along the grass *as if* on tiptoe (553).
> [as if young girls would *not* naturally run on tiptoe!]

> Her delicate head bowed *as if* under the weight of a mass of fair hair (555).

> The old man spoke *as if* startled (563).

As we have seen above, Conrad frequently uses expressions such as *from under, from behind*, and even *from out under*. But is it really necessary to be as precise as he is in *Nostromo* when he says that the dust raised by the galloping horses came *from under* their hoofs? (27) Or that the Indian girls "stared dully *from under* the square cut fringes on their foreheads?" (24)

In the *Outcast*, Conrad says of Aissa: "*from between* the long eyelashes, she sent out a sidelong look." (71) One wonders from where else her looks could come. Willems, on the other hand, glances at Almayer "ferociously *from under* his eyebrows." (73) Lakamba, in a mood of deep humility, equally looks at Abdulla "*from under* his eyebrows." (135) Lingard, furious at Almayer, stares at him "*from behind* his lowered eyebrows." (188) Other examples are:

> *From under* the house the thumping of wooden pestles husking the rice started with unexpected abruptness (237). (Why "from"?)

> Lingard stepped out *from behind* the tree (244).

His laugh ... seemed to be brought violently on the
surface *from under* his bitterness, his self-contempt,
from under his despairing wonder at his own nature
(274).

In the sentence, "the light of remote sun coming
victorious *from amongst* the dissolving blackness of the
clouds" (286) we notice not only the absence of an article
("remote sun") but also the use, so characteristic of Conrad, of a double preposition.

Many other illustrations of Conrad's anxiety to convey the clearest possible meaning could be mentioned.
They all prove the fact that this over-emphasis on clarity
often just led to an awkward turn of phrase. In a few
cases, it also produced a pleonasm, as in the sentence,
"He had been lying prone on the ground, either on his
back or on his face" (*Nostromo*, 497), where "prone" is
clearly used as a synonym to lying as opposed to standing.

Conrad's Choice of English

Conrad knew Polish well at the age of seventeen,
but during his period of maturation he was exposed for
four years to a French milieu, then, without preparation,
to an English speaking environment. He could not possibly have written in Polish, since as an adult he was
practically severed from Polish life and letters. He had
good reasons not to respond to his uncle's suggestions to
write about his travels in the Warsaw *Traveler*. He most
likely lacked even the necessary vocabulary to describe a
world so completely different. He would have found it
especially difficult, if not impossible, to render the nautical and geographical terms. Polish was definitely out of
the question.

Conrad might have written in French on the condition of being immersed long enough in the French
milieu. One must not forget that as a writer he would
have been handicapped by his lack of any formal schooling in the French language. French (like Polish, incidentally) is much more a formal language than English, and
we may believe Conrad when he wrote that he "would
have been afraid to attempt expression in a language so
perfectly 'crystallized'."[174] On the other hand, at least
some of his French letters are so idiomatic that one can
surmise that another five years of exposure to French

would have made all the difference, and that his literary French would then actually have been superior to the English of his first novels.

Hugh Clifford, a longtime friend of Conrad's (despite his criticisms of the latter's Malays), understood that Conrad had once hesitated between writing French or English. This statement was published in Hugh Walpole's *Joseph Conrad* (1916), to the great annoyance of Conrad who protested vehemently in a letter addressed to Walpole:

> I want to thank you at once for the little book and to tell you that I am profoundly touched . . . The only thing that grieves me and makes me dance with rage is the cropping up of the legend set afloat by Hugh Clifford about my hesitation between English and French as a writing language. For it is absurd. When I wrote the first word of *Almayer's Folly*, I had already for years and years been thinking in English. I began to think in English long before I mastered, I won't say the style (I haven't done that yet), but the mere uttered speech.[175]

Conrad then explained that writing in French would have meant translating from the English. This is certainly true of most of Conrad's writing, including his first books. On the other hand, some passages in *The Arrow of Gold* and in *The Rover* are definitely thought out in French, especially the speeches of Rita, Lieutenant Réal, Peyrol, and Scevola. Parts of "Prince Roman," "Amy Foster," and *The Sisters* were just as clearly conceived in Polish. Even in *Almayer's Folly* there are expressions which seem to have a Polish origin. Thus, " 'It [the sun] has set at last', said Nina to her mother" is possibly a reminiscence from *Konrad Wallenrod*, where we read, " 'It has set at last', said Alf to Halban." Both can hardly wait for the night to come.

Conrad would not have interspersed his English letters with so many French expressions, if he had never thought in French. Being exposed to an English speaking environment, with nobody ever speaking a word of French (except in Mauritius), he naturally thought mostly in English when in contact with others, but this may have been different in his frequent moments of solitude. A man who knows three languages never thinks in one language alone.

In his desire to emphasize his affection for English, Conrad, moved by his Polish propensity to pay exaggerated compliments, made some incongruous statements. What also attracted him to English, he said, was "the sheer appeal of the language, my quickly awakened love for its prose cadences, a subtle and unforeseen accord of my emotional nature with its genius." This is a very curious statement in view of the fact that he often complained about the erratic English phonetics with its badly enunciated vowels. He once said to his wife: "You English pronounce all vowels alike," and to Mégroz: "The phonetics of English is indeed a dismal thing for foreigners."[176] This does not sound like coming from one who is delighted at English prose cadences. We know that Flaubert's or Maupassant's prose appealed to him more. Conrad also pronounced the famous words that he had been "adopted by the spirit of the language" which "fashioned" his "still plastic character." Twice (in his letter to Hugh Walpole of 7 June 1918, and in his Author's Note to *A Personal Record)*, he solemnly declared that, had he not written in English, he would never have written a line for print at all. Here one is tempted to reply not "Amen," but "How do you know?"

In 1922, Conrad had a talk with Mégroz, during which he gave some information on how he picked up his English. He had been to Boult's Coaching School in London to prepare himself for his merchant Navy certificates, and there had learned the nautical terminology. He had also bought a green, one-volume edition of *Shakespeare's Complete Works* which he read through more than once. He also possessed Mill's *Political Economy,* which "pulled [his] English together," but also acted as a soporific! Much of his English Conrad claimed to have learned from the reading of good newspapers, especially *The Standard,* known for its great attention to style. Conrad told Mégroz that he experienced "enormous difficulties in learning the English language" because of "the many words pronounced alike and meaning different things."

We know that Conrad admired Dickens very much, but he did not mention this in his talk with Mégroz. We also know that he read Turgeniev in English. Apart from the talk of sailors and some other acquaintances, the language of his books is that learned from readings and refashioned by a strong individuality.

He had always abhorred grammar, he told Mégroz. He was very arbitrary in his use of "should" and "would." Being impervious to grammar, he could never learn Latin or German which, in Polish schools of his time, were taught predominantly in a grammatical way. He was best at composition and mathematics.

It must be said that Conrad was not always sure of his spelling. He made spelling mistakes in Polish, French, and English alike. In *Nostromo*, almost half of the numerous Spanish words are misspelled. A few are not even Spanish. His *Polish Memorandum*, written in 1914, contained a number of bad mistakes, even the word "Russia" (Rosja) was misspelled as Rossja! In French, he would often write *présant* for *présent*, *example* for *exemple*, and he was never sure about the ending *-ance* or *-ence*.[177] In English, words like *although* gave him trouble, as Garnett reported in his introduction to *Letters from Joseph Conrad*. These, of course, are minor blemishes only mentioned for the sake of completeness.

Conrad's Persona and Personality

There is no doubt that Conrad, seeing that he was unable to make a living as a ship's officer, resolved to become an English writer at all costs. The acceptance of *Almayer's Folly* and some favorable reviews showed that he had talent, so he decided to use it. Even so, it was a desperate and reckless attempt. Which foreigner, not schooled in English has ever become a successful writer of fiction? Wells did not exaggerate a bit when he wrote in his autobiography that Conrad "had set himself to be a great writer, an artist in words, and to achieve all the recognition and distinction that go with that ambition. He had gone literary with a singleness and intensity of purpose that made the kindred concentration of Henry James seem lax and large and pale"[178].

In order to achieve success, Conrad tried everything to build up a *persona*, i.e. an "image" of a great writer. We have already seen elsewhere to what lengths he was ready to go in this respect. Wells was very struck by the image Conrad tried to convey to him: "I found- ... something ... ridiculous in Conrad's *persona* of a romantic adventurous un-mercenary intensely artistic gentleman carrying an exquisite code of unblemished honor through a universe of baseness..."[179] Such, of course, was Wells' personal impression ironically expressed, covering only one aspect of Conrad's "duplex" personality. It has to be balanced against Garnett's description:

> There were two natures interwoven in Conrad: one, feminine, affectionate, responsive, clear-eyed: the other, masculine, formidably critical, fiercely ironical, dominating, intransigent. Often the sweet mood would change in a flash . . . His fine courtesy kept his Polish impetuosity in check in those early years, but he resented bad manners when addressed. When Conrad wanted to surrender himself to anybody, he did it singleheartedly.[180]

Indeed, Conrad was a *homo duplex* in more ways than one. His very nature was contradictory to such an extent that different people got to know him from quite different angles. He kept the habits of a Polish land squire, but also lived as a British "citizen." He never spoke the language properly. He was arbitrary, unpredictable, suffered no contradiction from wife or children; in short, he was as domineering as a Polish country squire of the last century. He considered himself a clever businessman, but was unable to manage his financial affairs. He was a gifted writer with an almost unique power of visualization; yet, he was not free from bad lapses of taste. He loved to live under the British flag, but thought that British politics were rotten, the parliamentary system with its two parties artificial, that all British politicians were unimaginative MacWhirrs unable to interpret the storm signs of the times. He despaired of Western civilization which accommodated itself with the fact that the noble Polish nation was kept captive and divided for almost a century and a half, and which had no answer to poverty, social divisions, national and racial prejudices, imperialism, and war. He foresaw that the British Empire and the Western civilization would be doomed unless drastic changes were made.

The Boer War almost drove him crazy. On one side, he wanted to be loyal to the country of his choice (as testified in his letter to Mme. Zagórska of 25 December 1899, where he admits that his feelings are "very complex");[181] on the other hand, the imperialistic take-over of a free republic reminded him too much of what had happened to his native country. His only hope was that the affair would be over quickly, for, as he wrote to

Cunninghame Graham on 14 October 1899, "if there's murder to be done in the next room and you can't stop it, you wish the head of the victim to be bashed in forthwith and the whole thing over for the sake of your own feelings." (*LL*, I, 285) In a letter to E. L. Sanderson, dated October 26, 1899, he expressed his conviction that this war was not going to solve any problems, since "the victory will have to be followed by ruthless repression" (*LL*, I, 285)—a clear allusion to Poland.

The Spanish-American War, preceding the Boer War by one year had already stirred Conrad's indignation—needless to say that his sympathies were all on the side of the weaker Latin race (*LL*, I, 236 and 243). At this moment, he once asked why Cunninghame Graham was writing for the English, "*une galère qui n'arrivera nulle part*," and what was the use of "flinging scorn, contempt and bitterness at this world," since "*l'ignoble boule roulera toujours portant des êtres infirmes et méchants dans un univers qui ne se comprend pas lui-même.*"

In 1898 especially, he poured out his heart to Cunninghame Graham, using the French language for some emphasis: "*La société humaine est essentiellement criminelle*"; men are "*fourbes, lâches, menteurs, voleurs, cruels,*" the accepted principle being "*Ôte-toi que je m'y mette.*" He saw the democratic idea as a *beau phantôme* leading to a world where mass instincts and "caesarism" would reign.

This was the period when Conrad first battled with *The Rescue*, when the Americans had won their victories over the Spaniards, when the British had a major military victory in the Sudan, and when the Boer War was in the offing.

It has often been said that Conrad's fundamental pessimism was due to his childhood experience and to the hopelessness of the Polish situation. This seems to be supported by Conrad's own words:

> *Moi, je regarde l'avenir du fond d'un passé très noir et je trouve que rien ne m'est permis hormis la fidélité à une cause absolument perdue, à une idée sans avenir. Aussi, souvent, je n'y pense pas. Tout disparaît.*

What added to Conrad's desperation and scorn, however, was also his disappointment with Western culture. Like Miss Haldin in *Under Western Eyes* and Stephen in *The Sisters*, he felt that Western civilization and Western politics were not based on fundamental principles or values, but on opportunism and greed. Therefore, they were actually working at their own destruction. Far from believing in the then prevalent idea of eternal progress, he saw everywhere signs of incompetency and even decay. Yet, as late as 1922, he told Mégroz: "All my hopes for Europe, as a lover of humanity, you understand, are centered on England."[182] But this did not do away with his disillusionment.

It had been difficult to define Apollo's conception of a good government; it is not easier in the case of Conrad. We know that he was an aristocrat at heart and disliked the British labour government. He believed that leading men should lead instead of being dependent on and responsible to the whims and instincts of the masses. He disliked socialism because for him it meant the rule of the masses, the dictatorship of mediocrity and uniformity, and the end of the enlightened, competent individual responsible to his own conscience and to humanity. In these conceptions, Conrad may have been guided by the image of Uncle Bobrowski who would have made a fine politician indeed. But on the whole, it must be said that, while Conrad knew very well what was wrong with the West in general and England in particular, he failed to come up with real answers. One has only to read his novel of a country in the making, *Nostromo*, to become aware of this.

But Conrad's cosmic irony and fundamental pessimism cannot be explained by the Polish reminiscences alone. His values—the "few simple ideas"—the idea of fidelity were not sufficient. In all his books, except *The Rover*, the characters are blindfolded in one way or another, and, therefore, work for their own undoing, if not for the ruin of their community. He saw the politicians of the West in much the same light—with the future of Western civilization at stake. Such convictions, coupled with the feelings that nothing could be done, necessarily led to pessimism, if not downright despair. They explain much bitter sarcasm and they might have ended in cynicism if Conrad had not been too much of a responsible individual to become a cynic.

With the example of his father and his country before his eyes, he could not believe in ideals. He was convinced that an idealist never wins. On the other hand, the so-called realist and pragmatist is only thinking in terms of money and power. Conrad was intensely interested in political affairs, but he did not like what he saw. Most of his friends (Shaw, Wells, Cunninghame Graham, and others) believed in "progress" and in some kind of socialist doctrine. Conrad maintained that socialism, once in power, would soon turn to "caesarism." (This expression is the exact equivalent of the word *hosudarstwo* which his father had used to designate czarism). Conrad was against any division and did not believe in class politics. "Class for me is by definition a hateful thing. The only class really worth consideration is the class of honest and able men to whatever sphere of human activity they may belong."[183] Even if started by men animated by the highest ideals, a revolution would invariably fall into the hands of power-hungry sociopaths who would then maintain their power by force, against the will of the people and even against the public interest. Conrad saw the West heading, not towards "progress," but towards an impasse. He had always opposed imperialism and colonialism in all its forms and he knew that these isms would soon be obsolete, but he did not see any constructive alternative forthcoming. Being an aristocrat of the mind, he did not believe in the infallibility of mass instincts, nor did he see anything but danger in arousing them. He abhorred mass culture. (How he would have hated TV!) He believed in the leadership of the responsible, honest, gifted individual committed to lead the country to a higher destiny, but the party system seemed to produce only political opportunists who were unable to see the writing on the wall. He never voted in an election because he rejected the imperialism and nationalism of the Conservatives, as well as the ideological obtuseness of the Liberals, and the narrow materialism of Labor.

Conrad was fundamentally a pessimist because he thought that human nature was intrinsically corruptible, blind for the real issues, stupid if not downright bad. He did not believe that human nature could be changed on a scale great enough to change the course of history. Since a change of system without a change of heart would not constitute real progress, the greatest political upheaval could only make things worse.

Much of what Conrad believed has been vindicated since. Of all English novelists of his time, few, if any, had the penetrating political insights and prophetic gifts of the son of the political idealist, Apollo. There was in him the soul of the Polish poet-seer. One wonders what he would have become had he remained in Poland, or how he would have written, had he not been obliged to write for material gain.

Conrad's indebtedness to the tradition of the great Polish classics who preceded him by two generations cannot be doubted. In 1904, a Frenchman, Edouard Schuré, gave this impression of the Polish Romantic poets:

> I am struck by the power of these poets. They all have something excessive and almost obsessive about them, but they are deeply original and their imagination carries the reader away. They are all bards, prophets, visionaries. With them one feels transported to an epoch when humanity was more savage, but where man had a greater stature, where heroes were more noble and poets more inspired.[184]

There is no need to point out here how much of this description applies to Conrad's writings as well. Even his villains appear to be more than life size! But the quotation may also help us to understand why the Poles, especially when reading *Lord Jim*, never fail to somehow sense the Polish quality of Conrad's inspiration.

XIII.

Conrad's Art

This book is the work of a psychiatrist interested in the workings of the literary mind in general, and of the *duplex* personality of Conrad in particular. We have tried to show how most of Conrad's themes ultimately derive from his Polish background, and that he was never far away from Poland when writing.

What compelled him to write as he did, and did he succeed in what he set out to do? We know that he wrote compulsively, like a slave. He was what Szondi calls the paroxysmal type. When he had finished a book, the paroxysm of work was normally followed by a paroxysm of gout. He was either driven ahead as if by an invisible whip, or he had no drive at all. At best, he had a unique power of creating an atmosphere and of making a reader "see;" at worst, he became verbose, commonplace, pseudo-profound, magazinesque.

We believe that, essentially, art is communication, and that Tolstoy was right when he wrote that "infectiousness" was the mark of great art. Unless we are seized by what the artist tries to convey, or—to use a term perhaps too dear to us—unless we can "identify" with what the artist describes, we are not confronted with great art. Still more, unless the artist's communication changes us (by providing new insights leading to a more humane and constructive attitude), his art has failed. This sounds extremely demanding, but with Conrad no lesser criterion will do.

Because different people are differently affected (and infected) by the same work of art, judgements of value may differ. Grubiński asked: "Could there be a book more Polish in spirit than *Almayer's Folly?*" Najder called *Lord Jim* "Conrad's most Polish novel." If we can identify with Jim, and, through him, with Conrad, we easily come to the conclusion that *Lord Jim* is Conrad's greatest novel, because it is the most intensely personal. If this participation fails, the novel will still appear interesting, even intriguing, but unnecessarily long-winded, contrived, unduly pessimistic, with an ending that will not seem compelling. The same remark applies to *Victory*, where it is even more difficult to identify with the hero—to say nothing of the misty figure of Lena. Failing such identification, one cannot but dismiss the whole story as too "melodramatic." Yet, we are certain that Conrad never intended the ending to be melodramatic, and that to him it was genuinely pathetic.

If art is considered to be the power to evoke a fictitious world having a consistency and pathos of its own, then *Nostromo* is the superior novel. Here we meet Bobrowski in disguise, writing his exhaustive *Memoirs*, a most honest man and real patriot, but one who must accept the fact that bribes *do* lubricate the political machinery. We get a glimpse of Apollo in the person of the ex-freedom fighter, Giorgio Viola. We become familiar with young Conrad, fresh from Marseilles, in the shape of Decoud and of the patriotic Ofelia Buszczyńska as Antonia Avellanos. We hear of civil war, repression and pacification, imprisonment and torture, military tyranny, deeds of valor and deeds of atrocity: it is the Polish history of the years of 1814 to 1867 all over again.

While we find it difficult to identify with any character of the novel, we are called to participate in the political events of a country that can only be itself if it is free. No less than in *Lord Jim*, Conrad tries to enlist our sympathy or to mobilize our powers of disgust and abhorrence. Here too, he wants to teach us something—that which Captain Mitchell will never learn—and thereby to change us. By placing his heroes in boundary situations, by facing them with ultimate questions and irrevocable decisions, he is constantly asking his reader: how would *you* have fared under these circumstances? It is the Pole who speaks to the Englishman who does not know what it means to have to fight for national survival against an enemy who has all the material power, to begin to write in a foreign language in a country where he had virtually no friends, or to be insulted by being called "a man without a country and without a language" (1908).

While we read Conrad's best books, our own personality is being challenged, weighed, exposed; our values are being questioned mercilessly. While we watch with bated breath the hero (Jim, or Marlow in *Heart of Darkness*, the crew in the *Nigger*, the captain in *The Secret Sharer* or the skipper in *The Shadow Line*) undergoing, in Jungian parlance, a process of individuation, we are actually submitted to that very same operation. If Conrad, in his own obsessive-compulsive way, insists on confronting us constantly with the ultimate, with life or death, good or evil, human nature and human fate, the ultimate meaning of human existence, what else can he want from us but to share his own quest? He wants us to learn, to acquire new insights, lose old prejudices, give a fuller meaning to our lives so that we, too, might change. If he forces us to face our own shadow and our own hidden self, it is because he does not want to fight alone when grappling with the ghosts and shades which assail him.

But the quest for the ultimate meaning of life is really a religious question. Man is a spiritual being who has to find a higher meaning to his life than a merely biological and material one. Only religion can provide the answer.

The Greeks made the favor and disfavor of the gods—if not their jealousies—responsible for what befell human beings. Their gods were a projection of man's aspirations, drives, and passions. In the Jewish-Christian view, the approach is different. Here, man is confronted with a divine order, a preordained order of things which, in its last absurd consequence, leads to the idea of predestination. Man's fate is determined by his acceptance or nonacceptance of God's order, God's authority, and God's love. In the Christian view, it is the meek, not the heroic, who inherit the kingdom of heaven. The word *hero* does not make sense, since all human achievement, unless done in fulfilment of God's will, is vain and perishable. Christ was not a hero. The hero is a pagan conception: he is the man who dares to defy the gods, even if he has to pay for it with his life. With Conrad, the accent is very much on defiance. The seaman who "gives back yell for yell to a westerly gale" (*The Nigger*); Lord Jim who, before dying, sends "a proud and unflinching glance" at the assembled natives he has betrayed; Heyst who stubbornly refuses to leave his island after the death of Lena and jumps into his burning house—these are perhaps the most conspicuous examples of "heroism."

Atonement by death is a pagan idea. In the Christian view, God does not want the death of the sinner but that he repent and live. Death may be the wages of sin, yet there is no redeeming power in a violent end.

Most of Conrad's "heroes" are people who are at variance with the order of things in which they grew up. Some are downright outcasts, others unhappy exiles trying to find another meaningful existence. Some succeed, for a time, to create a world of their own: Lingard organizes the Shore of Refuge, then Sambir. The Malay Archipelago is his second homeland. Lord Jim becomes the leader of Patusan. For quite a number, their boat and their range of action replace their country, to which they will never return. The "Rover," Peyrol, is about the only person in Conrad's works who succeeds in going back. As a rule, Conrad's heroes are so alienated from the country of their fathers, that they will never "go home," or only go home to die. But if there are no happy relationships with the father(land), there are no happy marriages either. In this respect, too, Conrad's heroes run foul of the divine order. It is as if, by losing their country, they had also lost their spiritual heritage and the inner security and moral strength it provides and without which marriage cannot work.

Nobody can doubt that Conrad's works are haunted by the shades of his Polish past. He, too, had left his homeland in defiance of his father's most sacred convictions. Apart from two short visits to his uncle in the Ukraine, he was for many years afraid of facing the verdict of his countrymen. In 1914, he did not visit the tomb of his father—half an hour's carriage drive from his Cracow hotel. He did not look at the house where his father died, although he passed near by when he went to see the Royal castle with his family. He never read his father's original works. He rejected the latter's religious convictions.

Nobody today would blame Conrad for having left Poland in 1874. He had the right to decide for himself which road to take, but he also had to bear the inevitable consequences of his alienation and to carry, besides the difficult Nałęcz heritage, the extra burden of a *homo duplex*.

The development of Conrad's personality was particularly difficult. He lost his parents very early, and when he left Poland, had only an adolescent Polish personality, i.e. a personality in the making. During the following three years, he was under strong "méridional" influence and adopted most of the Southern French mannerisms, including a strong Southern accent. This phase came to an abrupt end, and Conrad now had to adjust to an English way of life. No sooner had he developed the *persona* of a British mariner and captain, his seafaring career ended, and he set himself the task of becoming a leading English novelist. As a foreigner, he had to be either outstanding and unique, or remain a nobody. In order to be successful, he for many years thought it necessary to repress his Polish heritage.

When a person deliberately tries to keep at bay his national heritage, as Conrad did up to 1909, the repressed factors are bound to form an unconscious opposition within his conscious personality. In Jungian terms: while the writer develops a *persona* modelled on the prototypes he chooses from amongst his environment, he at the same time acquires a strong *shadow*. This shadow is made of the repressed, underdeveloped, "inferior" aspects of the personality. The stronger the repression, the stronger the *shadow*. Conrad spoke of his shadows as of "ghosts and shades." Repressed tendencies are bound to become more primitive and less controllable. They nearly always lead to unpredictable behavior. They maintain an inner tension which produces hostility and aggressivity expressing itself in violent "unmotivated" outbursts. Jessie Conrad has faithfully reported on this aspect of Conrad as reflected in his daily life. In his works, these ghosts and shades are probably responsible for the extraordinary number of violent deaths and the many unhappy marriages. Indeed, beginning with his first novel, all marriages in Conrad are unhappy because of an incompatibility of character, often accentuated by racial differences. These conflicts may well reflect the incompatibility of the writer's basic but repressed and underdeveloped *polonitas* with his acquired personality as an English novelist. Such incompatibility by necessity leads to dangerous confrontations and boundary situations. Moreover, the strong undercurrents opposing the *persona* confer a mysterious, ghostlike, uncanny quality to the events. They create a state of mind where people, torn by incompatible tendencies, no longer know their

own mind (a very Conradian theme!), where unconscious motives suddenly take precedence over rational
thought, and where the whole existence acquires a
dreamlike, twilight quality. There is very often a mystery
surrounding the decisions of Conrad's characters. The
discussion concerning these motives sometimes takes
much space, as in *Lord Jim*. Conrad succeeded in using
the interaction between the *shadow* and the *persona* as a
highly artistic device. In *The Nigger of the "Narcissus," The
Shadow Line*, and *The Secret Sharer*, the spell is finally
broken (the shadow is left behind); in *Heart of Darkness*,
Kurtz is completely engulfed by his shadow while Marlow manages to free himself from its deadly embrace.
That Conrad became a master of describing the struggle
between conscious personality and shadow can only be
explained, apart from his talent, by his own experience of the incompatible within himself.

Being able to make the reader "see" this conflict
may have been, for Joseph Conrad, a kind of self-cure.
In his later novels, at any rate, this kind of struggle is
absent. The *shadow* is now clearly projected on some bad
men (Schomberg, Mr. Jones, Scevola, etc.), which is the
conventional way of visualizing what actually is an inner
conflict.

Conclusion

Joseph Conrad, a writer of English prose, was a fascinating person. His life story is nothing short of miraculous. He experienced his first shipwreck at the age of four—the exile of his parents. The words of the prophet in Słowacki's *Anhelli*, "your home shall be a sinking ship," came true for him. His mother perished when he was eight, his father when he was not quite twelve. He was rescued by a wonderful uncle, a widower who had lost his brothers, his only sister and his one child, and for whom Conrad became "my dear boy." That Joseph Conrad finally made it was to a great extent Bobrowski's merit.

Conrad was a descendant of Poland's gentry and he shared most of their pronounced defects as well as some of their virtues. He had enormous difficulties in adjusting to school, learned poorly, and at the age of sixteen became a drop-out who liked to do as he pleased. Spoiled in his childhood because of alleged delicate health, missing whole months of school for some cure in a spa, in the mountains, or in the South, his health miraculously improved in Marseilles, where no more "illness gain" could be expected.

Apart from his uncle, the hard life of a sailor was his best educator. Here he learned to master his impulses, to stick to a job, to take responsibility, to sacrifice his whims for hard necessities. Finally, when he realized that he was not made for the sea after all, he took up the even more exacting and—for many years—more thankless occupation of a writer. On the *Torrens*, the sailors disdainfully called him "the scribbling mate." Bobrowski considered his English writing as a hobby. His first published novel sold extremely poorly.

For Conrad who, according to his uncle, had all the unreliability and changeability of the Nałęcz, writing became the last straw to which he clung with a perseverance which seemed contrary to his family tradition, but which may have been an avatar of that recklessness with which his father had pursued his political visions.

As if this were not enough, Conrad also went through the trying school of marriage. By a stroke of luck, he got the very wife he needed: placid, extremely patient, a proficient typist, a capable cook, a fine mother both to him and his children. There are not many women who could have made a success of a marriage with Joseph Conrad; Jessie succeeded with her devotion, her extreme flexibility, her common sense. His Polish side was always a riddle to her; she spelled his second Polish name wrong on his tombstone; she quoted a verse allegedly from Apollo's tomb in Cracow which is not there; she got the address of Apollo's last abode quite wrong too. In short, she was a genius for mixing up Polish things. Yet, she made a tolerable husband and a good father out of a man who had no talent for either.

A lot has been written about Conrad's pessimism. Most critics tend to attribute it to the atmosphere of sadness, mourning, if not despair, in which the boy grew up. But Conrad's pessimism is more than that. It is related to the seemingly hopeless fate of Poland. Conrad's country was artificially divided between three empires who did their best (or worst) to stamp out Polish identity. Poland was in fact an occupied country for 150 years. What infuriated the Poles was that the Western democracies took this state of affairs for granted. Already Conrad's father, like many others, had appealed to the conscience of the West, those cradles of freedom and liberalism. The appeal was in vain. Western eyes did not see and Western ears would not listen. It needed no less than a world war to make the West realize that Poland existed and wanted to live her own life. The hopeless situation of Poland was, we believe, the real source of Conrad's pessimism.

When Conrad once said to a Pole that wherever he traveled over the seas he was never far away from his country, or when he declared to another Pole: "The leading principle of my life was to help Poland,"[185] he was of course falling into the typically Polish habit of exaggerating. Yet there is some truth in his assertion if we realize that he had gone to sea in order to escape an intolerable Polish situation and to find a freedom for which the Poles were thirsting at home. Even the smuggling of arms to Spain (as the clandestine traffic of arms and gunpowder in Conrad's Malayan novels) has a Polish connotation: the smuggling of weapons had played an important part in the Polish uprisings, as did clandestine political plotting.

Conrad's *polonitas* pervades his work in a subtle fashion: in his outlook, in the peculiar quality of his inspiration, his interest in politics, in his often ferocious style, the musical cadence of many sentences, the choice of his similes, and often also in the choice of his topics. Contrary to what some readers may think, the present book was not written to dig out the Polish raisins in what is an essentially English cake. The raisins are there, but they have been pointed out less as curiosities than as symbolic proofs showing how much Conrad's heart, despite everything, remained rooted in his native soil.

NOTES

I. The Family Heritage

1. In Polish "Dla miłego grosza".
2. In Polish "Co robić z tym fantem?" The title in an allusion to the well-known society game where the players have to give a "pawn" for each mistake. In the end, the pawn has to be redeemed by a solo performance of a funny kind.
3. According to Taborski, *Apollo Korzeniowski*, 57-59.
4. According to Bobrowski's *Memoirs* I, 362.
5. Conrad uses the same simile in *The Rescue,* 96, and in *Nostromo,* 484.
6. On the cross which Mrs. Conrad showed me in 1929, I read *Virtute,* but the order is known as *Virtuti Militari.*
7. G. Jean Aubry, *Joseph Conrad: Life and Letters* (2 vols., New York and London, 1927), I, 290-1 (hereafter quoted as *LL*).
8. A picture of the cross was published in my *Polish Heritage of Joseph Conrad,* 16.
9. The parents of [Apollo] Korzeniowski were very honorable people and much respected in the neighborhood. The mother was a Dyakiewicz, honest, tyrannized by her husband, a good mother, but leading an existence of no importance. The father, Teodor, lieutenant in 1807, captain in 1831, fought well but had all the limitations of the gentry. He was convinced he was the first soldier in Europe, the best estate-manager, and the man of the highest merit in the whole country. As a matter of fact, he was an utopian, and a teller of yarns of that special kind who first lie to themselves, get to believe their own lies, and then pass them on to others and quarrel with those who will not believe them. Naturally, he considered himself as a great politician and first-class patriot, for without listening to common sense, he was always ready to saddle a horse and chase the enemy out of the coun-

308

try. [Conrad used this very passage in *A Personal Record*, 47: "He himself was that type of Polish squire whose only ideal of patriotic action was 'to get into the saddle and drive them out'."] And people listened to what he said and often even believed him, for everybody knew that the gentry had fought well in old times. Few people objected that they were equally good at inventing yarns of imaginary heroic deeds. After the loss of his wife's estate in the Vinnitsa district, he administered the estate Korytno, belonging to the government. But though the estate was beautiful and the lease low, and in spite of his being an industrious and devoted manager, he continued to live according to his illusions and lost the rest of his money there. For himself, he had a great respect, but for his sons he showed great admiration, especially when speaking of them to others. It was a habit with him— especially when he was angry which happened quite often—to treat them not as adults but as small boys, calling them idiots if nothing worse—treatment which they bore with the greatest respect, kissing their father's hand . . . Living in a world of personal, family and politico-patriotic illusions, the brave captain spent his old age in poverty, and in 1863 saw the consequence of his convictions. In Spring 1864, while looking after the estate of his son Hilary, his ruined life ended." *Memoirs*, I, 363-365.

10. Miss Jerry Allen has tried to save Conrad's honor by the premise that he served on the *Anna Frost* for eight days when the ship made a journey from London to Le Havre and back in June 1881. For such a short voyage he would not necessarily have been entered on the crew's list. When leaving the harbor of Le Havre in tow of a tug named *Napoléon*, the ship struck her bow on the portside against a granite wall, loosening several stones. The accident happened at night, and Jerry Allen surmises that Conrad was "thrown overboard by the force of the collision". The ship was only slightly damaged and reached London two days later. It appears that Conrad was on board and that he went to a hospital for a few days.

Two months after the presumed accident Conrad wrote to his uncle *stating that he had been shipwrecked and had lost all his belongings!*

Jerry Allen's explanation is hardly convincing. Nobody falls overboard because of a slight collision—he would have to be standing on top of the railing! Moreover, Conrad could not swim! Finally, even if he had fallen overboard, he would not have lost all his belongings in the mishap. Bobrowski, with his usual precision, noted in his "Document", "In August [1881], having learned about the shipwreck of *Anna Frost*, £10." The actual shipwreck of that vessel took place 3 September 1882, in the Atlantic. Conrad was then serving on the *Palestine*.

11. Bobrowski's letter was dated 30 July 1802: "[Teodor and Hilary] were always involved in various projects, most diverse in nature, mostly of a financial order—they hatched them in their imagination and were even offended when anyone criticized them—considering their opponents to be "idiots", but the facts most often gave the lie to their dreams, hence bitterness towards those who had seen more clearly. Your father was an idealistic dreamer. He certainly loved people and wanted them to be happy—although he usually applied two measures: he was a lenient judge of the poor and the weak of this world and very severe and pitiless towards the rich and powerful . . . They all had a high opinion of themselves and suffered much after their failures . . . you are also subject to these inherited shortcomings and you too bear their punishment. In your projects you let your imagination run away with you—you become an optimist, but when you encounter disappointment, you become easily despondent.

   Quoted from Najder's *Conrad's Polish Background*, 147-148. (with permission of Oxford University Press and the Conrad Estate). *Translation Halina Carroll*

12. *Edinburgh Review*, January 1925.

13. *Castles in Spain*, 82.

14. *Joseph Conrad: A personal Remembrance* 17 and 119.

15. According to the Bobrowski Document, published in Najder's *Conrad's Polish Background*, 202. See also p. 22, where the total inheritance is put at 16,200 roubles. Conrad destroyed all the papers pertaining to these financial matters and let his wife and his biographer Jean Aubry believe it had only been "a small capital".

16. Jitomir (as spelt by most biographers) is written Zhitomir in modern transcription. Conrad mentioned it as J— in *A Personal Record*, 58. Jitomir is all right if pronounced in the French fashion. The Polish name was Żytomierz. In both languages, the accent is on the o.

17. Probably an allusion to Mickiewicz's verse in *Forefathers' Eve*: "Someone, perhaps, seduced by gifts of state, betrays his free soul to the Czar for hire." Conrad would take up this subject in *Under Western Eyes*.

18. The ring was used as legitimation, as is a ring in *Lord Jim*, 233, and in *The Rescue*, 21 and 93.

19. The Polish rising against the Germans, in Warsaw, August 1944, followed closely the pattern of all Polish re-

volts. There was no sufficient preparation, and the decision was made hastily in the vain hope that the Allies would support them. The Poles at first fought superbly and threw the Germans out of Warsaw, but owing to lack of support from outside, the insurrection spent itself within weeks. The Germans retook the town and destroyed it, with the Russian army looking on from the other side of the Vistula.

20. Sentence as reported by Apollo himself, in *Fatherland* (Ojczyzna), Leipzig 1864, no. 29. This was a Polish weekly written for the numerous Polish exiles in Central Europe. The court sentence was dated 23 March 1862. It read literally: "Prikazano wyslat' Korzeniowskogo i zhenu jego na zhitelstwo v g[orodie] Perm, pod strogim nadzorom policii." (It is ordered that Korzeniowski and his wife be exiled to residence in the city of Perm, under rigorous police supervision). The sentence proves that his wife was condemned together with Apollo and had no other choice but to go with him. However, they were under no obligation to take Konradek with them.

21. Blue-eyed people: Polish people. In several Polish towns, such as Białystok, there were small demonstrations, soon repressed by the Cossacks, in honor of Apollo, as soon as the convoy arrived.

22. This reminds us of a passage in a letter Conrad wrote to Sir Hugh Clifford, dated 25 January 1919: "It is a great relief to my feelings to think that no single life has been lost on any of the fronts for the sake of Poland. The load of obligation would have been too great." (*LL*, II, 217).

23. Chernikov is spelled differently according to languages: Chernigov (Russian), Chernihov (Ukrainian, Czerników (Polish). Conrad mentions the town as T— (obviously for Tchernikov) in *A Personal Record*, 71.

24. How much Conrad shared the political opinions of his father concerning Poland's historic role, is shown by a letter he addressed to John Quinn on 24 March 1920, in which he mentions "Poland's old historical part of defender of civilization against the dangers of barbarism." (*LL*, II, 237).

25. Translated from *Outline of Polish Literature*, vol. IV, 83.

26. Translated from *The Living Conrad*, 145.

27. "What I saw with my own eyes was the public funeral, the cleared streets, the hushed crowds; but I understood perfectly well that this was a manifestation of the national spirit seizing a worthy occasion. That bareheaded mass of work people, youth of the University, women at the windows, school-boys on the pavement, could have known nothing positive about him except the fame of his

fidelity to the one guiding emotion in their hearts . . . this
great silent demonstration seemed to me the most
natural tribute in the world—not to the man but to the
idea. *A Personal Record*, Author's Note.

". . . small boy . . . following a hearse; a space kept clear
in which I walked alone, conscious of an enormous following, the clumsy swaying of the tall black machine, the
chanting of the surpliced clergy at the head, the flames
of tapers passing under the low archway of the [Florian]
gate, the rows of bared heads on the pavement with
fixed, serious eyes. Half the population had turned out
on that fine May afternoon. They had not come to honor
a great achievement, or even some splendid failure. The
dead and they were the victims of an unrelenting destiny
which cut them off from every path of merit and glory.
They had come only to render homage to the ardent
fidelity of the man whose life had been a fearless confession in word and deed of the creed which the simplest
heart in that crowd could feel and understand." *Notes on
Life and Letters*, 109.

II. Conrad's Education

28. Apollo sent his adaptation to the French to Kaszewski,
    but it was never published. See Lisiewicz, *The Living Con-
    rad*, 149.
29. Letter dated 6 September 1865 (Russian calendar). The
    quotation is from Taborski's *Apollo Korzeniowski*, 128.
30. Conrad wrote the name in full in his *A Personal Record*,
    64, but mentioned his Bobrowski relatives only as B.
31. Barbara Kocówna, *Reminiscences*, 38.
32. *Ibid.*, 39-40.
33. Jean-Aubry, *The Sea Dreamer*, 41. It seems that Konrad
    had epileptoid attacks until the age of 14. See also note 3
    on page 9 of Najder's *Conrad's Polish Background*. Najder
    seems to believe that these were genuine epileptic fits.
    We doubt this very much. Like every overprotected
    child, Konradek was nervous and unconsciously pro-
    tested by hysteriform attacks against the unnatural way
    he was brought up. There is an interesting parallel to
    this in Carl Gustav Jung's life story, as related in his
    Memories, Dreams, Reflections (30-32). Jung remembers
    that, after a fall, he had fainting spells whenever he did
    not want to go to school or to do his homework. He had
    to be taken out of school at the age of 12. One day, he
    overheard a doctor tell his father this might be epilepsy
    and incurable. The boy was scared and soon overcame
    his nervous fits. He applied himself at school and became
    a good scholar.

34. According to the "Bobrowski Document" (185), Konradek spent the winter 1866/67 with his grandmother in the mild climate of the Black Sea, near Odessa. On the way they passed through Kiev where a doctor was consulted. They obviously stayed at the "Liman," i.e. on one of the several former river estuaries cut off from the sea, where the water contains a high percentage of magnesium, calcium, iodine and bromine salts which had the reputation of curing rheumatism; skin diseases and nervous disorders. The fact that Conrad later stated that he saw the sea for the first time in Venice, in 1873, has given cause for quite some controversy among Polish critics. Yet Konradek was not brought to the health resort near Odessa in order to watch the sea and still less to bathe in it, but in order that the delicate and nervous boy might profit from the good air and the emanations from the *limans*.

35. This, of course, is a fantastic version of the accident Conrad had on board the *Highland Forest*. A fall from a mast would most likely be fatal.

36. Quoted from Kocówna, *Reminiscences* etc., 86-88.

37. In his article "Where did Conrad first see the sea and where did he go to school?" *Literary News*, Nr. 37, 1932.

38. "Conrad in Cracow" in *Trends* (Kierunki), Cracow, 19 January, 1958.

39. While in Topolnica, in summer 1868, Apollo wrote to his friend Kaszewski: "It is difficult to teach [Konradek] anything at all with his health in this state. He is already eleven and for almost two years has learned nothing." In October, Konradek still was unable to go to school. See also Jean-Aubry, *The Sea Dreamer*, 41-42.

40. This must have been in March to May 1869, as Apollo moved to Cracow only at the end of February.

41. Jean-Aubry, in his *LL*, gave the address as Poselska 136 and Barbara Kocówna accepted this. But the street is much too short for such a number. Jessie Conrad, on the other hand, in *Joseph Conrad and his Circle*, 251, gives Apollo's address as 9, Hospital Street (Szpitalna), but Konrad came to live there only after the death of his father, with his grandmother. Jessie Conrad, in the same book (279) also quotes an inscription on Apollo's tombstone which is simply not there. The fact is that neither Conrad nor his wife, in 1914, visited Poselska Street, nor Apollo's grave.

42. See *The Secret Agent*, 301.

43. Attribute of Viola in *Nostromo*.

44. According to the obituary in *Time*, Cracow, no. 117, 1869.

45. Communication made in 1890 by Mrs. Josephine Rejska, to Marguerite Poradowska. (*Letters of Joseph Conrad to Marguerite Poradowska,* 135).

46. Conrad always remembered Pulman with thankfulness. Of his last examinations (spring 1873), he wrote in *A Personal Record* (42-43): "The scholastic year came to an end. I took a fairly good place at the exams, which for me (for certain reasons) happened to be a more difficult task than for other boys."

47. "Nothing on our continent could give a greater idea of the forces of nature and the omnipotence of the Creator than a look at this immense vault of foaming waves, at this thundering mass of water which rushes to the abyss boiling, hissing, throwing up clouds of mist. Before this sight, man feels as small as nothing. No one can watch this raging tumult of unrestrained forces without being shaken to his innermost self. Even the blandest minds will be fascinated again and again by this tumult of water. One may have seen it a hundred times, yet the impact remains as strong and as fresh as for the first time. The spectator feels as if he were admitted to God's holy workshop. No longer conscious of himself, he is but eye and ear. The majestic stream splits up to a thousand springs, the springs to billions of water particles. The spectator sees the stream transform itself to water currents and water dust driven around like dry leaves before the wind. The firm soil trembles under his feet, the rocks overlooking the tumult of water shake their black heads as if scandalized at the fury of the angry element. The tremor of the earth, the thunder of the water tempest around, above, and below him pierces his soul like music of the Cherubs and the sounds of holy! holy! holy! roar and throb though his whole body . . . Thus the sight of the infinite forces and the majesty of nature, before which all human greatness vanishes like a drop falling into the sea, opens the trembling heart to the consoling religion, leading the weak mortal to faith in God and Eternity."

48. "If anything could induce me to revisit Sulaco . . . it would be Antonia—and the true reason for that—why not be frank about it?—the true reason is that I have modelled her on my first love. How we, a band of tallish schoolboys, the chums of her two brothers, how we used to look up at that girl just out of the schoolroom herself, as the standard-bearer of a faith to which we were all born, but which she alone knew how to hold aloft with an unflinching hope! She had perhaps more glow and less serenity in her soul than Antonia, but she was an un-

compromising Puritan of patriotism with no taint of the slightest worldliness in her thoughts. I was not the only one in love with her; but it was I who had to hear oftenest her scathing criticism of my levities—very much like poor Decoud—or stand the brunt of her austere, unanswerable invective. She did not quite understand—but never mind. That afternoon when I came in, a shrinking but defiant sinner, to say the final good-bye, I received a hand-squeeze that made my heart leap and saw a tear that took my breath away. She was softened at the last as though she had suddenly perceived (we were such children still!) that I was really going away for good, going very far away—even as far as Sulaco, laying unknown, hidden from our eyes, in the darkness of the Placid Gulf."

III. Conrad's Contacts with Poland

50. Had Conrad known of this, he would certainly have commented sarcastically on this holocaust of anything found in Bobrowski's mansion that was printed or written—in the name of a "cause." The episode could have been part of *Nostromo*.

51. The original of this letter in Conrad's hand is at the Library of the Polish Academy of Sciences (PAN) in Cracow. My translation.

52. Quoted from Barbara Kocówna, *Reminiscences*, etc., 117-120. Perłowski (1872-1941) published his memories on Conrad in the *Contemporary Review*, in 1937, forty-seven years after the event.

53. *LL*, I, 79, and Conrad's letters to Joseph, 82-83.

54. The fact that Conrad's contemporary Joseph, to whom all of Conrad's letters were addressed, used Spiridion as his surname has led Jean-Aubry to attribute the whole correspondence to "Spiridion Kliszczewski". But from the contents, it is clear that they were written not to the father Spiridion Kliszczewski but to his son Joseph. In I, *LL*, the person mentioned several times as "Spiridion" or "Spiridion Kliszczewski" is always Joseph Spiridion-Kliszczewski. The same ambiguity exists in Jean-Aubry's *The Sea Dreamer*, 106-107.

55. *In Joseph Conrad as I knew him* (42-43), Jessie Conrad writes that she finished typing the *Nigger* in November 1896, but Jean-Aubry states that the *Nigger* was finished on 19 February 1897 (*LL*, I, 165)

56. Chwalewik, to whom we owe all the details about the Spiridion family, published the results of his research in *Literary Scene*, 8, 1932. He also published Mee's article in full, in Polish!

57. *Joseph Conrad and his Circle*, 55.

58. Lutosławski's article is reproduced in B. Kocówna, *Reminiscences* etc., 11-15.

59. Translated from E. Jankowski's biography *Eliza Orzeszkowa*, Warsaw 1964, 486-487.

60. Garnett, *Letters from Joseph Conrad*, 235.

61. The Polish word *polskość* (the letters ś and ć represent swishing sounds somewhat between s and sh, respectively ts and ch) seems to have no equivalent in English. Conrad himself translated it by *polonism*, a word not in the Oxford Dictionary. The best translation would be *polonity*, a word that should be created for the sake of Conrad. Gillon used the term *Polishness* in quotation marks, others rendered the meaning by speaking of "the Polish spirit" or "the Polish character". In this book, we shall speak of Conrad's *polonitas*.

62. See the chapter "Three Landmarks" for a reminiscence of Grażyna in Conrad's *Victory*.

63. According to Ujejski (*Joseph Conrad*, 18), Aniela reported Conrad's words as follows: "Don't bring me anything from that shrew."

64. Jessie Conrad, *Joseph Conrad and his Circle*, 263 and 271. John Conrad, *Reminiscences* in *The Living Conrad*, 29.

65. It is a riddle why Conrad thought so much of Winawer's very mediocre works. He could have found much worthier objects to translate from Polish.

66. Jessie Conrad, *Joseph Conrad and his Circle*, 175.

67. Letter in Polish, dated 18.10.1914, to Dr. Kosch and published in L. Krzyżanowski, *Centennial Essays*, 139.

68. *Ibid.*, 143.

69. *LL*, II, 188, to Chr. Sandeman.

70. To the same, *LL*, II, 191.

71. Conrad continued: "The Polish question has been buried so long that its very political importance is not yet seen. In this war it had not been (even) of episodic importance. If the Alliances had been differently combined the Western powers would have delivered Poland to the German learned pig with as little compunction as they were ready to give it up to the Russian mangy dog. It is a great relief to my feeling to think that no single life has been lost on any of the fronts for the sake of Poland . . . The only justification for the reestablishment of Poland is political necessity . . . Nothing serious or effective will be done. Poland will have to pay the price of some pretty ugly compromise, as you will see. The mangy Russian dog having gone mad is now being invited to sit at the Conference table, on British initiative! . . . In a class contest there is no room for conciliation. The attacked class cannot save itself by throwing

honesty, dignity, and convictions overboard. The issue is simply life and death, and if anything can save the situation it is only ruthless courage." (*LL*, II, 216-217).

72. Quoted from Kocówna, *Reminiscences* etc., 122-123.

73. Paderewski's biographer, Charles Phillips (*Paderewski, the Story of a Modern Immortal*) erroneously places the meeting between Paderewski and Conrad in London and in 1924.

74. Jean-Aubry, *The Relationship of Joseph Conrad to Music* in the Polish paper *Muzyka*, nr. 5, 1926.

IV. The Lingard Trilogy

75. Both quotations from *Almayer's Folly*, 11 and 23.

76. In his Author's Note to *Tales of Unrest*, V.

77. This detail I have from Dr. I. Griffith, Chatham, Ontario, who had practised medicine in London, before emigrating to Canada. One of his English patients was an old sailor who had served under Conrad on the *Torrens* and who remembered that this was the nickname the crew had bestowed upon him. The sailors had no idea what he was writing. See also *A Personal Record*, 4, "What are you always scribbling there?"

78. The Dutch spelling of this name is Olmeijer. Conrad may never have seen the name written or he (if not Almayer himself) may have thought it more convenient to spell the name in a way which the English could pronounce.

79. *Almayer's Folly*, 10.

80. A locality with this name does not exist in the Malay Archipelago. Gillon (*The Eternal Solitary*, 48) has pointed out the similarity between Sambir and Sambor, the market town in the Ukraine (then in Eastern Galicia) where Conrad's former tutor practised medicine. Moreover, Gillon drew attention to the fact that Conrad, in a Polish letter addressed to Gustaw Sobotkiewicz and dated 28 March 1890 had written that Pulman was probably living in Sambir, meaning Sambor. The Ukrainians themselves pronounce Sambor as Sambir (and Lvov like Lviv). Whether Conrad knew the Ukrainian pronounciation is a matter of conjecture. The letter to Sobotkiewicz is reproduced in Krzyżanowski, *Centennial Essays*, 159. It was written during Conrad's sojourn at his uncle's Kazimierówka.

81. The symbol of the swimmer fighting (mostly uselessly) for his survival, occurs several times in Conrad's works: *Outcast*, 80-81, *Rescue*, 240, *Lord Jim*, 181, *The Secret Sharer* (last sentence). In *The Planter of Malatta*, Renouard com-

mits suicide by swimming out into the sea. Conrad's fondness for this metaphor stands in strange contrast to the fact that (as his son John revealed in *The Living Conrad*) he could not swim himself. In a letter to W. Blackwood of 1 September, 1900, Conrad wrote: "Surely if I go under I shan't have the consolation of railing bitterly at the unkindness of mankind . . . Anyhow, I shall try to swim as long as I am able." (*Letters to Blackwood*, 110).

82. A white eagle is Poland's centuries-old emblem. This is strictly a heraldic bird, since white eagles have never existed in Europe. Eagle-like white birds, however, live in the tropics and one can imagine Conrad's feelings when he first saw a live "white eagle." Here, the white eagle, of course, symbolizes the soul of Arsat's wife taking its flight to heaven—a simile very much in the tradition of Polish romantic literature.

83. *LL*, I, 164, note.

84. *LL*, I, 186

85. *LL*, I, 230

86. *LL*, I, 232

87. *LL*, I, 255

88. *LL*, I, 260

89. *LL*, II, 209

90. *LL*, II, 212

91. For the symbol of the swimmer, see note 81.

92. In an unsigned article, *The Genius of Mr. Joseph Conrad*, *North American Review*, June 1904. He sent Conrad his article, revealing his identity. Conrad agreed at once that he knew very little about Malays. See also *Author's Note* to *A Personal Record*, VI: "I don't know anything about Malays." He knew them mostly from books.

V. Lord Jim

93. Letters dated 18 resp. 21 July, 1900, published in *Letters to Blackwood*.

94. In a curious mix-up of cargo and captain, the Montreal *Gazette* published this cable on 23 August, 1880: "London, 22 August, Captain Pilgrim, who abandoned his vessel, the Jeddah, in the Red Sea, has had his certificate suspended for three years."

95. The boat was called *Antenor*, a name taken from Greek mythology. Antenor was connected with a story of treason, for according to one Greek tradition it was he who helped to betray Troy.

96. The principal owner of the Jeddah was a rich Arab of Armenian descent, named S. Muhammad Alsagoff. The name is well known in Singapore and a recent develop-

ment of apartment houses carries the name "Alsagoff Gardens."

97. For details, see Norman Sherry, *Conrad's Eastern World*, 41 ff.

98. My own translation from Freud, *Gesammelte Werke*, XIII, chapter V, 280.

99. When Conrad was in Corsica (1921), he met a young French dramatic writer interested in psycho-analysis, H. R. Lenormand, who tried to discuss with him the psycho-analytical implications of *Lord Jim*, *Almayer's Folly* etc. He also gave Conrad Freud's *Dream Interpretation* to read. To his astonishment, Conrad declared he had never read a word of Freud, did not believe in psycho-analysis and would not read *Dream Interpretation*. He spoke of Freud with "ironical disdain." Lenormand, *En Corse avec Joseph Conrad, Transatlantic Rev.* 2, 1924, and *Nouvelle Revue française*, 135, Dec. 1924.

100. The epithet dreamer has been applied to Apollo as well as to Conrad more than once.

101. Conrad once told R. Curle that Patusan was supposed to be in Sumatra. The name was invented by Conrad. In the *Times Literary Supplement* of 30 August, 1923, we read in an unsigned article (probably by Curle) that Patusan was meant to be on the South coast of NW Sumatra. More about this in Andrzej Braun, Album, III, 196-204 and *In Conrad's Footsteps*, 584.

102. *Conrad's Eastern World*, 45.

103. In his introduction to "Selected Novels by Conrad" (in Polish) Ossolineum, Wrocław 1957

104. *The Living Conrad*, 138.

105. *A Personal Record*, 121: "I verily believe mine was the only case of a boy of my nationality and my antecedents taking a, so to speak, standing jump out of his racial surroundings and associations."

106. This aspect has been studied by R. R. Hodges in his essay *Four Fathers of Lord Jim*, in *Universal Rev.*, Dec. 1964. Denver's sentence (LJ, 189): "For my own sake I had to tell a plausible lie at the club" seems a most Polish trait—this is exactly what Bobrowski would have done. Marlow once calls Jim "my dear boy" (Bobrowski's usual form of address), to which Jim responds with "old man" *LJ* 240-241).

VI. The Political Novels

107. Actually twenty-seven.

108. Cunninghame Graham knew South America and the Spanish language very well and would easily spot Conrad's many inaccuracies.

109. Dr. Monygham's torture and subsequent false confession are very probably modeled on Masterman's experiences, described in his *Seven Eventful Years in Paraguay* (1870). See E. K. Hay's *The Political Novels of Joseph Conrad*, 170. The similarity between the "pacifications" of Poland and the events in Paraguay must have struck Conrad.

110. Paul Hostowiec (*The Living Conrad*, 87-91) also discusses the influence of Ukrainian memories in Conrad's work. The country estate (*dwór*) with its paternalistic organization (e.g., Bobrowski's *Kazimierówka*) is clearly reflected in the hospitable country estates (haciendas) described on pp. 87-88. Conrad was also familiar with the Ukrainian towns (Zhitomir, Lwów) with their mixture of nations living harmoniously together under Polish leadership. Sulaco is built along the same pattern.

111. The name "The Isabels" is probably derived from *Isola Bella*, which Conrad must have visited in 1873.

112. Costaguana can be either interpreted as "Coast of manure" or as "Coast of palms." Guano means *palm* in South America.

113. Before his exile, Apollo used to finish his letters to political friends with an emphatic "*Pro Patria!*"

114. It is doubtful whether this is a French name, as Conrad pretends it to be. It much rather sounds like a fragment of a German word. Conrad knew enough German to be aware of the depreciative meaning of the prefix *ver-* (*verdammt, verflucht*, "damned" etc.). It is possibly from the German word *verlochen*: "to throw away in a hole" that Verloc is derived.

115. *Conrad's Western World*, 228 ff.

116. *Joseph Conrad*: A study in Non-conformity (Phil. Library, New York, 1959).

117. Geneva has been chosen as background by several English writers (Shelley, Ruskin, Meredith, and others). H. W. Haeusermann has written a study on the subject: *The Genevese Background*, London 1952.

118. We do not know where Conrad took the name from. It is not really a Russian name (the Russian alphabet has no letter H).

119. Perhaps Conrad had unhappy memories concerning Geneva. We know that during his first stay he courted a French girl who refused him.

120. *Forefathers' Eve*, part III, translation by Watson Kirkconnell.

VII. Shadows

121. "Of the foolish and the wise alike"—a reminiscence from the first part of Goethe's *Faust*, where Mephisto tells

Faust: "A complete contradiction remains mysterious to the wise and fools alike."

122. *University of Toronto Quart.*, July 1955.
123. *Portraits from Memory*, 84.
124. "The 'Unspeakable Rites' in *Heart of Darkness,*" Mod. Fiction Studies IX, no. 4, reprinted in M. Mudrick's *Conrad: Collection of Critical Essays,* 45-54.
125. Schomberg is a Jewish name. A Dr. Schomberg lived in London at the end of the century. His son emigrated to Canada.

VIII. Three Landmarks

126. Conrad began to write *The Rover* immediately after returning from Corsica (1921), where he had freshened up his Mediterranean memories.
127. According to John Conrad (*The Living Conrad*, 29) and Jessie Conrad, *Joseph Conrad and his Circle*, 263 and 271.

IX. Conrad's Polish Stories

128. In his article *"On Conrad and Kipling,"* *Contemporary Rev.*, Cracow 1937, reprinted in Kocówna, *Reminiscences* etc., 121.
129. *Literary News*, no. 566, 1934.
130. "Conrad and Yanko Goorall," *Literary News*, Warsaw, No. 574, 1934.
131. Jessie Conrad, *Joseph Conrad as I knew him*, 35 and *Joseph Conrad and his Circle*, 26.
132. *A Set of Six*, Author's Note, VII. See also Wacław Borowy, *Studies and Essays*, Wroclaw 1952 (Vol. II, 61-72). Borowy suggests that "conde" might be the Napolitan form of "conte". It is true that in the Napolitan dialect the word is pronounced "condo", but it is unlikely that anything else but good Italian was spoken in the better circles where the Count was known.
133. This is how Mickiewicz described Yankel:
In the centre of the [inn's] room stood the host, Jankiel, in a long gown reaching to the floor and fastened with silver clasps. One hand was tucked into his black silk girdle, with the other he stroked his beard in dignified fashion. (*Pan Tadeusz*, Book IV, verses 223-226)
In "Prince Roman," Conrad wrote:
The innkeeper, a portly dignified Jew, clad in a black satin coat reaching down to his heels and girt with a red sash, stood at the floor stroking his long silvery beard. (*Tales of Hearsay*, 39).
    Mickiewicz also wrote that Yankel "had the reputation" of "being a patriotic Pole" and "as he spoke [of

Polish affairs] he sobbed; the honest Jew loved his country like a Pole"; while Conrad put it this way: "He tried to keep down his excitement, for the Jew Yankel, innkeeper and tenant of all the mills on the estate, was a Polish patriot."

134. The main passage is the following: Prince Roman Sanguszko was the son of Eustache . . . he was married to a Potocka . . . who, having given him a daughter, Maria (later Countess Alfred Potocka), died just before the insurrection, in 1831. Prince Roman at that time served in the Russian Guards but when on a visit to his parents in Volhynia, joined the rising and later became a prisoner. When the investigating officer, who sympathized with the parents, during the inquest wrote that he joined the rising because he was despondent following the death of his wife and did not realize the consequences, Prince Roman [requested to sign this declaration, instead] wrote on the sheet: "I joined the rising from conviction." I have heard that the last two words were adopted as a motto by Prince Sanguszko, but I never saw them on the actual seal of the Prince (*Memoirs*, II, 372).

135. "The commission was composed of three officers. It sat in the citadel in a bare vaulted room behind a long black table. Some clerks occupied the two ends, and besides the gendarmes who brought in the Prince there was no one else there. Within those four sinister walls shutting out from him all the sights and sounds of liberty, all hopes of the future, all consoling illusions—alone in the face of his enemies erected for judges, who can tell how much love of life there was in Prince Roman? How much remained in that sense of duty, revealed to him in sorrow? (*Tales of Hearsay*, 51)

136. What happened at this preliminary examination is only known from the presiding officer. Pursuing the only possible course in that glaringly bad case he tried from the first to bring to the Prince's mind the line of defence he wished him to take. He absolutely framed his questions so as to put the right answers in the culprit's mouth, going so far as to suggest the very words: how, distracted by excessive grief after his young wife's death, rendered irresponsible for his conduct by his despair, in a moment of blind recklessness, without realizing the highly reprehensible nature of the act, nor yet of its danger and its dishonour, he went off to join the nearest rebels on a sudden impulse. And that now, penitently . . .
But Prince Roman was silent. The military judges looked at him hopefully. In silence he reached for a pen and wrote on a sheet of paper he found under his hand: "I joined the national rising from conviction."

Such was the written testimony of Prince Roman in the supreme moment of his life. I have heard that the Princes of the S— family, in all its branches, adopted the last two words: "From conviction" for the device under the armorial bearings of their house. I don't know whether the report is true. My uncle could not tell me. He remarked only, that naturally, it was not to be seen on Prince Roman's own seal. (*Ibid.*, 52-53)

137. In "Prince Roman," the name is Sergeant Peter. Bobrowski did not mention under which name the Prince served, but we know from Eustachy Sanguszko's *Memoirs* that his son used the name Stanislaw Lubartowicz, Stanisław being one of Prince Roman's first names and Lubartowicz the old family name later changed to Sanguszko. It was a particularly grave offense in Russia to adopt a false name.

138. *On Conrad and Kipling*, 1937, reprinted in Kocówna's *Reminiscences* etc., 122. In the same article, Perłowski (who became a Polish diplomat after 1918) calls Conrad's statements concerning Poland, both in *A Personal Record* and in "Prince Roman" "inconsistent and chaotic."

X. The English Shock

139. This fact is firmly established. Bobrowski had this information from such a reliable source as the shipowner, Mr. Délestang, himself. We know this from a letter from Bobrowski addressed to Buszczyński and published in Najder's *Conrad's Polish Background*, 176. This is the relevant passage: "Although Konrad had been absolutely certain of accompanying Captain Escarras on his next voyage, the Bureau de l'Inscription forbade him to go on grounds of his being a 21-year-old alien who was under the obligation of doing his military service in his own country. Then it was discovered that he had never had a permit [army leave] from his consul. The Ex-Inspector of the port of Marseilles was summoned who in the register had acknowledged the existence of such a permit. He was severely reprimanded and nearly lost his job—which was undoubtedly very unpleasant for Konrad. The whole affair became far too widely known and all endeavors [to allow Konrad to serve on the ship] by the captain and the shipowner proved fruitless (the shipowner, Mr. Délestang, himself told me all this) and Konrad was forced to stay behind with no hope of [ever] serving on French vessels." (Translated by Halina Carroll Najder).

140. In Jean-Aubry's biographies, the fiction of a duel is upheld, although we know from Bobrowski's letters, both to Conrad and to Buszczyński, that Conrad attempted suicide, but that everybody was told it had been a duel. Conrad shot himself and the bullet went right through but without touching the heart. Two of Conrad's heroes are killed by a shot through the chest: Willems and Jim.
141. According to John Conrad, in *Living Conrad*, 17.
142. In a letter to Galsworthy of 21 January 1905, *LL*, II, 9.
143. Instead of his usual "straight like an arrow", Conrad here chose a Polish simile.
144. David Lynn in *Daily News*.
145. *Literary News*, Warsaw, 1929, no. 51.
146. As far as we know, Conrad never called himself a "British subject," but always a "British citizen." This was in keeping with Polish tradition: the Poles had been citizens in independent Poland, but became subjects to foreign rulers following the partitions.

XI. Conrad's Works in Poland

147. Probably through Antoni Czarnecki, journalist in Chicago.
148. He just said that Conrad was already known to the readers.
149. Quotations from Kocówna, *Reminiscences* etc., 33-34. Already Rolle had called Apollo a dreamer-poet.
150. Conrad wrote to Blackwood on 22 December 1902: "The third [copy of *Youth*], I want to send to Poland, for the very young lions of an extremely modern literature review in Warsaw, called *The Chimera*. Let them chew it up and snarl over the flavor of the fossil." Letters to *Blackwood*, 174.
151. The Polish original of Conrad's letter was published in Pietrkiewicz, *Polish Prose and Verse*, University of London, the Athlone Press, 1956. Żeromski's preface to *Almayer's Folly* was reprinted in a posthumous volume of Żeromski's essays entitled *Elegies* (1928) and in Kocówna's *Reminiscences* etc. (1963).
152. Garnett, *Letters from Joseph Conrad*, 280-281.
153. Grabowski, *Studies on Joseph Conrad*, 1927, 114.
154. Ujejski, *Joseph Conrad* (French edition), 24.
155. Maria Młynarska, in *The Living Conrad*, 264.
156. So during the Warsaw rising in August/September 1944, as Maria Młynarska attests (see above). Conrad must have thought of the Polish *wieszcz* when he wrote, in his *Personal Record*, of "the poet as a seer." 93.
157. All quotations from *Jan Kott* are from his essay "The lay tragic spirit," in *Creativity*, Sept. 1945, 137-160. Kott later

became more tolerant. He now lives in the West. His *Sketches on Shakespeare* were translated into English as *Shakespeare our Contemporary*, London 1964.

XII. Man of Three Languages

158. Najder, *Conrad's Polish Background*, 177.
159. *Ibid.*, 180. Both remarks were addressed to Stefan Buszczyński.
160. Quoted in Kocówna, *Reminiscences* etc., 117.
161. *Conrad and his Contemporaries*, 66.
162. Preface to *Almayer's Folly* (1922), reprinted in **Elegies* (1928) and in Kocówna, *Reminiscences* etc., 180.
163. Kocówna, *Reminiscences* etc., 91.
164. *Conrad in Zakopane*, in *Polish Gazette*, no. 24, 1932.
165. "Conrad as a Critic of the Polish Translation of his Short Story 'Il Conde'," reprinted in Borowy's *Studies and Essays*, Wrocław 1952, vol. II, 61-72.
166. Kocówna, *Reminiscences* etc., 181.
167. *Polish Gazette*, no. 24, 1932.
168. *The Eternal Solitary*, 47.
169. *Conrad and his Contemporaries*, 110.
170. According to Taborski's notes in the latest edition of *Comedy* (1954).
171. Jean-Aubry in his article *Souvenirs* [de Joseph Conrad]: "*Il s'en est fallu de bien peu que nous ne comptions un grand écrivain de plus.*" *Nouvelle Revue Française*, 1 December 1924, 677.
172. Paul Valéry came from the South of France himself, "Conrad *parlait le français avec un bon accent provençal; mais l'anglais avec un accent horrible qui m'amusait beaucoup.*" *Nouvelle Revue Française*, 1 December 1924, 663.
173. *World Today*, no. 52, July 1928.
174. *A Personal Record*, Author's Note (VII) and *LL*, II, 206.
175. Letter dated 7 June 1918, in *LL*, II, 206.
176. Mégroz, *Joseph Conrad's Mind and Method*, 33.
177. René Rapin, *Lettres de Joseph Conrad à Marguerite Poradowska*, Genève 1966. Rapin found no less than 227 mistakes in these letters, of which 192 wrong accents. Conrad also wrote *vous* always with a capital, in the Polish fashion. Rapin also pointed out many anglicisms such as *oeuvre créative* (for *créatrice*). *réassurer* (for *rassurer*), *significance* (for *signification*), and even *large* (for *grand*). Jean-Aubry had corrected all these mistakes and incorrections for publication in *Conrad, Lettres françaises*.
178. *Experiment in Autobiography*, II, 615.
179. Wells, in the same book, quoted by Baines, 234.
180. *Letters from Joseph Conrad*, 10.
181. *LL*, I, 288.

182. *Joseph Conrad's Mind and Method*, 21.
183. In a letter to E. L. Adams, dated 12 November 1922 (*LL*, II, 285).
184. Quoted from Sarrazin, G., *Les grands poètes romantiques de la Pologne*, Paris 1904.
185. See Antoni Czarnecki, "An Evening with Conrad" in *Ameryka Echo*, Toledo, Ohio, 31 July 1924.

Bibliography

Primary Sources

Aubry, Jean G. *Joseph Conrad: Life and Letters*.
Garden City: Doubleday Page, 1927 (This
source is identified as *LL*, vol. I or II, fol-
lowed by the page number)
———— *The Sea Dreamer: a definite Biography of
Joseph Conrad*. same publisher, 1957
Conrad, Joseph *Works*. Kent Edition. Garden
City: Doubleday Page, 1925. (All quotations
from Conrad's works are from this edition,
with page number following the title, e.g.
Lord Jim, 75. The pagination is the same as
in the English edition by Dent and Sons).
———— *Lettres françaises*. Paris: Gallimard, 1930
———— *Lettres de Joseph Conrad à Marguerite
Poradowska*. Edition critique précédée d'une
étude sur le français de Joseph Conrad, par
René Rapin. Genève: Kundig, 1966
Garnett, Edward *Letters from Joseph Conrad 1895-
1924*. London and Indianapolis, 1928
Najder, Zdzisław (edit.) *Conrad's Polish
Background*: Letters to and from Polish
friends. London: Oxford University Press,
1964

Secondary Sources

American and English Publications

Bradbrook, Muriel. *Joseph Conrad: Poland's English
Genius*. Cambridge Univ. Press, 1941
Brady, C. A. "Conrad, a Polish palinurus."
America, Sept. 1957 vol. 97
Coleman, A. P. "Polonisms in the English of
Joseph Conrad." *Mod. Lang. Notes*, Nov.
1931, vol 46

Conrad, Jessie. *Joseph Conrad as I knew him*, Garden City: Doubleday Page, 1926
—— *Conrad and his Circle* N.Y.: Dutton, 1935
Cooper, Christopher. *Conrad and the Human Dilemma*. London: Chatto and Windus, 1970
Cox, C. B. *Joseph Conrad: the Modern Imagination* London: Dent and Sons, 1974
Curle, Richard. "The Personality of Joseph Conrad." *Edinburgh Rev.*, Jan. 1925, no. 241
—— "Joseph Conrad as I remember him." *Contemporary Rev.*, July 1959, no. 196
Fleishman, Avrom *Conrad's Politics: Community and Anarchy in the Fiction of Joseph Conrad*. Baltimore: John Hopkins Press, 1967
Gardner, M. M. "Joseph Conrad as a Pole." *Spectator*, 1 Aug. 1925, no. 135.
Gillon, Adam. "Conrad in Poland." *Polish Rev.*, vol. 19 (1974), nos. 3-4.
—— "The Merchant of Esmeralda—Conrad's Archetypal Jew." *Polish Rev.*, vol. 9 (1964)
—— *The Eternal Solitary: a Study of Joseph Conrad*. N.Y,: Twayne Publishers, 1966
Gose, E. B. jun. "Pure Exercise of Imagination: Archetypal Symbolism in Joseph Conrad." PMLA, (vol. 79) March 1964
Guerard, Albert *Conrad the Novelist*. Cambridge, Mass., Harvard Univ. Press, 1962.
Gurko, Leo *Joseph Conrad: Giant in Exile*. New York: Macmillan, 1962
Hay, Eloise K. *The Political Novels of Joseph Conrad*. Chicago and London: Chicago Univ. Press, 1963
Herndon, R. "The Genesis of Conrad's 'Amy Foster'." *Stud. Philology*, July 1960
Hewitt, Douglas. *Conrad: a Reassessment*. Bowes and Bowes, Cambridge, Engl., 1952.
Mencken, Henry L. "A Freudian Autopsy upon a Genius." [meaning Morf's *The Polish Heritage of Joseph Conrad*.] *Am. Mercury*, 1930, no. 23
Meyer, Bernhard C. *Joseph Conrad, a Psychoanalytical Biography*. Princeton: Princeton Univ. Press 1967
Morf, Gustav. *The Polish Heritage of Joseph Conrad*. London: Sampson, Low, 1930
Morgan, Gerald. *Sea Symbol and Myth in the Work of Joseph Conrad*. Ph.D. Thesis, Univ. of Montreal, 1963.
—— *Nauclerus: Joseph Conrad* (Typescript, 1974)

Moser, Thomas "The 'Rescuer' Manuscript, a Key to Conrad's Development and Decline." *Harvard Libr. Bull.*, Winter 1956.

———— *Joseph Conrad: Achievement and Decline.* Cambridge, Mass.: Harvard Univ. Press, 1957.

Pritchett, V. S. "Conrad: the Exile, the Isolated Man, the Master of Atmosphere." *New Statesman and Nation*, vol. 40, 31 Jan. 1950.

———— *Joseph Conrad*, London, 1959

———— "The Moralist of Exile." *New Statesman*, vol. 70, 1960.

Rosenfield, Claire *Paradise of Snakes*: an archetypal analysis of Conrad's political novels. Chicago and London: Chicago Univ. Press.

Said, Edward W. *Joseph Conrad and the Fiction of Autobiography*. Cambridge, Mass.: Harvard Univ. Press, 1966

Schultheiss, Thomas "Lord Hamlet and Lord Jim" *Polish Rev.* vol. 11, no. 4 (1966)

Sherry, Norman *Conrad's Eastern World* Cambridge (Engl.) Univ. Press, 1966

———— *Conrad's Western World* same publisher, 1971

Speare, M. E. *The Political Novel, its Development in England and America*. London: Oxford Univ. Press, 1924

Spender, St. "The Destructive Elements." *Atlantic Monthly*, 1936

Tanner, Tony Conrad: Lord Jim London: 1964

Thale, Jerome. "Marlow's Quest." *Univ. of Toronto Quart.* July 1955.

Thorburn, David *Conrad's Romanticism*. Newhaven and London: Yale Univ. Press 1974

Polish Sources
(Polish titles rendered in English)

Andrzejewski, Jerzy "Three Remarks on Lord Jim." *Creativity* (Warsaw) Feb. 1956

Blüth, R "The Evolution of Heroism in Conrad's Works." *Lit. Scene*, 1932, no. 4

———— "The Tragic Cracow Decision of Konrad Korzeniowski." *Verbum*, 1936, no. 2

Borowy, W "Did Conrad present a Polish mountain peasant?" *Lit. News*, no. 566 (1934)

———— "Conrad as a Critic of the Polish Translation of his Story 'Il Conde'." (In Borowy's
Studies and Essays, Wrocław: Ossolineum,
1952

Braun, Andrzej *Conrad—Contact with the East*. (A
collection of photographs representing the
locale of Conrad's Eastern stories) Warsaw:
A-G Publications, 1970.

———— *In Conrad's Footsteps* [in the East] Warsaw:
Czytelnik, 1972

Chwalewik, Witold "Is Conrad a Polish Writer?"
National Thought no. 391 (1926)

———— "Joseph Conrad in Cardiff." *Lit. Scene*, no.
8, 1932

———— "Conrad and the Literary Tradition [of
Poland]" (in Kocówna, *Reminiscences* etc. pp
439-456

Dąbrowska, Maria *Sketches in Conrad*. Warsaw:
PIW, 1959

Dąbrowski, Marian "An Interview with Conrad."
Ill. Weekly (Warsaw) 16 May 1914

Dyboski, Roman "English and Polish Elements in
Conrad's Thought." *Papers of the Polish Society for East European and Near East Studies* no.
11, 1933

Jabłkowska, Róza *Joseph Conrad*. Wrocław: Ossolineum, 1961

Kocówna, Barbara (edit.) *Reminiscences and Studies
on Conrad* Warsaw: PIW, 1963

———— *Conrad's Polonitas*. Cracow: LSW 1967

Najder, Zdzisław *On Conrad*. Warsaw: PIW, 1965

Prorok, Leszek "A Watch with Conrad." In: *Baltic
and other Sketches*, Wrocław: Ossolineum,
1972 (On the Polish reception of Conrad)

Sapieha, L. *"The Essence of Conrad's polonitas News*
(London) no. 183 (1949)

Tarnawski, Wit *Conrad: the Man—the Writer—the
Pole* (Collected Essays) London: Polish Cultural Foundation, 1972

Ujejski, Józef *Joseph Conrad*, Paris 1939 (transl.)

Zabierowski, Stefan *Conrad in Poland* Gdańsk:
WM, 1971

———— "The Polish Controversy about Conrad in
the Years 1945-1949." In: *Yearbook for
Studies on the History of Literature*. Warsaw,
1975

DATE DUE

	GRAD	AUG 1 3 1979	
GRAD	AUG 6 1979		
GAYLORD			PRINTED IN U.S.A.